THE CONTEMPORARY BAUMAN

The recent work of Zygmunt Bauman has received extraordinary attention in the social sciences. Widely recognized as one of the world's most influential social theorists and politically engaged public intellectuals, Bauman's theory of 'liquid modernity' presents a dramatic, dark portrait of the contemporary age.

This is the first book to provide a detailed critical assessment of Bauman's liquid turn in sociology. Anthony Elliott has selected representative extracts from Bauman's recent path-making work, ensuring *The Contemporary Bauman* provides critical appraisals of the theory of liquid modernity in terms of its implications for self-identity, interpersonal relationships, culture, communications and the broad-ranging institutional transformations associated with globalization.

Elliott has brought together a highly distinguished group of international contributors comprising Ann Branaman, Makenna Goodman, Michael Hviid Jacobsen, Charles Lemert, Poul Poder, Larry Ray, Janet Sayers, Keith Tester and Iain Wilkinson, thus making this volume an integral tool for both undergraduates and postgraduates studying contemporary social theory and cultural studies.

Anthony Elliott is Professor of Sociology at Flinders University, Australia.

The Contemporary Bauman

Edited by Anthony Elliott

LONDON AND NEW YORK

First published 2007
by Routledge
2 Park Square, Milton Park, Abingdon, Oxon OX14 4RN

Simultaneously published in the USA and Canada
by Routledge
270 Madison Ave, New York, NY 10016

Routledge is an imprint of the Taylor & Francis Group, an informa business

© 2007 Anthony Elliott

Typeset in Amasis and Universe by
Florence Production Ltd, Stoodleigh, Devon
Printed and bound in Great Britain by
MPG Books Ltd, Bodmin, Cornwall, UK

All rights reserved. No part of this book may be reprinted or reproduced or utilized in any form or by any electronic, mechanical, or other means, now known or hereafter invented, including photocopying and recording, or in any information storage or retrieval system, without permission in writing from the publishers.

British Library Cataloguing in Publication Data
A catalogue record for this book is available from the British Library

Library of Congress Cataloging in Publication Data

ISBN10: 0–415–40969–1 (hbk)
ISBN10: 0–415–40968–3 (pbk)
ISBN10: 0–203–94667–7 (ebk)

ISBN13: 978–0–415–40969–8 (hbk)
ISBN13: 978–0–415–40968–1 (pbk)
ISBN13: 978–0–203–94667–1 (ebk)

Contents

Notes on Contributors vii
Acknowledgements ix

INTRODUCTION 1

Anthony Elliott
EDITOR'S INTRODUCTION 3

Zygmunt Bauman
CRITIQUE – PRIVATIZED AND DISARMED 19

PART ONE
Liquid modernity 27

Zygmunt Bauman
ON BEING LIGHT AND LIQUID 29

Zygmunt Bauman
FROM HEAVY TO LIGHT MODERNITY 34

1 Anthony Elliott
THE THEORY OF LIQUID MODERNITY: A CRITIQUE OF
BAUMAN'S RECENT SOCIOLOGY 46

2 Larry Ray
FROM POSTMODERNITY TO LIQUID MODERNITY: WHAT'S
IN A METAPHOR? 63

3 Keith Tester
BAUMAN'S IRONY 81

CONTENTS

PART TWO
Liquid love   99

Zygmunt Bauman
FALLING IN AND OUT OF LOVE   101

Zygmunt Bauman
ON LIVING IN A LIQUID MODERN WORLD   107

4   Ann Branaman
    GENDER AND SEXUALITIES IN LIQUID MODERNITY   117

5   Poul Poder
    RELATIVELY LIQUID INTERPERSONAL RELATIONSHIPS
    IN FLEXIBLE WORK LIFE   136

6   Janet Sayers
    LIQUID LOVE: PSYCHOANALYSING MANIA   154

PART THREE
Liquid life   169

Zygmunt Bauman
TO EACH WASTE ITS DUMPING SITE   171

Zygmunt Bauman
THE REALITY PRINCIPLE AND THE PLEASURE PRINCIPLE
STRIKE A DEAL   187

7   Charles Lemert and Makenna Goodman
    LIQUID WASTE, BEING HUMAN, AND BODILY DEATH   198

8   Michael Hviid Jacobsen
    SOLID MODERNITY, LIQUID UTOPIA – LIQUID MODERNITY,
    SOLID UTOPIA: UBIQUITOUS UTOPIANISM AS A TRADEMARK
    OF THE WORK OF ZYGMUNT BAUMAN   217

9   Iain Wilkinson
    ON BAUMAN'S SOCIOLOGY OF SUFFERING: QUESTIONS FOR
    THINKING   241

AFTERWORD

Zygmunt Bauman
ON WRITING; ON WRITING SOCIOLOGY   257

INDEX   269

Contributors

Ann Branaman is Associate Professor of Sociology at Florida Atlantic University, USA. She has edited two books: with Charles Lemert, *The Goffman Reader* (1997) and *The Self and Society Reader* (2001).

Anthony Elliott is Chair of Sociology at Flinders University, Australia and Visiting Research Professor at the Open University, UK. His recent books include *Social Theory Since Freud: Traversing Social Imaginaries* (2004) and, with Charles Lemert, *The New Individualism* (2006).

Makenna Goodman is a student at Wesleyan University, USA. Her primary research interests are social theory and cultural studies.

Michael Hviid Jacobsen is Associate Professor and Chair of Sociology at Aalborg University, Denmark. Recent publications include: *Bauman Before Postmodernity: Invitation, Conversations and Annotated Bibliography, 1953–1989* (with Keith Tester, 2005) and *Bauman Beyond Postmodernity: Critical Appraisals, Conversations and Annotated Bibliography, 1989–2005* (with Sophia Marshman and Keith Tester, forthcoming).

Charles Lemert is Professor of Sociology at Wesleyan University, USA. His most recent books include *Durkheim's Ghosts: Cultural Logics and Social Things* (2006) and *Thinking the Unthinkable* (2007).

Poul Poder is Assistant Professor of Sociology at the University of Copenhagen, Denmark. He has published several articles and interviews on Bauman and a study entitled 'The Feelings of Power and the Power of Feelings: Handling Emotions in Organizational Change' (2004).

Larry Ray is Professor of Sociology at the University of Kent, UK. He is author of many books including *Theorizing Classical Sociology* (1999) and, with William Outhwaite, *Social Theory and Postcommunism* (2005).

Janet Sayers is Professor of Psychoanalytic Psychology at the University of Kent, UK. She has published extensively in psychoanalytic theory including *Kleinians: Psychoanalysis Inside Out* (2000) and *Psychoanalysis Retold* (2007).

Keith Tester is Professor of Cultural Sociology at the University of Portsmouth, UK, and Honorary Member of the Thesis Eleven Centre for Critical Theory at LaTrobe

University, Australia. He is the author of many books including *Conversations with Zygmunt Bauman* (2001) and *The Social Thought of Zygmunt Bauman* (2004).

Iain Wilkinson is Senior Lecturer in Sociology at the University of Kent, UK. He has published *Anxiety in a Risk Society* (2001) and *Suffering: A Sociological Introduction* (2005).

Acknowledgements

I wish to thank the input of various people, as well as acknowledge the support of a number of academic institutions, that have made this book possible. First among them, of course, is Zygmunt Bauman, whose willingness to travel considerable distances to give lectures or seminars continues to astonish. The book arose from a one-day workshop on Bauman's social theory at the University of Kent at Canterbury, which formed part of a wider series on public sociology. At Kent my co-convenor of the public sociology series, Frank Furedi, was unfailingly supportive and kind. I would also like to thank Keith Tester for his input into the workshop, as well as his very helpful advice regarding the planning of this book. Much of the actual preparation of the manuscript was undertaken at the Centre for Critical Theory in Bristol, through the unfailing support of Elizabeth Williams. Subsequently, in putting finishing touches to the book, I was particularly fortunate to have assistance from Daniel Chaffee, where we both profited from the energetic intellectual input of staff from the Department of Sociology at Flinders University. Finally, this book has benefited from the time, patience and goodwill of the following people: Janina Bauman, Gerhard Boomgaarden, Paul du Gay, Nicola Geraghty, Charles Lemert, Anthony Moran and Nick Stevenson.

Anthony Elliott
Adelaide, 2006

INTRODUCTION

Anthony Elliott
EDITOR'S INTRODUCTION   3

Zygmunt Bauman
CRITIQUE – PRIVATIZED AND DISARMED   19

Editor's Introduction

The twilight decades of the last century and arrival of the 2000s saw a myriad of turbulent debates throughout the social sciences concerning the major institutional transformations sweeping through advanced contemporary societies. The analysis and critique of modernity – including discussion of the multidimensional nature and future of contemporary societies – became a topic of fundamental significance both inside the academy and within wider public political debate. The heralding of a postmodern condition – transformational of self and society as well as the eclipse of Enlightenment values – was widely celebrated and critiqued in equal measure. The great debate over globalization – its conditions and consequences – prepared the way for a thoroughgoing reassessment of the complex relations between state, society and governance. Moreover, these institutional transformations – modernity, postmodernism and globalization – were kept high on the sociological agenda, partly as a result of the resurgence of Theory throughout the academy, and partly as a result of profound social transformations, from the East European revolutions of 1989–91 to the terrors of 9/11. It is against this intellectual and political backdrop that the work of Zygmunt Bauman has received extraordinary attention. In writings that span many decades, Bauman has developed a theoretical perspective on the condition and future of world society that has become immensely topical in disciplines ranging from sociology to political science, history to cultural studies. As a result of his novel sociological interventions into the debate over postmodernity during the 1990s, as well as his more recent writings on the liquidization of contemporary societies, Bauman has come to rank as one of the world's most influential social theorists and politically engaged public intellectuals.

My aim in this Introduction is to contextualize the work of Bauman in order to provide a sociological backcloth for the critical debates that follow. I shall begin, in the first section of the Introduction, by providing a brief overview of Bauman's sociological corpus. I note that I cannot – in such limited space – provide a comprehensive survey of his social theory: this has, in any event, been already accomplished elsewhere (Beilharz 2000; Smith 1999; Tester 2004). Moreover, the contributors to this volume, in reviewing specific aspects of Bauman's work, offer exceptionally lucid overviews of his most recent work. In contextualizing Bauman's work I shall focus here on his widely celebrated sociology of postmodernity, and then look at his more recent disenchantment with the notion of the postmodern as a measure for the critique of modernity. In the second section of the Introduction, I shall briefly examine Bauman's 'liquid turn' and then summarize the main arguments of the chapters in this volume.

Bauman before and after postmodernity

The intellectual breadth and sweep of Bauman's writings are a remarkable achievement. Notwithstanding the diversity and subtlety of his earliest sociological offerings from Poland (see Tester and Jacobsen 2005) as well as his middle-period contributions to the elaboration of a sociological hermeneutics (Bauman 1978), it has only been in more recent years – since the publication of *Modernity and the Holocaust* (1989), a series of works on the critique of modernity and postmodernism, and his subsequent breathtakingly original elaboration of the theory of liquid modernity – that Bauman's intellectual standing has become widely acknowledged. Certainly since his retirement from the University of Leeds in the early 1990s, Bauman's voice has been increasingly heard throughout and beyond the discipline of sociology, as one cautioning that our new globalized world is riddled with uncertainty, unpredictability and ambivalence. In Bauman's view, the global economy – based upon the communications revolution – creates radical new patterns of power and inequality, from which fresh opportunities and risks arise for everyone. During the last twenty or so years, Bauman has published an astonishing series of books that offer a trenchant sociological critique of modernity, from his highly acclaimed study *Legislators and Interpreters* (1987) to his more recent visionary arguments detailed in his trilogy *Liquid Modernity* (2000), *Liquid Love* (2003) and *Liquid Life* (2005). Certainly the great strength of this work is his tenacity in pursuing the idea of the postmodern, liquid modern and globalism through every shifting guise and mutation, from the economy to entertainment. He tracks cultural pressures, emotional torments and political dilemmas with a uniquely agile understanding, helping us to glimpse if not the solutions then at least the complexities of global transformations.

Bauman's interest in postmodernity, liquid modernization and globalization has come increasingly to the fore, but he was a leader of the cultural turn in sociology as far back as the 1970s. His first book published in English, *Between Class and Elite* (1972), took the British labour movement as its field of investigation. In the following years, in books such as *Culture as Praxis* (1973), *Socialism: The Active Utopia* (1976) and *Memories of Class* (1982), he established himself as a dazzlingly erudite analyst of the interconnections between class and culture. However Bauman's fame, as noted above, rests upon his more recent writings on modernity and postmodernization. *Modernity and the Holocaust* (1989), his masterwork, is a dark, dramatic study of the deathly consequences of Enlightenment reason. Auschwitz, in Bauman's eyes, was a result of the 'civilizing' mission of modernity; the Final Solution was not a dysfunction of modern rationality but its shocking product. The Holocaust, according to Bauman, is unthinkable outside the twin forces of bureaucracy and technology. In subsequent work, including *Modernity and Ambivalence* (1991) and *Postmodernity and Its Discontents* (1997), he moved from a concern with the historical fortunes of the Jews as victims of modernity to an analysis of the complex ways in which postmodern culture cultivates all of us as outsiders, strangers, others.

Bauman sprang from a marginalized position in post-war Poland. In many ways, his analysis of the dreads and dislocations of modernity and postmodernization might be read as a series of intellectual concerns developed from biographical experience. He is both Polish and English, sociologist and social theorist, modernist and postmodernist, high theoretician and anthropologist of the *Lebenswelt* of postmodern society. Born in 1925 in Poland and educated in Soviet Russia, Bauman became a soldier with the Red Army and fought against the Germans in the Second World War. His promising career in the military came undone in 1953 when he was summarily dismissed, a victim of an anti-Semitic purge. In going virtually overnight from insider of the Communist Party to marginalized outsider, it was as if he found – through his emergent dedication to sociology – an intellectual space for doubt within a society obsessed with ideological certitude. Indeed, Bauman's sociological fascination with ambivalence, ambiguity, difference and otherness arguably stems (in various senses) from his Polish background and the visceral anti-Semitism he encountered. And it was from this appreciation in particular of the dialectical interplay between order and otherness, between structure and ambivalence, that Bauman developed his comprehensively textured social theory of modernity and postmodernization.

Let me now turn to some of the central themes arising from the modernity/postmodernity debate in social theory – for it is my view that, in order to fully grasp the novel terrain and trajectory of Bauman's theory of global liquidization, the polarity which arose in social theory during the late 1980s and 1990s between modernity and postmodernity must be adequately set out and contextualized. The 'project of modernity' has been widely characterized as involving an institutionalization of unilinear history and meaning. Science, bureaucracy and technological expertise serve in the modern era as an orientating framework for the cultural ordering of meaning. A conception of history as having a single direction, the endeavour to develop a rational programme of collective emancipation, the grounding of diverse human experience and symbolic representation in reason: these are the hallmarks of modernity. And yet it is precisely these modernist aims for self-mastery and control that, paradoxically, fall victim to the very social processes they seek to colonize. Recent decades have powerfully shown that the ethos of modernity has come to haunt us. From the awesome destructive potential of nuclear arms to the massive risks of ecological catastrophe: the world in which we live today is fraught with dangers and risks, many of which arise directly as a consequence of the successes of science and the drive for progress. Such threats have powerfully served to highlight the gross limitations of modernist aims and perspectives, generating in turn the emergence of a new social and political agenda that seeks to counterbalance these oppressive features of modernity. This sphere of awareness is that of postmodernity.

Postmodernity confounds identity, theory and politics in a scandalous way, with its levelling of hierarchies, its dislocating subversion of ideological closure, its interpretative polyvalence, its self-reflexive pluralism. The world of postmodern culture is heterogeneous. On the one hand, postmodernism refers to certain currents of cultural and critical discourse which seek to deconstruct the ideological affinities of totalizing thought, the operations of power, the legitimating functions of knowledge and truth, and the discursive practices of self-constitution. On the other hand, however, postmodernism penetrates well beyond the boundaries of theory, at once inaugurating and designating new forms of personal and cultural experience. From a radical viewpoint, postmodern theories seek to demonstrate that the interconnections between self and society no longer depend upon the epistemological and ideological categories of modernity. Whilst postmodernists acknowledge that we are still living in a time of extraordinary social and political transformation, there is no longer a blind faith – or so it is argued – in metadiscourses of scientific knowledge and technological legitimation. Our growing appreciation of the limits of rationality has led to the wholesale abandonment of the epistemological illusions of emancipatory declarations – such as Freedom, Truth, Equality and Liberty. There has been, in short, a breakdown in the metanarrative of Enlightenment. For, as Lyotard puts this in *The Postmodern Condition*, (1984) postmodernity is defined as an 'incredulity toward metanarratives'. The grand narratives that unified and structured Western science and philosophy, grounding truth and meaning in the presumption of a universal subject and a predetermined goal of emancipation, no longer appear convincing or even plausible. Instead, the anti-totalizing, postmodern perspective reveals the generation of knowledge as singular, localized and perspectival. Knowledge is constructed, not discovered; it is contextual, not foundational. In this vision, truth-validation is itself explicitly recognized as entering into the pragmatics of intersubjective transmission.

One of the most challenging accounts of postmodernism – to which Bauman owes a considerable debt – is the *critique of simulated media culture*. This is a critique, influential within sociology and dominant in cultural and media studies, which announced an epochal rupture with modernity, which bid farewell to productivism and political economy and embraced instead ever-expanding, spiralling cycles of signs and codes. By disconnecting the modern and postmodern in this way, advocates of postmodernity as simulated media culture were to euphorically celebrate the play of signs, spectacles and simulacra in our media age; they cut loose communication technologies, entertainment and information from any relation to an external 'outside'; and, they dissolved the concepts of the political and society as mere metaphysical nostalgia. Jean Baudrillard, self-described 'intellectual terrorist' and one of the most important proponents of this viewpoint, famously announced the 'death of the social' and speculated about the emergence of what he termed 'fatal strategies' of melancholy, passivity, silence. In giving priority to the depthless, fragmented surfaces of postmodernist culture in this way, Baudrillard's suggestion is that critics must learn to view silence, apathy and passivity as signs of a potentially productive vitality of social life against its drive for seductive domination in an age of simulation and virtuality. For followers of Baudrillard's account of postmodernity as simulated media culture, there is nothing but pure surface.

A related, but quite distinct, critique of the postmodern involves the *analysis of global capitalist transformations*. Postmodernity as global capitalist transformations takes something from Baudrillard's emphasis on simulations and hyperreality, but mixes this critique with analytical attention to the worldwide economy, finance capital and new structural forces generating exploitation, repression and the like. Again, this is a standpoint on postmodernism to which Bauman owes something of a debt. From postmodern aesthetics, this critique adopts an emphasis on blendings of high and mass culture, the dissolution of art into everyday life and the acceleration of schizoid or fragmentary elements of self-constitution as such. But that is not all, for the critique of global capitalist transformations crosses its orientation to postmodern culture with a modernist impulse to unearth generalized structures of socio-economic domination as well as the search for political justice and human autonomy. This response to the global crisis of postmodernization is perhaps nowhere better dramatized than in American Marxist and literary critic Fredric Jameson's (1992) notion of 'cognitive mapping' – the working through for a resourceful critique of the subject's inability to mentally represent or locate themselves in the global postmodern, with a view to rewriting possible intermediate forms of connection between the conditions of identity on the one hand and the global economy on the other. In an age of image, information and identity, Jameson's political project is to refloat the question of the postmodern so that it may be considered as a historical-ontological condition from which deeper structural antinomies can be assembled, critiqued and transfigured.

Jameson's purchase on postmodernism as multinational global capitalism is not discussed by Bauman in any of his writings, and yet one suspects that there are various points of linkage between these two theorists of our contemporary cultural malaise. One key link might lie in the tracking of postmodern entertainment back to the economy. Yet for Bauman, as distinct from Jameson, the postmodern must be related not only to an economics of culture but also to the sociology of everyday practices. For what the wholesale aestheticization of culture will do to society in more general terms, as contemporary women and men find themselves increasingly seduced by the fetish of surface and style as well as the cult of hedonism and libidinal intensities as promoted by late capitalism, can only be adequately grasped through a more properly socio-structural critique of postmodernity. Indeed for the Bauman of the early 1990s, it is only a sociology of postmodernity, rather than the elaboration of a postmodern sociology, which can understand the global transformations that have shaped the society in which we live today. Rather than posit some intolerable conflict between modernity and postmodernity, Bauman suggests a two-way traffic between these two modalities of culture and critique. In bracketing off the issue of historical periodization, what is at stake here – under a response to the crisis of postmodernity as generalized social systems – is nothing less than a pluralization or liquidization of human ambivalence. What links modern and postmodern orders for Bauman is that for both, though in very distinct ways, ambivalence is key to social life and its reproduction. Modernity is less a description of a particular historical period than a kind of social practice seeking the erasure or prohibition of ambivalence by rationalizing classifications, an essentially permanent cultural possibility within which hegemonic patterns of compulsory inclusion and exclusion are rehearsed daily by women and men. The notion of the postmodern, in this sociological critique at least, is the reverse lining of modernity – and presents a very different response to ambivalence. For if societal ambivalence is here to stay – if we are, as it were, stuck with (or in) ambivalence – then the postmodern response seeks to fully acknowledge this, embracing ambiguity, difference and otherness as the basis for, or any result of, human creativity. Postmodernity is thus symptomatic of a ruthless and episodic existence, one in which thick global flows of cash and credit unleash staggering new possibilities and risks, novel forms of polarization between rich and poor and the globalization of Western modes of life in which structures of reflexivity and self-experimentation become increasingly dominant.

Bauman's discussion of the interconnections between modernity and postmodernity – sketched in *Modernity and Ambivalence* (1991) and *Intimations of Postmodernity* (1992) and developed throughout the 1990s – remains in my view extremely persuasive. Bauman is critical of those who celebrate the postmodern as a mark *beyond* modernity. Any such reading of postmodernity as a cultural phase beyond modernity, he argues, is itself an exercise in self-contained ordering. Rather than attempting a historical periodization of the modern and postmodern eras, Bauman argues that contemporary culture, not without certain tensions and contradictions, deploys both orders simultaneously. Contemporary society revolves around a modernist impulse for creating order, boundaries and classifications as well as a postmodern tolerance for plurality, difference and uncertainty. Contemporary society, it might be said, embraces and avoids ambivalence in equal measure. There is something in all of this which is deeply disturbing and problematic: the more society generates pluralism and ambivalence, the more this rebounds as a loss of orientation and meaning. To become more aware of personal and cultural contingency is to break with the hold of social-historical fixation and to court vulnerability. But this seemingly contradictory, and often confused, state of affairs is, in fact, one of the supreme values of postmodernity. 'Postmodernity', says Bauman, 'is modernity that has admitted the non-feasibility of its original project. Postmodernity is modernity reconciled to its own impossibility – and determined, for better or worse, to live with it. Modern practice continues – now, however, devoid of the objective that once triggered it off' (Bauman 1990: 98).

This leads directly to Bauman's central thesis: *postmodernity as modernity without illusions*. Postmodernity is an opening out to the complex, contradictory realm of human and social experience, in all its wonder and insecurity. The end of codes equals an encounter with experience, pure and unrestrained. The postmodern subject is preoccupied, among other things, with creative and pragmatic living, free of the distortion of unrealistic hopes and aspirations, of unrealizable goals and values. Beyond the self-mastery of modernity there exists a postmodern, cultural space which calls for, and indeed celebrates, difference and otherness. Rejecting the supra-individual authority of blank technologism, rationality, economic progress, causality and system, postmodern culture transmutes the foundations of identity and society as fluid, ambivalent and radically contingent.

Bauman adopts a postmodernist language stressing ambivalence and ambiguity, while being thoroughly suspicious of the whole terrain of postmodernism. Sociologically speaking, his work analyses the fissures between modernist cultural practices one the one hand and postmodern global transformations on the other, with particular emphasis on the deregulation and privatization of all things social. Any compressed reconstruction of the main arguments of Bauman's sociology of contemporary culture cannot possibly do justice to it as a whole, such is its sheer imaginative sweep and intellectual breadth. These include a liquid mode of experience – experience of the self and others, of space and time, of life's possibilities and risks – that is shared by women and men the world over; the separation of power and sovereignty from the politics of the territorial nation-state; the collapse of 'society' as a bounded complex, or set of structures, and thus the eradication of sociology's disciplinary self-evident client; and finally, the outsourcing of public political functions to non-political, deregulated market forces. This last is a central theme, and gives his work a radical political edge. Privatization or deregulation, according to Bauman, becomes a vital preoccupation of the postmodern age for a whole host of reasons. In the neo-liberal epoch, the drastically shrinking world of public political space may seem (and in various respects is) an upshot of transnational capitalism. Yet at the same time, privatization of life-experience and life-politics is policed and regulated by culturalist and sub-political processes that follow a kind of Weberian logic all their own, an institutional development which the discipline of sociology has been too slow to recognize. As Bauman develops this in his book *Society Under Siege*:

> Governments are today no less, if not more, busy and active than ever before in modern history. But they are busy in the TV Big Brother's style: letting the subjects play their own games and blame themselves in the event that the results are not up to their dreams. Governments are busy hammering home the 'there is no alternative' message, the 'security is dependency' and the 'state protection is disempowering' messages, and enjoining subjects to be more flexible and to love the risks (read: erratic and unpredictable) life-settings is fraught with.
> (Bauman 2002: 68)

Notwithstanding his suspicion of traditional institutional politics, Bauman is in various senses a collectivist thinker, the product of his training in the Polish sociological tradition with its affinities to Weberian-Marxism. What is striking about Bauman's sociology from the earliest texts is the scrupulous exactness with which he maps not just class power or social hierarchy, but social oppression and political domination in general. There were after all no ruling capitalists throughout central Europe after the Second World War, and this is undoubtedly one reason why Bauman became so finely attuned to various modes of 'ordering action' and forms of repression. Socialism, in the postindividualist sense of affective solidarity, can be seen as the collective unconscious motivating resistance to capitalism, a kind of 'counterculture of modernity', as he puts it in *Socialism: The Active Utopia* (1976).

Modernity is an obsessive project, marked by desire for constant change. Whatever is seen as old must be replaced by the new – always, and in itself, a sign of progress. Science and its technological offshoots are the central drivers of assigning an object, event or person to ever-new systems of rational classification; and in this way rationalization and science consequently merge in curious ways to further modernity's obsessive urge to control. Modernity is thus a high-brow, abstract affair, concerned above all with constant rationalizing and the logics of classification, at once distant and dismissive of the messiness and unpredictableness of the everyday. In fact, if modernity takes an interest in the dynamics of everyday life, this is primarily driven out of its obsessive quest for order, stability and consistency. If modernity and modernism in their various guises are interested by the everyday details of human ambivalence and ambiguity, the point of this interest is to strengthen the impulse for order. To keep things neat and tidy, with all glimmerings of ambivalence safely disowned, is key.

Bauman himself demonstrates something of an obsession with ambivalence, from *Modernity and Ambivalence* (1991) to *Wasted Lives* (2004), but he is able to connect this contemporary cult of the unpredictable to radical political ends. For Bauman, as for Sigmund Freud, ambivalence is essential to human subjectivity, at once enriching the affective texture of interpersonal experience and multiplying the complexity of social life itself. The more we become aware of ambivalence, undecidability and uncertainty as intrinsic to human life and forms of association, the more dense networks of social dependencies become. And yet modernity is the moment at which ambivalence becomes prohibited, constructed as both aberrant and abject. The modernist impulse to order is a regime governed by intolerance, inflexibility and symbolic violence, with regulating patterns of classificatory inclusion and exclusion serving less as a transparent rational medium than as a surreptitiously hegemonic form of repression.

There is a sense then in which Bauman initiates a postmodern recasting of the ordering ambitions of modernity, preferring to cobble together fragments of various modernist and postmodernist mentalities, orientations, dispositions and world views. He is certainly no enthusiast of post-structuralist or postmodernist versions of postmodernity, of what he terms 'the preachers and enthusiasts of the postmodern bliss' (Bauman, 2000: 339). 'It is simply', he says, 'a salutary decision to speak of postmodernity, rather than late modernity, without necessarily accepting every rubbish written in the name of postmodern theory' (Bauman 2001: 20). For him, everything postmodern is fashioned out of something modern. There is no definitive line of separation between the modern and the postmodern, as postmodernity is itself 'a self-conscious stage in the development of modernity' (Bauman 2001: 20). In the end, Bauman rejects pronouncements of the 'end of modernity' and yet – retaining the enthusiasm of some postmodernists – declares the postmodern a 'chance of modernity', a chance for tolerance, solidarity and autonomy. This sense of potential transfiguration, deriving from reflexive self-consciousness of the temporal and spatial flux of contemporary life, is what gives Bauman's portrait of the postmodern age its sociological distinctiveness.

This tension in Bauman's writing – between embracing and rejecting certain elements of the discourse of postmodernism – is the sign of a more familiar sociological dilemma. If the postmodern is a cultural phase beyond modernity, it is granted a special stamp of autonomy which is somehow free of ambivalence; if postmodernity represents a break with the modern, it displaces the modernist surgical ambition of social engineering but – in pluralizing the social and cultural pursuit of order – runs the risk of 'anything goes'. It is for this reason that Bauman resists the widespread tendency to historically periodize the modern and postmodern, and indeed the point of his sociology is to have it both ways: modernity and postmodernity mix, and necessarily so in various overlappings and criss-crossings. It is against this backcloth that Bauman can simultaneously proclaim the energizing dimensions of the postmodern, opening a space for the imaginative pluralization of structures of meaning, and critique the cultural consequences of modernity. Contemporary women and men aspire to power, to modernist dreams of certitude, order and structure; yet they equally seek to live without guarantees, trading yesterday's road maps for the sudden lurches of mood generated by today's high-tech globalism. We are neither one nor another, but potentially both, modern and postmodern.

If for Fredric Jameson postmodernism is a cultural dominant tendentially global in scope, it is for Bauman a more unstable affair, often on the brink of bringing itself undone. Indeed the postmodern, which for Bauman represents not transcendence but a societal turning back on the consequences of modernity, is everywhere evident (especially in popular culture, the plastic arts and new communication technologies) but nowhere supreme – such is the ruthless colonizing logic of modernist desires for homogeneity, control, order and certitude. At once akin and estranged, both inside and outside each other's culturalist or ideological range, modernity and postmodernity share in common the crisis of identity that afflicts life in the contemporary West. Yet if the postmodern world view – permeated with a sense of the ambivalence of existence – is premised upon a compact with reflexivity, it also involves a thoroughgoing dismantling of the normative force of standards, ideals and truths. This, one might immediately hasten to add, is not necessarily bad news politically speaking – as the following passage from Bauman regarding postmodern wisdom plainly indicates:

> What the postmodern mind is aware of is that there are problems . . . with no good solutions, twisted trajectories that cannot be straightened up, ambivalences that are more than linguistic blunders yelling to be corrected, doubts which cannot be legislated out of existence, moral agonies which no reason-dictated recipes can soothe, let alone cure. The postmodern mind does not expect any more to find the all-embracing, total and ultimate formula of life without ambiguity, risk, danger and error, and is deeply suspicious of any voice that promises otherwise. The postmodern mind is aware that each local, specialized and focused treatment, effective or not when measured by its ostensive target, spoils as much as, if not more than, it repairs. The postmodern mind is reconciled to the idea that the messiness of the human predicament is here to stay. This is, in the broadest outlines, what can be called postmodern wisdom.
> (Bauman 1993: 245)

Bauman's postmodernism here comes close to being a celebratory affair, but in a manner that sociologically delineates between postmodern world views (seen as potentially subversive) and postmodernity (a mix of opportunity and risk). There is, at any rate, a force at work in the postmodern habitat making for autonomy, even if, sociologically speaking, this movement towards autonomy is necessarily to collide with the more oppressive features of postmodernity as a social system.

Modernity and postmodernity are hence two key aspects of our contemporaneity, with the revisions and reversals of the postmodern rendering the self-formative process of human beings subject to intensive interrogations of the assumptions and aspirations of modernity. It is exactly this incessant criss-crossing of modern and postmodern life-strategies that Bauman sought to capture and elaborate during his engagement with the modernity/postmodernity debate of the 1990s, even though he subsequently came to acknowledge that his most systematic attempts to redefine the term 'postmodern' with greater sociological precision failed to outstrip mainstream or cruder formulations of postmodernism. As Bauman reflected upon these grave limitations of the postmodern discourse:

> 'Postmodern' was also flawed from the beginning: all disclaimers notwithstanding, it did suggest that modernity was over. Protestations did not help much, even as strong ones as Lyotard's ('one cannot be modern without being first postmodern') – let alone my insistence that 'postmodernity is modernity minus its illusion'. Nothing would help; if words mean anything, then a 'postX' will always mean a state of affairs that has leaved the 'X' behind.
>
> (Bauman 2002: 2/7)

The essential difference between Bauman's position and that of simplistic postmodernist standpoints, a difference which even the discipline of sociology was very slow to grasp in its manifold complexities, is that Bauman rejects the theme of a transcendence or end of modernity. Whether Bauman's formulation of the postmodern as modernity minus its illusion is persuasive or not, it is an idea that Bauman himself jettisons with the arrival of the 2000s. In its place comes the theory of liquid modernity.

Bauman's liquid turn

Seeking to free himself from the deadlocks of the modernity/postmodernity debate, Bauman announces in *Liquid Modernity* (2000), poignantly and provocatively, that ours is the age of liquefaction. The present-day condition of modernity, says Bauman, is one of liquidity, fluidity and drift, with the frailty, fading and short-termism of social relationships to the fore. As Bauman reflects on the contours of his revised constructive social theory:

> One attribute that liquids possess and solids don't, an attribute that makes liquids an apt metaphor for our times, is the fluids' intrinsic inability to hold their shape for long on their own. The 'flow', the defining characteristic of all liquids, means a continuous and irreversible change of mutual position of parts due to the faintness of inter-molecular bonds can be triggered by even the weakest of stresses. Fluids, according to *Encyclopedia Britannica*, undergo for that reason 'a continuous change in shape when subjected to stress'. Used as a metaphor of the present phase of modernity, 'liquid' makes salient the brittleness, breakability, ad-hoc modality of inter-human bonds. Another trait contributes to the metaphorical usefulness of liquids: their, so to speak, 'time sensitivity' – again contrary to the solids, which could be described as contraptions to cancel the impact of time.
>
> (Bauman 2002: 3/7)

If modernity in the age of industrialization was about the fixing and solidifying of fluid social things into a form of imagined permanence, modernity in the age of liquid globalism represents the full-blown embrace of impermanence and flow in inter-human bonds.

The theory of liquid modernity, detailed first in *Liquid Modernity* (2000) and elaborated exquisitely in *Liquid Love* (2003), *Liquid Life* (2005) and *Liquid Fear* (2006), has become a complex and comprehensive theoretical system. Bauman has refined the concept of liquidity, reworking the sociological critique of modernity, and linked it to an ever-widening terrain of pressing public political issues. In this volume, the chapters by Elliott, Ray and Tester address many of the central issues raised by Bauman's sociological approach. In Chapter 1, Elliott offers an analysis of Bauman's general approach. In developing a critique of the theory of liquid modernity, Elliott begins by noting several sociological shortcomings with Bauman's argument for the generality of societal liquidization. The argument is put that his analysis of liquefaction squeezes to the sidelines of sociological concern the ongoing force of early modernist codes and norms in the production of social life. This critique is then broadened to consider Bauman's earlier sociology of postmodernity. An argument is developed that there are valuable sociological emphases in Bauman's sociology of postmodernity that should be preserved for the analysis of liquid modernity. Finally, some general sociological issues are raised concerning Bauman's analysis of identity and subjectivity in the context of liquid societies. Some conceptual proposals are advanced for alternative ways of thinking sociologically about the complexity of identity to those detailed in the theory of liquid modernity. Throughout the chapter, Bauman's highly original contribution to sociology is underscored, and as such the critique developed of the theory of liquid modernity is made in a spirit of sympathy and admiration, in order to suggest alternative social-theoretical paths by which certain conceptual difficulties of Bauman's account might be overcome.

The status of generalizing social critique in Bauman's work is examined in the contribution by Larry Ray, 'From postmodernity to liquid modernity: what's in a metaphor?' (Chapter 2). He commences by sketching Bauman's shift from sociologist of postmodernity to liquid modernity, and traces the manner in which Bauman glosses and sometimes displaces issues surrounding the evidential basis of his more universalistic claims. According to Ray, Bauman's sociology lacks specificity as to where and how far processes of societal liquidization are occurring. Equally problematic, he contends, is that Bauman addresses 'surface experiences of the contemporary societies rather than asking questions about' them. Ray concludes by offering what he terms a 'defence of sociology *against* metaphor', one analytical consequence of which is the need for the discipline to be more finely tuned to the empirical foundations of generalizing social theory.

In Chapter 3, 'Bauman's irony', Keith Tester recasts C. Wright Mills's term 'the sociological imagination' to develop a brilliant reading of the place and function of irony in Bauman's writings. Looking at the influence of literature upon Bauman's sociology, in particular the writings of Balzac, Musil and Kundera, Tester argues that irony, paradox and ambiguity are central planks in Bauman's sociological efforts to reconfigure biography and society in the telling of contemporary social things. In

Bauman's sociological world view, says Tester, a measure of irony is needed for a world which has become inhospitable to autonomous subjectivity as well as creative engagement with social things. This argument is important in that it alerts us to the importance of Bauman's literary style, and in particular the point that Bauman's contemporary works are written both for and beyond the readership of disciplinary sociology. 'Since Bauman', writes Tester, 'is a practitioner of a sociological imagination, as opposed to a systematic sociologist, this means that his work frequently looks for inspiration outside the confines of the discipline.' Both condition and consequence in this viewpoint extend beyond sociology *narrowly conceived*, and this way of reading Bauman provides perhaps an important supplement to the type of critique concerning evidential accuracy raised by Larry Ray in this volume.

If the theory of liquid modernity offers fresh ways for thinking about the character and shape of contemporary institutional and organizational life, it also provides new insights into the plight of modern women and men seeking to bring their emotional, intimate needs into dialogue with the spirit of the age. From this angle, Bauman has sought to refine the concepts of liquidity and modernity and link them with the pervasive sense of uprootedness, anxiety and insecurity that increasingly influences structures of identity and subjectivity in conditions of globalization. Here Bauman argues that liquid modernity gives rise to the emergence of 'privatized identity' – of short-term, market-oriented, episodic fabrications of the self. In a series of recent books, from *Liquid Love* (2003) and *Identity* (2004) to *Liquid Life* (2005), Bauman's theoretical approach and substantive analyses paint a picture of self-identity as increasingly fractured, fluid and frail. Part Two of this book, 'Liquid love', focuses on these aspects of sociological analysis and moral critique in Bauman's work. The essays by Branaman, Poder and Sayers critically examine some of Bauman's key claims and insights into the changing nature of love, sexuality, gender, intimacy and interpersonal relationships.

Love, in the infamous summation of the French psychoanalyst Jacques Lacan, is the desire to give something you haven't got to someone who doesn't exist. From a psychoanalytic point of view, to love another is to desire what they lack, and thus in a sense to identify with nothing, self-destruction, the death wish. Love's promises are, it seems, always doomed to end in disappointment: contemporary men and women cannot desire where they love and cannot love where they desire. No wonder then that ambivalence – the coexistence in the same person of love and hate for the desired object – was regarded by Sigmund Freud as central to the diversity of our emotional lives. For Freud, the gap between desire and love is among other things a familiar psychological division between consciousness and the unconscious, pleasure and unpleasure, Eros and Thanatos. Freud understood society as a kind of trade-off: unfettered sexual desire and the urge towards violence are sacrificed for a sense of collective security. Self-expression is limited, held in check, in the name of social order; desire, in turn, climbing a complicated ladder of cultural sublimations, saturates personal bonds, friendships, loves, communities.

From our contemporary vantage point, to speak of culture in terms of security or order sounds somewhat quaint. Against the backdrop of persistent economic uncertainty, multiculturalism and the globalization of terrorism, Freud's cultural analysis looks increasingly out of date. In the current political climate, the freedom of the individual now reigns supreme, with the pleasure principle having firmly ousted the reality principle in the court of all social affairs. This is one of the central planks of Bauman's analysis of selfhood and identity in the current age. Bauman contends that, if Freud were analysing our cultural life today, he would need to reverse his sociological diagnosis. In today's world, says Bauman, the most common types of emotional troubles, anxieties and discontents stem not from too much repression, but from a surge in personal addictions – from drugs and gambling to episodic sex and love affairs. In *Liquid Love*, for example, Bauman suggests that the 'cultures of repression' which dominated during Freud's era have given way to today's 'cultures of desire'. Looking at how the glossy seductions of consumer culture may prove restrictive to an individual's way of life, Bauman dramatizes and critiques – in a series of moving fragments – the changing nature of intimacy in a world dogged with new uncertainties. Reminiscent of Roland Barthes's classic *A Lover's Discourse* (1978), Bauman's *Liquid Love* is witty, poetic, prophetic, full of vitality and enormously informative. Shifting the theory of liquid modernity away from institutional to personal transformations, Bauman tackles many issues: the collapse of 'till-death-do-us-part' marriages and of family ties that bind; the widespread neurotic obsession with youth, sex and the frantic urge to consume; the rush towards market solutions for private emotional dilemmas; and the progressive loosening (or, as Bauman prefers, liquidization) of human bonds and sexual relationships. This last is perhaps the most accomplished theme, and gives his work on identity its cutting political edge. With the metaphor of liquid coursing throughout his writings on identity and everyday life, Bauman applies his formidable sociological intellect to the reshaping of sex, intimacy and love through new information technologies. Today the flow of desire, says Bauman, unfolds against a high-tech backdrop – a world of mobile phones, Internet dating, relationship columns and self-help therapy. Present-day obsessions with surfing the Net, texting and networking are frantic attempts to create some kind of provisional union or bond – no matter how fleeting. Yet, as Bauman notes, 'the union only goes so far as the dialling, talking, messaging. Stop talking – and you are out. Silence equals exclusion *Il n'y a pas dehors du texte*, indeed – there is nothing outside the text – though not just in the sense meant by Derrida'.

In Chapter 4, 'Gender and sexualities in liquid modernity', Ann Branaman concentrates on the loosening or liquidization of gender norms for contemporary women and men as they face the challenges of living in a post-traditional world. Reviewing Bauman's writings on identity, love and intimacy, Branaman expertly unwraps how Bauman sees the global economy penetrating the deepest recesses of the mind. Increasingly, people want from relationships that which they derive from shopping at the mall: variety, novelty, disposability. Thus, 'lovers' are reclassified as 'sexual partners', and in turn assessed as potential risks to 'emotional investment' through cold, calculating cost/benefit analysis. Such liquidization represents, amongst other things, a massive weakening of the hold of gender categories and sexual norms: the authoritative codes of yesteryear (marriage 'till-death-do-us-part') are replaced by episodic sexual relationships ('until further notice'). Branaman traces out the sociological consequences of this shift to liquid love, and considers in detail its implications for feminism and related movements of sexual liberation. Rather than an analytical focus on liberation, she notes, Bauman's recent work highlights the ever-growing gap between the social obligations and pressures to self-assertion on the one hand and the capacity to control the socio-economic circumstances in which such claims to autonomy can be feasibly made on the other.

Poul Poder, in Chapter 5, 'Relatively liquid interpersonal relationships in flexible work life', builds upon these issues concerning today's increased fluidity in personal and professional relationships as discussed by Branaman – but takes a somewhat different sociological tack. According to Poder, the changing relationship between life, relationships and work might not be as corrosive as Bauman suggests in his recent work. That is to say, Poder wants to underscore some of the more positive features of liquid or flexible work life, and to contrast these enabling aspects of contemporary institutional life to the negative or constraining aspects highlighted by Bauman's theory of liquid modernity. In doing so, Poder reviews certain sociological trajectories across advanced societies in post-bureaucratic organization, in particular the development of novel work relations between managers and employees. He stresses aspects of empowerment arising from these post-bureaucratic managerial practices, though throughout the discussion continues to draw inspiration from Bauman as to the more oppressive features of liquid-life settings.

In Chapter 6, 'Liquid love: psychoanalysing mania', Janet Sayers subjects Bauman's writings on identity, desire and love to a psychoanalytic reading. For Sayers, Bauman's portrait of liquid life can be grasped as a lifting of 'manic consumerism' into the mind itself. From this angle, identity is framed as a kind of 'shopping list of manic desire'. Against the backdrop of the decline of stable marriages, Sayers reviews Bauman's musings on the rise of 'top-pocket relationships' – those you can use when you need to and dispose of just as easily. So too, she casts a psychoanalytic eye over Bauman's gloss on the highly compartmentalized worlds of SDCs (semi-detached couples), those postmodern romantics who maintain separate pads and separate lives. Whilst sympathetic to elements of this sociological critique, Sayers argues that Bauman's analysis is weakened considerably by an overestimation of the spread of manic individualism. Drawing from the psychoanalytic research of Donald Winnicott, Wilfred Bion and Julia Kristeva, Sayers considers other, alternative forms of identity-constitution and their relation to contemporary culture.

Part Three of the book, 'Liquid life', offers a reflective configuration of how the institutional and biographical play out through a consideration of various issues of pressing political importance. Charles Lemert and Makenna Goodman's 'Liquid waste, being human and bodily death' (Chapter 7) examines Bauman's analysis of tumultuous liquid worlds with reference to the themes of waste, destruction and death. After locating their analysis of liquid modernity through a comparison to the recent conceptual departures of Ulrich Beck and Anthony Giddens, Lemert and Goodman present Bauman's globalism as more open-ended and politically transgressive. 'Bauman', they write, 'thinks globally as opposed to thinking *about* globalization.' In this first part of the chapter, Lemert and Goodman show how Bauman keeps a critical distance from both Beck's and Giddens's 'liberal faith' in the modernist dream of autonomous individuality and progressive self-critique. Facing head-on the tragic realities of globalization, Bauman by contrast sees self-critique as a pathology of 'modernity's early attempts to present itself as solid when in fact it was always liquid'. In the second part of the chapter, Lemert and Goodman explore in detail the bulimic pathologies of our liquid age, focusing in particular on the dumping of humans in prisons, refugee camps and related sites of waste. In general, Lemert and Goodman extol the virtues of Bauman's sociology. However they do also suggest new pathways by which the themes of liquidity, globalism, waste and death might be more fruitfully developed in contemporary social theory. From this angle, they conclude that the haunting of contemporary culture is key to grasping liquidity – especially for understanding the play of symbolic death and ghosts in the ongoing expansion of advanced multidimensional capitalism.

In Chapter 8, 'Solid modernity, liquid utopia – liquid modernity, solid utopia', Michael Hviid Jacobsen examines some of the recent reformulations and revisions of Bauman's views on utopianism. Focusing primarily on the liquid turn in Bauman's theorizing, Jacobsen relates the presence and necessity of utopian thinking to the most ossified, dystopian elements of liquid modern societies and cultures. Taking aim at the beyond Left and Right political consensus of There Is No Alternative, Jacobsen unearths the subtle yet persistent message in Bauman's sociology that society does not have to be the way it is. Rereading Bauman's reflections on utopic constructs in social thought through the duality of solid and liquid modernities, Jacobsen maps with precision the complex ways in which modern utopias were intimately interwoven with the planning, regulation and governance of everyday life. The arrival of liquid modernity, says Jacobsen, means the abandonment of the grand utopic illusions of solid modernity – however this is less an end to utopia than its transformation. For one thing, utopia has now been appropriated by the entertainment industry and popular culture – what is termed the contemporary liquid utopia – as a kind of dystopia. Finally, Jacobsen tracks dormant utopian possibilities within the episodic and short-term logic of liquid modernity itself.

In Chapter 9, 'On Bauman's sociology of suffering: questions for thinking', Iain Wilkinson concentrates on the ethical dimensions of Bauman's work. Wilkinson returns to earlier formulations by Bauman that modernity is best grasped as involving the production of order and the elimination of ambivalence, and then traces the theme of human suffering throughout Bauman's recent writings – particularly the twin notions of 'wasted lives' and 'outcasts'. Wilkinson goes on to argue that Bauman's literary presentation of social suffering is of questionable character – that is, that it is focused too much on abstract, global issues and away from the concrete subjective experience of those that suffer. Bauman's sociology, says Wilkinson, 'affords little space for thinking with suffering'. In developing this argument, the chapter contrasts Bauman's work with the ethics of Hannah Arendt and seeks to connect the experience of suffering (however distantly observed in our global electronic age) with pressing public issues of moral and political reform.

The essays contained in this volume, notwithstanding the critical reflections developed in relation to the theory of liquid modernity, all recognize the fundamental significance of Bauman's recent work for social theory and social science. The critical appraisal of Bauman developed in this book highlights that one of the great strengths of the theory of liquid modernity lies in its reflective reconfiguration of the institutional and personal domains for the analysis of modern societies. Bauman, as I have suggested in this Introduction, mostly writes about a surge in conflicting desires to tighten interpersonal bonds yet keep them loose, which consequently allows him ample room to develop a hermeneutical sociological critique of our liquid modern lifestyles.

References

Bauman, Z. (1972) Between Class and Elite: The Evolution of the British Labour Movement: A Sociologically Study. Trans. Sheila Patterson. Manchester: Manchester University Press.
Bauman, Z. (1973) *Culture as Praxis*. London: Rutledge and Kegan Paul.
Bauman, Z. (1976) *Socialism: The Active Utopia*. London: Allen and Unwin.
Bauman, Z. (1978) *Hermeneutics and Social Science*. London: Hutchinson.
Bauman, Z. (1982) Memories of Class: The Pre-history and After-life of Class. London: Routledge and Kegan Paul.
Bauman, Z. (1987) Legislators and Interpreters: On Modernity, Post-modernity and Intellectuals. Cambridge: Polity Press.
Bauman, Z. (1989) *Modernity and the Holocaust*. Cambridge: Polity Press.
Bauman, Z. (1990) *Thinking Sociologically*. Oxford: Blackwell.
Bauman, Z. (1991) *Modernity and Ambivalence*. Cambridge: Polity Press.
Bauman, Z. (1992) *Intimations of Postmodernity*. London: Routledge.
Bauman, Z. (1993) *Postmodern Ethics*. Oxford: Blackwell.
Bauman, Z. (1995) *Life in Fragments*. Oxford: Blackwell.
Bauman, Z. (1997) *Postmodernity and its Discontents*. Cambridge: Polity Press.
Bauman, Z. (2000) *Liquid Modernity*. Cambridge: Polity Press.
Bauman, Z. (2001) *The Individualized Society*. Cambridge: Polity Press.
Bauman, Z. (2001) 'The Telos Interview', in Peter Beilharz (ed.) *The Bauman Reader*. Oxford: Blackwell.
Bauman, Z. (2002) *Society under Siege*. Cambridge: Polity Press.
Bauman, Z. (2003) *Liquid Love*. Cambridge: Polity Press.
Bauman, Z. (2004) *Wasted Lives: Modernity and Its Outcasts*. Cambridge: Polity Press.
Bauman, Z. (2004) *Identity*. Cambridge: Polity Press.
Bauman, Z. (2005) *Liquid Life*. Cambridge: Polity Press.
Bauman, Z. (2006) *Liquid Fear*. Cambridge: Polity Press.
Beck, U. (1999) *World Risk Society*. Cambridge: Polity Press.
Beilharz, P. (2000) *Zygmunt Bauman: Dialectic of Modernity*. London and Thousand Oaks, CA: Sage.
Jameson, F. (1992) Postmodernism, or The Cultural Logic of Late Capitalism. London: Verso.
Lyotard, J-F. (1984) *The Postmodern Condition: A Report on Knowledge*. Minneapolis: University of Minnesota Press.
Smith, D. (1999) *Zygmunt Bauman: Prophet of Postmodernity*. Cambridge: Polity Press.
Tester, K. (2004) *The Social Thought of Zygmunt Bauman*. London: Palgrave.
Tester, K. and Jacobsen, M. (eds) (2005) Bauman Before Postmodernity: Invitation, Conversations and Annotated Bibliography 1953–1989. Aalborg: Aalborg University Press.

ZYGMUNT BAUMAN

Critique – privatized and disarmed

Source: Zygmunt Bauman (2001) *The Individualized Society*,
Cambridge: Polity Press, pp. 99–108.[1]

What is wrong with the society we live in – said Cornelius Castoriadis – is that it has stopped questioning itself. This is a kind of society which no longer recognizes any alternative to itself and thereby feels absolved from the duty to examine, demonstrate, justify (let alone prove) the validity of its outspoken and tacit assumptions. This society did not suppress critical thought as such, neither did it make its members afraid of voicing it. The opposite is the case: it made the critique of reality, the disaffection with 'what is', both an unavoidable and an obligatory part of every member's life business. We are all engaged in 'life politics' – we are 'reflexive beings' who look closely at every move we take and are seldom satisfied with its results. Somehow, however, that reflexion does not reach far enough to embrace the conditions which connect our moves with their results and decide their outcomes. We are critically predisposed, but our critique is, so to speak, 'toothless', unable to affect the agenda set for our 'life-political' choices. The unprecedented freedom which our society offers its members has arrived, as Leo Strauss warned a long while ago, together with unprecedented impotence.

One sometimes hears the opinion that contemporary society (late modern or postmodern society, or, as Ulrich Beck has recently suggested, the society of 'second modernity') is inhospitable to critique. That opinion seems, however, to miss the nature of the ongoing change by assuming that the meaning of 'hospitality' itself is invariant. The point is, rather, that contemporary society has given 'hospitality to critique' an entirely new sense and invented a way to accommodate critical thought and action while itself remaining immune to the consequences of that accommodation and emerging unaffected and unscathed from the tests and trials of the open-house policy.

One can think of the kind of 'hospitality to critique' characteristic of present-day modern society as having the pattern of a camping site. The place is open to everyone who has their own caravan and money to pay the rent. Guests come and go, none taking much interest in how the site is run, providing that they have been allocated a plot big enough to park the caravan, that the electric sockets and water taps are in good order and that the passengers in nearby caravans do not make too much noise and turn down their portable hi-fi and TV speakers after 10 p.m. drivers bring their own homes attached to their cars, equipped with all the appliances they need for the short stay. Each driver has his or her own plans and own schedule, and wants from the site managers nothing more than to be left alone and not to be interfered with, promising in exchange not to break the site rules and to pay the rent. They pay and they demand. They tend to be quite adamant in claiming their rights to go their own ways and to demand that the promised services are on offer. On occasion, they may clamour for better service; if they are outspoken, vociferous and resolute enough, they may even obtain it. If they feel they are being short-changed or find that the managers' promises are not kept, campers may complain and demand their due – but it won't occur to them to challenge and renegotiate the managerial philosophy of the site. They may, at the utmost, make a mental note never to use the facilities again and not to recommend using them to their friends. When they leave, following their own itinerary, the site remains much as it was before their arrival – unaffected by past campers and waiting for the next to come – though if certain complaints go on being lodged repeatedly, the services provided may be modified to prevent similar discontents in the future.

As far as 'hospitality to critique' goes, our society follows the pattern of the *camping site* – while at the time 'critical theory' was put into shape by Adorno and Horkheimer it was another model – of a shared household, with its norms and rules, assignment of duties and supervised performance – in which, not without good reason, the idea of critique was inscribed. While hospitable to critique after the fashion of the camping site's hospitality to caravan owners, our society is definitely and resolutely *not* hospitable to critique in the mode which the founders of the critical school assumed and to which they addressed their theory. To put it in a nutshell, we may say that 'consumer-style critique' has come to replace the 'producer-style' one. That fateful shift cannot be explained merely by reference to a change of public mood, a common good and images of the good society, a fall in the popularity of political engagement or a rising tide of hedonistic and 'me first' sentiments – though all such phenomena are indeed signs of our times. The causes of the shift go deeper; they are rooted in a profound transformation of the public space and, more generally, in the fashion in which modern society works and self-perpetuates.

The kind of modernity which was the target, but also the cognitive frame, of classical critical theory appears in retrospect 'heavy' as against the contemporary 'light' modernity; better still, 'solid' as distinct from 'liquid' or 'liquefied'; condensed as against capillary; finally, *systemic* as distinct from *network-style*.

That was a kind of modernity pregnant with a totalitarian tendency; totalitarian society of compulsory and enforced homogeneity loomed constantly on the horizon as its ultimate destination, ineradicable threat or never fully exorcised spectre. That modernity was the sworn enemy of contingency, variety, ambiguity, waywardness and idiosyncrasy, and was bent on their annihilation; in the last account, it was freedom and autonomy that was expected to be the prime casualty of the crusade. The principal icons of that modernity were the *Fordist factory*, which reduced human activities to simple and routine and by and large predesigned moves, meant to be followed unquestioningly and mechanically without engaging mental faculties while keeping all spontaneity and individual initiative off-limits; *bureaucracy*, akin at least in its innate tendency to Max Weber's ideal model, in which the identities and social bonds of the officials were deposited in the cloakrooms on entry, together with hats, umbrellas and overcoats, so that solely the command and the statute book could guide the actions of the insiders so long as they stayed inside; the *panopticon*, with its watch-towers and residents who could never count on their surveillants having a momentary lapse of vigilance; the *Big Brother* who never dozes off, always quick and expeditious to reward the faithful and punish the infidels; and – finally – the *concentration camp* (later to be joined in the anti-Pantheon of modern demons by the *gulag*), the site at which the limits of human malleability are tested under laboratory conditions, while all those presumed not to be malleable enough are selected for gas chambers and Auschwitz crematoria.

Again in retrospect, we can say that critical theory was aimed at defusing, neutralizing and best of all turning off the totalitarian tendency of a society presumed to be contaminated with that tendency endemically and permanently. Defending human autonomy and the freedom to choose and self-assert was critical theory's principal target. Much as the early Hollywood melodramas presumed that the moment when the lovers find each other again and take marriage vows was the end of the drama and the beginning of the blissful 'living happily ever after', early critical theory saw the wrenching of individual liberty from the iron grip – or letting the individual out of the iron cage – of a society afflicted with insatiable totalitarian, homogenizing and uniformizing appetites as the ultimate task of emancipation and the end of human misery. Critique was to serve that purpose; it need not look beyond the moment of its attainment.

George Orwell's *1984* was at its time the canonical inventory of the fears and apprehensions which haunted modernity in its 'heavy' stage; once projected upon diagnoses of current troubles and causes of current sufferings, these fears set the horizons of the emancipatory programmes of the era. Come the real 1984, and Orwell's vision was expectedly drawn back into public debate and given once more (perhaps for the last time) a thorough venting. Most writers, again expectedly, sharpened their pens to pinpoint the truth and untruth in Orwell's prophecy as tested by the stretch of time Orwell gave his words to turn into flesh. In our times, when even the immortality of the greatest monuments of human cultural history is subject to continuous recycling, as they surface in public attention on the occasion of anniversaries or retrospective exhibitions, only to vanish from view and thought again once the exhibitions are over, the 'Orwell event' was not much different from the treatment accorded intermittently to the likes of Tutankhamen, Vermeer, Picasso or Monet. Even so, the brevity of *1984* celebration, the tepidness and rapid cooling of the interest it aroused and the speed with which Orwell's *chef d'oeuvre* sank into oblivion once the press hype ended – all that makes one pause and think; this book, after all, served for many decades (and still not that long ago) as the most authoritative catalogue of public fears, forebodings and nightmares; so why only passing interest in its brief flare-up? The only reasonable explanation is that those who discussed the book in 1984 felt lukewarm towards their subject because they no longer recognized their own chagrins and agonies in Orwell's dystopia. The book reappeared fleetingly in public debate, carrying a status plotted somewhere between that of Pliny the Elder's *Historia naturalis* and that of Nostradamus's prophecies.

For many years Orwell's dystopia, much like the sinister potentials of the Enlightenment unravelled by Adorno and Horkheimer, Bentham/Foucault's panopticon, or recurrent signals of a gathering totalitarian tide, came to be identified with the idea of 'modernity'. No wonder that once new fears, quite unlike the horrors of an impending *Gleichschaltung* and loss of freedom, came to the fore and forced their way into public debate, many observers hastened to proclaim the 'end of modernity' (or even, more boldly, the end of history itself – arguing that it had already reached its *telos* and made freedom, at least the type of freedom exemplified by consumer choice, immune to all further threats). And yet, to repeat after Mark Twain, the news of modernity's death is grossly exaggerated: the profusion of its obituaries does not make them any less premature. It seems that the kind of society which has been diagnosed and put on trial by the founders of Critical Theory (or, for that matter, by Orwell's dystopia) was but one of the forms modern society was to take. Its waning does not augur the end of modernity. Nor does it herald the end of human sufferings. Least of all does it presage the end of critique as intellectual task and vocation – even less does it render such critique redundant.

The society which enters the twenty-first century is no less 'modern' than the society which entered the twentieth; the most one can say is that it is modern in a somewhat different way. What makes it modern is what sets modernity apart from all other historical forms of human cohabitation: compulsive and obsessive, continuous and unstoppable *modernization*, the overwhelming and endemic urge for creative destruction (or destructive creativity, as the case might be: to 'clear the site' in the name of 'new and improved' design; to 'dismantle', 'cut out', 'phase out', 'downsize' for the sake of greater productivity or competitiveness). As Gotthold Lessing pointed out long ago, at the threshold of modern times we were emancipated from belief in the act of creation, in revelation and eternal condemnation; with such belief out of the way we, the humans, are 'on our own' – which means that there are no limits to improvement and self-improvement other than our own inherited or acquired gifts, nerve, resolve and determination. And whatever is man-made can be man-unmade. Being modern means being unable to stop, let alone to stand still. We move and are bound to keep moving not so much because of the 'delay of gratification', as Max Weber suggested – but due to the *impossibility* of being gratified: the horizon of satisfaction, the end of effort and restful self-congratulation move away faster than the fastest of the runners. Fulfilment is always in the future, and achievements lose their attraction and satisfying potential once achieved. Being modern means being perpetually ahead of oneself, in a state of constant transgression; it also means having an identity which can exist only as an unfulfilled project. In these respects, there is not much to distinguish between our grandfathers' and our own plights. Two features, nonetheless, make our situation – our form of modernity – novel and different.

The first is the collapse and decline of early modern illusions: namely, that there is an end to the road along which we proceed – a state of perfection to be reached tomorrow, next year or in the next millennium – something like a good society, just society, conflict-free society in any of its visualized forms: a state of steady equilibrium between supply and demand, of the satisfaction of all needs; a state of perfect order, in which everything is allocated to its right place and no place is in doubt; a state of affairs totally transparent, a control over the future, free from contingency, contention, ambivalence and unanticipated consequences of human undertakings.

The second seminal change is the deregulation and privatization of modernizing tasks and duties. What used to be seen as a task standing before human reason, seen as the collective endowment and property of the human species, has been fragmented – 'individualized', left to individual guts and stamina – and assigned to individually administered resources. Though the idea of improvement (or the modernization of the status quo) through legislating actions of the society as a whole has not been completely abandoned, the emphasis has shifted decisively towards the self-assertion of the individual. This fateful departure has been reflected in the shift of the ethical/political discourse from the 'just society' to 'human rights': that is, to the right of individuals to stay different and to pick and to choose at will their own models of happiness and proper lifestyle.

Instead of big money in governmental coffers, small change in the 'taxpayers' pockets'. The original modernity was top-heavy. The present-day modernity is light at the top at the expense of the middle and bottom layers, to which most of the burden of continuous modernization has been relegated. 'No more salvation by society,' famously proclaimed the spokesman for the new business spirit, Peter Drucker; 'there is no such thing as society,' declared yet more bluntly Margaret Thatcher. Do not look behind your back, or up; look inside, wherever your own cunning, will and power reside. There is no longer a 'Big Brother' watching you; it is now your task to watch Big Brothers and Big Sisters, closely and avidly, in the hope of finding a pattern to follow and guidance for coping with your problems, which, like their problems, need to be coped with individually. No more great Leaders to tell you what to do and to relieve you from responsibility for the consequences of your doings; in the world of the individuals, there are but other individuals from who you may draw examples of how to go about your own life business, bearing full responsibility for the consequences of investing your trust in this rather than that example.

We are all individuals now; not by choice, though, but by necessity. We are individuals *de jure* regardless of whether we are or are not individuals *de facto*: self-identification, self-management and self-assertion, and above all self-sufficiency in the performance of all these three tasks, are our duty whether or not we command the resources which the performance of the new duty demands (a duty by default rather than by design: simply, there is no other agency to do the job for us). Many of us have been individualized without truly becoming individuals, and many more yet are haunted by the suspicion that they are not really individuals enough to face up to the consequences of individualization. For most of us – as Ulrich Beck poignantly put it in *Risikogesellschaft (Risk Society)* – individualization amounts to 'the experts dumping their contradictions and conflicts at the feet of the individual and leaving him or her with the well-intention to judge all of this critically on the basis of his or her own notions'. As a result, most of us are compelled to seek 'biographic solutions to systemic contradictions'.

The modernizing impulse, in any of its renditions, means a compulsive critique of reality. The privatization of the impulse means compulsive *self-critique*: being and individual *de jure* means having no one to blame for one's own misery, seeking causes of one's own defeats nowhere except in one's own indolence and sloth, and looking for no remedies other than trying harder and harder still. Living daily with the risk of self-reprobation and self-contempt is not an easy matter. It generates ever greater supplies of the painful feeling of *Unsicherheit*. With eyes focused on one's own performance and thus diverted from the social space where the contradictions of individual existence are collectively produced, men and women are naturally tempted to reduce the complexity of their predicament. Not that they find 'biographic solutions' onerous and cumbersome: there are, simply, no 'biographic solutions to systemic contradictions', and so the dearth of solutions at their disposal needs to be compensated for by imaginary ones. Yet – imaginary or genuine – all 'solutions', to at least seem sensible and viable, must be in line and on a par with the 'individualization' of tasks and responsibilities. There is therefore a demand for individual pegs on which frightened individuals can collectively hang their individual fears, if only for a brief moment. Our time is auspicious for scapegoats – be they politicians making a mess of their private lives, criminals swarming out of the mean streets and rough districts, or 'foreigners in our midst'. Ours is a time of patented locks, burglar alarms, barbed fences, 'neighbourhood watches' and vigilantes, as well as 'investigative' tabloid journalists fishing for conspiracies to fill the threateningly empty public space and for plausible new causes for 'moral panics' to release the pent-up fear and anger.

There is a wide and growing gap between the plight of the 'individuals *de jure*' and their chances to become 'individuals *de facto*': to be in control of their fate and take the choices they truly desire. It is from that abysmal gap that the most poisonous effluvia contaminating the lives of contemporary individuals emanate. And that gap cannot be filled by individual efforts alone: not by the means and resources available within 'life politics'. Bridging that gap is a matter of politics. We may say that the gap has emerged and grown precisely because of the emptying of the public space, and particularly the *agora*, that public/private, intermediary site where 'life politics' meets Politics with a capital 'P': where private problems are translated as public issues and public solutions are sought, negotiated and agreed for private troubles.

The table has been turned; the task of critical theory has been reversed. It used to be the defence of private autonomy from the advancing troops of the public domain, almost wholly subsumed under the rule of the all-powerful, impersonal State and its many bureaucratic tentacles or smaller-scale replicas. It is now the defence of the vanishing public realm, or rather the refurnishing of the public space fast emptying due to desertion on both sides: the exit of the 'interested citizen' and the escape of real power into a territory which, for all the extant democratic institutions are capable of doing, can only be described as outer space.

It is no longer true that the 'public' is set on colonizing the 'private'. The opposite is the case: it is the private that colonizes the public space, squeezing out and chasing away everything which cannot be fully, without residue, translated into the vocabulary of private interests and pursuits. As de Tocqueville observed as much as two centuries ago – the individual is the citizen's worst enemy. Told repeatedly that he or she is the master of his or her own fate, the individual has little reason to accord 'topical relevancy' (Alfred Schütz's term) to anything which resists being engulfed within the self and being dealt with by the self's facilities; but having such a reason and acting upon it is precisely the trademark of the citizen.

For the individual, the public space is not much more than a giant screen on which private worries are projected without, in the course of magnification, ceasing to be private: the public space is where public confession of private secrets and intimacies is made. From the daily guided tours of the public space individuals return reinforced in their *de jure* individuality and reassured that the solitary fashion in which they go about their life business is what other 'individuals like them' do, and – again like them – do with their own measure of stumblings and (hopefully transient) defeats.

As to the power – it sails away from the street and the market-place, from assembly halls and parliaments, local and national governments, and beyond the reach of citizens' control, into the exterritoriality of electronic networks. Its strategic principles are nowadays escape, avoidance, disengagement and invisibility. Attempts to anticipate its moves and predict the unanticipated consequence of its moves (let alone to avert the undesirable among them) have all the practical effectiveness of a League to Prevent the Changes of Weather.

And so the public space is increasingly empty of public issues. It fails to perform its former role of a meeting-and-dialogue place for private troubles and public issues. On the receiving end of the individualizing pressure, individuals have been gradually but consistently stripped of the protective armour of citizenship and had their citizen skills and interests expropriated. As a result, the prospect of the individual-*de-jure* ever turning into the individual-*de-facto* (that is, one who commands the resources indispensable for genuine self-determination) becomes ever more remote.

The 'individual *de jure*' cannot turn into the 'individual *de facto*' without first turning into the *citizen*. There are no autonomous individuals without an autonomous society, and the autonomy of society requires deliberate and deliberated self-constitution, which may only be a shared accomplishment of its members. 'Society' has always stood in an ambiguous relation to individual autonomy: it has been, simultaneously, its enemy and its *sine qua non* condition. But the relative proportions of threats and chances in what is bound to remain an ambivalent relationship have radically changed in the course of modern history. Less than an enemy, society is the condition individuals strongly need yet badly miss in their vain and frustrating struggle to reforge their *de jure* status into a genuine autonomy and capacity for self-assertion.

This is, in the broadest of outlines, the predicament setting the present-day tasks of critical theory – and social critique in general. They boil down to once more tying together what the combination of formal individualization and the divorce between power and politics have torn asunder. In other words, to redesigning and repopulating the now largely vacant *agora* – the site of meeting, debate and negotiation between the individual and the common, private and public good. If the old objective of critical theory – human emancipation – means anything today, it means to reconnect the two edges of the abyss which has opened between the reality of the 'individual *de jure*' and the prospects of the 'individual *de facto*'. And individuals who have relearned the forgotten citizen skills and reappropriated the lost citizen tools are the only builders who are up to the task of this particular bridge-making.

Note

1 This essay was previously published in *Zeitschrift für Kritische Theorie* 9 (1999).

PART ONE

LIQUID MODERNITY

Zygmunt Bauman
ON BEING LIGHT AND LIQUID   29

Zygmunt Bauman
FROM HEAVY TO LIGHT MODERNITY   34

1 Anthony Elliott
   THE THEORY OF LIQUID MODERNITY: A CRITIQUE OF BAUMAN'S
   RECENT SOCIOLOGY   46

2 Larry Ray
   FROM POSTMODERNITY TO LIQUID MODERNITY: WHAT'S IN A
   METAPHOR?   63

3 Keith Tester
   BAUMAN'S IRONY   81

ZYGMUNT BAUMAN

ON BEING LIGHT AND LIQUID

Source: Zygmunt Bauman (2000) *Liquid Modernity*, Cambridge: Polity Press, pp. 1–8.

Liquids, unlike solids, cannot easily hold their shape. Fluids, so to speak, neither fix space nor bind time. While solids have clear spatial dimensions but neutralize the impact, and thus downgrade the significance, of time (effectively resist its flow or render it irrelevant), fluids do not keep to any shape for long and are constantly ready (and prone) to change it; and so for them it is the flow of time that counts, more than the space they happen to occupy: that space, after all, they fill but 'for a moment'. In a sense, solids cancel time; for liquids, on the contrary, it is mostly time that matters. When describing solids, one may ignore time altogether; in describing fluids, to leave time out of account would be a grievous mistake. Descriptions of fluids are all snapshots, and they need a date at the bottom of the picture.

Fluids travel easily. They 'flow', 'spill', 'run out', 'splash', 'pour over', 'leak', 'flood', 'spray', 'drip', 'seep', 'ooze'; unlike solids, they are not easily stopped – they pass around some obstacles, dissolve some others and bore or soak their way through others still. From the meeting with solids they emerge unscathed, while the solids they have met, if they stay solid, are changed – get moist or drenched. The extraordinary mobility of fluids is what associates them with the idea of 'lightness'. There are liquids which, cubic inch for cubic inch, are heavier than many solids, but we are inclined nonetheless to visualize them all as lighter, less 'weighty' than everything solid. We associate 'lightness' or 'weightlessness' with mobility and inconstancy: we know from practice that the lighter we travel the easier and faster we move.

These are reasons to consider 'fluidity' or 'liquidity' as fitting metaphors when we wish to grasp the nature of the present, in many ways *novel,* phase in the history of modernity.

I readily agree that such a proposition may give a pause to anyone at home in the 'modernity discourse' and familiar with the vocabulary commonly used to narrate modern history. Was not modernity a process of 'liquefaction' from the start? Was not 'melting the solids' its major pastime and prime accomplishment all along? In other words, has modernity not been 'fluid' since its inception?

These and similar objections are well justified, and will seem more so once we recall that the famous phrase 'melting the solids', when coined a century and a half ago by the authors of *The Communist Manifesto,* referred to the treatment which the self-confident and exuberant modern spirit awarded the society it found much too stagnant for its taste and much too resistant to shift and mould for its ambitions –

since it was frozen in its habitual ways. If the 'spirit' was 'modern', it was so indeed in so far as it was determined that reality should be emancipated from the 'dead hand' of its own history – and this could only be done by melting the solids (that is, by definition, dissolving whatever persists over time and is negligent of its passage or immune to its flow). That intention called in turn for the 'profaning of the sacred': for disavowing and dethroning the past, and first and foremost 'tradition' – to wit, the sediment and residue of the past in the present; it thereby called for the smashing of the protective armour forged of the beliefs and loyalties which allowed the solids to resist the 'liquefaction'.

Let us remember, however, that all this was to be done not in order to do away with the solids once and for all and make the brave new world free of them for ever, but to clear the site for *new and improved solids*; to replace the inherited set of deficient and defective solids with another set, which was much improved and preferably perfect, and for that reason no longer alterable. When reading de Tocqueville's *Ancien Régime,* one might wonder in addition to what extent the 'found solids' were resented, condemned and earmarked for liquefaction for the reason that they were already rusty, mushy, coming apart at the seams and altogether unreliable. Modern times found the pre-modern solids in a fairly advanced state of disintegration; and one of the most powerful motives behind the urge to melt them was the wish to discover or invent solids of – for a change – *lasting* solidity, a solidity which one could trust and rely upon and which would make the world predictable and therefore manageable.

The first solids to be melted and the first sacreds to be profaned were traditional loyalties, customary rights and obligations which bound hands and feet, hindered moves and cramped the enterprise. To set earnestly about the task of building a new (truly solid!) order, it was necessary to get rid of the ballast with which the old order burdened the builders. 'Melting the solids' meant first and foremost shedding the 'irrelevant' obligations standing in the way of rational calculation of effects; as Max Weber put it, liberating business enterprise from the shackles of the family-household duties and from the dense tissue of ethical obligations; or, as Thomas Carlyle would have it, leaving solely the 'cash nexus' of the many bonds underlying human mutuality and mutual responsibilities. By the same token, that kind of 'melting the solids' left the whole complex network of social relations unstuck – bare, unprotected, unarmed and exposed, impotent to resist the business-inspired rules of action and business-shaped criteria of rationality, let alone to compete with them effectively.

That fateful departure laid the field open to the invasion and domination of (as Weber put it) instrumental rationality, or (as Karl Marx articulated it) the determining role of economy: now the 'basis' of social life gave all life's other realms the status of 'superstructure' – to wit, an artefact of the 'basis' whose sole function was to service its smooth and continuing operation. The melting of solids led to the progressive untying of economy from its traditional political, ethical and cultural entanglements. It sedimented a new order, defined primarily in economic terms. That new order was to be more 'solid' than the orders it replaced, because – unlike them – it was immune to the challenge from non-economic action. Most political or moral levers capable of shifting or reforming the new order have been broken or rendered too short, weak or otherwise inadequate for the task. Not that the economic order, once entrenched, will have colonized, re-educated and converted to its ways the rest of social life; that order came to dominate the totality of human life because whatever else might have happened in that life has been rendered irrelevant and ineffective as far as the relentless and continuous reproduction of that order was concerned.

That stage in modernity's career has been well described by Claus Offe (in 'The Utopia of the Zero Option', first published in 1987 in *Praxis International):* 'complex' societies 'have become rigid to such an extent that the very attempt to reflect normatively upon or renew their 'order', that is, the nature of the coordination of the processes which take place in them, is virtually precluded by dint of their practical futility and thus their essential inadequacy'. However free and volatile the 'subsystems' of that order may be singly or severally, the way in which they are intertwined is 'rigid, fatal, and sealed off from any freedom of choice'. The overall order of things is not open to options; it is far from clear what such options could be, and even less clear how an ostensibly viable option could be made real in the unlikely case of social life being able to conceive it and gestate. Between the overall order and every one of the agencies, vehicles and stratagems of purposeful action there is a cleavage – a perpetually widening gap with no bridge in sight.

Contrary to most dystopian scenarios, this effect has not been achieved through dictatorial rule, subordination, oppression or enslavement, nor through the 'colonization' of the private sphere by the 'system'. Quite the opposite: the present-day situation emerged out of the radical melting of the fetters and manacles rightly or wrongly suspected of limiting the individual freedom to choose and to act. *Rigidity of order is the artefact and sediment of the human agents' freedom.* That rigidity is the overall product of 'releasing the brakes': of deregulation, liberalization, 'flexibilization', increased fluidity, unbridling the financial, real estate and labour markets, easing the tax burden, etc. (as Offe pointed out in 'Binding, Shackles, Brakes', first published in 1987); or (to quote from Richard Sennett's *Flesh and Stone*) of the techniques of 'speed, escape, passivity' – in other words, techniques which allow the system and free agents to remain radically disengaged, to by-pass each other instead of meeting. If the time of systemic revolutions has passed, it is because there are no buildings where the control desks of the system are lodged and which could be stormed and captured by the revolutionaries; and also because it is excruciatingly difficult, nay impossible, to imagine what the victors, once inside the buildings (if they found them first), could do to turn the tables and put paid to the misery that prompted them to rebel. One should be hardly taken aback or puzzled by the evident shortage of would-be revolutionaries: of the kind of people who articulate the desire to change their individual plights as a project of changing the order of society.

The task of constructing a new and better order to replace the old and defective one is not presently on the agenda – at least not on the agenda of that realm where political action is supposed to reside. The 'melting of solids', the permanent feature of modernity, has therefore acquired a new meaning, and above all has been redirected to a new target – one of the paramount effects of that redirection being the dissolution of forces which could keep the question of order and system on the political agenda. The solids whose turn has come to be thrown into the melting pot and which are in the process of being melted at the present time, the time of fluid modernity, are the bonds which interlock individual choices in collective projects and actions – the patterns of communication and coordination between individually conducted life policies on the one hand and political actions of human collectivities on the other.

In an interview given to Jonathan Rutherford on 3 February 1999, Ulrich Beck (who a few years earlier coined the term 'second modernity' to connote the phase marked by the modernity 'turning upon itself', the era of the *soi-disant* 'modernization of modernity') speaks of 'zombie categories' and 'zombie institutions' which are 'dead and still alive'. He names the family, class and neighbourhood as the foremost examples of that new phenomenon. The family, for instance:

> Ask yourself what actually is a family nowadays? What does it mean? Of course there are children, my children, our children. But even parenthood, the core of family life, is beginning to disintegrate under conditions of divorce . . . [G]randmothers and grandfathers get included and excluded without any means of participating in the decisions of their sons and daughters. From the point of view of their grandchildren the meaning of grandparents has to be determined by individual decisions and choices.

What is happening at present is, so to speak, a redistribution and reallocation of modernity's 'melting powers'. They affected at first the extant institutions, the frames that circumscribed the realms of possible action-choices, like hereditary estates with their no-appeal-allowed allocation-by-ascription. Configurations, constellations, patterns of dependency and interaction were all thrown into the melting pot, to be subsequently recast and refashioned; this was the 'breaking the mould' phase in the history of the inherently transgressive, boundary-breaking, all-eroding modernity. As for the individuals, however – they could be excused for failing to notice; they came to be confronted by patterns and figurations which, albeit 'new and improved', were as stiff and indomitable as ever.

Indeed, no mould was broken without being replaced with another; people were let out from their old cages only to be admonished and censured in case they failed to relocate themselves, through their own, dedicated and continuous, truly life-long efforts, in the ready-made niches of the new order: in the *classes,* the frames which (as uncompromisingly as the already dissolved *estates)* encapsulated the totality of life conditions and life prospects and determined the range of realistic life projects and life strategies. The task confronting free individuals was to use their new freedom to find the appropriate niche and to settle there through conformity: by faithfully following the rules and modes of conduct identified as right and proper for the location.

It is such patterns, codes and rules to which one could conform, which one could select as stable orientation points and by which one could subsequently let oneself be guided, that are nowadays in increasingly short supply. It does not mean that our contemporaries are guided solely by their own imagination and resolve and are free to construct their mode of life from scratch and at will, or that they are no longer dependent on society for the building materials and design blueprints. But it does mean that we are presently moving from the era of pre-allocated 'reference groups' into the epoch of 'universal comparison', in which the destination of individual self-constructing labours is endemically and incurably underdetermined, is not given in advance, and tends to undergo numerous and profound changes before such labours reach their only genuine end: that is, the end of the individual's life.

These days patterns and configurations are no longer 'given', let alone 'self-evident'; there are just too many of them, clashing with one another and contradicting one another's commandments, so that each one has been stripped of a good deal of compelling, coercively constraining powers. And they have changed their nature and have been accordingly reclassified: as items in the inventory of individual tasks. Rather than preceding life politics and framing its future course, they are to follow it (follow *from* it), to be shaped and reshaped by its twists and turns. The liquidizing powers have moved from the 'system' to 'society', from polities' to 'life policies' – or have descended from the 'macro' to the 'micro' level of social cohabitation.

Ours is, as a result, an individualized, privatized version of modernity, with the burden of pattern-weaving and the responsibility for failure falling primarily on the individual's shoulders. It is the patterns of dependency and interaction whose turn to be liquefied has now come. They are now malleable to an extent unexperienced by, and unimaginable for, past generations; but like all fluids they do not keep their shape for long. Shaping them is easier than keeping them in shape. Solids are cast once and for all. Keeping fluids in shape requires a lot of attention, constant vigilance and perpetual effort – and even then the success of the effort is anything but a foregone conclusion.

It would be imprudent to deny, or even to play down, the profound change which the advent of 'fluid modernity' has brought to the human condition. The remoteness and unreachability of systemic structure, coupled with the unstructured, fluid state of the immediate setting of life politics, change that condition in a radical way and call for a rethinking of old concepts that used to frame its narratives. Like zombies, such concepts are today simultaneously dead and alive. The practical question is whether their resurrection, albeit in a new shape or incarnation, is feasible; or – if it is not – how to arrange for their decent and effective burial.

ZYGMUNT BAUMAN

FROM HEAVY TO LIGHT MODERNITY

Source: Zygmunt Bauman (2000) *Liquid Modernity*, Cambridge: Polity Press, pp. 113–29.

The era of *hardware,* or *heavy* modernity – the bulk-obsessed modernity, 'the larger the better' kind of modernity, of 'the size is power, the volume is success' sort. That was the *hardware* era; the epoch of weighty and ever more cumbersome machines, of the ever longer factory walls enclosing ever wider factory floors and ingesting ever more populous factory crews, of ponderous rail engines and gigantic ocean liners. To conquer space was the supreme goal – to grasp as much of it as one could hold, and to hold to it, marking it all over with the tangible tokens of possession and 'No trespassing' boards. Territory was among the most acute of modern obsessions, its acquisition among the most compulsive of modern urges – while guarding the boundaries figured high among the most ubiquitous, resilient and relentlessly growing modern addictions.

Heavy modernity was the era of territorial conquest. Wealth and power was firmly rooted or deposited deep inside the land – bulky, ponderous and immovable like the beds of iron ore and deposits of coal. Empires spread to fill every nook and cranny of the globe: only other empires of equal or superior strength set limits to their expansion. Anything lying between the outposts of competing imperial realms was seen as masterless, a no man's land, and so *an empty space* – and empty space was a challenge to action and reproach to idlers. (The popular science of the time grasped the mood of the era perfectly when informing laymen that 'Nature suffers no void.') Even more off-putting and less bearable was the thought of the globe's 'blank spots': islands and archipelagos as yet unheard of and unadumbrated, landmasses waiting to be discovered and colonized, the untrodden and unclaimed interiors of continents, the uncounted 'hearts of darkness' clamouring for light. Intrepid explorers were the heroes of the new, modern versions of Walter Benjamin's 'sailor stories', of childhood dreams and adult nostalgia; enthusiastically cheered on their departure and showered with honours on their return, expedition after expedition wandered through the jungle, bush or permafrost in search of as yet uncharted mountain range, lake or plateau. Also the modern paradise, like James Hilton's Shangri-La, was 'out there', in a still 'undiscovered' place, hidden and inaccessible, somewhere beyond the unpassed and impassable mountain masses or deadly deserts, at the end of a trail yet to be blazed. Adventure and happiness, wealth and might were geographical concepts or 'land estates' – tied to their place, immovable and untransferable. All that called for impenetrable walls, dense and tight checkpoints, unsleeping borderguards, and secrecy of the locations. (One of the most closely guarded secrets of World War II, the American air base from which the murderous raid on Tokyo was to be launched in 1942, was nicknamed 'Shangri-La'.)

Wealth and might which depend on the size and the quality of hardware tend to be sluggish, unwieldy and awkward to move. Both are 'embodied' and fixed, tied in steel and concrete and measured by their volume and weight. They grow by expanding the place they occupy and are protected by protecting that place: the place is, simultaneously, their hotbed, their fortress and their prison. Daniel Bell described one of the most powerful and most envied and emulated of such hotbeds/fortresses/prisons: the General Motors 'Willow Run' plant in Michigan.[1] The site occupied by the plant was two-thirds by a quarter of a mile. All the materials needed to produce cars were gathered under one gigantic roof, in a single monstrous cage. The logic of power and the logic of control were both grounded in the strict separation of the 'inside' from the 'outside' and a vigilant defence of the boundary between the two. Both logics, blended in one, were embodied in the logic of size, organized around one precept: bigger means more efficient. In the heavy version of modernity, progress meant growing size and spatial expansion.

It was the routinization of time that held the place whole, compact and subject to homogeneous logic. (Bell invoked the principal tool of routinization when calling such time 'metric'.)

In the conquest of space, time had to be pliant and malleable, and above all shrinkable through the increased 'space-devouring' capacity of each unit. To go around the world in eighty days was an alluring dream, but to do it in eight days was infinitely more attractive. Flying over the English Channel and then over the Atlantic were the milestones by which progress was measured. When, however, it came to the fortification of the conquered space, to its taming, colonization and domestication, a tough, uniform and inflexible time was needed: the kind of time that could be cut in slices of similar thickness fit to be arranged in monotonous and unalterable sequences. Space was truly 'possessed' when controlled – and control meant first and foremost the 'taming of time', neutralizing its inner dynamism. In short, the uniformity and coordination of time. It was wonderful and exciting to reach the sources of the Nile before other explorers managed to find it, but a train running ahead of schedule or automobile parts arriving on the assembly line ahead of other parts were heavy modernity's most gruesome nightmares.

Routinized time joined forces with high brick walls crowned with barbed wire or broken glass and closely guarded gates in protecting the place against intruders; it also prevented all those inside the place from leaving it at will. The 'Fordist factory', that most coveted and avidly pursued model of engineered rationality in times of heavy modernity, was the site of face-to-face meeting, but also a 'till death us do part' type of marriage vow between capital and labour. The wedding was of convenience or necessity, hardly ever a marriage of love – but it was meant to last 'for ever' (whatever that might have meant in terms of individual life), and more often than not it did. The marriage was, essentially, mono-gamic – and for both partners. Divorce was out of the question. For better or worse, the partners in marriage were bound to stay in each other's company; neither could survive without the other.

Routinized time tied labour to the ground, while the massiveness of the factory buildings, the heaviness of the machinery and, last but not least, the permanently tied labour 'bonded' the capital. Neither capital nor labour was eager, or able, to move. Like any other marriage that lacked the safety valve of painless divorce, the story of cohabitation was full of sound and fury, fraught with violent eruptions of enmity and marked by somewhat less dramatic, but more relentless and persistent, day in, day out, trench war. At no time, however, did the plebeians think of leaving the city; the patricians were no more free to do so. Menenius Agrippa's oratory was not needed to keep either in place. The very intensity and perpetuity of conflict was a vivid evidence of commonality of fate. The frozen time of factory routine, together with the bricks and mortar of factory walls, immobilized capital as effectively as it bound the labour it employed. It all changed, though, with the advent of software capitalism and 'light' modernity. The Sorbonne economist Daniel Cohen put it in a nutshell: 'Whoever begins a career at Microsoft has not the slightest idea where it will end. Whoever started it at Ford or Renault, could be well-nigh certain that it will finish in the same place.'[2]

I am not sure whether in both of the cases described by Cohen the use of the term 'career' is legitimate. 'Career' brings to mind a set trajectory, not unlike the American universities' 'tenure tracks', with a sequence of stages marked in advance and accompanied by moderately clear conditions of entry and rules of admission. The 'career paths' tend to be shaped by coordinated pressures of space and time. Whatever happens to the employees of Microsoft or its countless watchers and imitators, where all concern of the managers is 'with looser organizational forms which are more able to go with the flow', and where business organization is increasingly seen as a never conclusive, ongoing attempt 'to form an island of superior adaptability' in a world perceived as 'multiple, complex and fast moving, and therefore as "ambiguous", "fuzzy" or "plastic"',[3] militates against durable structures, and notably against structures with a built-in life expectation commensurable with the customary length of a working life. Under such conditions the idea of a 'career' seems nebulous and utterly out of place.

This is, though, merely a terminological quibble. Whether the terms are correctly or wrongly used, the main point is that Cohen's comparison grasps unerringly the watershed-like change in the modern history of time and hints at the impact it is beginning to make on the human existential condition. The change in question is the new irrelevance of space, masquerading as the annihilation of time. In the software universe of light-speed travel, space may be traversed, literally, in 'no time'; the difference between 'far away' and 'down here' is cancelled. Space no more sets limits to action and its effects, and counts little, or does not count at all. It has lost its 'strategic value', the military experts would say.

All values, as Georg Simmel observed, are 'valuable' in so far as they are to be gained 'only by forgoing other values'; it is the 'detour to the attainment of certain things' which is the cause to 'regard them as valuable'. Without using these words, Simmel tells the story of a 'value fetishism': things, wrote Simmel, 'are worth just what they cost'; and this circumstance appears, perversely, 'to mean that they cost what they are worth'. It is the obstacles which need to be negotiated on the way that lead to their appropriation, 'the tension of the struggle for it' which makes values valuable.[4] If no time needs to be lost and forgone – 'sacrificed' – to reach even the remotest of places, places are stripped of value in the Simmelian sense. Once distances can be spanned (and so the materially distant parts of space acted upon and affected) with the velocity of electronic signals, all references to time appear, as Jacques Derrida would put it, *'sous rature'*. 'Instantaneity' apparently refers to a very quick movement and very short time, but in fact it denotes the absence of time as a factor of the event and by the same token as an element in the calculation of value. Time is no longer the 'detour to the attainment', and thus no longer bestows value on space. The near-instantaneity of software time augurs the devaluation of space.

In the era of hardware, of heavy modernity, which in Max Weber's terms was also the era of instrumental rationality, time was the means which needed to be husbanded and managed prudently so that the returns of value, which were space, could be maximized; in the era of software, of light modernity, the effectiveness of time as a means of value-attainment tends to approach infinity, with the paradoxical effect of levelling up (or rather down) the value of all units in the field of potential objectives. The question mark has moved from the side of the means to that of the ends. If applied to the time–space relation, this means that since all parts of space can be reached in the same time span (that is in 'no-time'), no part of space is privileged, none has 'special value'. If all parts of space can be reached at any moment, there is no reason to reach any of them at any particular moment and no reason to worry about securing the right of access to any. If you know that you can visit a place at any time you wish, there is no urge to visit it often or to spend money on a valid-for-life ticket. There is even less reason to bear the expenditure of perpetual supervision and management, of laborious and risk-fraught husbandry and cultivation of lands which can be easily reached and as easily abandoned following the shifting interests and 'topical relevances'.

The seductive lightness of being

The insubstantial, instantaneous time of the software world is also an inconsequential time. 'Instantaneity' means immediate, 'on-the-spot' fulfilment – but also immediate exhaustion and fading of interest. Time-distance separating the end from the beginning is shrinking or vanishing altogether; the two notions, which were once used to plot the passing, and so to calculate the 'forfeited value, of time, have lost much of their meaning, which – as all meanings – arose from the starkness of their opposition. There are only 'moments' – points without dimensions. But is such a time, time with the morphology of an aggregate of moments, still time 'as we know it'? The expression 'moment of time' seems, at least in certain vital respects, an oxymoron. Perhaps, having killed space as value, time has committed suicide? Was not space merely the first casualty in time's frenzied rush to self-annihilation?

What has been described here is, of course, a *liminal* condition in the history of time – what seems to be, at its present stage, that history's ultimate *tendency*. However close to zero is the time needed to reach a spatial destination, it has not yet quite arrived. Even the most advanced technology armed with ever more powerful processors has still some way to go to attain genuine 'instantaneity'. Nor has the logically following irrelevance of space truly and fully happened, nor has the weightlessness, the infinite volatility and flexibility of human agency, been achieved. But the condition described is indeed the developmental horizon of light modernity. More importantly yet, it is the ever-to-be-pursued though (or is it because?) never-to-be-reached-in-full ideal of its major operators, one that in the avatar of a new norm pervades and saturates every organ, tissue and cell of the social body. Milan Kundera portrayed 'the unbearable lightness of being' as the hub of modern life's tragedy. Lightness and speed (together!) have been offered by Italo Calvino, the inventor of those totally free characters (free completely, owing to their being uncatchable, unensnarable, elusive, impossible to lay hold of) – the tree-jumping baron and the bodyless knight – as the fullest, ultimate incarnations of the eternal emancipatory function of literary art.

More than thirty years ago (in his classic *Bureaucratic Phenomenon*) Michel Crozier identified domination (in all its varieties) with the closeness to the sources of uncertainty. His verdict still holds: people who manage to keep their own actions unbound, norm-free and so unpredictable, while normatively regulating (routinizing, and thereby rendering monotonous, repetitive and predictable) the actions of their protagonists, rule. People whose hands are untied rule over people with tied hands; the freedom of the first is the main cause of the unfreedom of the second – while the unfreedom of the second is the ultimate meaning of the freedom of the first.

Nothing has changed in this respect with the passage from heavy to light modernity. But the frame has filled with a new content; more precisely, the pursuit of the 'closeness to the source of uncertainty' has narrowed down to, and focused on, one objective – instantaneity. People who move and act faster, who come nearest to the momentariness of movement, are now the people who rule. And it is the people who cannot move as quickly, and more conspicuously yet the category of people who cannot at will leave their place at all, who are ruled. Domination consists in one's own capacity to escape, to disengage, to 'be elsewhere', and the right to decide the speed with which all that is done – while simultaneously stripping the people on the dominated side of their ability to arrest or constrain their moves or slow them down. The contemporary battle of domination is waged between forces armed, respectively, with the weapons of acceleration and procrastination.

Differential access to instantaneity is crucial among the present-day versions of the everlasting and indestructible foundation of social division in all its historically changing forms: the differential access to unpredictability, and hence to freedom. In a world populated by ground-plodding serfs, tree-jumping was for the barons a foolproof recipe for freedom. It is the facility of the present-day barons to behave in a fashion akin to jumping the trees which keeps the successors of the serfs in place, and it is these successors' enforced immobility, boundedness to the ground, that allows the barons to go on jumping. However deep and depressing the serfs' misery, there is no one in sight to rebel against, and had the serfs rebelled they would not have caught up with the fast-moving targets of their rebellion. Heavy modernity kept capital and labour in an iron cage which none of them could escape.

Light modernity let one partner out of the cage. 'Solid' modernity was an era of mutual engagement. 'Fluid' modernity is the epoch of disengagement, elusiveness, facile escape and hopeless chase. In 'liquid' modernity, it is the most elusive, those free to move without notice, who rule.

Karl Polanyi (in *The Great Transformation: The Political and Economic Origin of our Time,* published in 1944) proclaimed the treatment of labour as 'commodity' to be a fiction and unwrapped the consequences of the social arrangement based on that fiction. Labour, Polanyi pointed out, cannot be a commodity (at least not a commodity like other commodities), since it cannot be sold or bought separately from its carriers. The labour which Polanyi wrote about was indeed *embodied* labour: labour which could not be moved around without moving the labourers in the flesh. One could hire and employ human labour only together with the rest of the labourers' bodies, and the inertia of the hired bodies set limits to the freedom of the employers. To supervise labour and to channel it according to the design, one had to manage and supervise the labourers; to control the work process, one had to control the workers. That requirement brought capital and labour face to face and kept them, for better or worse, in each other's company. The result was much conflict, but also a lot of mutual accommodation: acrimonious charges, bitter struggle and altogether little love lost, but also tremendous ingenuity in designing the moderately satisfying or just bearable rules of cohabitation. Revolutions and welfare state were both the unanticipated but unavoidable outcome of the condition which precluded the disengagement from being a feasible and viable option.

We now live through another 'great transformation', and one of its most prominent aspects is a phenomenon exactly opposite to the condition which Polanyi took for granted: the 'disembodiment' of that type of human labour which serves as the principal source of nourishment, or the grazing ground, of contemporary capital. Panopticon-like, bulky, clumsy and awkward installations of surveillance and drill are no longer necessary. Labour has been let out of the Panopticon, but, most importantly, capital has shed the vexing burden and exorbitant costs of running it; capital got rid of the task which tied it to the ground and forced it into direct engagement with the agents exploited for the sake of its self-reproduction and self-aggrandizement.

The disembodied labour of the software era no longer ties down capital: it allows capital to be exterritorial, volatile and fickle. Disembodiment of labour augurs weightlessness of capital. Their mutual dependency has been broken unilaterally; while the capacity to labour is as before incomplete and unfulfillable if left alone, and dependent on the presence of capital for its fulfilment, the reverse does not apply any more. Capital travels hopefully, counting on brief profitable adventures and confident that there will be no shortage of them or of partners to share them with. Capital can travel fast and travel light and its lightness and motility have turned into the paramount source of uncertainty for all the rest. This has become the present-day basis of domination and the principal factor of social divisions.

Bulkiness and size are turning from assets into liabilities. For capitalists who would rather exchange massive office buildings for hot-air balloon cabins, buoyancy is the most profitable and the most cherished of assets; and buoyancy can be best enhanced by throwing overboard every bit of non-vital load and leaving the non-indispensable members of the crew on the ground. One of the most cumbersome items of ballast which needs to be disposed of is the onerous task of management and supervision of a large staff – a task which has an irritating tendency to swell incessantly and to put on weight through the addition of ever new layers of commitments and obligations. If the 'managerial science' of heavy capitalism focused on keeping the 'manpower' in and forcing or bribing it to stay put and to work on schedule, the art of management in the era of light capitalism is concerned with letting 'humanpower' out and better still forcing it to go. Brief encounters replace lasting engagements. One does not plant a citrus-tree grove to squeeze a lemon.

The managerial equivalent of liposuction has become the paramount stratagem of managerial art: slimming, downsizing, phasing out, closing down or selling out some units because they are not effective enough and some others because it is cheaper to let them fight for survival on their own than to undertake the burdensome, time-taxing managerial supervision, are this new art's principal applications.

Some observers have hastened to conclude that 'bigger' is no longer considered to be 'more efficient'. In such generalized rendition, though, this conclusion is not correct. The downsizing obsession is, as it happens, an undetachable complement of the merger mania. The best players in the field are known to negotiate or enforce mergers in order to acquire more scope for downsizing operations, while the radical, 'right to the bare bone' 'stripping of assets' is widely accepted as the vital precondition for the success of the merger plans. Merger and downsizing are not at cross-purposes: on the contrary, they condition each other, support and reinforce. This only appears to be a paradox; the apparent contradiction dissolves once the 'new and improved' rendition of Michel Crozier's principle is considered. It is the blend of merger and downsizing strategies that offers capital and financial power the space to move and move quickly, making the scope of its travel ever more global, while at the same time depriving labour of its bargaining and nuisance-making power, immobilizing it and tying its hands ever more firmly.

Merger augurs a longer rope for the lean, buoyant, Houdini-style capital which has made the major vehicles of its domination out of evasion and escape, the substitution of short-term deals and fleeting encounters for lasting commitments, and keeping the option of the 'disappearing act' permanently open. Capital acquires more room for manoeuvre – more shelters to hide in, a larger matrix of possible permutations, a wider assortment of available avatars, and so more strength to keep the labour it deploys in check together with the cost-saving ability to wash its hands of the devastating consequences of successive rounds of downsizing; this is the contemporary face of domination – over those who have been already hit and those who fear they are in line for future blows. As the American Management Association learned from a study it commissioned, 'The morale and motivation of workers dropped sharply in the various squeeze plays of downsizing. Surviving workers waited for the next blow of the ax rather than exulting in competitive victory over those who were fired.'[5]

Competition for survival, to be sure, is not just the fate of the workers – or, more generally, of those on the receiving side of the changed time and space relationship. It penetrates the obsessively dieting and slimming company of light modernity from top to bottom. Managers must downsize worker-employing outfits to stay alive; top managers must downsize their managerial offices in order to earn the recognition of the stock exchange, gain shareholders' votes and secure the right to the golden handshake when the current round of hatchet jobs has been completed. Once embarked upon, the 'slimming' trend develops its own momentum. The tendency becomes self-propelling and self-accelerating, and (like Max Weber's perfectionist businessmen who no longer needed Calvin's exhortations to repent in order to keep going) the original motive – increased efficiency – becomes increasingly irrelevant; the fear of losing in the competition game, of being overtaken, left behind or put out of business altogether are quite sufficient to keep the merging/downsizing game going. This game becomes, increasingly, its own purpose and its own reward; or, rather, the game no longer needs a purpose if staying in the game is its only reward.

Instant living

Richard Sennett was for a number of years a regular observer of the worldwide gathering of the high and mighty, held annually in Davos. Money and time spent on Davos trips paid handsomely; Sennett brought from his escapades quite a few striking and shocking insights into the motives and character traits which keep the present-day top players of the global game on the move. Judging from his report,[6] Sennett was particularly impressed by the personality, performance, and publicly articulated life-creed of Bill Gates. Gates, says Sennett, 'seems free of the obsession to hold on to things. His products are furious in coming forth and as rapid in disappearing, whereas Rockefeller wanted to own oil rigs, buildings, machinery, or railroads for the long term.' Gates repeatedly announced that he preferred 'positioning oneself in a network of possibilities rather than paralyzing oneself in one particular job'. What seems to have struck Sennett most was Gates's unashamed, outspoken, even boastful willingness to 'destroy what he has made, given the demands of the immediate moment'. Gates appeared to be a player who 'flourishes in the midst of dislocation'. He was cautious not to develop attachment (and particularly a sentimental attachment) or lasting commitment to anything, including his own creations. He was not afraid of taking a wrong turn since no turn would keep him going in one direction for long, and since turning back or aside remained constantly and immediately available options. We may say that, except for the widening range of accessible opportunities, nothing else was accumulating or accruing along Gates's life-track; the rails kept being dismantled as soon as the engine moved a few yards further, footprints were blown away, things were dumped as quickly as they were put together – and forgotten soon after.

Anthony Flew quotes one of the characters impersonated by Woody Allen: 'I don't want to achieve immortality through my work, I want to achieve immortality by not dying.'[7] But the meaning of immortality is derivative of the sense attached to the admittedly mortal life; the preference for 'not dying' is not so much a choice of another form of immortality (an alternative to 'immortality through one's works'), as a declaration of unconcern with eternal duration in favour of *carpe diem*. Indifference to duration transforms immortality from an idea into an experience and makes of it an object of immediate consumption: it is the way you live-through-the-moment that makes that moment into an 'immortal experience'. If 'infinity' survives the transmutation, it is only as a measure of the depth or intensity of the *Erlebnis*. The boundlessness of possible sensations slips into the place vacated in dreams by infinite duration. Instantaneity (nullifying the resistance of space and liquefying the materiality of objects) makes every moment seem infinitely capacious; and infinite capacity means that there are no limits to what could be squeezed out of any moment – however brief and 'fleeting'.

The 'long term', though still referred to by habit, is a hollow shell carrying no meaning; if infinity, like time, is instantaneous, meant to be used on the spot and disposed of immediately, then 'more time' can add little to what the moment has already offered. Not much can be gained from the 'long-term' considerations. If 'solid' modernity posited eternal duration as the main motive and principle of action, 'fluid' modernity has no function for the eternal duration to play. The 'short term' has replaced the 'long term' and made of instantaneity its ultimate ideal. While promoting time to the rank of an infinitely capacious container, fluid modernity dissolves – denigrates and devalues – its duration.

Twenty years ago Michael Thompson published a pioneering study of the convoluted historical fate of the durable/transient distinction.[8] 'Durable' objects are meant to be preserved for a long, long time; they come as close as possible to embody and tokenize the otherwise abstract and ethereal notion of eternity; in fact, it is from the postulated or projected antiquity of the 'durables' that the image of eternity is extrapolated. Durable objects are assigned special value and are cherished and coveted thanks to their association with immortality – that ultimate value, 'naturally' desired and requiring no argument or persuasion to be embraced. The opposite of the 'durable' objects is 'transient' ones, meant to be used up – consumed – and to disappear in the process of their consumption. Thompson points out that 'those people near the top . . . can ensure that their own objects are always durable and those of others are always transient . . . [T]hey cannot lose.' Thompson takes it for granted that the desire to 'make their own objects durable' is the constant wish of 'those people near the top'; perhaps even that ability to make objects durable, to amass them, keep them, insure against their theft and spoliation, best of all monopolize them, is what puts people 'near the top'.

Such thoughts rang true (or at least credible) amidst the realities of solid modernity. I suggest, though, that the advent of fluid modernity has radically undermined their credibility. It is Bill Gates-style capacity to shorten the time span of durability, to forget about the 'long term', to focus on the manipulation of transience rather than durability, to dispose of things lightly in order to clear the site for other things similarly transient and similarly meant to be instantly used up, that is nowadays the privilege of the top people and which makes them the top people they are. Being stuck with things for a long time, beyond their 'use up and abandon' date and beyond the moment when their 'new and improved' replacements and 'upgrades' are on offer, is, on the contrary, the symptom of deprivation. Once the infinity of possibilities empties the infinity of time of its seductive power, durability loses its attraction and turns from an asset into a liability. Perhaps more to the point is to observe that the very borderline dividing the 'durable' from the 'transient', once a focus of intense contention and engineering bustle, has been by now all but deserted by the border police and building battalions.

The devaluation of immortality cannot but augur a cultural upheaval, arguably the most decisive turning point in human cultural history. The passage from heavy to light capitalism, from solid to fluid modernity, may yet prove to be a departure more radical and seminal than the advent of capitalism and modernity themselves, previously seen as by far the most crucial milestones of human history at least since the neolithic revolution. Indeed, throughout human history the work of culture consisted in sifting and sedimenting hard kernels of perpetuity out of transient human lives and fleeting human actions, in conjuring up duration out of transience, continuity out of discontinuity, and in transcending thereby the limits imposed by human mortality by deploying mortal men and women in the service of the immortal human species. Demand for this kind of work is nowadays shrinking. The consequences of falling demand remain to be seen and are difficult to visualize in advance, since there are no precedents to recall and to lean on.

The novel instantaneity of time radically changes the modality of human cohabitation – and most conspicuously the way in which humans attend to (or do not attend to, as the case may be) their collective affairs, or rather the way in which they make (or do not make, as the case may be) certain affairs into collective ones.

The 'public choice theory' currently making truly phenomenal advances in political science aptly grasped the new departure (though – as often happens when new human practices set a new stage for the human imagination – it hurried to generalize relatively recent developments into the eternal truth of the human condition, allegedly overlooked, neglected or belied by 'all past scholarship'). According to Gordon Tullock, one of the most distinguished promoters of the new theoretical fashion, 'The new approach begins by assuming that voters are much like customers and that politicians are much like businesspeople.' Sceptical about the value of the 'public choice' approach, Leif Lewin caustically retorted that the thinkers of the 'public choice' school of thought 'depict political man as . . . a myopic cave man'. Lewin thinks this is utterly wrong. It might have been true in the troglodyte's era, 'before man 'discovered tomorrow' and learned to make long-term calculations', but not now, in our modern times, when everyone knows, or most of us, electors and politicians alike, know, that 'tomorrow we meet again' and so credibility is 'the politician's most valuable asset'[9] (while the allocation of trust, we may add, is the elector's most eagerly used weapon). To support his critique of 'public choice' theory, Lewin refers to numerous empirical studies, showing that few electors own up to voting with their wallets, while most of them declare that what guides their voting behaviour is the state of the country as a whole. This is, Lewin says, what could have been expected; this is, as I would rather suggest, what the interviewed voters thought they were expected to say and what would be *comme il faut* for them to say. If one makes the necessary allowances for the notorious disparity between what we do and how we narrate our actions, one would not reject off-hand the claims of 'public choice' theorists (as distinct from the universal and extemporal validity of those claims). In this case, their theory might have actually gained in insight by cutting itself loose from what has been taken, uncritically, for 'empirical data'.

It is true that once upon a time the cavemen 'discovered tomorrow'. But history is a process of forgetting as much as it is a process of learning, and memory is famous for its selectivity. Perhaps we will 'meet tomorrow again'. But then again, perhaps we will not, or rather the 'we' who will meet tomorrow won't be the 'we' who met a moment ago. If this is the case, are the credibility and the allocation of trust assets, or liabilities?

Lewin recalls Jean-Jacques Rousseau's parable of stag hunters. Before men 'discovered tomorrow' – so the story goes – it could happen that a hunter, instead of waiting patiently for the stag to emerge from the woods, might have been distracted by his appetite for a rabbit running by, despite the fact that his share of meat in the jointly hunted stag would have been greater. Indeed so. But it so happens that today few hunting teams stay together for as long as it takes for the stag to appear, so whoever puts her or his trust in the benefits of the joint enterprise may be bitterly disappointed. And it so happens that, unlike the stags which, to be trapped and caught, require hunters who close ranks, stand arm to arm and act in solidarity, the rabbits fit for individual consumption are many and different and need little time to be shot, skinned and cooked. These are also discoveries – *new* discoveries, perhaps as pregnant with consequences as the 'discovery of tomorrow' once was.

'Rational choice' in the era of instantaneity means *to pursue gratification while avoiding the consequences,* and particularly the responsibilities which such consequences may imply. Durable traces of today's gratification mortgage the chances of tomorrow's gratifications. Duration changes from an asset into a liability; the same may be said about everything bulky, solid and heavy – everything that hinders and restricts the move. Giant industrial plants and corpulent bodies have had their day: once they bore witness to their owners' power and might; now they presage defeat in the next round of acceleration and so signal impotence. Lean body and fitness to move, light dress and sneakers, cellular telephones (invented for the use of the nomad who needs to be 'constantly in touch'), portable or disposable belongings – are the prime cultural tokens of the era of instantaneity. Weight and size, and above all the fat (literal or metaphorical) blamed for the expansion of both, share the fate of durability. They are the dangers one should beware of and fight against, and best of all steer clear of.

It is difficult to conceive of culture indifferent to eternity and shunning durability. It is similarly difficult to conceive of morality indifferent to the consequences of human actions and shunning responsibility for the effects these actions may have on others. The advent of instantaneity ushers human culture and ethics into unmapped and unexplored territory, where most of the learned habits of coping with the business of life have lost their utility and sense. As Guy Debord famously put it, 'Men resemble their times more than their fathers.' And present-day men and women differ from their fathers and mothers by living in a present 'which wants to forget the past and no longer seems to believe in the future'.[10] But the memory of the past and trust in the future have been thus far the two pillars on which the cultural and moral bridges between transience and durability, human mortality and the immortality of human accomplishments, as well as taking responsibility and living by the moment, all rested.

Notes

1 See Daniel Bell, *The End of Ideology* (Cambridge, Mass.: Harvard University Press, 1988), pp. 230–5.

2 Daniel Cohen, *Richesse du monde, pauvretés des nations* (Paris: Flammarion, 1997), p. 84.

3 Nigel Thrift, 'The rise of soft capitalism', *Cultural Values*, April 1997, pp. 39–40. Thrift's essay can only be described as eye-opening and seminal, but the concept of 'soft-capitalism' used in the title and throughout the text seems a misnomer – and a misleading characterization. There is nothing 'soft' about software capitalism of light modernization. Thrift points out that 'dancing' and 'surfing' are among the best metaphors to approximate to the nature of capitalism in its new avatar. The metaphors are well chosen, since they suggest weightlessness, lightness and facility of movement. But there is nothing 'soft' about daily dancing and surfing. Dancers and surfers, and particularly those on the overcrowded ballroom floor and on a coast buffeted by a high tide, need to be tough, not soft. And they are tough – as few of their predesecessors, able to stand still or move along clearly marked and well-serviced tracks, ever needed to be., Software capitalism is no less hard and tough than its hardware ancestor used to be. And liquid is anything but soft. Think of a deluge, flood or broken dam.

4 See Georg Simmel, 'A chapter in the philosophy of value', in *The Conflict in Modern Culture and Other Essays*, trans. K. Peter Etzkorn (New York: Teachers College Press, 1968), pp. 52–4).

5 As reported in Eileen Applebaum and Rosemary Batt, *The New American Workplace* (Ithaca: Cornell University Press, 1993). Here quoted after Richard Sennett, *The Corrosion of Character: The Personal Consequences of Work in the New Capitalism* (New York: W.W. Norton & Co., 1998), p. 50.

6 Sennett, *The Corrosion of Character*, pp. 61–2.

7 Anthony Flew, *The Logic of Mortality* (Oxford: Blackwell, 1987), p. 3.

8 See Michael Thompson, *Rubbish Theory: The Creation and Destruction of Value* (Oxford: Oxford University Press, 1979), particularly pp. 113–19.

9 Leif Lewin, 'Man, society, and the failure of politics', *Critical Review*, Winter-Spring 1998, p. 10. The criticized quotation comes from Gordon Tullock's preface to William C. Mitchell and Randy T. Simmons, *Beyond Politics: Markets, Welfare, and the Failure of Bureaucracy* (Boulder, Col.: Westview Press, 1994), p. xiii.

10 Guy Debord, *Comments on the Society of the Spectacle*, trans. Malcolm Imrie (London: Verso, 1990), pp. 16, 13.

CHAPTER ONE

The theory of liquid modernity

A critique of Bauman's recent sociology

Anthony Elliott

The analysis and critique of modernity, which has been a central preoccupation of recent social theory, has generated an impressive literature of a truly interdisciplinary nature. In the writings of most major contemporary theorists, from Habermas to Touraine to Giddens, the claim that we are living in 'new times', or in transformed social conditions, has been powerfully explored. The transformations associated with modernity have been generated, it has been argued, by a wide variety of social processes – industrial upheavals, worldwide capitalist expansions, techno-scientific discoveries and the advent of globalization. Such processes are sometimes referred to apocalyptically in the sociological literature, as suggestive of the collapse of Western patterns of social development ('post-industrialism', 'postmodernism', 'post-capitalism'). Yet such processes have also been conceptualized positively, as referring to the constitution of a new type of social system (such as the 'information society' or 'reflexive modernization'). In this latter intellectual approach there is one figure of outstanding social and political significance, the Polish born sociologist Zygmunt Bauman. He made his debut to the debate over modernity in his award-winning *Modernity and the Holocaust* (1989) with a spectacular contention: the Nazi Final Solution, he argued, was not a dysfunction of modern rationality but its shocking product. Next, he transformed received understandings of postmodernism by tracking manifestations of postmodernity as a social system through its every shifting guise and mutation, from the economy to entertainment. Most recently, having retreated from the discourse of postmodernity, he has advanced a highly original formulation of modernity as liquid – in a social theory which differs substantially from most current sociological discussions. The theory of liquid modernity proposed by Bauman has already exerted considerable influence in his own country – the United Kingdom – and has gained a wide audience in Europe, the United States and Australia as well.

This chapter does not seek to provide a general introduction to the work of Bauman; there are already several accomplished such surveys (see Smith 1999; Beilharz 2000; Tester 2004). Rather, the chapter is restricted to a synthesizing exposition of Bauman's recent theory of liquid modernity, referring only where necessary to other aspects of his corpus. Following this brief exegesis, the second section of the chapter is more critical and reconstructive in character, and I seek to assess some of his central concepts and claims. In developing a sympathetic critique of Bauman's recent work on societal liquidization, I shall try to indicate some alternative social-theoretical ways in which certain conceptual difficulties of his account might be overcome.

Outline of the theory of modernity

Liquidization: from heavy to light modernity

Bauman's account of societal liquidization, or 'liquefaction', arises from his critique of the theoretical presuppositions and political consequences of recent debates over postmodernity, the 'end of history', 'late modernity', 'second modernity' and 'surmodernity'. (See, amongst others, Jameson 1992; Fukuyama 1993; Giddens 1991; Beck 1999). To acknowledge that sociology can say more about the state of the world than that modernity is over is to engage with what Bauman calls a positive account of the *novelty* of contemporary social processes. To this end, he deploys the metaphor of 'liquid' to capture the present-day state of modernity. Liquids for Bauman do not keep any shape for long and are constantly prone to alteration. Liquids, unlike solids, undergo continuous changes of shape. Liquids make salient the fractured, brittle nature of human bonds today: there are compelling reasons, writes Bauman, 'to consider "fluidity" or "liquidity" as fitting metaphors when we wish to grasp the nature of the present, in many ways *novel*, phase in the history of modernity' (2000: 2). What is important in the social dimension of liquidity is not its specific gravity but rather the looseness fluids possess. 'What is a truly novel feature of this social world, and makes it sensible to call the current kind of modernity "liquid" in opposition to the other, earlier known forms of modern world', argues Bauman, 'is the continuous and irreparable fluidity of things which modernity in its initial shape was bent on solidifying and fixing' (Bauman in Gane 2004: 19–20).

This focus on liquidization provides a conceptual plank from which Bauman reformulates some of the central preoccupations of social-theoretical accounts of modernity, particularly accounts which focus on the production and reproduction of modernization. Many key features associated with modernization and industrialization are recast as instances of what he calls, provocatively and poignantly, 'heavy modernity'. This notion of modernity as 'heavy', or 'hardware modernity', appears throughout his recent writings in different contexts, depending upon the topic under discussion, although its central attributes can be spelt out as follows. Modernity as 'heavy' assumes a dominant role with the development of industrialization and the intensification of modernization throughout the West. Vast machinery, huge factories, massive workforces: economic success defined in terms of size, and symbolic power defined in terms of volume, are central to the contours of heavy modernity. 'Heavy capitalism', writes Bauman (2000: 58), 'was obsessed with bulk and size, and, for that reason, also with boundaries, with making them tight and impenetrable.'

The heavy version of modernity appears, in the view of Bauman, as a certain type of society subsumed to a specific organization of space and time. The conquering of space was fundamental to the ordering ambitions of heavy modernity: spatial expansion was deeply interwoven with the logic of social control and the logic of symbolic power. Space was to be tamed, colonized, domesticated – indeed, devoured. Referencing the work of Daniel Bell, Bauman writes of the 'space-devouring' monstrous cage of General Motors 'Willow Run' plant in Michigan. This infamous General Motors' site measured some two-thirds by a quarter of a mile, with all factory workers and plant machinery contained under the one gigantic roof. Bauman interprets General Motors' colonization of space as reflective of the modernist ideology that 'bigger means more efficient'; but he also argues that such spatial expansionist logic which informed activities of large economic enterprises became inscribed in daily social practice itself. The 'Fordist factory' was heavy modernity's ideal model of engineered rationality. 'Fordism', writes Bauman (2000: 57) 'was the self-consciousness of modern society in its "heavy", "bulky", or "immobile" and "rooted", "solid" phase.' This socially engineered delineation of space existed, argues Bauman, through a concomitant regularization of time: 'It was the routinization of time that held the place whole, compact and subject to homogeneous logic. . . In the conquest of space, time had to be pliant and malleable' (Bauman 2000: 115). This space/time binding of heavy modernity produced, in turn, the immobilization of labour and capital. 'The frozen time of factory routine, together with the bricks and mortar of factory walls', writes Bauman (2000: 116), 'immobilized capital as effectively as it bound the labour it employed.'

The space/time coordinates which secured the efficacy of heavy modernity, paradoxically, contained the seeds of its own failure however. The era of heavy modernity for Bauman was slowly but steadily undermined by an intrinsic contradiction: the social ordering ambitions, ethical ideals and economic and political goals of heavy modernity were presented as foundational, transcendent and eternal, but were in fact counterproductive and corrosive. This spelt the beginning of the end for heavy modernity. Bauman consequently introduces the notions of 'light modernity' and 'software capitalism' as superseding those of 'heavy modernity' and 'hardware capitalism': he refers to the unprecedented power of *liquidization* in objective alterations of the private and public domains of contemporary societies. The alteration in question springs from, amongst other social forces, the technological explosion of new information systems; the rise of multinationals and transnational conglomerates; the outsourcing of manufacturing operations from the West to the 'developing world'; and the large-scale shift in investment from industrial manufacture to the communications, finance and service sectors. These developments, according to Bauman, have produced a new 'weightlessness of capital' and concomitant 'liquidization of life' – in business cycles, employment patterns, family relationships, communal fates, political horizons.

Where 'heavy modernity' was the era of instrumental rationality, concerned as it was with the cultivation of seemingly endless spatial expansion and the management of time, 'light modernity' signifies a 'new irrelevance of space' and killing off of time. 'In the software universe of light-speed travel', writes Bauman (2000: 117), 'space may be traversed, literally, in "no time"; the difference between "far away" and "down here" is cancelled. Space no more sets limits to action and its effects, and counts little, or does not count at all.' Liquidization assumes different forms across the space/time zonings of contemporary institutional life, from 24-hour finance markets to media-ridden culture. Yet liquidity for Bauman can be said to be culturally dominant to the extent that social life is organized in and through the 'insubstantial, instantaneous time of the software world' (2000: 118).

The concepts of heavy and light modernity, which must be interrelated as distinct institutional frames of order-aimed social regulation, comprise the key dimensions of Bauman's theory of societal liquidization. The transition from hardware societies of social engineering based on industrialization, of ever-expanding accumulation and its management of heavy machinery and massive workforces, to liquid societies of light modernity, based on the instant flight of exterritorial capital and socio-economic deregulation, is the conceptual backcloth from which Bauman specifies processes of the reproduction of asymmetrical relations of power. The maintenance of domination in heavy modernity, according to Bauman, was Panoptican-like – factory routine, rooted on-site management, immobile capital. As he puts this (2000: 57), 'capital, management and labour were all, for better or worse, doomed to stay in one another's company for a long time to come, perhaps for ever'. This no longer holds for our own time. As Bauman contends (2000: 58): 'Nowadays capital travels light – with cabin luggage only, which includes no more than a briefcase, a cellular phone and a portable computer.' In his more recent political tracts, including *Globalization: The Human Consequences* (1998), *Community* (2001) and *Society Under Siege* (2002), Bauman deploys this conceptualization of liquidity as domination in order to confront current debates surrounding global order. Any compressed reconstruction of the main arguments of Bauman's political sociology would not do justice to it as a whole, such is the imaginative sweep of his contribution, but some of the key issues he stresses include: the separation of power and sovereignty from the politics of the territorial nation-state; the collapse of 'society' as a bounded complex, or set of structures; and, the outsourcing of public political functions to non-political, deregulated market forces. This last is a central theme, and gives his work a radical political edge. Privatization and deregulation, according to Bauman, becomes a vital preoccupation of the current age for a whole host of reasons. In conditions of neo-liberalism, in which global capitalism drastically shrinks public political life, the privatization of life-experience and life-politics becomes ever more regulated by culturalist and sub-political processes that follow a kind of Weberian logic all their own, an institutional development which Bauman believes the discipline of sociology has been too slow to recognize. As he develops this:

> Governments are today no less, if not more, busy and active than ever before in modern history. But they are busy in the TV Big Brother's style: letting the subjects play their own games and blame themselves in the event that the results are not up to their dreams. Governments are busy hammering home the 'there is no alternative' message, the 'security is dependency' and the 'state protection is disempowering' messages, and enjoining subjects to be more flexible and to love the risks (read: erratic and unpredictable) life-settings is fraught with'.
>
> (Bauman 2002: 68)

Liquid moderns: identity, love, ambivalence

The intensification of processes of liquidization does not only reshape social institutions; it also penetrates to the core of the self and the fabric of everyday life. These are issues that Bauman addresses directly in a number of recent works, including *Liquid Love* (2003), *Identity* (2004) and *Liquid Life* (2005). Life and identity in conditions of liquid modernity are for Bauman increasingly fluid, fractured, flexible and frail. As he develops this perspective:

> Liquid life is a precarious life, lived under conditions of constant uncertainty. The most acute and stubborn worries that haunt such a life are the fears of being caught napping, of failing to catch up with fast-moving events, of being left behind, of overlooking 'use by' dates, of being saddled with possessions that are no longer desirable, of missing the moment that calls for a change of tack before crossing the point of no return. Liquid life is a succession of new beginnings – yet precisely for that reason it is the swift and painless endings . . . that tend to be its most challenging moments and most upsetting headaches. Among the arts of liquid modern living and the skills needed to practise them, getting rid of things takes precedence over their acquisition.
>
> (Bauman, 2005: 2)

Small wonder that in such circumstances the newly constituted terrain of 'privatized identity' comes to bear a heavy burden of expectations, hopes and fears in a world where traditional social bonds are loosening their chokehold.

In formulating his account of 'liquid life' through an analysis of the ways in which a pervasive sense of uprootedness, anxiety and insecurity become increasingly global in scope, Bauman relies on recent social theories of individualization. In this context, and at various points of his writings, he cites the work of Beck, Melucci and Giddens. He tries to elucidate some of the basic assumptions of the individualization thesis, in particular the complex ways in which identity is becoming disembedded from social structures, as well as the disengagement of individual actions and choices from collective ways of doing things and community projects. It is Bauman's view that the privatizing of life-strategies transforms identity 'from a given into a task' (2001: 144), with social responsibility for self-determination now falling 'primarily on the individual's shoulders' (2000: 7–8). Bauman does not just 'apply' the individualization thesis, however; he also tries to tease out the kinds of reasoning which are increasingly taken for granted by individuals today. According to Bauman, the uncanny frailty of individualized society, particularly the feelings of insecurity generated by societal liquidization, promotes desperate attempts by men and women to shore up what is missing in their private and public lives. Experiencing ever-weaker social bonds, individuals must constantly negotiate the 'until-further-notice' of today's social relations. People now drift from one episodic encounter to the next, seeking to nail down a sense of identity – however provisional or fleeting. Such anxiety-provoking activity Bauman sees everywhere in the individualizing societies of the West: individuals reaching for mobile phones, addictively texting; surfing the Net, flitting from one chat room to another; speed dating, moving ever faster between relationships. Yet, as Bauman notes, 'the union only goes so far as the dialling, talking, messaging. Stop talking – and you are out. Silence equals exclusion. *Il n'y a pas dehors du texte*, indeed – there is nothing outside the text – though not just in the sense meant by Derrida'.

Consumer capitalism, with its ideology of 'want-now' consumption and the ever-new, plays a basic role in furthering individualization. In particular, Bauman is troubled by the societal rush towards market solutions for private dilemmas. In an age increasingly defined by a cultural obsession with youth, sex and the frantic urge to consume, individuals want from relationships that which they derive from shopping at the mall: variety, novelty, disposability. Accordingly, 'lovers' are reclassified as 'sexual partners', and in turn assessed as potential risks to an individual's 'emotional investment' through cold, calculating cost/benefit analysis. Bauman searches high and low in obscure corners of both academia and the media for telling clues of such trends. From marriage guidance journals, he tracks the rise of 'top-pocket relationships' – those you can use when you need to and dispose of just as easily. From the Sunday newspaper supplements, he monitors the highly compartmentalized worlds of SDCs (semi-detached couples), those postmodern romantics who maintain separate pads and separate lives. On and on run the contemporary examples.

Bauman's sociological scope: a critique

Few today would dispute the sociological importance of Bauman's writings. His account of an ever-spiralling societal liquidity is developed as a series of fragmentary sketches that link and contrast episodes, moments, movements, ideas or cultures – the method of which Bauman terms 'sociological hermeneutics' (Bauman 1978, 2000). For some, it is this lightness of touch which gives Bauman's sociology its critical edge (Beilharz 2000; Tester 2004). He discusses the notion of liquid modernity not as a systematic grand theory, but rather as sociological fragments or prefigurations – looking at developments in, amongst other domains, morality, ethics, individualization, love, sexuality, human rights, social exclusion, globalization and terrorism. In formulating the operational contours of liquid modernity, Bauman cross-references – both implicitly and explicitly – many sociological practitioners and systematic theoretical positions. Whilst this cross-referencing is far from forming a closed system, it does mean that one must read Bauman with constant reference to the basic coordinates of individualization and globalization informing the modernity/postmodernity debate. One need only compare the different elements and themes of, say, Anthony Giddens, Ulrich Beck, Richard Sennett and Cornelius Castoriadis as recapitulated in Bauman's writings on liquid modernity. From Giddens, Bauman takes the insight that modernity does its work in the reflexivity of daily life, yet in his hands this is now recast in terms of questions concerning privatization and commercialization; from Beck, an insistence on risk and other instrumental modes of calculability, but now dramatized within symbolic systems of media (mis)information and persuasion; from Sennett, the episodic pursuit of reinvention and new strategies of identity, yet now blended with a properly sociological concern for social structure; and from Castoriadis, a positive conception of imagination, as an underpinning for autonomy.

However one might probe, question and critique the sources of Bauman's sociological eclecticism (see Beilharz 2000; Tester and Jacobsen 2005), it is very difficult not to be impressed with his assortment of takings from Giddens, Beck, Sennett and Castoriadis, not to mention his reworking of themes from Levinas, Adorno, Deleuze, Baudrillard and Maffesoli. 'There is a multitude', writes Tester and Jacobsen (2005: 26), 'of sources of inspiration, affinities, fads, references, predecessors, contemporaries and intellectual kinships, spiritual and sociological soul mates in Bauman's writings. Mixing, combining, uniting, utilising, bending, joining, modifying, supporting, critiquing, forging and transforming these constant presences makes up much of the sociological skeleton that he has gradually constructed and developed.' Yet Bauman's accomplishment extends well beyond an inspirational integration of diverse classical and current traditions of social thought. The important fact is rather Bauman's connecting of abstract issues of social theory on the one hand with concrete sociological issues and contemporary political concerns on the other. From this angle, his work on, say, social marginalization, exclusion and human waste as well as on love, intimacy and sexuality – together with his more theoretical reflections on postmodernization and liquid modernity – are surely of enduring significance to sociology.

In mobilizing such disparate theoretical orientations and conceptual thematics to bolster the theory of liquid modernity, it is as if Bauman seeks new ground for the sociologist. For the fractured rhythms of Bauman's sociological imagination – combining a poetic hermeneutics with impassioned introspections that are acutely sensitive to the sociological problems of the contemporary era – manage to scoop up and absorb so many of these leading currents in social theory, thus in turn providing a kind of *unstructured systematic analysis* of modernity that might otherwise remain elusive and diffuse in Bauman's work. The sociology itself is concrete – directed at the social and spatial stratifications of power, poverty, persecution and the public political sphere – yet rich in theoretical intensity as well, demonstrating an overriding faith in the possibility of alternative social futures. We are dealing, in short, with a sociologist of extraordinary intellectual power and scope.

Bauman's recent sociology, sketched briefly in the preceding discussion, has the outstanding merit of highlighting the political significance of the demise of the 'long term', as liquidization or liquefaction, in contemporary social processes. There are, however, various problems with Bauman's social theory. Here I shall restrict myself to considering those areas where Bauman's ideas seem to me open to question. As someone generally sympathetic to Bauman's work, I will try to indicate ways in which the broad direction of his social theory might be more profitably developed and pursued. Put in a nutshell, my critique commences from the following questions: How successful has the transition in Bauman's work from a sociology of postmodernity to a sociology of liquid modernity been? Do the accomplishments of Bauman's recent writings match the sociological inspiration and strength of his earlier work on postmodernization?

Modernity as liquid?

One criticism most forcefully made against Bauman's account concerns the *adequacy* of his sociological diagnosis of liquid modern times. There are both *strong* and *weak* versions of this critique. The strong version of this criticism rests upon the misgiving that a liquidization of human bonds cannot provide a generalizable model for the sociological analysis of global institutional change as well as forms of sociality in contemporary societies. For example, Ray (see Chapter 2) rejects the plausibility of Bauman's recent work on such grounds, arguing that the theory of liquid modernity 'illustrates a tendency within sociology to view theories as metaphors to be judged on grounds of appropriateness rather than truth claims judged on grounds of explanatory power'. What one sees in this strong critique is a suspicion of developing social theory from the putative experiences of people's interactions in social contexts, as well as an implicit assumption that concepts, theories and frameworks are really only of use to sociologists when empirically grounded in observable processes of human agency and institutional patterns. There is then disagreement not only over what liquid modernity is, but over whether the term 'liquid' is relied upon to do too much conceptual work in Bauman's argument. Like almost every other general social theory, according to this strong critique, Bauman analyses all current social phenomena through an undifferentiated prism – that of liquidization – and as a consequence must write off whatever fails to conform to it. Bauman, in short, fails to specify how to tread a sociological line from the analysis of very diverse phenomena (work, love, identity) that suggest liquidity to the specific global properties of liquid modernity. A related point has been made from the vantage point of post-structuralist and deconstructive sociology: the social cannot be limited to the generalizability of single-factor forces. Best (1998), for example, contends that Bauman's notion of 'the social' is unduly restrictive, premised as it is upon modernist assumptions.

Perhaps the more difficult issue suggested by this strong critique of Bauman's theory of liquid modernity, namely that the theory does not provide an adequate general account of the complexity of Western modernity, is this: even if liquidization is an apt metaphor for the social processes spawned by globalized capitalism, how might the notion serve to help sociologists rethink global order and particularly the relations between north and south, core and periphery, the First and Third worlds? Whilst the criticism to date is nowhere developed in detail, one might reasonably question Bauman's account along these lines by invoking the discourses of multiculturalism and postcolonialism. For postcolonial critics, Bauman's portrait of liquid modernity – like most sociologies of a predominantly Western orientation – might be interpreted as highlighting certain developments and processes prevalent throughout the First World and projecting them worldwide, including onto the distinct geopolitical space of the Third World. As a result, or so the argument might run, the hard political differences of geopolitical space are diminished and the 'modernity differential' between the First and the Third World is erased (Chesneaux 1992: 57). Such a line of criticism might well suggest that the appeal of liquid modernity in the West proceeds from its streetwise, sceptical culture – a culture of irony which is far from evident in, say, sub-Saharan Africa. For example, Paolini (1999) has provocatively suggested that modernity, in all its heterogeneity, produces a very different set of experiences and demands in the Third World to that of the West; one reason this is so, he argues, referencing Third World critiques of modernity, are the ongoing attractions of old-style modernization to vast numbers in Third World populations. From the standpoint of the theory of liquid modernity, however, it is hard to speak, let alone interpret, such Others of the capitalist world system: Bauman's diagnosis, so it might appear, better captures what is occurring in London than Lisbon, Boston than Bombay. A foregrounding of liquidization, plasticity, dismantling, destabilization – all this, it might be argued, smacks of a distinctively Western world view and culture.

These are certainly forceful lines of critique, but stated thus they overemphasize particular strands (explicit or implicit) in Bauman's sociology. In the face of various critiques of social theory and the philosophy of social science, Bauman has defended his version of sociological hermeneutics as the recovery of the possibilities of human choosing, of meanings, in the frame of structured experiential dimensions of social reality (Bauman 1972, 2000). From this angle, the principal shortcoming of the strong critique of liquid modernity then follows from its assumption that sociology is part of a managerial ethos aimed at predicting instrumental forms of calculation or the routinization of actors in the social world. But this is precisely the role for sociology that Bauman rejects, preferring as he does artistry over predictabilities, the open-endedness of choosing over the positivism of 'behaviour' (Tester and Jacobsen 2005: 206–10). To return therefore to the central questions: Does the notion of an increasing liquidization of lives, loves, bonds and human relations adequately capture the shape of worldwide social change today? Are human bonds really defined *in toto* by liquid modern impulses and the social forces of liquid modernity? Within the terms of Bauman's sociological hermeneutics – specifically, his aim to unravel, describe and evaluate what people actually experience in social life – my inclination is to answer these questions with a qualified 'Yes'. The qualification which is necessary to note is that Bauman points out, repeatedly, that today's liquid modern anxieties and risks of living together, and apart, take the individualizing form they do predominantly in the expensive, postmodern cities of the West. But this does not mean that he is inattentive to the hard social differences of geopolitical space. For Bauman has insisted, at various points in his writings, that various Others – from the marginalized and migrants within the West to those starving to death in the Third and Fourth Worlds – remain locked out from the new political economy of liquid modernity. Certainly criticism might be made that Bauman is not sufficiently attentive to the specificities of such geopolitical processes: the 'other side' of liquid modernity remains, for the most part, out of view in Bauman's own account. But this is not to say that his social theory is incapable of addressing such political concerns; in fact, one of the most striking features of liquid modernity is that it appears to be novel and post-industrial, but in actuality passes itself off as such only by exporting manufacture and production to the cheap labour zones of the Third World.

This brings us to the weak version of the critique of Bauman's theory of liquid modernity. In this kind of reading of Bauman, whilst the reworking of modernity in terms of liquidization is broadly received as challenging, there remains some doubt about the wider social and cultural contextualization of his social theory. Here the criticism is that, by focusing attention on the liquidization of the self, social relations and everyday life in a globalized world, Bauman tends to neglect the ongoing significance of more structured, solid forms of sociality. To a great extent, Bauman's many examples of our liquid modern times are drawn from daily experiences familiar to inhabitants of, say, North America or Europe – that is, of life lived in the high divorce and remarriage society, of relationships structured with reference to mobile telecommunications, and of intimacy guided by therapy culture. Some social theorists see in such social processes the arrival of a post-traditional society (Giddens 1992, 1994), while others lament the decline of the power of tradition (Furedi 2004). But what Bauman may well be accused of neglecting are the many ways in which liquid modern societies still depend on traditions, world views, regimes of discourse, modes of power as well as structures of feeling that are characteristic of organized or 'hardware' modernity. Why, for example, do we find the forces of liquid modernity more at work in some sectors of the economy – say, finance and the communications sectors – than others? The ordering ambitions of modernity – centred upon structure, classification, hierarchy and control – remain vital to various private life-strategies and social practices of the contemporary era. That the organizing and organized impulses of modernism have been squeezed to the sidelines by liquidized forms of social life in more recent years does not preclude the ongoing force of modernist world views from exerting an impact upon the contemporary era.

The significance of liquidization can, in short, be exaggerated. We can begin to unfold the sociological implications of this criticism by considering the ways in which critics have marshalled various kinds of empirical evidence to call into question the thesis of societal liquidization. Smart and Shipman (2004), for example, have examined in detail the lives of various transnational families living in Britain whose values and practices do not fit easily with ideas of liquid modern relationships. The analysis set out by Smart and Shipman of the ongoing power of marriage as a cultural ideal, and of the complex ways in which self-control and interpersonal commitment are negotiated across generations, differs substantially from the liquid frame of 'until-further-notice' relationships of which Bauman speaks. A rather similar critique is developed by Gross (2005), who distinguishes between 'regulative' and 'meaning-constitutive' traditions of the social field governing intimacy. Whilst acknowledging that the regulative tradition of lifelong marriage as an ideal has declined in strength across the West in recent years, Gross argues that the organizing tradition of romantic love (and its ideology of coupledom) remains central to current social arrangements throughout the West. Here liquidization is thus viewed as only a *partial* transformation of social life.

Whatever the force of these criticisms, it would be quite misleading to suggest that Bauman simply overlooks or ignores the role that earlier modernist forms of ideology or world views still play in the shaping of social life. Indeed, arguably, the thesis of increasing societal liquidization only makes sense in a rigorously sociological way if it is interpreted against the backdrop of the diversity of modernist socio-symbolic forms in the reproduction of social life. That said, there is no reason why a more comprehensive approach to social theory should not attend to the ongoing role of early modernist world views, codes and norms in the production of cultural life while incorporating the theory of intensified societal liquidity as developed by Bauman.

Liquidization and the renewal of postmodernity?

In a related vein, one can question the shift in terminology from 'postmodernity' to 'liquid modernity' in Bauman's sociology. With the benefit of hindsight, it is not difficult to see why Bauman retracted from this deployment of the term 'postmodernity' to define certain aspects of contemporary social experience. By the late 1990s, the label 'postmodern' had everywhere – from academia to popular culture – become coterminous with a form of cultivated relativism in which 'everything goes'. It was, ironically, this very flattened and generalized view of the postmodern that Bauman wished to distance himself from with his influential idea of 'postmodernity as modernity minus illusions'. In contrast to post-structuralist or postmodern interpretations of postmodernism (Lyotard 1979; Baudrillard 1983; Smart 1992), Bauman developed a path-breaking understanding of postmodernity as a generalized social system – in which the postmodern did not function as a point *beyond* modernity, but rather as reflection upon the guiding assumptions of modernity itself. 'Postmodernity', in Bauman's celebrated formulation (1990: 98), 'is modernity that has admitted the non-feasibility of its original project. Postmodernity is modernity reconciled to its own impossibility – and determined, for better or worse, to live with it. Modern practice continues – now, however, devoid of the objectives that once triggered it off.' It was from this highly original formulation that Bauman came to examine in detail the ambivalent character of postmodernity in terms of current and future prospects of the self, social relations and everyday life. In the intervening period, however, the postmodern interpretation of postmodernity as 'everything goes' had become increasingly dominant, and Bauman felt the need for new terminological descriptions of contemporary culture. As Bauman has said: 'The postmodernity debate may have been a "fleeting affair", but in its time it was indispensable. Like many other good intentions, it went astray' (Bauman in Tester and Jacobsen 2005: 149).

Bauman's theoretical and political response to this implosion of the modernity/postmodernity debate was, as discussed above, to outline the contours of a 'liquid modern condition'. The issue which I now wish to raise is whether certain productive emphases in Bauman's novel deployment of the concept of postmodernity have not been sidelined in his new account of liquid modernity. That is to say, it seems to me that Bauman's thought-provoking analysis on how postmodernity promotes ambivalence – of societal opening and closure in equal measure – becomes somewhat blurred in the theory of liquid modernity. For the notion of liquid modernity appears to appertain to the fragmentation of (1) life-strategies as processes of individualization and (2) the 'long term', transformed today as slices of experience or episodicity. Yet viewed against the backcloth of Bauman's sociology of postmodernity, the theory of liquid modernity may be seen as lacking a normative political edge from which to call into question those aspects of societal liquidization Bauman is concerned to critique and contest.

This is not the place to pursue the theoretical complexities of Bauman's sociology of postmodernity, a topic which has already generated various volumes. But let us briefly consider the emphasis that Bauman puts on the idea that postmodernity means standing apart, however ambivalently, from the operational confines of modernity. In *Modernity and Ambivalence* (1991), Bauman conceived of the postmodern reflection upon modernity in terms of engagement with the complexities of the modernist dream to impose a systematic grid of order, control, classification and hierarchy upon social life. Such postmodern reflection, argued Bauman, is necessarily ambivalent, fragmented, disjointed; and yet he did insist this postmodern perspective contained various utopic possibilities. 'Postmodernity', wrote Bauman (1991: 98), 'means a resolute emancipation from the characteristically modern urge to overcome ambivalence and promote the monosemic clarity of the sameness.' Such 'postmodern wisdom', in Bauman's terms, arose from the personal and social capacity to become immersed in social life without the need for blueprints, codes or guidelines, and with remarkable tolerance for ambiguity and confusion. Interweaving Cornelius Castoriadis's notion of autonomy with Richard Rorty's conceptualization of solidarity, Bauman dramatized the political possibilities of the postmodern in terms of freedom, diversity and tolerance. This was no more and no less than what Bauman termed 'the chance of postmodernity'.

The issue which arises from this is of a very general and political kind. What happens to these utopic, potentially autonomous, creative energies and innovative life-strategies in the theory of liquid modernity? Given the importance of these issues in Bauman's earlier sociology, it may come as something of a surprise to find that they receive little analytical attention in *Liquid Modernity* (2000) and *The Individualized Society* (2001). There are, it is true, various references to the sociological imagination and of the public political orientation of social theory. But Bauman does not, in his more recent work, consider in detail the sorts of self-questioning practices and forms of self-interrogation that he explicitly theorized in terms of certain values and potentialities associated with postmodernity. This is a serious omission, in my view, because the coupling modernity/postmodernity provided sociology – as Bauman formulated the relation at any rate – with the normative means from which to challenge and contest the media-ridden, consumerist imperatives of globalized capitalism. By dissolving these dual aspects of modernity and postmodernity, Bauman risks flattening the force of his critical account: the danger is that liquid modern practices appear as just ways of duping human agents. In terms of the theory of liquid modernity, it is difficult to see how to follow Bauman's earlier lead that recognized the enormous vitality and imaginative possibilities of postmodernity, while simultaneously deploring the damage modernity wreaks on its unsuspecting subjects. How to explain this? Given the shift from the 1990s into the 2000s, there was no doubt a range of political factors implicated in Bauman's reappraisal of social theory. In reformulating the contours of his revised sociology of liquid modernity, Bauman may well have been swayed by the destructive force of global political events early in the twenty-first century. Global pandemics, 9/11 and the war on terrorism, the neo-liberalization of global markets: there is no shortage of evidence that rage, destructiveness and negativity defines the institutional spaces of modernity and its consequences. And yet Bauman's shift in approach – away from what he once termed 'postmodern wisdom' (1993: 245) – carries important implications for the utopic dimensions of social theory; it also raises the question of reintegrating the notion of postmodernity – as a kind of counter-culture of liquid modernity – into social theory.

Identity and subjectivity

At this point I want to return to Bauman's texts and take up again the question of identity and subjectivity. In my view Bauman is right to emphasize the metaphor of 'liquid' for grasping key aspects of contemporary social processes and for calling attention to the complex ways in which everyday life and social experience are becoming light, flexible and more mobile. I further think that Bauman is right to stress the intimate connection between liquid modernity and liquid life. The liquidity conditions of contemporary institutional processes – the continuous fluidity of information, signs, money and people in the global age – reshape and transform the various ways individuals experience identity and interpersonal bonds. Life in a liquid modern world, as Bauman provocatively suggests, means that individuals must work at the never-ending task of shaping fluids as well as the continuous work of reshaping liquids. Against this backdrop, 'relationships' are increasingly replaced by the activity of 'relating', 'connections' are increasingly replaced by the activity of 'connecting'.

So far I am in agreement with the thrust of Bauman's social theory. Where his account runs into difficulties, as I try to demonstrate, is in his contention that liquid life is an inherent subjective corollary of liquid modernity. There are many aspects of the connections he posits between identity and society that could be questioned in this respect. For example, some critics have disputed the details of Bauman's account of the relations between consumerism, popular culture and identity; in doing so, these critics have expressed serious reservations with the idea that consumer culture results in the production of only liquidized or privatized identities (cf. Patterson 2006). Others have raised important concerns about Bauman's predominantly negative interpretation of identity formation in the current age, suggesting that the idea of 'privatized identity' fails to do justice to the exciting opportunities generated by today's identity-politics – particularly the rich complexity of gay, lesbian, queer, ethnic and racial identities (Gane 2004). Other critics have raised doubts concerning the psycho-social adequacy of Bauman's portrayal of liquid identity, pointing out that the stress on 'manic individualism' in this account jostles uneasily with other aspects of personality development in mania and narcissism as portrayed in psychoanalysis (Sayers, Chapter 6; see also Clarke and Moran 2003).

The issue on which I want to focus my critical comments, however, relates not to the sociological or psycho-social accuracy of Bauman's portrayal of liquid identity, but rather to the question of why he extends this thesis to cover all forms of self-definition and life-strategies in contemporary societies. My reservation concerning Bauman's approach is that, by conceptualizing liquid lives as the dominant mode of identity constitution in the current era, he tends to neglect other modes of self-constitution. Liquidized forms of experience and identity, with their emphasis on short-termism and relentless self-transformation, are undoubtedly characteristic of large areas of contemporary cultural life – particularly through the world of commodified images in the media and new information technologies. On the other hand, contemporary social life permits the development of various critical, cosmopolitan identities, many of which contain possibilities for transcending the rigid determinations of identity – class, gender, race – associated with industrial capitalism (du Gay and Hall 1996; Habermas 2001; Beck 2006). The constitution of identities, nonetheless, involves much more than this – and certainly cannot be reduced to an either/or, contrasting modernity's liquidity of narcissistic identities with the cultivation of more cosmopolitan forms of subjectivity. For the analysis of identity and subjectivity – even accepting the main parameters of Bauman's account of key institutional transformations associated with liquid modernity – is best conceptualized, I argue, through a dual psycho-social focus. On the one hand, this involves attention to private life, the psyche, emotions, memories and desire; on the other hand, it involves attention to social changes such as those associated with globalization, neo-liberalism, processes of social exclusion, and on and on. Whilst Bauman's analysis is finely honed on the latter of these concerns, the adequacy of his conceptualization of the former is open to question.

Let us consider these points in a little more detail. Recent research in social theory, sociology and psycho-social studies highlights the extraordinary diversity of modes of identity-constitution in the global age (Taylor 1989; Giddens 1992). Such diversity has been studied not only in terms of cognition, but also performativity, affectivity, receptiveness to difference and engagement with otherness (Butler 1993; Bhabha 1994; Lemert 2002). How might this complex, contradictory core of identity-constitution in the current age be best approached? Is there a way in which such personal and social differences can be apprehended from within the theory of liquid modernity? What is quite exquisitely detailed in Bauman's account is an appreciation of the ambivalence of modernity as it operates through identities, and yet the responses of subjects and especially alternative and non-conformist subjectivities are disowned too often in this sociological approach. For example, is 'liquid life' only a means of adjusting narcissistic individuals to the dictates of late capitalism? Is this liquidization of identity always a defensive closure at the level of private life, against the range of possibilities and perils inaugurated by globalization? What of identities resistant to the short-term temper of liquid modernity, of those individuals who reject cultural pressures towards change and flexibility? Due to the generality and sweep of the theory of liquid modernity, what threatens to recede into the shadows is the point that all of us have multiple identities, some overlapping, some contradictory, and that at any moment these identities are interacting with – incorporating, resisting and transforming – broader social values and cultural differences, shaping and being shaped by modernity. Following from this point, we might also ponder the location of the sociological critic, and of those readers who adopt a similarly critical stance, towards the episodic nature of liquid life. Given the sharply critical dimension of Bauman's analysis, and given the wide influence of the theory of liquid modernity within and beyond the discipline of sociology, why have individuals and institutions not decried the corrosive character of liquefaction in a more systematic and widespread way?

A more detailed account of the link between liquidization and identity would require a more systematic analysis of the complexity of subjectivity and its relation to modernity. I have already sought to provide such an analysis elsewhere (Elliott 1996), and so here I shall confine myself to a few key points. First, liquid identity – in its pursuit of the ever-new and cult of the short-term – should be regarded as one among many modes of identity-constitution in the contemporary period. Second, the connections between liquid modernity and the formation and expression of liquid life strategies are worthy of sociological attention; the subjectivities of liquid life, however, should not be approached as only epiphenomena, the products of external forces operating outside those individuals who help to create such identities. Here we should recognize that individuals co-create their personal settings of daily action through direct engagement with their wider social conditions of action. Third, this means for social theory, as regards the analysis of identity and subjectivity, that individuals cannot be homogenized into an undifferentiated mass – whose experiences and identities will be pre-set by the dominant social and cultural forces of modernity. The activities of individuals – however much seemingly liquid and narcissistic in character – are never the actions of ciphers, and to interpret subjectivity thus runs the risk of ignoring emotional conflicts, social contradictions, as well as tensions that people increasingly experience in respect of transformations affecting family, sexuality, work and politics (see Elliott and Lemert 2005).

Conclusion

In conclusion, let me briefly summarize the central points of this chapter. After outlining the main parameters of Bauman's social theory of liquid modernity, I focused on three key areas of sociological concern, criticizing and reconstructing the arguments upon which they depend. I suggested, first, that there are shortcomings with Bauman's argument for the generality of societal liquidization; that his thesis of liquid modernity is, at various points in his writings, exaggerated; and that his analysis of liquefaction squeezes to the sidelines of sociological concern the ongoing force of early modernist codes and norms in the production of cultural life. I argued, second, that there are various emphases in Bauman's earlier sociology of postmodernity that should be preserved for the analysis of liquid modernity, specifically as regards issues of autonomy and social transformation. In the final section I raised some general questions about Bauman's analysis of identity in the context of liquid societies and offered some constructive remarks concerning alternative ways of thinking sociologically about the complexity of human subjectivity. Whatever the difficulties and shortcomings of the theory of liquid modernity, there can be little doubt that it is among Bauman's major achievements to have set much of the wider agenda for social theory in these early days of the twenty-first century. For in his exquisitely heterodox and imaginatively capacious sociology, Bauman's is a dazzlingly virtuoso performance, and one which is likely to influence the direction of the social sciences for many years to come.

References

Baudrillard, J. (1981). *For a Critique of the Political Economy of the Sign*. Trans. with an introduction by Charles Levin, St. Louis, MO: Telos Press.

Baudrillard, J. (1983) *Simulations*. Trans. Paul Foss, Paul Patton and Philip Beitchman. New York: Semiotext(e).

Bauman, Z. (1972) Between Class and Elite: The Evolution of the British Labour Movement: A Sociological Study. Trans. Sheila Patterson. Manchester: Mancheser University Press.
Bauman, Z. (1978) *Hermeneutics and Social Science*. London: Hutchinson.
Bauman, Z. (1989) *Modernity and the Holocaust*. Cambridge: Polity Press.
Bauman, Z. (1990) *Thinking Sociologically*. Oxford: Blackwell.
Bauman, Z. (1991) *Modernity and Ambivalence*. Cambridge: Polity Press.
Bauman, Z. (1992) *Intimations of Postmodernity*. London: Routledge.
Bauman, Z. (1993) *Postmodern Ethics*. Oxford: Blackwell.
Bauman, Z. (1995) *Life in Fragments*. Oxford: Blackwell.
Bauman, Z. (1998) *Globalization: The Human Consequences*. Cambridge: Polity Press.
Bauman, Z. (2000) *Liquid Modernity*. Cambridge: Polity Press.
Bauman, Z. (2001) *The Individualized Society*. Cambridge: Polity Press.
Bauman, Z. (2001) Commodity: Seeking Safety in an Insecure World. Cambridge: Polity Press.
Bauman, Z. (2002) *Society under Siege*. Cambridge: Polity Press.
Bauman, Z. (2003) *Liquid Love*. Cambridge: Polity Press.
Bauman, Z. (2004) *Wasted Lives: Modernity and Its Outcasts*. Cambridge: Polity Press.
Bauman, Z. (2004) *Identity*. Cambridge: Polity Press.
Bauman, Z. (2005) *Liquid Life*. Cambridge: Polity Press.
Beck, U. (1999) *World Risk Society*. Cambridge: Polity Press.
Beck, U. (2006) *Cosmopolitan Vision*. Cambridge: Polity Press.
Beilharz, P. (2000) *Zygmunt Bauman: Dialectic of Modernity*. London and Thousand Oaks, CA: Sage.
Best, S. (1998) 'Zygmunt Bauman: Personal Reflections within the Mainstream of Modernity', *British Journal of Sociology*. 49 (2) June: 311–20.
Bhabha, H. (1994) *The Location of Culture*. London: Routledge.
Butler, J. (1993) *Bodies That Matter*. London: Routledge.
Chesneaux, J. (1992) *Brave Modern World: The Prospects for Survival*. London: Thames and Hudson.
Clarke, S. and Moran, A. (2003) 'The Uncanny Stranger: Haunting the Australian Settler National Imagination', *Free Associations*. 10, Pt 1 (53): 165–89.
Du Gay, P. and Hall, S. (eds) (1996) *Questions of Cultural Identity*. London: Sage.
Elliott, A. (1996) *subject to Ourselves: Social Theory, Psychoanalysis, and Postmodernity*. (Second edition 2004). Boulder, CO: Paradigm Press.
Elliott, A. and Lemert, C. (2005) The New Individualism: The Emotional Costs of Globalization. London: Routledge.
Fukuyama, F. (1993) *The End of History and The Last Man*. London: Penguin.
Furedi, F. (2004) *Therapy Culture*. London: Routledge.
Gane, N. (ed.) (2004) *The Future of Social Theory*. London: Routledge.
Giddens, A. (1991) *Modernity and Self-Identity*. Cambridge: Polity Press.
Giddens, A. (1992) The Transformation of Intimacy: Sexuality, Love and Eroticism in Modern Societies. Cambridge: Polity Press.
Giddens, A. (1994) 'Living in a Post- Traditional Society', in Ulrich Beck, Anthony Giddens and Scott Lash (eds) *Reflexive Modernization: Politics, Tradition and Aesthetics in the Modern Social Order*. Stanford, CA: Stanford University Press.
Gross, N. (2005) 'The Detraditionalization of Intimacy Reconsidered', *Sociological Theory*, 23 (3): 286–311.
Habermas, J. (2001) *The Postnational Constellation*. Cambridge: Polity Press.
Jameson, F. (1992) Postmodernism, or The Cultural Logic of Late Capitalism. London: Verso.

Lemert, C. (2002) *Dark Thoughts*. New York: Routledge.
Lyotard, J-F. (1979) *The Postmodern Condition: A Report on Knowledge*. Trans. G. Bennington and B. Massumi. Minneapolis: University of Minnesota Press, 1984.
Paolini, A. (1999) Navigating Modernity: Postcolonialism, Identity and International Relations. Boulder, CO: Lynne Rienner.
Patterson, M. (2006) *Consumption and Everyday Life*. London: Routledge.
Smart, B. (1992) *Modernity Conditions, Postmodern Controversies*. London and New York: Routledge.
Smart, C. and Shipman, B. (2004) 'Visions in Monochrome: Families, Marriage and the Individualization Thesis', *British Journal of Sociology*. 55 (4): 491–509.
Smith, D. (1999) *Zygmunt Bauman: Prophet of Postmodernity*. Cambridge: Polity Press.
Taylor, C. (1989) *Source of the Self: The Making of the Modern Identity*. Cambridge, MA: Harvard University Press.
Tester, K. (2004) *The Social Thought of Zygmunt Bauman*. London: Palgrave.
Tester, K. and Jacobsen, M.H. (eds) (2005) Bauman Before Postmodernity: Invitation, Conversations and Annotated Bibliography 1953–1989. Denmark: Aalborg University Press.

CHAPTER TWO

From postmodernity to liquid modernity

What's in a metaphor?

Larry Ray

Bauman is one of the most influential contemporary sociologists whose recent work joins with that of Ulrich Beck and others in offering a broad-brush depiction of the central cultural trends in the world today. Bauman's work has undergone a number of conceptual shifts over the four decades in which he has been writing sociology – his early work (Bauman 1972) was an analysis of class and elite in the British labour movement; later he developed theories of structure and action (Bauman 1973 and 1976); then he became one of the leading theorists of modernity and postmodernity weaving together knowledge of western and central-eastern European societies with an encyclopedic grasp of social theory (Bauman 1989, 1991, 1992, 1993). However the theme of fragmentation and uncertainty that characterizes much of his work in the 1990s offered a new twist as the sociologist of postmodernity abandoned the language of the postmodern (though not necessarily his stance on the current state of the social) and became instead the sociologist of 'liquid modernity' (Bauman 2000). This trajectory seems to embody a desire to encapsulate the uniqueness of the present in concepts that transcend earlier and rapidly outmoded ways of seeing. It is not surprising then that early in *Liquid Modernity* Bauman quotes Beck's critique of sociology that clings to 'zombie categories', such as family, class and neighbourhood that are 'dead but still alive' (Bauman 2000: 6)[1]. The presumption here is that sociology enters into a conceptual dialectic with the pace of social change – unable to stand still, always revolutionizing its own frameworks – its very concepts change with the pace of social development itself. The risks here though are that we will be led to see as novel things that are actually ephemeral or superficial and that we will prematurely reject the insights from existing theories, especially those of classical sociology (see for example Turner 2006 on this).

This chapter will examine Bauman's transition from sociologist of postmodernity to theorist of liquid modernity, particularly with reference to his style of sociological writing and the evidential debates that he by and large eschews. Two serious problems with Bauman's theory will be identified. First, there is a lack of specificity as to where these putative changes are occurring (and therefore where they are not) and, second, it takes at face value surface experiences of the contemporary societies rather than asking questions about underlying processes. This chapter offers a defence of sociology *against* metaphor and defends precisely the sociological approaches that are dismissed by Bauman and other contemporary theorists such as Urry and Beck. It argues that in order to develop sociological approaches adequate for understanding the social world and intervening effectively in public debate, we need to be finely tuned to the empirical foundation for our theoretical generalities and recognize that the complexity of the contemporary social world must escape attempts at encapsulation within any overarching metaphors.

Metaphor or sociological theory?

In an interview with Harald Welzer in 2002 Bauman commented that to read Habermas 'was a waste of time' since his theory was a 'world populated by concepts not people . . . theoretical fetishism . . . separate from the real world'. Now this may well be a judgement others would share. But aside from the point that this is a criticism to which much sociology, including Bauman's, could be subject, the sentiment is symptomatic of a direction taken by social theory in the past two decades. Habermas's two-volume *Theory of Communicative Action*, published in the 1980s, was a monumental critical synthesis that offered sociology the opportunity to overcome transcendental illusions of the twentieth century, an *objective* at least shared by Bauman, while retaining theoretical complexity. But several leading sociologists chose a different path in which theories became metaphors describing dimensions of human experience often involving generalized attempts to capture the meaning of the contemporary life. This practice is also advocated by Urry (2000: 18) who seeks to 'develop through appropriate metaphors a sociology which focuses upon movement, mobility and contingent ordering, rather than upon stasis, structure and social order'. Certainly, metaphors are valuable ways of conceptualizing large-scale social processes and of reflecting back into our understanding of the present some key tendencies that place specific events in a wider context. However, the key attribute of a metaphor is allegorical appropriateness rather than validity or truth, in terms of correspondence between propositions and an externally knowable reality. Metaphoric sociology entails a significant loss of interest in the role of empirical research as a standard against which to establish the adequacy of theories, in which context it is notable that Bauman's *Thinking Sociologically* (1990) makes no specific reference to social research or empirical evidence as an element of sociological thinking[2].

Implicit in this issue is an important debate about the nature of social as opposed to sociological theory. Harrington (2005: 2) points out that although the term 'social theory' did not exist in any language before the twentieth century, social theory as an intellectual activity emerged with modernity and was largely equated with an attitude of critical thinking, and the desire for knowledge through 'a posteriori' methods of discovery, rather than 'a priori' methods of tradition. However, abstract and generalized theorizing was subject to critique from different sources in (what has become known as) classical sociology. Marx was critical of the abstract and 'spiritual' concepts used by the Hegelians, such as Zeitgeist, Objective Mind and Consciousness, and called instead for the study of 'real living men' (e.g. Marx 1970). Durkheim regarded sociological theory as generating testable hypotheses and crucially being able to account for different outcomes (such as variations in the rate and nature of suicide over time and space) while capturing the central processes operating within European society at an abstract level. Weber, though methodologically eclectic, was committed to grounding his theoretical claims in empirical (often historical) data and probably his most influential work, *The Protestant Ethic and the Spirit of Capitalism*, is tied to a specific set of claims that became the subject of debate in Weber's lifetime and the ensuing hundred years. Even highly abstract sociological theorists such as Parsons and Habermas insisted at least in principle that the evaluation of their theories should depend on empirical verifiability (as Habermas for example says repeatedly in *Theory of Communicative Action*). Thus sociology as a systematic discipline claimed to develop theories that would refer to empirically based observations and be testable with reference to empirical evidence, however this was understood. Now this may appear to be labouring the obvious. But *social* theory by contrast functions inherently in an interdisciplinary manner, as it uses ideas from and contributes to a plethora of disciplines such as anthropology, economics, theology, history and many others. It refers to the use of theoretical frameworks to explain and analyse social patterns and large-scale social structures but makes little use of empirical evidence. Its propositions thus become more like metaphors of social experiences and they will in particular have cultural resonance and tap into widely shared perceptions of the world. Bauman for example says of contemporary cultural experience that it is

> disorderly, to wit plural, rhizomically growing, devoid of direction . . . It is this new cultural experience . . . which has been distilled in the postmodern view of the world as a self-constituting and self-propelling process, determined by nothing but its own momentum, subject to no overall plan – 'of the movement toward the "Second Coming"', 'universalization of human condition', 'rationalization of human action'.
>
> (Bauman 1992: 35)

So the *experience* of the world in these terms (by who we are not told) is distilled (presumably that is, condensed or refined) into the theory of postmodernism. Theory is then an abstract representation of widely held cultural experiences – the articulation of a kind of Zeitgeist. But this is open to the objection that it revives abstract speculation rather than empirically founded validity claims. It also risks faddishness – representing as global and epochal trends that are actually rather spatially and socially limited experiences, without addressing the underlying processes. In any event, if a theorist is developing claims about social transformation (as Bauman is) then the question of how statements about the social world can be validated still is relevant.

The shift in Bauman's conceptual framework from sociology of postmodernity to liquid modernity is an illustration of theory as metaphor and parallels Beck's dichotomy between first and second modernity (Beck and Lau 2005). Having become one of the foremost advocates of sociological postmodernism in the early 1990s, albeit as Rengger (1995: 179) suggested of a 'soft-sceptical' variety, Bauman now appears to renounce his earlier postmodernism when he claims that 'the society which enters the twenty-first century is no less "modern" than the society which entered the twentieth' (Bauman 2000: 28). The contrast between 'heavy' and liquid' modernity is essentially a contrast between Fordist, bureaucratic, centralized societies of nation-states engaged in military-territorial competition on the one hand and post-Fordist, globalized, fluid, post-bureaucratic societies on the other. The former was the world of the *Konzlager* in which the limits of human malleability were tested under laboratory conditions (Bauman 2000: 25) as he argued previously in *Modernity and the Holocaust* (1989). Likewise Communism was situated within 'heavy' and post-communism within 'liquid' modernity in which there has been a 'dissipation of politburos' and individuality has replaced the collective. So for Bauman the fall of Communism signalled the wider transition from heavy to liquid modernity, and after Communism so ended utopianism, legislative reason, productivism (especially in Soviet systems the 'steel per head' celebration of production) along with other grand social designs.

Bauman's assessment of the state of contemporary society has not fundamentally changed between postmodernist and liquid modernist phases nor was the shift prompted by any explanatory inadequacy of postmodernist sociology. The world of liquid modernity is much the same as that of postmodernity. Why did this transition in Bauman's thinking occur? The core reasons arose from concerns about the adequacy of the postmodern metaphor. In an interview in 2002 Bauman says:

> I've some time ago distanced myself from the 'postmodern' grid of the world-map. A number of reasons contributed . . . the concept of 'postmodern' was but a stop-gap choice, a 'career report' of a search – still on-going and remote from completion. That concept signalled that the social world had ceased to be like the one mapped using the 'modernity' grid . . . but was singularly un-committal as to the features the world had acquired instead. . . . About the qualities of the present-day world we can say now more than it is unlike the old familiar one. We have, so to speak, matured to afford (to risk?) a positive theory of the novelty.
> (Bauman and Yakimova 2002)

He previously described postmodernity as 'an aspect of a fully fledged, viable social system which has come to replace the "classical" modern, capitalist society and thus needs to be theorized according to its own logic' (Bauman 1992: 52).

Now, however, the

> 'Postmodern' was . . . flawed from the beginning: all disclaimers notwithstanding, it did suggest that modernity was over. Protestations did not help much, even as strong ones as Lyotard's ('one cannot be modern without being first postmodern') – let alone my insistence that 'postmodernity is modernity minus its illusion'. Nothing would help; if words mean anything, then a 'postX' will always mean a state of affairs that has left the 'X' behind.
> (Bauman and Yakimova 2002)

The themes of flexibility and uncertainty of the present survive in the concept of liquid modernity but there is now a clearer attempt to work through the 'logic' of the new social system of the present.

Not that this should involve straightforward periodization. Postmodern sceptics saw modernist views of time, linear time, as oppressive and the attempt to periodize

Derrida called 'chronophonism'. Bauman too tried to avoid over-simple temporal dichotomies of modern/postmodern. Although he depicted modernity in Promethean terms, which were contrasted with the fluid, differentiated and aestheticized cultural forms of post or liquid modernity, he also insisted that postmodernism was not a stage beyond so much as the exhaustion of modernity, or 'modernity coming to terms with its own impossibility' (Bauman 1990: 26). Again, in *Postmodern Ethics* (1993) the postmodern represents the beginning and not the end for a truly human ethics that abandons the legislative stance, accepts humans' moral ambivalence and lives without guarantees and transcendence. Similarly, liquidity is offered as a better metaphor for contemporary experience rather than a better *theory* in a more traditional sociological sense.[3]

The heavy-liquid metaphor is carried through several areas of social life, which are summarised in Table 2.1. The politics of emancipation abandons the idea of a *telos* of history, a state of perfection based in class politics and legislative reason, to privatization, and closure of the public sphere. The idea of a 'state of perfection' it might be noted was associated with certain social movements, notably Communism, rather than characteristic of modernity per se. Most liberals from theoretical positions as varied as Sigmund Freud, Frederick von Hayek and Karl Popper regarded the pursuit of perfectibility a dangerous illusion. Anyway, for Bauman at the level of individuality, liquidity means a transition from instrumental producer, to consumer in which sources of self-identity are derived more from shopping than from occupation but with heightened uncertainty and instability. Similarly, discussing the end of Communism from the standpoint of postmodern sociology, Bauman claimed that 'confronted by a . . . consumer society in the west, the obsolete steel-per-head philosophy proved no match for the lure of the narcissistic culture of self-enhancement, self-enjoyment, instant gratification' (Bauman 1992: 169). Time and space become detached and the investment of power in space (territory) gives way to the disembodied, empty (cyber) space of mobility and transience. The world of work is transformed from the stability of Fordist secure employment to post-Fordist flexibility and fluidity of short-term contracts and rapid technological change. The 'heavy' nationally solidaristic communities give way to liquid communities of post-national sentiments, which Bauman calls 'cloakroom communities' because like clothes donned for a special occasion, these are fleeting, disposable and ephemeral. None of this is terribly surprising and these claims have become tropes in which contemporary (western) societies are routinely described. But this analysis does rather leave unanswered the question of how, amid all this transitory fluidity, social life gets done at all or what bonds of sociability might bind people together for long enough to be able to get from home to work. One could argue of course (as I think I would) that the greater informality and mobility of contemporary life requires more complex and in a way durable bonds of solidity than in an earlier period of greater formality and stability.

Social integration can be achieved in different ways but to simply point to fluidity and flexibility without examining the persistence of social bonds is one-sided. Notions of solidarity based on class, nation, religion and local community (a somewhat idealized picture of mid-twentieth century Europe) may have weakened. The post-national constellation (Habermas 2001) seeks forms of identity, collective

Table 2.1 Bauman's typology of heavy and liquid modernity

	Heavy modernity	Liquid Modernity
Emancipation	Utopian – reality shaped by designers and planners Legislative reason Class politics Critique of reality Public 'colonizing' private	End of utopian visions Individualization Self-critique of individual Private colonizes public
Individuality	Means-ends calculation Certainty and stability	Prioritizing ends Uncertainty and instability
Time/space	Territorial conquest – wealth and power in *land* Hardware, bulk-obsessed, fixed, sluggish Panoptic surveillance	Extra-territorial, cyber-space, 'disembodied' Light, aesthetic, bricoleur Post-panoptic
Work	Fordist Careers Welfare Capital and labour	Post-Fordist Rapid movement and change, 'saturated with uncertainty' Fluid contracts and individual identities
Community	Nation-states Locales Nationalism	Nations retreat behind communities Ephemeral 'community' Ethnic violence and cleansing

agreement, cosmopolitanism and right-based integration. Even so, there are some (e.g. Smith 1997) who would claim that national solidarity based on quasi-sacred commitment to land and community is no less strong now than in the recent past. However, even if we accept that these traditional 'heavy' loyalties are in decline, social life still gets fixed in multiple ways through institutional structures, complex relations of dependence and exchange that can be local or stretch across continents,[4] the 'dull compulsion of economic relations' (Marx 1974: 689) that binds people in relations of inequality, along with social relations of family, friendship and locality. Beneath this the structures of the lifeworld constitute tacit, normative and largely unspoken knowledge of how social relations are conducted.

Bauman follows many later twentieth-century sociologists in pointing (in effect) to a 'crisis of meaning' as common-sense 'knowledge' of the social world is increasingly called into question so that no interpretation, no range of possible actions can be accepted any longer as the only true and unquestionably right one. Luckmann (1996) for example claims that individuals are faced with the question,

> whether they should not have lived their lives in a completely different manner than they actually did. This is experienced on the one hand as a great liberation, as an opening of new horizons and possibilities of life, leading out of the confines

of the old, unquestioned mode of existence. The same process is, however, often experienced as oppressive (often by the same people) – as a pressure on the individual to repeatedly make sense of the new and unfamiliar in their reality.

Some may relish this uncertainly while others may 'feel insecure and lost in a confusing world full of possibilities'. It is claimed that the range of taken-for-granted assumptions shrinks to a relatively small core, a process driven particularly by technological-economic forces. But while this view is consistent with Bauman's liquid individuality and Beck's reflexive individualization, the extent to which social relations have been fluidized can also be exaggerated.

A good example of these issues is the debate over the social consequences of the Internet. Most of the data on Internet use and long-distance social relationships for example indicates that people are able to sustain distanced interactions through the development of complex distanced sociality. The Internet is an important 'test case' because it epitomizes fluidity, liquidity and post-space social relations. Nie and Erbring (2000) famously argued that the Internet created a lonely crowd in cyberspace because it necessarily took time away from friends but considerable evidence points to the opposite conclusion. Kraut *et al.* (1998) found that Internet users have larger social networks than non or infrequent users and that rather than being isolating, Internet communities offer multiple supports. Further, the Internet can be viewed as an interactive and social activity in its own right indicating a change of medium rather than of substance in people's interactions. Katz *et al.* (2001) found that the more time people spend online the more likely they are to engage in offline activities, and Hampton and Wellman's (2002) Electronic Village Study challenges the notion that there is an absence of intimate personal acquaintanceship on the Web but argues on the contrary that the longer people spend online the more likely they are to build social capital. The Internet allows both asynchronous and direct one-to-one and one-to-many broadcasts and has become another communication tool among many ways in which people can interact. Asynchronous communication is a low-cost way for people to organize their lives but is not a distinct social system separate from existing foci of activity. They conclude that the Internet has intensified the volume and range of neighbourly relations rather than reducing social connections. So post-space sociality does not necessarily mean the end of social bonds, reciprocity and interaction rules of the kind traditionally studied by sociologists.

Problems with the heavy/liquid dichotomy

The heavy/liquid distinction like modernity/postmodernity is a binary contrast concept that is unlikely to capture the multiple complexities and diversity of contemporary life. The broad contours of what was described as postmodern and now liquid are the same. One troubling issue with this shift is that if one can just as easily describe contemporary society as 'postmodern' or 'liquid' modern there is some specificity missing in both concepts – the main difference between them seems to be their connotations of temporality and the future. Sociology has seen a lot of generalized attempts to capture the essence of the contemporary and we need more work on the concrete diversity of social forms of the contemporary world. Indeed, in *Globalization* (1998a) Bauman emphasizes how globalization is accompanied by increasing heterogeneity and difference and that global social relations are inscribed in a highly uneven and unequal way in locales. So it is surprising that *Liquid Modernity* is totalizing and undifferentiated with relatively little acknowledgement that the configurations of the modern manifest in contradictory and highly uneven ways.

Bauman seems uncertain as to quite how to understand modernity. The concept is open to many modes of specification – that may be temporal (modernity as the period that follows traditional society) technological (modernity as industrial society), and cultural-organizational (post-traditional individualization and rationalization). The latter view has been elaborated by Habermas into a multi-layered theory of modernity as a dual process of rationalization – at the level of system (expansion of steering via money and power) and lifeworld (expanding the potential for moral autonomy, post-traditional norms of validity and democratic will formation). But the complexity of these changes allows for many differences of emphasis. Bauman (like Giddens) suggests that 'Modernity starts when space and time are separated from living practice and from each other and so become ready to be theorized as distinct and mutually independent categories of strategy and action' (Bauman 2000: 8). But this arguably began to happen once transport technology began to move people faster than walking pace or when communications could transcend space. The pre-Roman Celts in Europe developed a road network for horse-drawn carts and the Romans of course developed speed through horse-drawn chariots. The first recorded use of homing pigeons used to send a message was in 776 BC to announce the winner of the Olympic Games to the Athenians. Between 200–100 BC human messengers on foot or horseback were common in Egypt and China and messenger relay stations were built. Sometimes fire messages were used to communicate from relay station to station rather than using human runners, and in AD 37 the Roman Emperor Tiberius used heliographs – the first recorded use of mirrors – to send messages. Each of these indicates a kind of triumph of time over space. Does this mean we should date modernity in classical antiquity?[5] Presumably not, but this does suggest the need for more clarity on quite what are the core characteristics of 'the modern'.

Again, modernity is (or was) an assault on the nomadic in that citizenship, and membership of the paradigmatic modern institution, the nation-state, was tied to permanent residence and settlement. But now, Bauman suggests, we are witnessing the 'revenge of the nomadic' in new forms of mobility – tourism, migration, modern transnational corporations as new 'absentee landlords' and a culture in which whatever is smaller, lighter and more portable constitutes progress. But this claim conflates several different processes. The 'absenteeism' of the transnational corporation was a feature of heavy modernity too, surely, and if anything the contemporary organizational culture of TNCs often emphasizes the importance of local knowledge and involvement – such as HSBC, whose slogan is 'The world's local bank'. There is clearly a commercial preoccupation with mobility and speed but these are facilities for people who are based somewhere and have the means to buy the technologies of actual and virtual mobility – not for those who are poor or homeless and have nowhere to go in a hurry. Some borders then are liquid or permeable and some very heavy and cannot be crossed with ease.

Bauman himself has drawn attention to this, distinguishing between 'tourists' and 'vagabonds'. The former move through choice, choose their destinations, move easily, and despise and fear the vagabond, who in turn moves through necessity, does not choose where to go, moves with difficulty, and admires and envies the tourists. 'The tourists travel *because they want to*; the vagabonds because *they have no other bearable choice*' (Bauman 1998b: 94). Again these are metaphors for postmodern (liquid) modernity in that both involve chaotic (as opposed to regular) mobility. The vagabond, he says, is a pilgrim without a destination, a nomad without an itinerary; while the tourist pays 'for their freedom; the right to disregard native concerns and feelings, the right to spin their own web of meanings . . . The world is the tourist's oyster . . . to be lived pleasurably – and thus given meaning' (Bauman 1993: 241). Both vagabonds and tourists travel through other people's spaces and both involve the separation of physical closeness from moral proximity, and both set standards for happiness and the good life. For Bauman the good life has come to be thought of as somewhat akin to a 'continuous holiday' (1993: 243) and the vagabond is a 'flawed consumer' (1998a: 77).

However, the implication that because both tourism and forced migration involve travel across borders they are somehow both manifestations of a nomadic liquidity is superficial and does not recognize the different social and economic processes that generate a global culture of consumer tourism on the one hand and some 10 million migrants and 25 million displaced persons on the other. Both are processes of global significance but arise in very different ways. Tourism is one of the largest global industries[6] but is premised not on mobility as such but rather on temporary sojourn in which many 'home comforts' and familiar forms of consumption will be available. Not all tourism is cross-border and in China for example internal tourism is a major source of revenue for local businesses (Sklair 2002: 264). On the other hand, migration itself is a highly differentiated process – that includes temporary migrant workers, highly skilled voluntary migrants, forced and trafficked migrants and refugees – generated by different sets of social relationships. Underlying economic migration is the way in which capital increasingly defines labour costs in terms of lowest global costs and through subcontracting in home and overseas markets is able to achieve lowest costs in some sectors, such as textiles. Low-cost and often forced labour migration is a crucial facet of global mobilities (Papastergiadis 2000: 40). The presence of undocumented workers in advanced capitalist economies has the important effect of reducing costs in sectors that are structurally dependent upon them, such as textiles, minicabs, cleaners, food service and agriculture (Rivera-Batiz 1999). The implication of this for Bauman is that the metaphors of 'vagabond' and 'tourist' conceal more than they reveal while the patterns of global population movement can be accounted for in terms of existing theories and concepts of global capital, and class, gender and racial structures.

A further difficulty with the heavy/liquid dichotomy is that while Bauman articulates some well-known contrasts between industrial and post-industrial society, the distinctions are painted very broadly and are too general to give much purchase on the explanation of change in particular locales. When certain sorts of changes occur (for example dismantling the welfare and industrial institutions) these are manifestations of a wider trend, which they both exemplify and intensify. There is an unacknowledged tension between the centrality of agency in Bauman's writing and the inevitability of his depiction of social processes. Welfare restructuring is a political strategy that is not necessarily dictated by external events or circumstances such as globalization – this means that actors (at any rate institutional actors) have choices and that therefore the processes Bauman describes are contingent rather than necessary. If social outcomes are contingent (which they should be if subjects have agency) then in what ways do contemporary societies vary and why?

It is questionable how thoroughly contemporary life has been 'liquidified' anyway. For Bauman, what is novel about the present (liquid) moment is the sense that the old social bonds of family and community are being replaced by concepts of identity that are by their nature fluid and flexible. Modernity originally aimed to break primordial social bonds only to reform and relocate individuals in even stronger, new bonds such as the nation, or the nuclear family. Liquid modernity means that there are no longer any strong bonds. But even if the transition in family structure (that is occurring largely in western countries) were to become universal, this liquefaction does not apply to other aspects of social life. For billions of people, strong bonds of identity, centred on religion, family, nationality and ethno-linguistic particularity, are still at the core of social being. Even in the states in Europe where 'marriage is passé', there are strong movements to limit or cancel immigration from the south and the east in the interest of preserving national identity.

Further, it is possible to point to areas of organizational life in western societies where autonomy and uncertainty has given way to increased routinization and regulation. An illustrative example is the growth of the audit culture especially in public sector professional life. In the pre-audit period of 'heavy' modernity professions (such as medicine and teaching) exercised autonomy that was legitimated in terms of ethically based control over the conditions of application of their knowledge and skills. Durkheim saw this as a model for solidaristic work organization, in which the market and class-based antagonism between managers and workers would be regulated through morally integrative codes of practice (Durkheim 1957). Jamous and Pelloille (1970) wrote about the 'indeterminacy' of expert knowledge that had a high tacit and inexpressible dimension so that professional–client relations were based on high levels of trust. This was contrasted with the technicality of codifiable and replicable knowledge. Friedson (1971) saw physicians having 'charismatic' as well as formal-rational authority based on expertise since their authority to define an 'emergency' enabled them to override bureaucratic procedures. This power was rooted in the class and status systems of 'heavy' modernity and the occupational structure that differentiated professions from trades and unskilled workers. The irony though is now that in a supposedly liquid modernity in which the systems of deference and authority that made professional autonomy possible have been partially eroded there is more formality, fixity and routine application of codifiable accountability. The audit culture has arisen with the growth of internal markets and commercialization of the public sector but this has brought not greater fluidity but rule by targets, administrative imperative, quasi-sacred templates, formulaic report writing and obsessive attention to predefined categories. The internal market has not created increased autonomy and fluidity but on the contrary a deep suspicion of any non-quantifiable and standardized measures of performance.

Throughout Bauman's thesis there are claims that are dependent on implicit but unjustified empirical claims. For example:

> Work has changed its character. More often than not, it is a one-off act: a ploy of a bricoleur, a trickster, aimed at what is at hand and inspired and constrained by what is at hand . . . more the outcome of chance than the product of planning and design.
>
> (Bauman 2000: 139)

There are similar arguments in Beck, who Bauman frequently quotes with approval. There is indeed a widespread view that permanent employment associated with traditional employment patterns has been fundamentally undermined with the advent of the 'new economy'. Industrial restructuring is said to have given way to more precarious forms of employment characterized by short-term jobs. However, such perceptions are challenged by the analysis of long-term employment and industrial, occupational change in the European workforce. They are flawed on at least two counts. First, the idea of standard employment in 'heavy' industrial society is exaggerated. It arguably pertained in developed capitalist economies during the period of post-war expansion (1954–65) but applied mostly to privileged white, male, skilled workers while women, migrants and semi- and unskilled workers were largely excluded. Further, where job security did exist (in western societies) this was not an essential feature of the heavy industrial system but was hard fought for by organized unions against casual labour practices. Second, contrary to the arguments of Beck, Castells and Sennet, as well as Bauman, the evidence suggests a more complex picture and even that labour market change in the European Union is moving in the opposite direction with significant *increase* in long-term employment across member states (Doogan 2005).

Even so, this increase might be at the expense of intensified exploitation (Carnoy 2000: 143). Bauman (like Beck) deploys highly general categories that amalgamate disparate forms of risk and compact together diverse employment experiences. Far from being directed by a universal axis of insecurity, labour market inequalities follow the patterns created by traditional forms of stratification (Mythen 2005). It is possible then that contrary to the liquidity metaphor there is little evidence for an acceleration of labour market 'churning' but rather there is evidence of stagnation of decline in labour market flexibility since the 1970s combined with intensification of labour market inequalities. The latter has been evident in marked differences in sectoral job security with some service sector jobs becoming more unstable but others less so (Erlinghagen and Knuth 2004). Again detailed analysis of changes in the workplace needs to be related to specific organizational practices. These are being altered by changes in technology and international pressures but this does not mean that traditional ('heavy') work has been eradicated, but rather dispersed to developing economies (Morris 2004).

Moreover, despite Bauman's (and Beck's) aspirations to be 'critical' the analysis of work uses concepts employed by managers – flexibility, empowerment, performance management (Bradley *et al.* 2000: 4). This is not a critical sociology but reflects more an alliance between academics in business and management schools and managers that extends increasingly across many areas of university life. The rejection of classical sociology and in particular the concept of class is symptomatic of a managerial view that major productive and work-based conflicts have now ended. Similarly, one of the core claims made about postmodern/liquid modernity is the dominance of consumption over production, which reflects what Sklair (2002) calls the 'culture-ideology of consumerism' that the market really does bring expanded choice and that through consumer choices people can freely assert their identity. Further, there is considerable evidence for the growth of a 'long hours culture' in which people work 12-hour days and weekends and attend 'optional' meetings and training courses, while ubiquitous mobile phones mean that the activities of the office spill over into the train, pub, restaurant and living room (Bradley *et al.* 2000: 135). Now while Bauman does acknowledge this (Bauman 1998b: 34) many studies of work suggest that rather than being confined to a professional-managerial elite, this cult of work is expanding to millions of ordinary working people. Further, while this may be resented by many there is also evidence that for workers in both professional and less glamorous types of jobs important aspects of identity, self-esteem and social contact are derived from working life (Bradley *et al.* 2000: 135–7).

This discussion raises a central question as to whose experience is being generalized in the liquidity metaphor? Bauman has been criticized here for implicitly basing his analysis on the experience of western internationally mobile elites. Amardeep Singh for example comments that

> In *Liquid Modernity* . . . Bauman himself is guilty of thinking about globalisation's effect on space and time from the international airport (or worse, from the hotel swimming pool), rather than from the city street or the impoverished farms of the world's rural hinterlands. For people without money, without a visa, etc. modernity is not liquid, it's hard.
>
> (Singh 2004)

One could add that the sweep of contemporary sociology through Giddens, Beck, Ritzer, Urry and others on globalization and mobility assumes a standpoint that unashamedly engages in epochal generalization from the limited experiences of mobile elites. But this may not be entirely justified. Bauman does argue that the current state of modernity is one of increasing polarization and in the liquid consumer (as opposed to 'heavy' producer) society 'The poor . . . have very little mobility, while the affluent . . . have a high degree of mobility' (1998a: 77). Consumers 'live in time' and have choice while the poor do not, a theme developed in *Wasted Lives* (2004). Actually data on geographic mobility suggests that the poor are more mobile than the rich or affluent and that (aside from holidays) the latter are more likely to remain in one locale and occupation for longer[7]. But either way mobility is structured by socio-economic status. However, if Bauman is simply saying that the rich have more choices than the poor – this is obviously true though it is odd that sociologists needed to be told this at all and that we apparently do is perhaps a comment on the current state of of the discipline.

Tradition and the vicissitudes of modernity

There are further questions to ask about the way Bauman depicts 'modernity'. In a wide range of works from *Modernity and the Holocaust* (1989) through *Intimations of Postmodernity* (1992) and *Liquid Modernity* (2000) he has tended to associate modernity (latterly 'heavy' modernity) with totalitarian systems in which 'the limits of human malleability were tested under laboratory conditions' (2000: 26). Thus he argued that Communism, along with fascism, was the epitome of modernity, albeit in one of its most nightmarish forms (Bauman 1992: xvii). Thus the collapse of Communism portends a crisis of (heavy) modernity per se. However, this is open to question since in many ways Communism and fascism harked back to pre-modern societies and contained strong themes of anti-modernism – including military codes of honour, devotion to the leader, the warrior ethos of violence, collectivism, and negation of the individual. 'In placing the interests of the group above those of the person and social values above individual ones,' says Todorov (2003: 41), 'totalitarianism harks back to traditional societies and in that respect must be conservative and anti-modern.' A similar theme is developed by Elias (1996) who argued that in Germany a peculiar conjuncture of circumstances following the First World War established a 'de-civilizing process' – a resurgence of warrior values, decay of the state's monopoly of force, middle-class resistance to the Weimar Republic, and an escalating double-bind of violence and counter-violence that ended in Hitler's rise. Moreover, Communism and Nazism were the opposite of Weber's notion of modernity of disenchanted detached scepticism in which ethics become the private matter of individuals and public life the realm of formal-legal decisions. Bauman's response to this might be to argue that modernity dethroned gods only to replace them with new abstract totalities and orders – of the people, state, class, etc. But the Nazi rebellion was a rebellion *against* modernity epitomized by the anti-semitic stereotype of the Jews as classical strangers – rootless, cosmopolitan, dealing in finance across national borders. This invoked substantive values of pre-modern blood, belonging and volk, not those of sceptical and secular instrumental rationality. Further, as I have argued elsewhere (e.g. Ray 1996 and 1997), it was as the Soviet systems relied less on heroic ideology and more on instrumental rationality to establish legitimacy and efficiency that the underlying functional and legitimacy crises became more acute. If conventional modernization and expansion of decentralized steering through the market and democratization contributed to the formation of crises in Soviet systems then it is difficult to regard them as the epitome of 'modern' systems of any variety.

The concept of *modernity* itself has an uneven history. Although the concept of the *modern* has a long history and was used by Christianized Romans to differentiate the new age (*modernus*) from the pagan, moder*nity* was not widely used until the end of the nineteenth century, and then more as a cultural than sociological term. In mid-century sociology the concept of modern*ization* was widely used until the demise of modernization theory in the 1970s. For a time modernity concepts were regarded as overly loose compared especially with Marxist and Weberian concepts of social relations, such as mode of production, social class, patrimonialism, patriarchy, rationalization and so forth. But with the subsequent cultural turn and of course the appearance of postmodernism, 'modernity' came back into its own in sociology. Arguably, though, modernity has been required to do more work in sociological theory than was useful or justifiable, while the complexity and multilayered nature of the social means that it is particularly difficult to periodize the modern within defensible boundaries. Many attributes of aesthetic post/liquid modernity can be located in modernity too, which is actually replete with multiple possibilities – a point that Habermas has consistently attempted to establish. Similar problems dogged the distinction between modernity and postmodernity. Charles Lemert comments that irony is the discursive form of postmodern theory since 'irony is the only and necessary attitude for theory today' (Lemert 1992: 17). But then irony came into its own in eighteenth-century literature and philosophy especially in the German Romanticism of the Schlegel brothers and Novalis. Irony is significant because it connotes a changed relationship between human subjects and recognition of the gap between the subject and object of thought that can be approached only reflexively. Thus in turn it requires a different kind of reading in which the meanings of the text have to be inferred through reflexive understanding of the author's intentions – as for example in Montesquieu's ironic defence of slavery or indeed the whole genre of Enlightenment satire. Ironic distance could then be as crucial to modernity per se as to post/liquid forms[8].

In some ways we should take seriously Bauman's and others' rejection of chronophonism because this enables us to begin to see multiple modernities or potentials in contemporary society folding into alternative possibilities. However this comes with a need to research systematically the differentiated ways complex global sociality instantiates itself in manifold local social relationships. From this point of view there would be no more stages or sequences to social development since thinking in terms of temporal transitions ignores the way in which particular outcomes are the product of configurations of global and local circumstances. Neither Bauman's view that the fall of the USSR represented the triumph of post/liquid/modernity nor Habermans's view (1992) that post-communism offers hope of renewed modernity is adequate. The post-communist world is one in which the play of modernization, modernity and otherness has become both intense and unstable and to understand actual and possible outcomes we need more specifically refined concepts of social relations. We should not view 'modernity' in any of its vicissitudes as an agent causing things to happen in the social arena but as the outcome of multiple structures, forces and processes that need systematic analysis in their own right.

Partisanship, scholarship, and the public sphere

Bauman ends *Liquid Modernity* with a call for partisanship: 'There is no choice between "engaged" and "neutral" ways of doing sociology. A non-committal sociology is an impossibility'. The job of sociology' he says, 'is to see to it that the choices [faced daily by human beings] are genuinely free, and that they remain so, increasingly so, for the duration of humanity' (Bauman 2000: 216). While this will rightly resonate with many sociologists, the pursuit of perfection seems to have crept back in to sociology, which is surely premised on choices never being free from the social contexts and structures in which they are made. Further, we should acknowledge that partisanship could be an obstacle to our effective engagement in public debates unless we are able to relate theoretical claims to focused and empirically grounded analyses. Take for example the question of globalization and inequality. This is a highly polarized debate in which advocates of economic globalization, especially from international bodies such as the World Bank (2006), argue that globalization is good for international business but also the best way to empower poor people and poor countries. On the other hand, critics argue that globalization enriches a global elite at the expense of labour, poor countries and the environment, while eviscerating the ability of national governments to respond. This debate is driven by the old partisanship of the push and pull of distributive vs. market advocating politics. There is an urgent need for sociologists and other social scientists to reflect on these debates and bring increased clarity as well as complexity based on a more sophisticated understanding of the issues. For example as sociologists know very well, measurement is crucial to how the evidence for each position here is advanced. Depending on which measures of globalization are used – global flows of finance and trade for example, or openness of countries' regulatory regimes to investment – one will get different results as to the extent and effects of globalization. Similarly, inequality within and between nations can be measured in many ways – for example in terms of market exchange rates, purchasing power parity and the Gini coefficient – and the combination of measures used will support different positions (Brune and Garrett 2005).

Now, social theory might not want to get into this level of debate but stay with broader themes and trends, which is reasonable to a point. However, if the existence of global trends is being asserted there should at least be some acknowledgement of the complexity of research issues and of the probability that no trend is uniform and will manifest differently in different locales. When the World Bank claims that poverty has decreased during the last two decades of the twentieth century then to engage effectively in public debate we will need to be able to offer nuanced and detailed responses rather than generalized metaphors. However useful metaphors may be in stimulating imaginative enquiry they are not a substitute for rigorous conceptualization and research into the social.

Notes

1 The original reference, to 'zombie categories' that were 'dead long ago but [are] still haunting people's minds' is in Beck (2000).
2 In Bauman (1992: 105) empirical sociology is seen as being tied to the interests of state bureaucracy that with the decline of the nation-state will face lack of funding. This was a poor prediction in view of levels of social science funding in Europe, at any rate, in

the intervening period but it also reflects a rather narrow view of empirical social science and its purposes.
3 Whether the typology of heavy and liquid does avoid chronological transition is questionable. Bauman never abandons the terms 'modernity' and 'modernization', but the concept still maps chronologically and conceptually to the idea of postmodernity he is now questioning.
4 As for example in the case of global family ties where emotional and financial exchanges are organized across long distances.
5 Adorno and Horkheimer (1973) did famously date the 'origin of the modern bourgeois' with the shift they identify from a mythical to rational world view in Ancient Greece, which is an allusion Bauman could have picked up and elaborated although he does not.
6 Figures produced by the World Travel and Tourism Council (WTTC) indicate that tourism generates 11 per cent of global gross domestic product (GDP), employs 200 million people, and transports nearly 700 million international travellers per year – a figure that is expected to double by 2020. International tourism accounts for 36 per cent of trade in commercial services in advanced economies and 66 per cent in developing economies; constitutes 3–10 per cent of GDP in advanced economies and up to 40 per cent in developing economies; generated US$464 billion in tourism receipts in 2001; and is one of the top five exports for 83 per cent of countries and the main source of foreign currency for at least 38 per cent of countries. See http://www.uneptie.org/pc/tourism/library/mapping_tourism.htm
7 See for example Donovan, N. *et al. Geographic Mobility* Performance & Innovation Unit, 2002 http://www.strategy.gov.uk/downloads/su/gmseminar/gm_analytical.pdf
8 Irony was also incidentally regarded as subversive of the staid formality and seriousness of Soviet ideology and was therefore used by many anti-communist movements – such as Orange Alternative in Poland – in the 1980s (see Outhwaite and Ray 2004: 100–1).

References

Adorno, T. and Horkheimer, M. (1973) *Dialectic of Enlightenment*. London: New Left Books.
Bauman, Z. (1972) Between Class and Elite: The Evolution of the British Labour Movement. A Sociological Study Manchester: Manchester University Press.
Bauman, Z. (1973) *Culture as Praxis*. London: Routledge.
Bauman, Z. (1976) *Towards a Critical Sociology*. London: Routledge.
Bauman, Z. (1989) *Modernity and the Holocaust*. Cambridge: Polity Press.
Bauman, Z. (1990) Thinking Sociologically. An Introduction for Everyone. Cambridge, MA: Blackwell.
Bauman, Z. (1991) *Modernity and Ambivalence*. Cambridge: Polity Press.
Bauman, Z. (1992) *Intimations of Postmodernity*. London: Routledge.
Bauman, Z. (1993) *Postmodern Ethics*. Oxford: Blackwell.
Bauman, Z. (1998a) *Globalization*. Cambridge: Polity Press.
Bauman, Z. (1998b) Work, Consumerism and the New Poor. Cambridge: Polity Press.
Bauman, Z. (1998c) 'What Prospects of Morality in Times of Uncertainty', *Theory, Culture and Society* 15(1): 11–22.
Bauman, Z. (2000) *Liquid Modernity*. Cambridge: Polity Press.
Bauman, Z. (2004) *Wasted Lives: Modernity and its Outcasts*. Cambridge: Polity Press.
Bauman, Z. and Yakimova, M. (2002) 'A Postmodern Grid of the Worldmap?' *Critique and Humanism* published online by Eurozine: http://www.eurozine.com/article/2002-11-08-bauman-en.html

Beck, U. (2000) 'The Cosmopolitan Perspective: The Sociology of the Second Modernity', *Sociology* 51 (1): 79–106.

Beck, U. and Lau, C. (2005) 'Second Modernity as a Research Agenda: Theoretical and Empirical Explorations in the "meta-change" of modern society', *British Journal of Sociology* 56 (4): 526–57.

Bradley, H., Erickson, M., Stephenson, C. and Williams, S. (2000) *Myths at Work* Cambridge: Polity Press.

Brune, N. and Garrett, G. (2005) 'The Globalization Rorschach Test: International Economic Integration, Inequality and the Role of Government', *Annual Review of Political Science* 8: 399–423.

Carnoy, M. (2000) Sustaining the new economy: Work, Family and Community in the Information Age. Cambridge, MA: Harvard University Press.

Doogan, K. (2005) 'Long-term Employment and the Restructuring of the Labour Market in Europe', *Time and Society* 14 (1): 65–87.

Durkheim, E. (1957) *Professional Ethics and Civic Morals*. London: Routledge and Kegan Paul.

Elias, N. (1996) *The Germans* Cambridge: Polity Press.

Erlinghagen, M. and Knuth, M. (2004) 'In Search of Turbulence – Labour Market Mobility and Job Stability in Germany', *European Societies* 6 (1): 49–70.

Friedson, E. (1971) *Profession of Medicine*. New York: Dodd and Mead.

Habermas, J. (1992) 'Citizenship and National Identity: Some Reflections on the Future of Europe', *Praxis International* 12 (1): 1–19.

Habermas, J. (2001) *The Postnational Constellation*. Cambridge: Polity Press.

Hampton, K. and Wellman, B. (2002) 'The Not so Global Village of Netville', in B. Wellman and C. Haythornthwaite (eds) *The Internet and Everyday Life*. Oxford: Blackwell.

Harrington, C. (2005) *Modern Social Theory: An Introduction* Oxford: Oxford University Press.

Jamous, H. and Pelloille, B. (1970) 'Changes in the French University Hospital System', in J. A. Jackson (ed.) *Professions and Professionalization* London: Cambridge University Press.

Katz, J., Rice, R. E. and Aspden, P. (2001) 'The Internet, 1995–2000: Access, Civic Involvement, and Social Interaction', *American Behavioral Scientist* 45 (3): 405–20.

Kraut, R., Patterson, M., Lundmark, V., Kiesler, S., Mukopadhyay, T. and Scherlis, W. (1998) 'Internet Paradox – A Social Technology that Reduces Social Investment and Psychological Well-being', *American Psychologist* 53 (9): 1017–31.

Lemert, C. (1992) 'General Social Theory, Irony and Postmodernism', in S. Seidman and D.G. Wagner (eds) *Postmodernism and Social Theory*. Oxford: Blackwell.

Luckmann, T. (1996) 'Some Problems of Pluralism in Modern Societies': http://stud.unisg.ch/~cems/review/luckmann.html

Marx, K. (1970) *Critique of Hegel's Philosophy of Right* (1843). Cambridge: Cambridge University Press.

Marx, K (1974) *Capital*. London: Lawrence and Wishart.

Morris, J (2004) 'The Future of Work: Organizational and International Perspectives', *International Journal of Human Resource Management* 15 (2): 263–75.

Mythen, G. (2005) 'Employment, Individualization and Insecurity: Rethinking the Risk Society Perspective', *Sociological Review* 53 (1): 129–49.

Nie, N. H. and Erbring, L. (2000) 'Internet and Society: A Preliminary Report', *IT & Society* 1 (1): 275–83.

Outhwaite, W. and Ray, L. (2004) *Social Theory and Postcommunism*. Oxford: Blackwell.

Papastergiadis, N. (2000) *The Turbulence of Migration*. Cambridge: Polity Press.

Ray L. J. (1996) Social Theory and the Crisis of State Socialism. Cheltenham: Edward Elgar.
Ray L. J (1997) 'Post-Communism: Post-Modernity or Modernity Revisited?', *British Journal of Sociology* 48 (4): 543–60.
Rengger, N. (1995) Political Theory, Modernity, and Postmodernity: Beyond Enlightenment and Critique. Oxford: Blackwell.
Rivera-Batiz, F. (1999) 'Undocumented Workers in the Labor Market', *Journal of Population Economics* 1: 91–116.
Singh, A. (2004) 'Zygmunt Bauman's Doubts about "postmodernism"': http://www.lehigh.edu/~amsp/2004/06/zygmunt-baumans-doubts-about.html
Sklair, L. (2002) *Globalization, Capitalism and its Alternatives*. Oxford: Oxford University Press.
Smith, A (1997) 'Towards a Global Culture?', in M. Featherstone (ed.) *Global Culture, Nationalism, Globalization and Modernity*. London: Sage.
Todorov, T. (2003) Hope and Memory: Reflections on the Twentieth Century. London: Atlantic Books.
Turner, B. S. (2006) 'Classical Sociology and Cosmopolitanism: A Critical Defence of the Social' *British Journal of Sociology* 57 (1): 133–51.
Urry, J. (2000) Sociology Beyond Societies: Mobilities for the Twenty-First Century. New York: Routledge.
Welzer, H. (2002) 'On the Rationality of Evil: An Interview with Zygmunt Bauman', *Thesis Eleven* 70: 100–12.
World Bank (2006) *World Development Indicators. Washington* DC: The International Bank for Reconstruction and Development/The World Bank.

CHAPTER THREE

Bauman's irony

Keith Tester

It is the purpose of this chapter to provide an insight into the distinctive and compelling sociological imagination that informs and shapes the work of Zygmunt Bauman. The use of the term *sociological imagination* is quite deliberate and helps situate Bauman's work. Of course, C. Wright Mills first put the term into currency, and he defined the sociological imagination as 'a quality of mind' that, 'enables its possessor to understand the larger historical scene in terms of its meaning for the inner life and the external career of a variety of individuals' (Mills 1970: 11).

That is precisely the task and promise that runs through Bauman's work. He has said that 'what sociologists can do for us' is, 'show us how our *individual* biographies intertwine with the *history* we share with fellow human beings' (Bauman 1990: 10). The motivation behind this task is the promise that men and women will become better and more responsibly able to understand their individual and common lives and therefore: 'One could say that the main service the art of thinking sociologically may render to each and every one of us is to make us more *sensitive*' (Bauman 1990: 16).

If that is the promise of the sociological imagination, at least a part of its task is making men and women wish to attend to its insights. The problem is that through the emphasis on the link between biography and society, the sociological imagination upsets common-sense notions that the way things are is the way that things must be. The sociological imagination tells men and women that actually the world, and they themselves, could become very different. This presents sociology with a challenge since, 'Questioning and disrupting the routine may not be to everybody's liking' (Bauman 1990: 15). But one of the steadfast qualities of Zygmunt Bauman's work is that, despite his keen awareness of the problems that it might cause, nevertheless the practice of a sociological imagination has to go on if the world is going to be fit for humans to live in. Bauman's work is important because it is *committed* and never deviates from its *dedication to human freedom*.

It is the suggestion of this chapter that, in this way, Bauman's work can be identified as a committed and devoted attempt to add a measure of irony to a world that has otherwise become inhospitable to human being. Bauman's work is an attempt to make the world ambiguous, so that it can also become more human. But since Bauman is a practitioner of a sociological imagination, as opposed to a systemic sociologist, this means that his work frequently looks for inspiration outside the confines of the discipline. Indeed, one of the most obvious qualities of Bauman's work is the extent to which it draws inspiration from European literature. It is with a discussion of that aspect of Bauman's work that this chapter begins.

The uses of irony

Now, Milan Kundera is one of the more reflective of novelists. He does not simply write fiction; he also spends a lot of time thinking about the stakes and circumstances of what it is that he does. In particular, Kundera is absolutely committed to his work being identified as a contribution to a specifically European tradition of the novel. According to Kundera, this tradition is an exploration of how the meaning of the world has been transformed, from the place of wide open adventure into which Don Quixote rode, to the place of petty yet life-threatening officialdom and administrative opacity in which Kafka's unheroic heroes are consigned to dwell. How has it been that the transformation of a man into a beetle, which for Don Quixote would have been a call to arms, by the beginning of the twentieth century, has become just one more family embarrassment?

According to Kundera the tradition of the novel reveals a paradox. Kundera says that what he calls the Modern Era commenced when reason released the human world from supernatural power so that meanings were to be made rather than found (made in the spirit of adventure symbolized by Don Quixote). But by the commencement of the twentieth century, 'just when reason wins a total victory, pure irrationality . . . seizes the world stage, because there is no longer any generally accepted value system to block its path' (Kundera 1986: 10). In other words, the Modern Era (in Kundera's phrase) is a time in which the meaning of things has flipped over. With Musil the most intelligent men of the Austro-Hungarian Empire are so wrapped up in their plans for the long-term future that they cannot see the war that is about to break out, and with Hasek war itself has become a comedy. And of course before them, in the middle of the nineteenth century, Flaubert showed how the much-vaunted bourgeois progress consists in the most incredible stupidity. This is the condition of the *terminal paradoxes* which, at their heart, signify a transformation of the relationship of men and women to history: 'it no longer has anything to do with the train the adventurers used to ride; it is impersonal, uncontrollable, incalculable, incomprehensible – and it is inescapable' (Kundera 1986: 11). Don Quixote set out on a journey that led to the doors of Kafka's Castle.

As Kundera admits, his argument is heavily indebted to Hermann Broch and in particular to the latter's novel *The Sleepwalkers* (Broch 1986). There Broch developed the thesis that the contemporary West has been subjected to a disintegration of values that has been so profound that now human life has lost any meaning. Don Quixote went out so that his life would make whatever sense he imposed upon it, and when that world fought back then *it* was wrong. But Broch was driven to ask much more fundamental questions: 'Is this distorted life of ours still real? Is this cancerous reality still alive? The melodramatic gesture of our mass movement towards death ends in a shrug of the shoulders, men die and do not know why.' For Broch this leads to a terminal paradox: 'An age that is softer and more cowardly than any preceding age suffocates in waves of blood and poison-gas' (Broch 1986: 373).

As Hannah Arendt noted, Broch concluded that the only way out of this hell was a reintegration of values that was both redemptive and utopian. For this reason he ultimately turned away from literature; for him literature in the end achieved nothing (Arendt 1973: 149).

That is where Kundera leaves Broch, although the former never says as much. But what Kundera and Broch do share is a concern to try to recover something human from a world, 'where the external determinants have become so overpowering that internal impulses no longer carry weight' (Kundera 1986: 26). This then is the greatest of the terminal paradoxes. The Modern Era lived according to the principle of human freedom, but now distinctively human qualities have been completely overwhelmed in the course of that very era. Despite Broch, Kundera is committed to the tradition of the novel as a way out of the trap, since according to him the novel precisely deals with those human qualities of ambiguity, complexity, uncertainty, mistake, that Don Quixote represents but which the great train of History has crushed. Kundera identifies – and can be identified – with a tradition in which the novel is, 'the ironic, irreverent counter-culture to the technological-scientific culture of modernity, that culture of ordering passion, neat divisions and taut discipline' (Bauman 1997: 119). It can be said that Kundera's work represents, 'a continuous training session for living with the ambivalent and the mysterious' (Bauman 1997: 119).

That is also what the work of Zygmunt Bauman is concerned to try to achieve. It is a sustained exploration of the paradox that is mulled over by Milan Kundera: How is it that the free human adventure has produced a world that is a trap for human freedom? That question is the essence of the sociological imagination. Moreover, Bauman's work shares the commitment of Kundera to, 'tolerance and equanimity towards the wayward, the contingent, the not-wholly determined, the not-wholly understood and the not-wholly predictable' (Bauman 1997: 119). Indeed, and at the risk of identifying a link between Kundera and Mills where there is none (there is no evidence that Kundera has read Mills, and there is every reason to believe that Kundera would actually be fairly dismissive of sociology), Mills opened *The Sociological Imagination* with the announcement that: 'Nowadays men often feel that their private lives are a series of traps. They sense that within their everyday worlds, they cannot overcome their troubles, and in this feeling, they are often quite correct' (Mills 1970: 9).

This argument that Bauman shares certain affinities with Milan Kundera makes it possible to explain one of the aspects of Zygmunt Bauman's work that makes it so very different from the work of most other sociologists. Whereas most sociologists are very likely to wheel on statistics or 'facts' to support an argument, Bauman is more likely to refer to literature. It is quite clear that Zygmunt Bauman's sociological work is inspired to a considerable degree by literature. Bauman has quite rightly said that: 'Understanding human dilemmas and torments is not the sociologists' privilege. Learning sociological methods may guarantee a job, but not wisdom and insight', and he followed this train of thought to identify who, for him, can be identified as exemplars of 'wisdom and insight': 'I personally learned more about the society we live in from Balzac, Zola, Kafka, Musil, Frisch, Perec, Kundera, Beckett . . . than, say, from Parsons' (Bauman in Blackshaw 2002: 2). These are exactly the kinds of names that Kundera would also be likely to list. These are all writers who in one way or another are keen to show that it is in ambiguity and not routine orderliness that the human *adventure* lays, and that the human *condition* consists in the coming together of these contradictory pressures. Sociology thereby becomes the analytic of that condition, and validly can draw on any resources that the human world offers in order to develop its interpretation of the present condition of the trap of the world.

The kind of literature that Bauman's work embraces is that which, just like Milan Kundera's novels, unsettles the commonplace by making it *ironic*. Indeed, irony is an integral component of Bauman's style as well as one of his fundamental principles. For example, towards the beginning of *Globalization* Bauman says that he cannot pretend that the book is, 'asking the right questions, all the right questions, and, most important, all the questions that have been asked' (Bauman 1998a: 5). The very first sentence of *Wasted Lives* is similarly disconcerting: 'There is more than one way in which the story of modernity . . . can be told. This book is one of such stories' (Bauman 2004: 1). Not *the* story, just *a* story, *one* story from amongst many. It is also worth noting that Bauman identifies his book as a *story*, not an *analysis*. There is the distinct sense that with these comments, Bauman is trying deliberately to *irritate*. But this is irritation of a special sort. It is not the irritation of causing annoyance; rather it is the irritation of denying the reader the confidence that in these – or for that matter any other – pages, she or he is going to find the truth unrolled like a velvet carpet on a hard floor. Peter Beilharz has put it especially well. He says that Bauman's readers are, 'both attracted and irritated, for he both pokes you in the eye and expects you to follow through, to stay awhile, and ponder, talk, and listen' (Beilharz 2001: 2). This is right. Bauman is calling upon his reader to do some work by disturbing the relationship of the reader to the text. In short, Bauman is being *ironist*: 'Irony irritates. Not because it mocks or attacks but because it denies us our certainties by unmasking the world as an ambiguity' (Kundera 1986: 134). With his deliberate doubt Bauman unmasks the ambiguity of the world by unsettling the relationship of his reader to the text.

It is possible to find other signs of Bauman's irony. For example, it has been noted that when he was still Professor at the University of Leeds, Zygmunt Bauman kept in his office a reproduction of Picasso's painting of Don Quixote. From this observation, Richard Kilminster and Ian Varcoe not unreasonably reach a conclusion about Bauman's own sociological work. According to them the picture shows, 'Don Quixote tilting at windmills, which clearly symbolized one of . . . [Bauman's] major identifications' (Kilminster and Varcoe 1996: 7). Actually, the Picasso picture is a lot more ironic (irritating, ambiguous) than that. In the picture the Don and Sancho Panza are on a hill, looking down at the windmills – or giants – that are striding across the plain. Yes, it is possible that the Don is shown preparing himself and Rocinante for the attack, but then again Picasso might have painted the moment after the assault, when Don Quixote and Sancho are reflecting on this latest misadventure, before setting off on another. Is Picasso's picture a depiction of innocence or experience? Indeed is Don Quixote a hero or a fool? Is Sancho Panza the voice of reason or defeat? Or, as Kafka once pondered, is Sancho Panza the secret master of this story and not the servant he appears. Is it all just an invention of Sancho so that he might succeed in 'diverting his devil'? (Kafka 1979: 112). And if that is the case is Sancho a realist or a dreamer in a barren world? Then again, are these the right questions to ask of the picture? It is impossible to know, and so Picasso's picture is left to irritate. *Don Quixote is ironic*. Consequently, the message of the picture on the study wall is not just that Bauman tilts at windmills; it is also, if not more powerfully, that the human adventure is ambiguous. The adventure begins when God is dethroned and when human being in the world is required to explore, 'the world as ambiguity, to be obliged to face not a single absolute truth but a welter of contradictory truths . . . to have as one's only certainty the *wisdom of uncertainty*' (Kundera 1986: 7). Or at least, the human adventure is ambiguous when left to itself, the meaning of the journey to be decided after arrival and not before departure (assuming that arrival is possible if there is no antecedently given destination).

Bauman carries through the ironic sense of the ambiguity of the human adventure to his book, *Society Under Siege* (2002). He makes it clear that the adventure is a journey that is pressing into the future (here then there is resonance with Bauman's utopianism; for discussions of this aspect of Bauman's work see Jacobsen 2003; Tester 2004). Bauman writes that one of the defining features of humanity is to measure life as it is by the yardstick of what it ought to be. This means that, for men and women, what it means to be human is always in the future, always an adventure of the making and not a process of discovery and revelation: 'Human being-in-the-world means being ahead-of-the-world'. He goes on: 'The "human" in "human being" is what "sticks out", runs ahead from the rest of being – while "the world" is that rest which has been left behind' (Bauman 2002: 222). Human being, then, is ironic because it is an irritation of the world that otherwise is all too likely to be taken for granted, accepted as common sense.

It is important not to push the connection of Bauman and Kundera – or for that matter Bauman and Don Quixote – too far. Their work is quite different, and they would be among the first to insist on this. *Kundera is a novelist and Bauman is a sociologist.* They are happy and willing to be given those labels for two reasons. First, the labels coincide with self-understanding. Second, both Bauman and Kundera know that it is only because of the location of their work in a distinctive tradition of thought and work that it is able to raise the questions that it does. But Bauman's relationship to the sociological tradition is suitably ambiguous.

Sociology: imagination and tradition

Bauman's commitment to literature as a tool of irony, and therefore of the unsettling of the determinations of common sense, shows that he is extremely aware that the sociological imagination is quite independent of the discipline of sociology. One can be a paragon of the discipline and possess no sociological imagination whatsoever (all of the clues are that Bauman sees Parsons in these terms; see Bauman 1978), and by reversal one can have read few works produced within the discipline and yet practice the sociological imagination in the most subtle and penetrating ways (for Bauman, Georges Perec would seem to fall into this category). Indeed, Bauman has rather implied that he is not a good exemplar of the discipline of sociology because he has never learnt 'respect and reverence for "canonical texts"' and is therefore weak at exegesis and at slavishly following the letter, as opposed to the spirit of the 'classics' (Bauman and Tester 2001: 23). But even though Bauman admits that much, it is perfectly clear that he is not terribly concerned by it, since he is confident that his work is possessed of a sociological imagination.

This position compares with Kundera's proposition that not all novelists write novels. Kundera talks about the state of literature in Communist Russia, and argues that although thousands of books were published in huge editions, nevertheless they were not novels in the sense that derives from the adventure of Don Quixote. This is because they, 'add nothing to the conquest of being. They discover no new segment of existence; they only confirm what has already been said; furthermore: in confirming what everyone says . . . they fulfil their purpose, their glory, their usefulness to that society' (Kundera 1986: 14). Kundera says that novels of this kind (and similar productions can be found in bookshops anywhere in the world; their ghastly ilk is not peculiar to the time and place of Soviet Russia), 'are *novels that come after the history of the novel*' (Kundera 1986: 14, original emphasis). By extension, it might be suggested that there is a sociology that comes after the history of sociology in that these works merely confirm the commonplace and commonsensical (compare the comments of Turner and Rojek on the rise of what they call 'decorative sociology'; Turner and Rojek 2001). Kundera wants to write novels that take their place in the history of the novel, in the history of that interrogation that seeks to recover the ambiguity of all things human from the trap that the world has become. Similarly, Zygmunt Bauman wants to write sociology in terms of a distinctive understanding of the history of sociology, in terms of a tradition.

Bauman's commitment to tradition is made quite clear when he says that: 'Being part of the cultural tradition defines the fashion in which one seeks knowledge and understanding: respect for reality, self-control and self-criticism'. In particular, examples and exemplars of the sociological tradition can be identified as the compass points, 'which sociological discourse needed so badly if it was to stay on course in spite of the cross-waves of collective amnesia and the cross-wind of Columbus complexes' (Bauman 1987a: 1. Bauman often castigates the Columbus complex that consists in getting bored with problems before solving them: see for example Bauman and Tester 2001: 41). It is the sociological tradition that, 'defines the values that enlighten the road to knowledge: rationality, truth and self-understanding' (Bauman 1987a: 1). For Bauman the sociological tradition is important for precisely the same reasons that were established by C. Wright Mills. The tradition points to the task and the promise with which sociology must grapple if it is going to be relevant: 'to grasp history and biography and the relations between the two within society' (Mills 1970: 12). In this way, the classical texts that constitute the tradition are not to be confronted like exhibits in the museum; rather they are living storehouses of inspiration, insight and purpose. For the sociological imagination, the tradition lives (see Bauman 1993).

When Mills was writing, the only way in which sociology could be made relevant once again was if the imagination were emancipated from the twin irrelevances of grand theory and abstracted empiricism, and reinvigorated by the addition of a large dose of the tonic that is provided by the tradition, all the time that it is not approached as a series of classics but as a vibrant contributor to a conversation about the human condition. As Mills said: 'The nuance and suggestion that students of sociology can find in their traditions are not to be briefly summarized, but any social scientist who takes them in hand will be richly rewarded' (Mills 1970: 32). In this light it is unsurprising that Bauman identifies Mills as one of a small band (which also includes Lewis Coser and Tom Bottomore) who saw that: 'given the direction the academic adaptation of social science had taken, the resuscitation of sociological tradition and the return to the orientations and the concerns of the classics were progressive steps and revolutionary tasks' (Bauman 1987a: 3). Indeed, it is quite noticeable that, apart from Durkheim, Bauman only ever talks about the classical founders of the discipline in understanding terms and as partners in a conversation. There is room to wonder whether his consistent condemnation of Durkheim might not owe something to the once hegemonic reading of Durkheim as a structural functionalist, and of structural functionalism as a version of sociology as social science that denies the ambiguous and justifies the commonplace. There is more than a hint of Mills to all of this. (For Bauman on the importance of Mills, see Bauman and Tester 2001: 27–8. For Bauman's critique of Durkheim, see for example, Bauman 1976).

The tradition, this history in which Bauman places himself and with which his work identifies, is one of the sociological imagination and not really one of the discipline of sociology at all. It is a tradition that Bauman has tied to specifically Polish roots. He has argued that one of the unique qualities of Warsaw sociology during the 1950s was its *openness* (it might be said that another word for 'openness' is 'irony). Bauman has said that Warsaw sociology was 'suspicious of, and resistant to, all monopoly claims' of the kinds put forward by Parsons and his followers (Bauman and Tester 2001: 23). It was an irritant, and it irritated monopoly claims. Those monopoly claims might be made by common sense or by disciplinary orthodoxy. Yet Bauman understands himself as drawing on what is insightful, interesting, revealing, rather than on what is defined as right and proper by the guardians of disciplinary orthodoxy. Once again then, Bauman becomes a practitioner of the sociological imagination as opposed to a good sociologist. He becomes an irritant, an ironist. And the sociological imagination, in its turn, can be identified as an example of the attitude of *liberal ironism* that has been outlined by Richard Rorty.

According to Rorty, a *liberal* is someone who believes that cruelty is the worst action that humans can carry out. Cruelty does not just involve the causing of physical harm; it also means the deliberate and intentional destruction of the little world of things that humans construct around themselves. Rorty argues that, 'the best way to cause people long-lasting pain is to humiliate them by making the things that seemed most important to them look futile, obsolete, and powerless' (Rorty 1989: 89). Precisely this vision can be found in Bauman's work. It can be found in his condemnation of poverty when he says that: 'nothing humiliates more than poverty, and no poverty humiliates more than poverty suffered amidst people bent on fast and accelerating enrichment' (Bauman and Tester 2001: 153). This point is also found in Bauman's discussion of what he called the 'flawed consumers' of contemporary capitalism, who know that poverty, 'means being excluded from whatever passes for a "normal life". It means being "not up to the mark". This results in a fall of self-esteem, feelings of shame or feelings of guilt'. Bauman continues: 'Poverty also means being cut off from the chances of whatever passes . . . for a "happy life" . . . this results in resentment and aggravation, which spill out in the form of violent acts, self-deprecation, or both' (Bauman 1998b: 37). These are people who do not possess the material resources to respond to the needs that are created by consumer capitalism, and therefore who are consigned to live in the knowledge that, even according to their own desires, the things that they possess are 'futile, obsolete, and powerless' (to recall Rorty), and who are thereby put into a situation of being humiliating even to themselves.

However, it is also the question of humiliation that explains why men and women might be reticent about embracing the promise of the sociological imagination. Since sociological work seeks to ironize the world and, in so doing, show to men and women that what they have always taken for granted is not really necessary and inevitable at all, it is not unreasonable to conclude that those men and women will want to keep sociological insight at bay. This is because they, 'may feel humiliated: what they have known and were proud of has now been devalued, perhaps even shown worthless and ridiculed' (Bauman 1990: 15). But, for Bauman as with Rorty, this is no reason to give up on the task of ironization, although for both of them the chance of humiliation does mean that the task has to be carried out carefully and, most importantly, *sensitively and respectfully*. For Bauman the aim is not to show to men and women that everything that they hold dear is trivial; the point absolutely is to neither sneer nor condescend. Rather, the point is always to bear in mind, and communicate, the promise of the sociological imagination, that lives could be lived with 'more self-awareness, more comprehension – perhaps also with more freedom and control' (Bauman 1990: 15) and, therefore, with much less of a sense of the trap.

Once again, then, the assault of Bauman's sociological imagination on common sense comes to the fore. It is an assault that is worth discussing in some depth. In *Towards a Critical Sociology* (1976), Bauman contended that, 'commonsense is the ultimate object of sociological exploration in the same inescapable way as nature is the ultimate object of natural science'. Common sense, then, is what the sociological imagination seeks to render ironic, but it is also the precondition of that work of irritation. Without common-sense assumptions about the way that the world 'must be' there could be no sociological work that seeks to show that 'things could be different than this'. For Bauman this meant that, 'commonsensical experience will always remain the locus in which sociological queries and concepts are gestated – and the umbilical cord binding the knowledge of human affairs to commonsense will never be cut'. (Bauman 1976: 28).

Much the same argument was being made some fourteen years later when, in *Thinking Sociologically*, Bauman wrote that: 'Perhaps more than other branches of scholarship, sociology finds its relation with common sense (that rich yet disorganized, non-systematic, often inarticulate and ineffable knowledge we use to conduct our daily business of life) fraught with problems decisive for its standing and practice' (Bauman 1990: 8). He went on to explain that it is precisely because of this closeness of common sense and sociology that it is important to be quite clear about what distinguishes the latter from the former. Bauman identifies four ways in which common sense and sociology are different, four ways in which sociology is identifiable and cohesive. These might also be identified as four principles of irony. First, sociology ought to be responsible; it ought only to make claims that can be corroborated and ought to refuse to accept anything that is said to be true because 'I know it is true'. Sociology is analytical not assertive. Second, sociology draws its material from a wider field than common sense. Common sense draws on the everyday, the close at hand and the self-evident, while sociology draws upon a broader field of material; it widens horizons. Third, common sense makes sense of the world through the prism of the sovereign individual acting in almost glorious isolation in terms of her or his own will. Meanwhile, sociology is the analysis of the social and cultural determinants and situation of that action (this is the nub of the sociological imagination as defined by C. Wright Mills). Finally, common sense is a knowledge that confirms the world and its arrangements (Bauman says that common sense is immune to questioning), whereas it is the business of the sociological to 'defamiliarise the familiar'. Sociological analysis is not about confirmation at all. It is in the business of irritation. (This list of the differences between common sense and sociology is drawn from Bauman 1990: 12–15).

By this token, to think sociologically is to recover the ambiguity of the human adventure from the trap that the world has become thanks to common sense. That stake is stated with great clarity at the end of *Liquid Modernity*: 'Sociologists may deny or forget the . . . effects of their work, and the impact . . . on human singular or joint actions, only at the expense of forfeiting that responsibility of choice which every other human being faces daily'. Bauman wrote that: 'The job of sociology is to see to it that the choices are genuinely free, and that they remain so, increasingly so, for the duration of humanity' (Bauman 2000: 216; these paragraphs on common sense draw on the discussion in Tester 2004).

But back to Rorty. He believes that a liberal *ironist* is someone who is incapable of providing a non-circular justification for the argument that cruelty is the worst thing that humans are capable of doing (Rorty 1989: xv). Rorty consequently does not mean that the condemnation of cruelty is nothing more than a personal preference that cannot be validated. Instead what he is saying is that a liberal ironist is someone who knows that the justification for the abhorrence of cruelty is not to be found in some ahistorical foundation of human being in the world that can be discovered once all distractions have been got out of the way, but rather it is a call to be made through a commitment to a human solidarity that lies in the future and which will embrace the principle that cruelty is to be condemned. This is precisely the kind of commitment that runs all the way through Bauman's work (in particular, here it is hard not to recall Bauman's comment about the human always running ahead of the world). Liberal ironism, then, is the knowledge that the abhorrence of cruelty cannot be justified here and now, but is a call to look towards a utopian future in which cruelty has been replaced with solidarity:

> In my utopia, human solidarity would be seen not as a fact to be recognized by clearing away 'prejudice' or burrowing down to the previously hidden depths but, rather, as a goal to be achieved. It is to be achieved not by inquiry but by imagination, the imaginative ability to see strange people as fellow sufferers.
> (Rorty 1989: xvi)

This is the sensibility that runs through what is the closest thing to Bauman's statement of method (Bauman 1978).

One of the most valuable tools in the generation of that 'imaginative ability' is literature (and it is worth noting that the literature to which Rorty refers is markedly European). According to Rorty works of literature are confronted by ironists as acquaintances who hold out the possibility of opening up worlds that were previously invisible or unknown to the reader. In other words, books are irritants that cause the reader to realize that who she or he was previously, before this particular book was encountered, is different to who she or he will become, having made the acquaintance of this particular work. Books are not objective treasuries of 'facts' and neither are they dead 'classics'. Consequently, Rorty says that ironists pay little or no heed to the library classifications of books into separate disciplines. The ironist does not think that the classification of books is based on different objects of knowledge: 'Ironists see . . . [libraries] as divided according to traditions, each member of which partially adopts and partially modifies the vocabulary of the writers who he has read. Ironists take the writings of all the people with poetic gifts . . . as grist to be put through the same dialectical mill' (Rorty 1989: 75–6). Or put another way, the sociologist can derive much more human insight from a sensitive poem than from all the methodology books that have ever been published.

To put the point in an even more focused manner: Bauman's work is situated within a sociological tradition that is ironic about the status of sociology, which sees no reason to avoid certain books simply because they are found in different parts of the library, and which is concerned to recover the ambiguity of the human adventure from any trap into which it might fall or be pushed. But that recovery will only bear fruit in the future, not today. And so sociological work is about ceaselessly and with commitment *preparing* the way for a human world that is always not-yet rather than announcing its arrival today (or its once-and-for-ever loss yesterday). Bauman's is a paradoxical *liberal ironist* sociological imagination (just like Mills's, *avant le lettre*).

But, to repeat, however much his work illustrates Rorty's liberal ironism, Bauman identifies himself as a sociologist and, therefore, his contribution to the tradition of liberal ironism possesses a distinctly – and distinctive – sociological core. Yet it is worth noting that, in the spirit of ironism, this is not a core that Bauman is capable of justifying in any non-circular way.

Ironic foundations

In a 1967 article that is rather important to understanding the foundations of Bauman's sociological work, he argued that all sociological work is predicated upon what he called a 'cognitive *a priori*'. This a priori is, 'an intellectual image of investigated world which is prior to any research endeavour' (Bauman 1967: 12). Behind all sociological work then, there is an assumption about the world from which all understanding is deduced. What then was Zygmunt Bauman's cognitive a priori? Upon what assumptions was his sociological work based?

Bauman's a priori was an *image of man* (his phrase) that is intrinsically ironic. Bauman's sociological work was built on an a priori that sought to make the world ambiguous despite and because of the tendency of common sense to make it routine and predictable. By contrast, Bauman identified a 'mechanistic' view of man in contemporary life, and opposed himself to it. In this Bauman was allying himself with C. Wright Mills's opposition to, 'social science as a set of bureaucratic techniques' (Mills 1970: 27) and also showing the extent to which his imagination was shaped by Julian Hochfeld and, in particular, Stanislaw Ossowski. Bauman always makes it clear that he learnt a great deal from Hochfeld and Ossowski and, not least, they put the moral iron into his sociological soul: 'I guess that they found the prime sense of sociological vocation in the fact that humans suffer and that seeing through the social causes of their suffering may help them to mitigate their misery or even make the social production of misery grind to a halt' (Bauman and Tester 2001: 21). This is a version of sociological practice that is very far removed from bureaucratic technique; it is sociology as a moral mission. (The influence of Hochfeld and Ossowski on Bauman's work is explored in much greater detail in Tester 2004: chapter 2.)

Bauman identified in contemporary sociology two different images of man, which push in quite contrary directions. The mechanistic image either seeks to generate probabilistic knowledge through the analysis of how human behaviour responds to external stimuli, or to develop a systemic knowledge that identifies the foundations of societal equilibrium so that disturbances to that condition might be specified and managed all the more efficiently. Whereas this mechanistic image identifies human action as a response to external stimuli, Bauman advocated instead an 'activistic' image in which it is presumed that: 'Human acts are not only "reactions", but also "procreations". If we remove from the human act all what is possibly determined by the value of "input" variables still something will be left'. Bauman identified this residue as that which, 'distinguishes any human being from any machine and is responsible for the fact that the human behaviour is only partly predictable' (Bauman 1967: 14). Consequently, whenever action is predictable, as it is when it is routinized and managed, some damage must have been done to what it is that makes human being different from anything else in the world. From this it is no surprise when Bauman's cognitive a priori emerges as identification with 'the less managerial, even anti-managerial, more traditional, humanistic variation of sociology' and as one that, 'aims at making the human behaviour less predictable by activating inner, motivational sources of decision – supplying the human beings with ampler knowledge of their situation and so enlarging the sphere of their freedom of choice' (Bauman 1967: 15. Compare the comments from the end of *Liquid Modernity* that were quoted above). For Bauman then, to be human is to be unpredictable, and in unpredictability lies freedom. His sociological work was – and largely remains – organized around this deeply ironic cognitive a priori that quite obviously embraces ambiguity (or, as Bauman was later to have it, ambivalence) over and above the clear-cut.

However the point is that Bauman's adoption of this starkly ironic cognitive a priori cannot be justified in any non-circular fashion. As Bauman said of any and every cognitive a priori: 'The pre-empirical image of man is not so much a regrettable "bias" as indispensable pre-condition of any research. One cannot do without it' (Bauman 1967: 13). The image of man that is presumed in any sociological work is not the voice with which that work speaks; more strongly it is the very *ability* of that work to speak.

But in 1967 Bauman was not sufficiently ironic entirely to give up on the attempt of justification. Rorty contends that one becomes an ironist when one begins to have doubts about the validity of the vocabulary to which one has become accustomed:

> The ironist spends her time worrying about the possibility that she has been initiated into the wrong tribe, taught to play the wrong language game. She worries that the process of socialization which turned her into a human being by giving her a language may have given her the wrong language, and so turned her into the wrong kind of human being.
>
> (Rorty 1999: 75)

Through the 1960s it is possible to see exactly these kinds of worries in the contemporary work of Bauman. He was in an ambiguous situation in which there was a conviction that there was 'something wrong' with his vocabulary, and yet he could not give up on it if he were going to be able to carry on communicating with others. During this period he moved into the camp of humanistic Marxism, and therefore into a position of political opposition to the state, precisely in an attempt to recover Marxism from being tied to the 'wrong language' of actually existing socialism. His essay on the images of man that underpin sociological work is a product of this time. What Bauman is doing is thinking through his doubts about the sociological language with which he has become familiar and which can be used all too unthinkingly as a common sense, and he is in the process of becoming an ironist. (This phase of Bauman's work is discussed and contextualized in Tester 2004.) But he has not yet become a fully fledged ironist. Bauman knows that the cognitive a priori cannot be justified, but still he tries to do exactly that.

Bauman tried to argue that there are in fact external and non-circular criteria upon which the a priori image of man might be justified. He pointed to three such criteria. First, the images of man that are presumed by the sociological work, 'may be more or less empirically relevant, that means they can serve better or worse their basic function of ordering and explaining available research data and inspiring cognitively fruitful questions'. Second, Bauman identified a criterion of particularity. He suggested that the validity of a cognitive a priori could be judged to the extent that it transcends the particular interests of 'human groups discriminated by their cultural, class, national and similar peculiarities'. Third, the competing images of man that are available to sociology and sociological work, 'may be more or less approvable ethically, that means they can sponsor and corroborate or contradict given moral ideology the scholar or his public subscribe to'. (These three justifications, and these quotations, all come from Bauman 1967: 13.)

The irony, of course, is that all three of these justifications fail. They do not constitute non-circular justifications for the adoption of any given image of man as opposed to any other. The first justification fails because it presumes that there is an external realm of research data that is ontologically independent of the image of man, but that would lead to the conclusion that the cognitive a priori is either induced from facts (in which case it is not an a priori at all) or an optional philosophical gloss that ought to be subjected to the strictures of Occam's Razor. Second, the argument that an image of man can be justified on account of its universality presupposes the identification of criteria of particularity (such as class, nation, ethnicity or, although Bauman did not mention this, gender) that are themselves theoretically dependent and only empirically identifiable to the extent that they are pre-identified as relevant. Bauman himself denied the principle of justification by universality when he wrote that: 'Methodological devices in the study of man are coined to match and fit a particular research programme, and this programme is determined in all its significant dimensions at the very moment the image of man is . . . chosen' (Bauman 1967: 20). Third, justification by ethical approval fails because the criteria of ethical approval or disapproval are themselves deduced from the same cognitive a priori, from the same image of man, that they purportedly judge. This too is circular reasoning. This difficulty multiplies when Bauman says that the a priori may, 'corroborate or contradict given moral ideology the scholar or his public subscribe to'. The identification of such a 'moral ideology' is itself either circular or, like Bauman's first defence (empirical relevance), it fails because it presumes the a priori relevance of the empirical sphere that the conception of the cognitive a priori necessarily refutes.

Bauman's sociological imagination focuses upon an activistic image of man because, in the last instance, Bauman made *a choice* that it would, and that choice was itself immune to sociological justification. But Bauman's immediate rejoinder to any attack from the direction that therefore his work is unscientific would be that, unlike the attacker, at least he is clear about his ultimate values, at least he is clear about the status of his activity. Here then there is an aspect of Socratic irony. In 1967, Bauman identified two different kinds of sociologists. First there are those, like himself, who, 'are aware of their theoretical assumptions and so try to select carefully, taking into account all their implications' and second there are, 'those who disdain stubbornly or disbelieve that what they do is saturated with "philosophical" notions and so are helpless and disarmed while facing the real choice' (Bauman 1967: 21).

Sociology against kings

The *real* choice . . . .

For Bauman what makes these choices of cognitive a priori of pressing importance is the relationship of the chosen image of man to political power. Again, there is an echo of C. Wright Mills about this. Running through Bauman's essay on the cognitive a priori in sociology is the identification of the mechanistic image of man with the horizons and needs of bureaucracy. The mechanistic approach, with its concern to identify the links between external stimuli and human reactions, is especially well suited to the question of what needs to be done to build an orderly society, say, in which each and any individual will behave in a predictable manner. Mills identified a trap in which, 'The individual social scientist tends to become involved in those many trends of modern society that make the individual a part of a functionally rational bureaucracy' (Mills 1970: 199). In short, mechanistic sociology is of great use and interest to power, and the sociologist who works in the terms of this a priori quickly, and usually happily, becomes 'an adviser to the king' (Mills 1970: 199). As Bauman has rather nicely yet sardonically remarked: 'Proletarians of all countries refused to follow Marx's call, but there seems to be a well-entrenched and thriving International of establishment lovers' (Bauman and Tester 2001: 27). In Kundera's terms, meanwhile, such a mechanistic sociology, and such a mechanistic cognitive a priori, cannot possibly tolerate human ambiguity or accord respect to and for the individual (Kundera 1986: 164), while in Richard Rorty's language, the mechanistic image of man and mechanistic sociology is nothing other than a common sense since it takes it for granted that statements that are constructed in terms of behavioural responses to external stimuli are sufficient to describe the (re)actions and beliefs of humans (Rorty 1989: 74).

Bauman's activistic a priori leads him to make a different choice, and it leads him to work in a manner that is incompatible with advising kings, intolerance or common sense. Bauman's sociological work is a prime example of the kind that was applauded by Mills. Mills supported an approach to sociology that, 'is to remain independent, to do one's work, to select one's own problems, but to direct this work *at* kings as well as *to* "publics"' (Mills 1970: 200). The problem is that kings can be quite adept at making sure that they can also *use* work that is directed *at* them. Bauman quickly learnt that power is not amorphous but is, instead, structured and systemic in such a way that it thrives on the input of information that is then absorbed and turned to ends that the producers might never have imagined or suspected: 'Since the system "is interested" in its own survival, it is *eo ipso* "interested" in absorbing all achievable and relevant information' (Bauman 1971: 22). This means that sociology is in a quite different and much more difficult position than that which Kundera identifies with the tradition of the novel. Even if the novelist accepts that power is an information-absorbing system, she or he can respond to this situation by writing fiction that is too ambiguous to be absorbed in any determinate way. For Kundera this points to a novel that is quite incapable of being translated into the 'apodictic and dogmatic discourse' of power (Kundera 1986: 7). But sociology cannot of itself take that oppositional stance precisely because the knowledge that it produces *can* be absorbed. Any and all knowledge of social life can be put to systemic use. As such, the ambiguity of sociology points towards the ethical commitment of the sociologist. It becomes a vocational responsibility to ensure that one's work is never absorbed by the system. (For Bauman's continued commitment to a sociology that renounces any manipulation of men and women, see Bauman 1998c.)

Moreover, kings change. Bauman's work emerged in the totalitarianism of Communist Poland, and through enforced exile was relocated in consumer capitalism. Whereas the Communist power system dealt with information through absorption, consumer capitalism deals with it through the expedient of the market taking over the values about which systemic politics has become indifferent: 'freedom of choice, sovereignty of the individual, autonomy of decision, mastery over one's life-world. It is as a consumer that the individual becomes free, sovereign, autonomous' (Bauman 1987b: 21). Such a situation places demands on the sociologist. First, she or he must ensure that her or his work attends to freedom, sovereignty and autonomy and casts ironic doubt upon the common-sense meanings of these values. This is an ironization of common sense about which Bauman is keenly aware of and, as Rorty puts it: 'The opposite of irony is common sense' (Rorty 1989: 74). In this way, the sociologist must ensure that her or his work acts as an irritant on the otherwise well-moisturized skin of consumer culture. Second, the sociologist must take care to ensure that she or he does not her or him self become a reflection of this world. The sociologist must take care that her or his own choices do not become mimetic or legitimatory. (This is the nub of Bauman's commitment to a sociology of postmodernity, and his rejection of a postmodern sociology; Bauman 1992.) Bauman has steadfastly sought to do this by letting his work make its own way in the world, and by a consistent and committed refusal to restrict its absolute ambiguity by the citation of some authorial authority.

Consequently, the sociologist as the producer of the work of the sociological imagination is called upon permanently to be on guard against the encroachments and allures of power of whatever kind. It is not enough to *do* sociology; one must also *be* a sociologist. This is a lesson that Bauman learnt from Stanislaw Ossowski.

Ossowski believed that the social researcher – that is to say, the *sociologist* – has a duty to be *disobedient* towards those who are in power. Ossowski said that if the social researcher alters his views in line with the commands of an external authority, if he writes and speaks in a way that is contrary to his thoughts, he is shirking his duty. Ossowski condemns such an obedient researcher for being nothing more than a clerk, whereas: 'Disobedient thinking is one of the duties of the research worker. The research worker works towards the social cause and that means that he must not think obediently when doing his job.' Ossowski put himself on the side of those, 'whose activities are turned towards values which do not die as soon as the political tactics have changed. These . . . people owe their authority to the opinion that respect for truth, not mutable tactics or obedience, controls their words' (Ossowski 1998: 93). This is a position that compares with the principle of Mills that the sociologist ought to act on the basis of reason alone (Mills 1970: 200), as well as with a statement that Bauman once made about Polish circumstances in the 1960s: 'sociology is looked upon by the broad public not as an occupation or even a branch of science, but as a vocation or mission; as the vocation of those men and women who are morally responsible for discovering truth and making it available to all people' (Bauman 1968: 171).

Conclusion

In his inaugural lecture at the University of Leeds, and using terms that seem – well – *ironic* when read in the context of his later positions, Bauman spoke about: 'Our devotion to reason and our belief in the possibility of a rational, improved, more congenial organization of human life' (Bauman 1972: 203: in Rorty's terms, this statement by Bauman has become ironic, not because he has moved away from those commitments but because he would now describe them in the terms of a rather different vocabulary). Devotion means that the attractions of fashion and the market-place must be avoided. The sociologist must not become a celebrity since important sociological work always remains to be done. As Bauman once said: 'more than ever we must beware of falling into the trap of fashions which may well prove much more detrimental than the malaise they claim to cure' (Bauman 1972: 203).

By this argument then, Bauman's ironic sociological imagination, which seeks to recover the ambiguity of the human adventure from the routinized trap that the world has become, is rooted in an existential commitment, in a *vocation* to recover and nurture the human adventure. He speaks up against a world that, 'loathe[s] the sliminess of ambiguity and thus let[s] the endemic dialectics of human existence go unnoticed' (Bauman 1972: 188). And the sociologist who recovers this dialectics will come to appreciate that she or he shares with the heirs to the tradition of the European novel a 'unique responsibility': 'Responsibility not toward "truth" sufficiently abstract to be unable to vindicate its rights, but toward human culture, welfare, culture. The feeling of responsibility lends bitterness to their critique, and heat to their desires' (Bauman 1972: 200).

What then can sociologists learn from Bauman's ironic work? At the risk of over-schematization, there are three lessons to be learnt, and therefore three guiding principles for sociological work that can be taken from Bauman:

1 First, sociology is a vocation that makes demands upon the sociologist. The sociologist must develop respectfulness towards men and women, sensitivity towards the humiliations that they suffer, and outrage at what it is that humiliates.
2 Second, the sociologist should be an irritant and not sycophantic to the way things presently are.
3 Third, sociological work ought to be guided by a concern to emancipate the ambiguous human adventure from the constraints of common sense, power and fashion.

In short, the lesson to be learnt from Bauman is that the place of the sociologist is alongside Don Quixote.

References

Arendt, Hannah (1973) *Men in Dark Times*, Harmondsworth: Penguin.
Bauman, Zygmunt (1967) 'Image of Man in the Modern Sociology (Some Methodological Remarks)', *Polish Sociological Bulletin*, 1: 12–21.
Bauman, Zygmunt (1968) 'Macrosociology and Social Research in Contemporary Poland', in *The Social Sciences: Problems and Orientations*, The Hague: Mouton/Unesco.
Bauman, Zygmunt (1971) 'Uses of Information: When Social Science Information Becomes Desired', *Annals of the American Academy of Political and Social Science*, 1: 20–31.
Bauman, Zygmunt (1972) 'Culture, Values and Science of Society', *University of Leeds Review*, 15(2): 185–203.
Bauman, Zygmunt (1976) Towards a Critical Sociology. An Essay on Commonsense and Emancipation, London: Routledge and Kegan Paul.
Bauman, Zygmunt (1978) Hermeneutics and Social Science. Approaches to Understanding, London: Hutchinson.
Bauman, Zygmunt (1987a) 'The Importance of Being Marxist', in William Outhwaite and Michael Mulkay (eds) *Social Theory and Social Criticism: Essays for Tom Bottomore*, Oxford: Basil Blackwell.

Bauman, Zygmunt (1987b) 'Unstately Pleasure Dome', *New Statesman*, 23 October: 20–1.
Bauman, Zygmunt (1990) *Thinking Sociologically*, Oxford: Blackwell.
Bauman, Zygmunt (1992) *Intimations of Postmodernity*, London: Routledge.
Bauman, Zygmunt (1993) 'Philosophy for Everyday – Though not for Everyone', *Economy and Society*, 22(1): 114–22.
Bauman, Zygmunt (1997) *Postmodernity and its Discontents*, Cambridge: Polity Press.
Bauman, Zygmunt (1998a) *Globalization: The Human Consequences*, Cambridge: Polity Press.
Bauman, Zygmunt (1998b) *Work, Consumerism and the New Poor*, Buckingham: Open University Press.
Bauman, Zygmunt (1998c) 'Sociological Enlightenment – For Whom, About What?' *Dansk Sociologi*, 9: 43–54.
Bauman, Zygmunt (2000) *Liquid Modernity*, Cambridge: Polity Press.
Bauman, Zygmunt (2002) *Society Under Siege*, Cambridge: Polity Press.
Bauman, Zygmunt (2004) *Wasted Lives: Modernity and its Outcasts*, Cambridge: Polity Press.
Bauman, Zygmunt and Tester, Keith (2001) *Conversations with Zygmunt Bauman*, Cambridge: Polity Press.
Beilharz, Peter (2001) 'Reading Zygmunt Bauman', in Peter Beilharz (ed.) *The Bauman Reader*, Oxford: Blackwell.
Blackshaw, Tony (2002) 'Interview: with Professor Zygmunt Bauman', *Network: Newsletter of the British Sociological Association*, no. 83, October: 1–3.
Broch, Hermann (1986) *The Sleepwalkers*, trans. Willa and Edwin Muir, London: Quartet.
Jacobsen, Michael Hviid (2003) *Utopianism in the Work of Zygmunt Bauman – Towards a Sociology of Alternative Realities*, Sociologisk Arbejdspapir no. 16, Aalborg Universitet: Sociologisk Laboratorium.
Kafka, Franz (1979) *Description of a Struggle and Other Stories*, Harmondsworth: Penguin.
Kilminster, Richard and Varcoe, Ian (1996) 'Introduction: Intellectual Migration and Sociological Insight', in Richard Kilminster and Ian Varcoe (eds) *Culture, Modernity and Revolution. Essays in Honour of Zygmunt Bauman*, London: Routledge.
Kundera, Milan (1986) *The Art of the Novel*, trans. Linda Asher, London: Faber and Faber.
Mills, C. Wright (1970) *The Sociological Imagination*, Harmondsworth: Penguin.
Ossowski, Stanislaw (1998) 'The Researcher's Duty: Obedience in Thinking and Social Duty of a Scientist', *Polish Sociological Review*, 2(122): 93–4.
Rorty, Richard (1989) *Contingency, Irony, and Solidarity*, Cambridge: Cambridge University Press.
Tester, Keith (2004) *The Social Thought of Zygmunt Bauman*, Basingstoke: Palgrave Macmillan.
Turner, Bryan S. and Rojek, Chris (2001) Society and Culture. Principles of Scarcity and Solidarity, London: Sage.

PART TWO

LIQUID LOVE

Zygmunt Bauman
FALLING IN AND OUT OF LOVE   101

Zygmunt Bauman
ON LIVING IN A LIQUID MODERN WORLD   107

4 Ann Branaman
   GENDER AND SEXUALITIES IN LIQUID MODERNITY   117

5 Poul Poder
   RELATIVELY LIQUID INTERPERSONAL RELATIONSHIPS IN
   FLEXIBLE WORK LIFE   136

6 Janet Sayers
   LIQUID LOVE: PSYCHOANALYSNG MANIA   154

ZYGMUNT BAUMAN

FALLING IN AND OUT OF LOVE

Source: Zygmunt Bauman (2003) *Liquid Love*, Cambridge: Polity Press, pp. viii–xii, 20–4, 36–7.

In our world of rampant 'individualization' relationships are mixed blessings. They vacillate between sweet dream and a nightmare, and there is no telling when one turns into the other. Most of the time the two avatars cohabit – though at different levels of consciousness. In a liquid modern setting of life, relationships are perhaps the most common, acute, deeply felt and troublesome incarnations of ambivalence. This is, we may argue, why they are firmly placed at the very heart of the attention of liquid modern individuals-by-decree and perched at the top of their life agenda.

'Relationship' is these days the hottest talk of the town and ostensibly the sole game in town worth playing, despite its notorious risks. Some sociologists, used to composing theories out of questionnaire statistics and the commonsensical beliefs such statistics record, hurry to conclude that their contemporaries are all out for friendships, bonds, togetherness, community. In fact, however (as if following Martin Heidegger's rule that things reveal themselves to consciousness only through the frustration they cause – going bust, disappearing, behaving out of character or otherwise belying their nature), human attention tends nowadays to be focused on the satisfactions that relationships are hoped to bring precisely because somehow they have not been found fully and truly satisfactory; and if they do satisfy, the price of the satisfaction they bring has often been found to be excessive and unacceptable. In their famous experiment, Miller and Dollard saw their laboratory rats ascending the peak of excitement and agitation when 'the adiance equalled the abiance' – that is, when the threat of electric shock and the promise of tasty food were finely balanced . . .

No wonder that 'relationships' are one of the main engines of the present-day 'counselling boom'. The complexity is too dense, too stubborn and too difficult to unpack or unravel for individuals to do the job unassisted. The agitation of Miller and Bollard's rats all too often collapsed into a paralysis of action. An inability to choose between attraction and repulsion, between hopes and fears, rebounded as an incapacity to act. Unlike the rats, humans who find themselves in such circumstances may turn for help to the expert counsellors offering their services, for a fee. What they hope to hear from the counsellors is how to square the circle: to eat the cake and have it, to cream off the sweet delights of relationship while omitting its bitter and tougher bits; how to force relationship to empower without disempowering, enable without disabling, fulfilling without burdening . . .

The experts are willing to oblige, confident that the demand for their counsels will never run dry since no amount of counselling could ever make a circle non-circular and thus amenable to being squared . . . Their counsels abound, though more often than not they do little more than raise common practice to the level of common knowledge, and that in turn to the heights of learned, authoritative theory. Grateful recipients of advice browse through 'relationship' columns of glossy monthlies and weeklies and weekly supplements of serious and less serious dailies to hear what they have been wishing to hear from people 'in the know', since they were too timid or ashamed to aver it in their own name; to pry into the doings and goings on of 'others like them' and draw whatever comfort they can manage to draw from the knowledge endorsed-by-experts that they are not alone in their lonely efforts to cope with the quandary.

And so the readers learn, from other readers' experience recycled by the counsellors, that they may try 'top-pocket relationships', of the sort they 'can bring out when they need them' but push deep down in the pocket when they do not. Or that relationships are like Ribena: imbibed in concentration, they are nauseating and may prove dangerous to their health – like Ribena, relations should be diluted when consumed. Or that SDCs – 'semi-detached couples' – are to be praised as 'relationship revolutionaries who have burst the suffocating couple bubble'. Or that relationships, like cars, should undergo regular MOTs to make sure that they are still roadworthy. All in all, what they learn is that commitment, and particularly long-term commitment, is the trap that the endeavour 'to relate' should avoid more than any other danger. One expert counsellor informs readers that 'when committing yourself, however half-heartedly, remember that you are likely to be closing the door to other romantic possibilities which may be more satisfying and fulfilling'. Another expert sounds blunter yet: 'Promises of commitment are meaningless in the long term . . . Like other investments, they wax and wane.' And so, if you wish 'to relate', keep your distance; if you want fulfilment from your togetherness, do not make or demand commitments. Keep all doors open at any time.

The residents of Leonia, one of Italo Calvino's *Invisible Cities,* would say, if asked, that their passion is 'the enjoyment of new and different things'. Indeed, each morning they 'wear brand-new clothing, take from the latest model refrigerator still unopened tins, listening to the last-minute jingles from the most up-to-date radio'. But each morning 'the remains of yesterday's Leonia await the garbage truck' and one is right to wonder whether the Leonians' true passion is not instead 'the joy of expelling, discarding, cleansing themselves of a recurrent impurity'. Otherwise why would street cleaners be 'welcomed like angels', even if their mission is 'surrounded by respectful silence', and understandably so – 'once things have been cast off nobody wants to have to think about them further'.

Let us think . . .

Are not the residents of our liquid modern world, just like the residents of Leonia, worrying about one thing while speaking of another? They say that their wish, passion, aim or dream is 'to relate'. But are they not in fact mostly concerned with how to prevent their relations from curdling and clotting? Are they indeed after relationships that hold, as they say they are, or do they, more than anything else, desire those relationships to be light and loose, so that after the pattern of Richard

Baxter's riches that were supposed to 'lie on the shoulders like a light cloak' they could 'be thrown aside at any moment'? When everything is said and done, what sort of advice do they truly want: how to tie the relationship, or how – just in case – to take it apart without harm and with a clear conscience? There is no easy answer to that question, though the question needs to be asked and will go on being asked, as the denizens of the liquid modern world go on smarting under the crushing burden of the most ambivalent of the many ambivalent tasks they daily confront.

Perhaps the very idea of 'relationship' adds to the confusion. However hard the hapless relation-seekers and their counsellors try, the notion resists being fully and truly cleansed of its disturbing and worrying connotations. It stays pregnant with vague threats and sombre premonitions; it tells of the pleasures of togetherness in one breath with the horrors of enclosure. Perhaps this is why, rather than report their experience and prospects in terms of 'relating' and 'relationships', people speak ever more often (aided and abetted by the learned advisers) of connections, of 'connecting' and 'being connected'. Instead of talking about partners, they prefer to speak of 'networks'. What are the merits of the language of 'connectedness' that are missed by the language of 'relationships'?

Unlike 'relations', 'kinships', 'partnerships' and similar notions that make salient the mutual engagement while excluding or passing over in silence its opposite, the disengagement, 'network' stands for a matrix for simultaneously connecting and disconnecting; networks are unimaginable without both activities being simultaneously enabled. In a network, connecting and disconnecting are equally legitimate choices, enjoy the same status and carry the same importance. No point in asking which of the two complementary activities constitutes 'the essence' of network! 'Network' suggests moments of 'being in touch' interspersed with periods of free roaming. In a network, connections are entered on demand, and can be broken at will. An 'undesirable, yet unbreakable' relationship is the very possibility that makes 'relating' as treacherous as it feels. An 'undesirable connection', however, is an oxymoron: connections may be, and are, broken well before they start being detested.

Connections are 'virtual relations'. Unlike old-fashioned relationships (not to mention 'committed' relationships, let alone long-term commitments), they seem to be made to the measure of a liquid modern life setting where 'romantic possibilities' (and not only 'romantic' ones) are supposed and hoped to come and go with ever greater speed and in never thinning crowds, stampeding each other off the stage and out-shouting each other with promises 'to be more satisfying and fulfilling'. Unlike 'real relationships', 'virtual relationships' are easy to enter and to exit. They look smart and clean, feel easy to use and user-friendly, when compared with the heavy, slow-moving, inert messy 'real stuff'. A twenty-eight-year-old man from Bath, interviewed in connection with the rapidly growing popularity of computer dating at the expense of singles bars and lonely-heart columns, pointed to one decisive advantage of electronic relation: 'you can always press "delete"'.

As if obedient to Gresham's law, virtual relations (renamed 'connections') set the pattern which drives out all other relationships. That does not make the men and women who surrender to the pressure happy; hardly happier than the practising of pre-virtual relations made them. You gain something, you lose something else.

[. . .]

'Top-pocket relationship', explains Catherine Jarvie, commenting on the opinions of Gillian Walton of London Marriage Guidance,[1] is so called because you keep it in your pocket so that you can bring it out when you need it.

A successful top-pocket relationship is sweet and short-lived, says Jarvie. We may suppose that it is sweet *because* it is short-lived, and that its sweetness dwells precisely in that comforting awareness that you do not need to go out of your way or stretch yourself over backwards to keep its sweetness intact for a longer time; in fact, you need not do anything at all to enjoy it. 'Top-pocket relationship' is instantaneity and disposability incarnate.

Not that your relationship would acquire those wondrous qualities without certain conditions having first been met. Note that it is *you* who must meet those conditions; another point in the 'top-pocket' relationship's favour, to be sure, since it is on you and only you that success depends, and so it is you and only you who is in control – and stays in control throughout the 'top-pocket' relationship's short life.

First condition: the relationship must be entered in full awareness and soberly. No 'love at first sight' here, remember. No *falling* in love . . . No sudden tide of emotions that leave you breathless and gasping: neither the emotions we call 'love', nor those we soberly describe as 'desire'. Don't let yourself be overwhelmed and shaken off your feet, and above all don't let your calculator be torn out of your hand. And don't allow yourself to mistake what the relationship you are about to enter is about, for what it neither is nor should be about. Convenience is the sole thing that counts, and convenience is a matter for a clear head, not a warm (let alone overheated) heart. The smaller your mortgage loan, the less insecure you'd feel when exposed to the fluctuations of the future housing market; the less you invest in the relationship, the less insecure you'd feel when exposed to the fluctuations of your future emotions.

Second condition: keep it this way. Remember that convenience needs little time to turn into its opposite. So don't let the relationship escape from the head's supervision, don't allow it to develop its own logic and particularly to acquire rights of tenure – to fall out of your top pocket where it belongs. Be on the alert. Don't let your vigilance take a nap. Watch closely even the slightest changes in what Jarvie calls 'emotional undercurrents' (obviously, emotions tend to become 'undercurrents' once they have been left out of the calculation). If you note something that you did not bargain for and would not care for – know that 'it's time to move on'. Travelling cautiously would spare you the ennui of arrival. It is the traffic that holds all the pleasure.

So keep your top pocket free and ready. You will soon need to put something there, and – keep your fingers crossed – you will . . .

The 'Relationships spirit' section of the *Guardian Weekend* is worth reading every week, but it is even better to read it many weeks in a row.

Each week it offers advice on how to proceed when confronting a 'problem' most men and women (mainly *Guardian* readers) are expected, and so duly expect, sooner or later to confront. One week, one problem; but over a succession of weeks the dedicated and attentive reader can gain much more than certain specific life-political skills that may come in handy in certain specific situations in tackling certain specific problems; skills that, once acquired and combined, could help to *create* the kinds of situations they have been conceived to deal with and to spot and locate the problems they have been designed to tackle. A regular and dedicated reader blessed with a longer memory-span than a single week can draw and fill in a complete map of the life in which 'problems' tend to crop up, register the complete inventory of 'problems' that do, and form an opinion of their relative frequency or rarity. In a world where the gravity of a thing or an event is represented only in numbers, and so can only be grasped that way (the quality of a hit in the number of sold records, of a public event or performance in the number of TV watchers, of a public figure in the number of people passing by the coffin, of the intellectuals in public view in the numbers of quotes and mentions), the high frequency with which some 'problems' keep returning to the column, in various guises, week after week after week, is all the testimony one needs to their relevance to a successful life, and so to the importance of the skills designed to tackle them.

So, when it comes to the relationships as seen through the prism of the 'Relationships spirit' column, what can a faithful reader learn about the relative importance of things and the techniques of handling them?

The reader may learn quite a few useful hints about the places where would-be relationship partners can be found in larger than usual quantities, and about the situations in which, once found, they are more likely to be prevailed upon or cajoled to assume the partner's role. And he or she would know that entering a relationship is a 'problem'; that is, it presents a difficulty which spawns confusion and brings about unpleasant tension which, in order to be fought against and chased away, needs a certain amount of knowing and know-how. This would be learnt – without swotting, just by following regularly, week by week, the *Guardian Weekend* version of the relationship spirit.

This won't be, however, the main lesson likely to trickle down and take root in the regular reader's vision of life and life politics. The art of *breaking up* the relationship and emerging out of it unscathed, with few if any festering wounds needing a lot of time to heal and a lot of care to limit the 'collateral damage' (like estranged friends, or circles where one would not be welcomed or which one would wish to avoid), beats the art of *composing* relationships hands down – by the sheer frequency of being vented.

It seems that Richard Baxter, the fiery Puritan prophet, were he instead a prophet of life strategy fit for the liquid modern era, would say of relationships what he did of the acquisition and care of external goods – that they 'should only lie on the shoulders like a light cloak, which can be thrown aside at any moment', and that one should beware more than anything else their turning, unintentionally and surreptitiously, into 'a steel casing' . . . You won't take your riches with you to the grave, the prophet-saint Baxter admonished his flock, rehearsing the common sense of the people who lived their life as handmaiden of the afterlife. You won't take your relations into the next episode, the expert-counsellor Baxter would admonish his clients, in unison with the premonitions-turned-certainties of the wise-after-the-fact people whose lives have been sliced into episodes lived through as handmaidens of the episodes yet to come. Your relationship is likely to break up well before the episode ends. But if it doesn't, there will hardly be another episode. Certainly not another episode to savour and enjoy.

[...]

This week, 'Living' is devoted to SDCs – 'semi-detached couples', 'relationship revolutionaries', who 'have burst the suffocating "couple bubble"' and 'go their own ways'. Their twosome-ness is part-time. They abhor the idea of sharing home and household, preferring to keep their separate abodes, bank accounts and circles of friends, and share time and space when they feel like it – but not when they don't. Like the old-style work that has split nowadays into a succession of flexible times, odd jobs or short-term projects, and like the old-style property purchase or lease that tends to be replaced these days with time-share occupation and package holidays – the old-style 'till death us do part' marriage, already elbowed out by the self-admittedly temporary 'we will see how it works' cohabitation, is replaced by a part-time, flexible-times 'comings together'.

Experts, as the well-known habit of experts would lead readers to expect, are divided. Their opinions range from a welcoming of the SDC model as the long-sought nirvana (squaring the circle of genuine giving and taking unpaid for by the loss of independence) finally come true, all the way to the condemnation of SDC practitioners for their cowardice: their unwillingness to face up to the tests and hardships that the creation and perpetuation of fully fledged relationships necessarily entail. Pros and cons are painstakingly traced, solemnly pondered and scrupulously weighed, though the effect of the SDC lifestyle on the SDC's human environment (curiously, considering the ecological sensitivity of our age) appears on none of the balance sheets. Subsections called 'Health', 'Well-being', 'Nutrition' (note: separate from 'Food', 'Restaurants' and 'Wine') and 'Style' (fully made up of furniture commercials). The section is completed with the 'Horoscope' part – in which, depending on their birth dates, some readers are advised to 'forget plodding – mobility is essential now. You have to scoot about, jabber into your mobile and do deals', while others are told that 'it's just your kind of time – new beginnings all round and not too much old business to weigh down your ever optimistic soul'.

Note

1 *Guardian Weekend*, 9 March 2002.

ZYGMUNT BAUMAN

ON LIVING IN A LIQUID MODERN WORLD

Source: Zygmunt Bauman (2005) *Liquid Life*, Cambridge: Polity Press, pp. 1–14.

In skating over thin ice, our safety is in our speed.
Ralph Waldo Emerson, On Prudence

'Liquid life' and 'liquid modernity' are intimately connected. 'Liquid life' is a kind of life that tends to be lived in a liquid modern society. 'Liquid modern' is a society in which the conditions under which its members act change faster than it takes the ways of acting to consolidate into habits and routines. Liquidity of life and that of society feed and reinvigorate each other. Liquid life, just like liquid modern society, cannot keep its shape or stay on course for long.

In a liquid modern society, individual achievements cannot be solidified into lasting possessions because, in no time, assets turn into liabilities and abilities into disabilities. Conditions of action and strategies designed to respond to them age quickly and become obsolete before the actors have a chance to learn them properly. Learning from experience in order to rely on strategies and tactical moves deployed successfully in the past is for that reason ill advised: past tests cannot take account of the rapid and mostly unpredicted (perhaps unpredictable) changes in circumstances. Extrapolating from past events to predict future trends becomes ever more risky and all too often misleading. Trustworthy calculations are increasingly difficult to make, while foolproof prognoses are all but unimaginable: most if not all variables in the equations are unknown, whereas no estimates of their future trends can be treated as fully and truly reliable.

In short: liquid life is a precarious life, lived under conditions of constant uncertainty. The most acute and stubborn worries that haunt such a life are the fears of being caught napping, of failing to catch up with fast-moving events, of being left behind, of overlooking 'use-by' dates, of being saddled with possessions that are no longer desirable, of missing the moment that calls for a change of tack before crossing the point of no return. Liquid life is a succession of new beginnings – yet precisely for that reason it is the swift and painless endings, without which new beginnings would be unthinkable, that tend to be its most challenging moments and most upsetting headaches. Among the arts of liquid modern living and the skills needed to practice them, getting rid of things takes precedence over their acquisition.

As the *Observer* cartoonist Andy Riley puts it, the annoyance is 'reading articles about the wonders of downshifting when you haven't even managed to upshift yet'.[1]

One needs to hurry with the 'upshifting' if one wants to taste the delights of 'downshifting'. Getting the site ready for 'downshifting' bestows meaning on the 'upshifting' bit, and becomes its main purpose; it is by the relief brought by a smooth and painless 'downshifting' that the quality of 'upshifting' will be ultimately judged . . .

The briefing which the practitioners of liquid modern life need most (and are most often offered by the expert counsellors in the life arts) is not how to start or open, but how to finish or close. Another *Observer* columnist, with a tongue only halfway to his cheek, lists the updated rules for 'achieving closure' of partnerships (the episodes no doubt more difficult to 'close' than any other – yet the ones where the partners all too often wish and fight to close them, and so where there is unsurprisingly a particularly keen demand for expert help). The list starts from 'Remember bad stuff. Forget the good' and ends with 'Meet someone new', passing midway the command 'Delete all electronic correspondence'. Throughout, the emphasis falls on forgetting, deleting, dropping and replacing.

Perhaps the description of liquid modern life as a series of new *beginnings* is an inadvertent accessory to a conspiracy of sorts; by replicating a commonly shared illusion it helps to hide its most closely guarded (since shameful, if only residually so) secret. Perhaps a more adequate way to narrate that life is to tell the story of successive *endings*. And perhaps the glory of the successfully lived liquid life would be better conveyed by the inconspicuousness of the graves that mark its progress than by the ostentation of gravestones that commemorate the contents of the tombs.

In a liquid modern society, the waste-disposal industry takes over the commanding positions in liquid life's economy. The survival of that society and the well-being of its members hang on the swiftness with which products are consigned to waste and the speed and efficiency of waste removal. In that society nothing may claim exemption from the universal rule of disposability, and nothing may be allowed to outstay its welcome. The steadfastness, stickiness, viscosity of things inanimate and animate alike are the most sinister and terminal of dangers, sources of the most frightening of fears and the targets of the most violent of assaults.

Life in a liquid modern society cannot stand still. It must modernize (read: go on stripping itself daily of attributes that are past their sell-by dates and go on dismantling/shedding the identities currently assembled/put on) – or perish. Nudged from behind by the horror of expiry, life in a liquid modern society no longer needs to be pulled forward by imagined wonders at the far end of modernizing labours. The need here is to run with all one's strength just to stay in the same place and away from the rubbish bin where the hindmost are doomed to land.

'Creative destruction' is the fashion in which liquid life proceeds, but what that term glosses over and passes by in silence is that what this creation destroys are other forms of life and so obliquely the humans who practise them. Life in the liquid modern society is a sinister version of the musical chairs game, played for real. The true stake in the race is (temporary) rescue from being excluded into the ranks of the destroyed and avoiding being consigned to waste. And with the competition turning global, the running must now be done round a global track.

The greatest chances of winning belong to the people who circulate close to the top of the global power pyramid, to who space matters little and distance is not a bother; people at home in many places but in no one place in particular. They are as light, sprightly and volatile as the increasingly global and extraterritorial trade and finances that assisted at their birth and sustain their nomadic existence. As Jacques Attali described them, 'they do not own factories, lands, nor occupy administrative positions. Their wealth comes from a portable asset: their knowledge of the laws of the labyrinth.' They 'love to create, play and be on the move'. They live in a society 'of volatile values, carefree about the future, egoistic and hedonistic'. They 'take novelty as good tidings, precariousness as value, instability as imperative, hybridity as richness'.[2] In varying degrees, they all master and practise the art of 'liquid life': acceptance of disorientation, immunity to vertigo and adaptation to a state of dizziness, tolerance for an absence of itinerary and direction, and for an indefinite duration of travel.

They try hard, though with mixed success, to follow the pattern set by Bill Gates, that paragon of business success, who Richard Sennett described as marked by 'his willingness to destroy what he has made' and his 'tolerance for fragmentation', as 'someone who has the confidence to dwell in disorder, someone who flourishes in the midst of dislocation' and someone positioning himself 'in a network of possibilities', rather than 'paralysing' himself in 'one particular job'.[3] Their ideal horizon is likely to be Eutropia, one of Italo Calvino's *Invisible Cities* whose inhabitants, the day they 'feel the grip of weariness and no one can any longer bear his job, his relatives, his house and his life', 'move to the next city' where 'each will take a new job, a different wife, will see another landscape on opening the window, and will spend his time with different pastimes, friends, gossip'.[4]

Looseness of attachment and revocability of engagement are the precepts guiding everything in which they engage and to which they are attached. Presumably addressing such people, the anonymous columnist of the *Observer* who hides under the pen name of the Barefoot Doctor counselled his readers to do everything they do 'with grace'. Taking a hint from Lao-tzu, the oriental prophet of detachment and tranquillity, he described the life stance most likely to achieve that effect:

> Flowing like water . . . you swiftly move along, never fighting the current, stopping long enough to become stagnant or clinging to the riverbank or rocks – the possessions, situations or people that pass through your life – not even trying to hold on to your opinions or world view, but simply sticking lightly yet intelligently to whatever presents itself as you pass by and then graciously letting it go without grasping . . .[5]

Faced with such players, the rest of the participants of the game – and particularly the involuntary ones among them, those who don't 'love' or cannot afford 'to be on the move' – stand little chance. Joining in the game is not a realistic choice for them – but neither have they the choice of not trying. Flitting between flowers in search of the most fragrant is not their option; they are stuck to places where flowers, fragrant or not, are rare – and so can only watch haplessly as the few that there are fade or rot. The suggestion to 'stick lightly to whatever presents itself and 'graciously let it go' would sound at best like a cruel joke in their ears, but mostly like a heartless sneer.

Nevertheless, 'stick lightly' they must, as 'possessions, situations and people' will keep slipping away and vanishing at a breathtaking speed whatever they do; whether they try to slow them down or not is neither here nor there. 'Let them go' they must (though, unlike Bill Gates, with hardly any pleasure), but whether they do it graciously or with a lot of wailing and teeth-gnashing is beside the point. They might be forgiven for suspecting some connection between that comely lightness and grace paraded by those who glide by and their own unchosen ugly torpidity and impotence to move.

Their indolence is, indeed, unchosen. Lightness and grace come together with freedom – freedom to move, freedom to choose, freedom to stop being what one already is and freedom to become what one is not yet. Those on the receiving side of the new planetary mobility don't have such freedom. They can count neither on the forbearance of those from who they would rather keep their distance, nor on the tolerance of those to who they would wish to be closer. For them, there are neither unguarded exits nor hospitably open entry gates. They *belong:* those to who or with who they belong view their belonging as their non-negotiable and incontrovertible *duty* (even if disguised as their inalienable *right*) – whereas those who they would wish to join see their belonging rather as their similarly non-negotiable, irreversible and unredeemable *fate*. The first wouldn't let them go, whereas the second wouldn't let them in.

Between the start and the (unlikely ever to happen) arrival is a desert, a void, a wilderness, a yawning abyss into which only a few would muster the courage to leap of their own free will, unpushed. Centripetal and centrifugal, gravitational and repelling forces combine to keep the restless in place and stop the discontented short of restlessness. Those hot-headed or desperate enough to try to defy the odds stacked against them risk the lot of outlaws and outcasts, and pay for their audacity in the hard currency of bodily misery and psychical trauma – a price which only a few would choose to pay of their own free will, unforced. Andrzej Szahaj, a most perceptive analyst of the highly uneven odds in contemporary identity games, goes as far as to suggest that the decision to leave the community of belonging is in quite numerous cases downright unimaginable; he goes on to remind his incredulous Western readers that in the remote past of Europe, for instance in ancient Greece, exile from the *polis* of belonging was viewed as the ultimate, indeed capital, punishment.[6] At least the ancients were cool-headed and preferred straight talk. But the millions of *sans papiers,* stateless, refugees, exiles, asylum or bread-and-water seekers of our times, two millennia later, would have little difficulty in recognizing themselves in that talk.

At both extremes of the hierarchy (and in the main body of the pyramid locked between them in a double-bind) people are haunted by the problem of identity. At the top, the problem is to choose the best pattern from the many currently on offer, to assemble the separately sold parts of the kit, and to fasten them together neither too lightly (lest the unsightly, outdated and aged bits that are meant to be hidden underneath show through at the seams) nor too tightly (lest the patchwork resists being dismantled at short notice when the time for dismantling comes – as it surely will). At the bottom, the problem is to cling fast to the sole identity available and to hold its bits and parts together while fighting back the erosive forces and disruptive pressures, repairing the constantly crumbling walls and digging the trenches deeper. For all the others suspended between the extremes, the problem is a mixture of the two.

Taking a hint from Joseph Brodsky's profile of materially affluent yet spiritually impoverished and famished contemporaries, tired like the residents of Calvino's Eutropia of everything they have enjoyed thus far (like yoga, Buddhism, Zen, contemplation, Mao) and so beginning to dig (with the help of state-of-the-art technology, of course) into the mysteries of Sufism, kabbala or Sunnism to beef up their flagging desire to desire, Andrzej Stasiuk, one of the most perceptive archivists of contemporary cultures and their discontents, develops a typology of the 'spiritual lumpenproletariat' and suggests that its ranks swell fast and that its torments trickle profusely down from the top, saturating ever thicker layers of the social pyramid.[7]

Those affected by the 'spiritual lumpenproletarian' virus live in the present and by the present. They live to survive (as long as possible) and to get satisfaction (as much of it as possible). Since the world is not their home ground and not their property (having relieved themselves of the burdens of heritage, they feel free but somehow disinherited – robbed of something, betrayed by someone), they see nothing wrong in exploiting it at will; exploitation feels like nothing more odious than stealing back the stolen.

Flattened into a perpetual present and filled to the brim with survival-and-gratification concerns (it is gratification to survive, the purpose of survival being more gratification), the world inhabited by 'spiritual lumpenproletarians' leaves no room for worries about anything other than what can be, at least in principle, consumed and relished on the spot, here and now.

Eternity is the obvious outcast. Not infinity, though; as long as it lasts, the present may be stretched beyond any limit and accommodate as much as once was hoped to be experienced only in the fullness of time (in Stasiuk's words, 'it is highly probable that the quantity of digital, celluloid and analogue beings met in the course of a bodily life comes close to the volume which eternal life and resurrection of the flesh could offer'). Thanks to the hoped-for infinity of mundane experiences yet to come, eternity may not be missed; its loss may not even be noticed.

Speed, not duration, matters. With the right speed, one can consume the whole of eternity inside the continuous present of earthly life. Or this at least is what the 'spiritual lumpenproletarians' try, and hope, to achieve. The trick is to compress eternity so that it may fit, whole, into the timespan of individual life. The quandary of a mortal life in an immortal universe has been finally resolved: one can now stop worrying about things eternal and lose nothing of eternity's wonders – indeed one can exhaust whatever eternity could possibly offer, all in the timespan of one mortal life. One cannot perhaps take the time-lid off mortal life; but one can (or at least try to) remove all limits from the volume of satisfactions to be experienced before reaching that other, irremovable limit.

In a bygone world in which time moved much slower and resisted acceleration, people tried to bridge the agonizing gap between the poverty of a short and mortal life and the infinite wealth of the eternal universe by hopes of reincarnation or resurrection. In our world that knows or admits of no limits to acceleration, such hopes may well be discarded. If only one moves quickly enough and does not stop to look back and count the gains and losses, one can go on squeezing into the timespan of mortal life ever more lives; perhaps as many as eternity could supply. What else, if not to act on that belief, are the unstoppable, compulsive and obsessive reconditioning, refurbishment, recycling, overhaul and reconstitution of identity for? 'Identity', after all, is (just as the reincarnation and resurrection of olden times used to be) about the possibility of 'being born again' – of stopping being what one is and turning into someone one is not yet.

The good news is that this replacement of worries about eternity with an identity-recycling bustle comes complete with patented and ready-to-use DIY tools that promise to make the job fast and effective while needing no special skills and calling for little if any difficult and awkward labour. Self-sacrifice and self-immolation, unbearably long and unrelenting self-drilling and self-taming, waiting for gratification that feels interminable and practising virtues that seem to exceed endurance – all those exorbitant costs of past therapies – are no longer required. New and improved diets, fitness gadgets, changes of wallpaper, parquets put where carpets used to lie (or vice versa), replacements of a mini with an SUV (or the other way round), a T-shirt with a blouse and monochromatic with richly colour-saturated sofa covers or dresses, sizes of breasts moved up or down, sneakers changed, brands of booze and daily routines adapted to the latest fashion and a strikingly novel vocabulary adopted in which to couch public confessions of intimate soul-stirrings . . . these will do nicely. And, as a last resort, on the vexingly far horizon loom the wonders of gene overhaul. Whatever happens, there is no need to despair. If all those magic wands prove not to be enough or, despite all their user-friendliness, are found too cumbersome or too slow, there are drugs promising an instant, even if brief, visit to eternity (hopefully with other drugs guaranteeing a return ticket).

Liquid life is consuming life. It casts the world and all its animate and inanimate fragments as objects of consumption: that is, objects that lose their usefulness (and so their lustre, attraction, seductive power and worth) in the course of being used. It shapes the judging and evaluating of all the animate and inanimate fragments of the world after the pattern of objects of consumption.

Objects of consumption have a limited expectation of useful life and once the limit has been passed they are unfit for consumption; since 'being good for consumption' is the sole feature that defines their function, they are then unfit altogether – useless. Once unfit, they ought to be removed from the site of consuming life (consigned to biodegradation, incinerated, transferred into the care of waste-disposal companies) to clear it for other, still unused objects of consumption.

To save yourself from the embarrassment of lagging behind, of being stuck with something no one else would be seen with, of being caught napping, of missing the train of progress instead of riding it, you must remember that it is in the nature of things to call for vigilance, not loyalty. In the liquid modern world, loyalty is a cause of shame, not pride. Link to your internet provider first thing in the morning, and you will be reminded of that sober truth by the main item on the list of daily news: 'Ashamed of your Mobile? Is your phone so old that you're embarrassed to answer it? Upgrade to one you can be proud of.' The flipside of the commandment 'to upgrade' to a state-of-consumer-correctness mobile is, of course, the prohibition any longer to be seen holding the one to which you upgraded last time.

Waste is the staple and arguably the most profuse product of the liquid modern society of consumers; among consumer society's industries waste production is the most massive and the most immune to crisis. That makes waste disposal one of the two major challenges liquid life has to confront and tackle. The other major challenge is the threat of being consigned to waste. In a world filled with consumers and the objects of their consumption, life is hovering uneasily between the joys of consumption and the horrors of the rubbish heap. Life may be at all times a living-towards-death, but in a liquid modern society living-towards-the-refuse dump may be a more immediate and more energy-and-labour-consuming prospect and concern of the living.

For the denizen of the liquid modern society, every supper – unlike that referred to by Hamlet in his reply to the King's inquiry about Polonius's whereabouts – is an occasion 'where he eats' *and* 'where he is eaten'.[8] No longer is there a disjunction between the two acts. 'And' has replaced the 'either-or'. In the society of consumers, no one can escape being an object of consumption – and not just consumption by maggots, and not only at the far end of consuming life. Hamlet in liquid modern times would probably modify Shakespeare's Hamlet's rule, denying the maggots' privileged role in the consumption of the consumers. He would perhaps start, like the original Hamlet, stating that 'we fat all creatures else to fat us, and we fat ourselves . . .' – but then conclude: 'to fat other creatures'.

'Consumers' and 'objects of consumption' are the conceptual poles of a continuum along which all members of the society of consumers are plotted and along which they move, to and fro, daily. Some may be cast most of the time particularly near to the commodities' pole – but no consumer can be fully and truly insured against falling into its close, too close for comfort, proximity. Only as commodities, only if they are able to demonstrate their own use-value, can consumers gain access to consuming life. In liquid life, the distinction between consumers and objects of consumption is all too often momentary and ephemeral, and always conditional. We may say that role reversal is the rule here, though even that statement distorts the realities of liquid life, in which the two roles intertwine, blend and merge.

It is not clear which of the two factors (attractions of the 'consumer' pole, or the repulsion of the 'waste' pole) is the more powerful moving force of liquid life. No doubt both factors cooperate in shaping the daily logic and – bit by bit, episode by episode – the itinerary of that life. Fear adds strength to desire. However attentively it focuses on its immediate objects, desire cannot help but remain aware – consciously, half-consciously or subconsciously – of that other awesome stake hanging on its vigour, determination and resourcefulness. However intensely concentrated on the *object* of desire, the eye of the consumer cannot but glance sideways at the commodity value of the desiring *subject*. Liquid life means constant self-scrutiny, self-critique and self-censure. Liquid life feeds on the self's dissatisfaction with *itself*.

Critique is self-referential and inward directed; and so is the reform which such self-critique demands and prompts. It is in the name of such inward-looking and inward-targeted reform that the outside world is preyed upon, ransacked and ravaged. Liquid life endows the outside world, indeed everything in the world that is not a part of the self, with a primarily instrumental value; deprived of or denied a value of its own, that world derives all its value from its service to the cause of self-reform, and by their contribution to that self-reform the world and each of its elements are judged. Parts of the world unfit to serve or no longer able to serve are either left outside the realm of relevance and unattended, or actively discarded and swept away. Such parts are but the waste from self-reforming zeal, the rubbish tip being their natural destination. In terms of liquid life's reasoning their preservation would be irrational; their right to be preserved for their own sake cannot be easily argued, let alone proved, by liquid life's logic.

It is for that reason that the advent of liquid modern society spelled the demise of Utopias centred on society and more generally of the idea of the 'good society'. If liquid life prompts an interest in societal reform at all, the postulated reform is aimed mostly at pushing society further towards the surrender, one by one, of all its pretences to a value of its own except that of a police force guarding the security of self-reforming selves, and towards the acceptance and entrenchment of the principle of compensation (a political version of a 'money back guarantee') in case the policing fails or is found inadequate. Even the new environmental concerns owe their popularity to the perception of a link between the predatory misuse of the planetary commons and threats to the smooth flow of the self-centred pursuits of liquid life.

The trend is self-sustained and self-invigorating. The focusing on self-reform self-perpetuates; so does the lack of interest in, and the inattention to, the aspects of common life that resist a complete and immediate translation into the current targets of self-reform. Inattention to the conditions of life in common precludes the possibility of renegotiating the setting that makes individual life liquid. The success of the pursuit of happiness – the ostensible purpose and paramount motive of individual life – continues to be defied by the very fashion of pursuing it (the only fashion in which it can be pursued in the liquid modern setting). The resulting unhappiness adds reason and vigour to a self-centred life politics; its ultimate effect is the perpetuation of life's liquidity. Liquid modern society and liquid life are locked in a veritable *perpetuum mobile*.

Once set in motion, a *perpetuum mobile* will not stop rotating on its own. The prospects of the perpetual motion arresting, already dim by the nature of the contraption, are made still dimmer by the amazing ability of this particular version of the self-propelling mechanism to absorb and assimilate the tensions and frictions it generates – and to harness them to its service. Indeed, by capitalizing on the demand for relief or cure which the tensions incite, it manages to deploy them as high-grade fuel that keeps its engines going.

A habitual answer given to a wrong kind of behaviour, to conduct unsuitable for an accepted purpose or leading to undesirable outcomes, is education or re-education: instilling in the learners new kinds of motives, developing different propensities and training them in deploying new skills. The thrust of education in such cases is to challenge the impact of daily experience, to fight back and in the end defy the pressures arising from the social setting in which the learners operate. But will the education and the educators fit the bill? Will they themselves be able to resist the pressure? Will they manage to avoid being enlisted in the service of the self-same pressures they are meant to defy? This question has been asked since ancient times, repeatedly answered in the negative by the realities of social life, yet resurrected with undiminished force following every successive calamity. The hopes of using education as a jack potent enough to unsettle and ultimately to dislodge the pressures of 'social facts' seem to be as immortal as they are vulnerable . . .

At any rate, the hope is alive and well. Henry A. Giroux dedicated many years of assiduous study to the chances of 'critical pedagogy' in a society reconciled to the overwhelming powers of the market. In a recent conclusion, drawn in cooperation with Susan Searls Giroux, he restates the centuries-old hope:

> In opposition to the commodification, privatization, and commercialization of everything educational, educators need to define higher education as a resource vital to the democratic and civic life of the nation. The challenge is thus for academics, cultural workers, students, and labour organizers to join together and oppose the transformation of higher education into a commercial sphere . . .[9]

In 1989, Richard Rorty spelled out, as desirable and fulfillable aims for the educators, the tasks of 'stirring the kids up' and instilling 'doubts in the students about the students' own self-images, about the society in which they belong'.[10] Obviously, not all the people employed in the educator's role are likely to take up the challenge and adopt these aims as their own; the offices and the corridors of academia are filled with two kinds of people – some of them 'busy conforming to well-understood criteria for making contributions to knowledge', and the others trying 'to expand their own moral imagination' and read books 'in order to enlarge their sense of what is possible and important – either for themselves as individuals or for their society'. Rorty's appeal is addressed to the second kind of people, as only in that category are his hopes vested. And he knows well against what overwhelming odds the teacher likely to respond to the clarion call will need to battle. 'We cannot tell boards of trustees, government commissions, and the like, that our function is to stir things up, to make our society feel guilty, to keep it off balance', or indeed (as he suggests elsewhere) that higher education 'is also not a matter of inculcating or educing truth. It is, instead, a matter of inciting doubt and stimulating imagination, thereby challenging the prevailing consensus.'[11] There is a tension between public rhetoric and the sense of intellectual mission – and that tension 'leaves the academy in general, and the humanistic intellectuals in particular, vulnerable to heresy hunters'. Given that the opposite messages of the promoters of conformity are powerfully backed by the ruling *doxa* and the daily evidence of commonsensical experience, it also, we may add, makes the 'humanistic intellectuals' sitting targets for the advocates of the end of history, rational choice, 'there is no alternative' life policies and other formulae attempting to grasp and convey the current and postulated impetus of an apparently invincible societal dynamic. It invites charges of unrealism, utopianism, wishful thinking, daydreaming – and, adding insult to injury in an odious reversal of ethical truth, of irresponsibility.

Adverse odds may be overwhelming, and yet a democratic (or, as Cornelius Castoriadis would say, an autonomous) society knows of no substitute for education and self-education as a means to influence the turn of events that can be squared with its own nature, while that nature cannot be preserved for long without 'critical pedagogy' – education sharpening its critical edge, 'making society feel guilty' and 'stirring things up' through stirring human consciences. The fates of freedom, of democracy that makes it possible while being made possible by it, and of education that breeds dissatisfaction with the level of both freedom and democracy achieved thus far, are inextricably connected and not to be detached from one another. One may view that intimate connection as another specimen of a vicious circle – but it is within that circle that human hopes and the chances of humanity are inscribed, and can be nowhere else.

Notes

1 See *Observer Magazine*, 3 Oct. 2004.
2 Jacques Attali, *Chemins de sagesse. Traité du labyrinthe* (Fyand, 1996), pp. 79–80, 109.
3 See Richard Sennett, The Corrosion of Character: The Personal Consequences of Work in the New Capitalism (W.W. Norton, 1998), p. 62.
4 Italo Calvino, *Le città invisibili*, quoted here after the translation by William Weaver, *Invisible Cities* (Vintage, 1997), p. 64.
5 See 'Grace under pressure', *Observer Magazine*, 30 Nov. 2003, p. 95.
6 Andrzej Szahaj, *E pluribus unum?* (Universitas, 2004), p. 81.
7 See Andrzej Stasiuk, 'Duchowy lumpenproletariat' ('Spiritual lumpenproletariat') and 'Rewolucja czyli zagłada' ('Revolution, or extermination'), in *Tekturowy Samolot* (Wydawnictwo Czarne, 2002).
8 See Shakespeare, *Hamlet*, Act IV, scene iii.
9 See Henry A. Giroux and Susan Searls Giroux, *Take Back Higher Education* (Palgrave, 2004), pp. 119–20.
10 See Richard Rorty, 'The humanistic intellectual: eleven theses', in *Philosophy and Social Hope* (Penguin, 1999), pp. 127–8.
11 In 'Education as socialization and as individualization', in *Philosophy and Social Hope* (Penguin, 1999), p. 118.

CHAPTER 4

Gender and sexualities in liquid modernity

Ann Branaman

Introduction: the melting of liquid modern identities

Gender, in Bauman's analysis, is one of a number of frameworks of identity that increasingly lose normative hold over the lives of individuals as they are subjected to the melting powers of liquid modernity. 'Identity' becomes a problem and a source of deep anxiety in liquid modernity; gender and sexual identity, like other bases of identity, become destabilized and deregulated, open to an unprecedented degree of individual experimentation and choice. The currently dominant tendency in sociology, shaped by feminist analyses, is to view this increase in choice as liberatory and desirable. In this view, the increasing indeterminacy of gender and sexual identities marks a progression towards achievement of the aims of gender and sexual liberation movements, as individuals are increasingly released from the oppressive burden of gender and sexual regulation. Although feminist positions vary on the question of the causal priority of gender regulation and gender inequality, most assume a strong connection between them, such that a reduction in one will contribute to, coincide with, or follow from a reduction in the other. For Bauman, however, deregulation is a limited foundation for reducing inequality. The loosening of norms may make life easier for those whose conformity (or failure of conformity) to regimes of gender and sexual regulation has proven uncomfortable, but Bauman emphasizes that the lifting of normative regulation of identity and desire is fully consistent with the intensification of social inequality on a global scale. Deregulation of identity and desire, furthermore, means very little for the many in the world whose freedom and self-determination is limited by lack of resources. In an increasingly unequal world in which politics have escaped local and national boundaries, power (i.e. the power of the global capitalist class) is indifferent to and unaffected by the increasing freedoms of individuals in their everyday lives, except insofar as these contribute to consumerism. Accordingly, Bauman believes that critical theory, in the current period, needs to be reoriented away from its traditional emphasis on liberation, an emphasis shared by gender and sexual liberation movements, and instead focused on what he sees as the most basic challenge for contemporary politics: the gap between 'individuality de jure' and 'individuality de facto'. The main contradiction of liquid modernity, he argues, is the 'yawning gap between the right of self-assertion and the capacity to control the social settings which render such self-assertion feasible or unrealistic' (2000: 38).

Not only is Bauman suspicious of the value of gender and sexual deregulation in this context, but he also points to the challenges that the loosening of gender and sexual norms pose for contemporary individuals as they face the task of constructing their self-identities. Central to Bauman's analysis of liquid modernity is his distinction between two phases of modernity: 'heavy modernity' and 'liquid modernity'. In the earlier heavy phase, according to Bauman, self-determining individuals faced the task of finding their niche in society and acting in conformity with clearly defined codes of conduct. In liquid modernity, by contrast, clearly defined, stable, and authoritative codes of conduct are impossible to find. When, in the heavy modern period, hereditary estates with their 'no-appeal-allowed allocation-by-ascription' were subjected to modernity's 'melting powers', individuals, Bauman says, could be excused for failing to notice: 'they came to be confronted by patterns and figurations which, albeit "new and improved", were as stiff and indomitable as ever' (2000: 6–7). Individuals were set free from old cages, but admonished to quickly 'find the appropriate niche and to settle there through conformity: by faithfully following the rules and codes of conduct identified as right and proper for the location' (2000: 7). Class and gender, in heavy modernity, were solid and confining social cages as much, if differently, as they were in pre-modern times. In liquid modernity, the hold of class and gender weakens.

In heavy modernity, individuals needed only to find or achieve their *placement* within an established and stable range of *places*. In the current period, the social types, models of conduct, patterns, and norms of behavior lose their solidity and are no longer sufficient to anchor an individual's self-identity over a lifetime. In the liquid modern era, it is 'not just the individual *placements* in society, but the *places* to which individuals may gain access and in which they may wish to settle are melting fast and can hardly serve as targets for "life projects"' (2001: 146). The issue for earlier modern individuals was to *insert* themselves into a fairly narrow range of established and stable social positions – occupation, marriage, church, community – and to behave in accordance with established expectations. For contemporary individuals, by contrast, the positions themselves are less stable and the expectations attached to them less clear. With awareness of a far greater range of possible identities, occupations, relationships, priorities, values, and ways of living *and* of the likelihood that none of these will be durable enough to anchor self-identity for long, an individual's self-identity is less likely to rest peacefully within any one.

So, whereas the earlier modern individual may have experienced anxiety over *attainment* of social class status or *fulfillment* of gender ideals, the anxiety of the liquid modern individual centers more on doubts about the long-term viability of any attained status, the worthiness of any set of ideals, or the possibility that some other direction one might take in life would yield more satisfaction than the current path. Applying Bauman's more general point to gender, liquid modern men and women worry far less about being appropriately masculine or feminine and much more about how to choose from competing and imperfectly scripted gender models and how to chart a successful course to meet standards that often are vague, volatile, or impossible. With the rapid pace of social change, further 'holding on' to identity becomes problematic; individuals can no longer assume, in other words, that an identity chosen at a given point of time, will continue to be workable or 'marketable' in the future. Contemporary life conspires 'against distant goals, life-long projects, lasting commitments, eternal alliances, immutable identities' (1996: 51).

This is not to say, Bauman notes, that there are not social types, models of conduct, patterns, and normative standards that continue to shape and constrain individuals' behavior and construction of identity. Gender remains a significant and constraining category; now, as much as ever, one can't shake gender. Even if a person alters gender by means of cross-dressing or sexual reassignment surgery, as is increasingly common, the deeply felt need to look, act, and dress 'like a man' or 'like a woman' is clear evidence of the continuing significance of gender and its powerful constraint. We continue to be constrained to *be* men *or* women. Now, however, more than in the earlier modern era, there is a much more expansive range of possible ways to be a man or a woman.

There are still Joneses to keep up with, as Bauman puts it, and, we might add, *gendered* Joneses. There are models of masculinity and femininity, or of ways of being a man or a woman, which capture the imagination and shape the aspirations of contemporary boys and girls and men and women. But there are such a variety of Joneses, Bauman argues, that the individual is unable to select and follow one model of conduct without nagging doubts that one's current model will fall out of fashion or that some other model might be more worthy or provide more satisfaction. Any particular model of conduct, in other words, loses its authoritative power – even if there remains a considerable degree of authority over most people to pick models from within their own gender.

An important difference between earlier modern gender ideals and contemporary ones, however, is that the power of contemporary (gender) ideals lies in seduction, not authority or regulation. In the same way that most people in advanced capitalist societies cannot avoid the seduction of consumerism, most cannot avoid being taken in by at least some of the gender models on offer. The increased freedom of contemporary men and women to choose what sort of men and women they wish to be, Bauman suggests, might be likened to the consumers' freedom (if they have the necessary resources) to select from a variety of consumer products on offer – but not the freedom to escape consumerism (or gender) altogether.

Gender, sexuality, and anxiety in the post-panoptical society

Bauman characterizes liquid modernity as a 'post-panoptical society', in which normative regulation becomes an unnecessary means of social control and domination (2000, 2001). No longer do contemporary individuals live in fear of 'Big Brother'; the detailed monitoring, normative judgment, and disciplining of everyday behavior characteristic of the panoptic institutions described in Foucault's *Discipline and Punish* (1977) no longer aptly describe liquid modern life. Normative regulation becomes inessential, in Bauman's view, for a couple of reasons. First, because the power-holders of the contemporary world are increasingly mobile, unattached to any particular location and to the workers who live there, they find it unnecessary and impractical to spend time and money disciplining the population. In the earlier phase of modernity, in which capital and labor were more mutually dependent,

Foucault's analysis of panoptical social control was more fitting. In the current period, the dependence of the weaker and more territorially bound working class on the resources of the increasingly mobile global elite, and the precariousness of their position in the face of this asymmetry of dependence, is typically sufficient to secure cooperation. Not only is it unnecessary and impractical for the global elite to expend resources in the training and discipline of workers, but it is also *undesirable* from the perspective of the global elite to produce a highly disciplined and normatively regulated population. Disciplined, normatively regulated individuals, in particular, those whose desires are regulated by objective possibilities, make bad consumers. The success and dominance of consumerism depends on the free flow of desire and the proliferation of wishes. Certainly, following Foucauldian logic, to be good consumers, contemporary individuals must receive training to freely follow wishes and desires and to focus these wishes and desires on goods and experiences purchasable in the consumer market; this is no more natural, and perhaps less so, than controlling desires and keeping expectations in line with objective possibilities. Even if we recognize this too as normative regulation, however, its nature is very different from the kind of normative regulation characteristic of heavy modernity.

Not only is it unnecessary to discipline workers as workers, but the normative regulation of sexuality (which, according to Foucault's analysis, was a central objective of modern disciplinary control) is also abandoned. If, as Freud argued, the maintenance of all civilizations up to his own required a significant degree of repression of sexual instinct, Bauman argues that this is no longer the case in liquid modernity. Foucault (1976) challenged Freud's analysis of sexual repression, arguing that sexuality in the modern era is highly regulated, but that repression is an inappropriate way to understand this regulation. Instead, he viewed the idea of repressed impulses as a fiction constructed with the aim of intensifying self-monitoring and self-judgment according to prevailing standards of psychological and sexual normalcy. The latter, in his view, was a 'productive', not a repressive, form of social control. From Bauman's perspective, however, neither Freud's nor Foucault's conceptions capture the relationship between sexuality and social control in the contemporary era. In Bauman's view, authoritative standards of sexual normality are dissolving.

No longer are the distinctions between healthy and perverse sexuality, drawn sharply and applied vigorously during the modern era, meaningful in the same way to liquidly modern individuals.

> for *homo sexualis* inserted in the liquid modern setting the boundary separating the 'healthy' and the 'perverse' manifestations of sexual instincts is all but blurred. All forms of sexual activity are not just tolerated, but often suggested as useful therapy for one or another psychological ailment, increasingly accepted as legitimate routes in the individual pursuit of happiness, and encouraged to be displayed in public.
>
> (Bauman 2003: 56)

Building on Foucault's assumption of a link between capitalist production and the repressive social control of sexuality, Bauman attributes this deregulation of sexuality to lack of interest on the part of the powers-that-be, given the 'fast fading demand for the employment of spare sexual energy' in the service of production (2003: 56). Sexuality continues to be exploited in liquid modern society, but in the interests of increasing consumption rather than production. Now, sexual energy is allowed and encouraged to run rampant, 'guided by seduction by the objects of sexual desire on offer rather than by any coercive pressures' (2003: 57).

For Bauman, there are still standards that apply to sexuality, but these sorts of standards are qualitatively different and different in their implications than the distinctions between 'normal' and 'abnormal' or 'healthy' and 'pathological' characteristic of the earlier modern period. The standards of heavy modernity were less variable and more authoritative, but were standards that everyone understood and most could meet. Current standards are more variable and less authoritative, controlling instead by seduction, but, at the same time, they are much more difficult, even impossible, to meet. The current preoccupation with 'fitness' illustrates this well. According to Bauman, the demand for 'fitness' has replaced the modern demand for 'health'. The difference is that health was a clearly demarcated and attainable state, defined by and large by an *absence* of pathology. Fitness, by contrast, is 'inherently open-ended and the criteria for achievement undefined. "Being fit" means to have a flexible, absorptive and adjustable body, ready to live through sensations not yet tried and impossible to specify in advance' (2000: 77); 'if health is about "sticking to the norm", fitness is about the capacity to break all norms and leave every already achieved standard behind' (2000: 77–8).

Sexuality, in the era of liquid modernity, is approached not as a matter of 'normal' versus 'pathological', as it was in heavy modernity, with concern only directed toward cases of sexual deviance. In liquid modernity, Bauman suggests, the concept of sexual deviance loses meaning. With the exception of pedophilia, Bauman points out, there are no sexual acts, desires, or orientations that are culturally off limits; quite the contrary, the capacity to experience new and different sensations, along diverse avenues, is a mark of fitness. Individuals are free, at least normatively, to move from one world of desire/orientation to another in search of more intense or different sexual sensation. But, if standards of normality and pathology no longer apply to sexuality to the extent that they once did, the contemporary demand for fitness, applied to sexuality, causes individuals to question whether their pleasures and sensations measure up (to an inherently indefinable and impossible standard). The consequence is heightened anxiety around sexuality. Never sure if sexual pleasure has been maximized, liquid modern individuals may wonder if they might find heightened pleasure by pursuing untried directions. 'What yesterday was considered normal and thus satisfactory may today be found worrying, or even pathological and calling for remedy' (2000: 79).

Bauman views anxiety as a pervasive affliction of liquid modern individuals. In contrast to Freud's view that psychic misery stemmed from the overwhelming pressure of ideals and the repression of desire and individual freedom, Bauman, in Durkheimian fashion, views contemporary individuals as tormented more by the *absence* of ideals (2001: 43).

This postmodern anxiety pervades many areas of life, including gender and sexuality. As indicated by Bauman's discussion of fitness, liquid modern individuals have every reason to be insecure about their sexuality, but in a quite different way than a person of the earlier modern era. Sexual insecurity in the earlier modern era, Bauman suggests, manifested itself in the form of fear of repressed desires or transgression of sexual norms. The sort of sexual insecurity Bauman sees as increasingly prominent in the current period, however, is insecurity concerning the capacity of one's own expressions, experiences, and orientations of sexuality to generate the most complete satisfaction. The nagging doubt is that one's own sexuality is somehow limited and that 'precious kinds of sensations have been missed' (2001: 232). It is not worry about being perverted or not fitting the mold, but rather the new kind of worry may be about being *too normal* (or, according to liquid modern standards, too limited). According to the logic of liquid modernity, 'normal' sexuality is more cause for insecurity than is the practice of more varied and 'unconventional' sexualities. In the same way that the ability to enjoy a diverse cuisine is valued as an indication of a more expansive and refined capacity for enjoyment, so it is with sexuality. In liquid modernity, everyone wants to be a gourmet.

According to liquid modern rationality, gender and sexual identities are alterable, transient, and non-final. This too, as Bauman sees it, is cause for anxiety.

> There is always a suspicion – even if it is put to sleep and dormant for a time – that one is living a lie or a mistake; that something crucially important has been overlooked, missed, neglected, left untried and unexplored; that a vital obligation to one's own authentic self has not been met, or that some chances of unknown happiness completely different from any happiness experienced before have not been taken up in time and are bound to be lost forever if they continue to be neglected.
>
> (Bauman 2004: 55)

On the one hand, the fear of missed pleasures or of 'wrong' orientation may create a feeling of unsettledness and fear of commitment in relationships. On the other hand, the anxiety-provoking awareness of the possibility of superior sensations and sexual experiences may also be self-protective, allowing the individual to deflect blame when relationships fail. Rather than attributing relationship breakup to communication failure, bad behavior, or, in general, failure to seize the opportunities for fulfillment within it, the individual can, with a clearer conscience, blame it on mistaken choice (possibly a mistaken choice of sexual orientation but, more commonly, a mistaken choice of partner). Both tendencies – fear of commitment and suspicion of mistaken choice as a cause of relationship dissatisfaction – contribute to the precariousness of human bonds.

Liquid modern relationships and gender equality: contradictions and discontents

Drawing on the terminology of Anthony Giddens (1992), Bauman speaks of the 'pure relationship', 'confluent love', and 'plastic sexuality' as manifestations of the commoditization and consumerization of human relationships. Giddens sees these tendencies as vehicles of emancipation, taking the burdensome component of obligation out of intimate partnerships, instead promoting mutual satisfaction as the sole basis for continuation of partnerships. Because each individual in a partnership maintains the freedom to opt out of the relationship if not satisfied, Giddens believes that the pure relationship makes for more egalitarian relationships. If both partners are free to leave if they are unsatisfied, it becomes far less likely that one may dominate, exploit, or ignore the wishes of the other without consequence; freedom to choose, seemingly, places an inherent limit on inequality.

Even if the new relational model increases gender equality in relationships, however, Bauman seems less than enthusiastic about its promises and possibilities. First, as this new relational model increases expectations for satisfaction in intimate relationships and makes increasingly available the option of opting out, intimate partnerships become more vulnerable. At least a portion of the increased rates of divorce in contemporary societies in comparison to earlier modern societies can be attributed to increased expectations of happiness in relationships and social acceptability of breaking commitments, a point Giddens fully acknowledges. But if this represents increased freedom of choice and opportunity to pursue fulfilment, one might argue, is this not a good thing? Maybe, but Bauman points out that freedom of choice, when exercised to terminate a relationship, is rarely a free choice of *both* partners: 'changing identity may be a private affair, but it always includes cutting off certain bonds and canceling certain obligations; those on the receiving side are seldom consulted, let alone given the chance to exercise free choice' (2003: 89–90).

Second, while the emergence of this new relational model affects intimate bonds at all class levels, Bauman argues that socioeconomic position shapes the experience of this new freedom to exercise choice; some are freer than others to exercise choice and are better equipped to bear the consequences of bad choices. The 'pure relationship' may be more emancipating and less threatening, Bauman suggests, for the lavishly endowed mobile elite who have sufficient resources to 'cut their losses', working out divorce settlements and financial provisions that leave everybody involved financially secure, comfortable, and well-equipped to move on with their lives. If the elite possess the resources to take the financial sting out of what may be emotionally painful to the less willing partner (and the children), however, the new relational model places those with a more modest endowment of financial resources in a much more precarious situation. Among the 'poor and the powerless,' Bauman points out, 'the new style partnership with its fragility of marital contract and the "purification" of the union of all but the "mutual satisfaction" function spawns much misery, agony and human suffering and an ever-growing volume of broken, loveless and prospectless lives' (2003: 90).

Taking the issue of resources out of the equation, however, the consumerization of intimacy and sexuality produces its own contradictions and discontents, in Bauman's analysis. When we treat human relationships as we do any other object of consumption, the prospects for long-term commitments are undermined. Liquid modern individuals are trained to adopt the model of shopping and the patterns of contemporary consumerism in just about every facet of their lives. In the same way that we are unskilled in maintaining and repairing consumer goods, tending to throw away and buy new, so are we lacking in the kind of life training and the mindset that would facilitate the long-term maintenance and repair of human relationships. Our stance towards committed intimate relationships is ambivalent and contradictory. On the one hand, yearning for intimacy and looking to relationships to relieve loneliness, insecurity, and uncertainty, many may wish for a 'till-death-do-us-part' sort of guarantee. On the other hand, long-term commitments *create* a great deal of insecurity, often threatening our sense of autonomy, in part by constraining our ability to remain full-fledged shoppers. Long-term commitments contradict the logic of consumerism, and we may find the restrictions thereby placed on our ability to remain open to new and more satisfying romantic possibilities or even to alternative self-identities to be jarring. For similar reasons, Bauman argues, many men and women experience great anxiety around the choice of whether or not to have children; children, as Bauman puts it, 'compromise the priorities of one's own preferences' (2003).

In addition to the contradiction between committed relationships and the logic of consumerism, another difficulty in human partnerships stems from their normative deregulation. As institutionalized patterns of human relationships lose legitimacy, contemporary partnerships may become increasingly embattled. Bauman (2001) refers to 'family violence' as an example of a distinctively 'postmodern' or 'new' form of violence, increasingly experienced as a threat in contemporary families. What makes family violence new is that its definition stems from the delegitimation of previously unquestioned patterns of relationships – i.e. male dominance and parental authority. Given the delegitimation of institutionalized coercion in family relationships, what once was unquestioned in the past is now increasingly recast as violence. Domestic violence, marital rape, and child abuse are literal examples, as these are phenomena that have come to be understood as violence as male dominance and unconditional parental authority have become less legitimate. But Bauman's use of the term violence here is not only literal, but also includes a wide range of relational behavior that might be interpreted as violating, disrespectful, selfish, or hurtful. Until legitimacy is established, one partner's selfishness or inconsiderateness, for example, may be seen as a sort of violence, using Bauman's non-literal definition of the term. Even if a relational pattern is accepted for a time as legitimate, it may at any time be reclassified as illegitimate (and, hence, violent in Bauman's sense) at the point that one partner no longer accepts the established pattern. Bauman suggests that the fluid, flexible, and non-patterned nature of contemporary relationships results in widespread use of 'reconnaissance by battle' strategies, where partners test their will against one another in an attempt to establish the legitimacy of a desired pattern.

The disruption of the unquestioned legitimacy of power hierarchies in human partnerships has been one of the central aims of feminism and may be welcomed, from a feminist perspective, not only for increasing gender equality but also for enhancing intimacy. Not addressing explicitly the question of the relationship between the disruption of institutionalized coercion and gender equality, however, Bauman highlights the emotional and interpersonal costs of embattlement and heightened suspicion of violence. 'The suspicion of violence is itself an ample source of anxiety: as the problem of legitimacy stays permanently unsolved and debatable, no demand likely to arise from the circumstances of sharing space, home or life is free from the charge of overt or hidden violence' (2001: 214).

Liquid sexualities: contradictions and discontents

Whereas the 'pure relationship' rests solely on the mutual satisfaction and feelings of love of the partners and implies no commitment beyond the point when mutual satisfaction ceases or love wanes, 'pure sex' rests on less than this. What Bauman calls the 'erotic revolution' has advanced the pursuit of sexual pleasure as an end in itself to the level of a cultural norm (2001: 223). In the earlier period of modernity, eroticism was limited, at least in its more socially respectable outlets, to sex in its reproductive function or, alternatively, linked to love and not to sex (2001: 222). In the liquid modern era, however, eroticism has been liberated from both sexual reproduction and love as a general cultural norm. This erotic revolution has occurred, according to Bauman, for a couple of reasons: first, because of the decline of the panoptic model for maintaining social order and the rise of social integration through seduction, advertising, and need creation (2001: 224–5); and second, because of a wider postmodern cultural transformation involving a tendency to cut off the present from both past and future (2001: 230).

Like pure relationships, however, pure sex is itself a source of anxiety, uncertainty, contradiction, and disappointment. One source of anxiety/disappointment stems from the gap between the dominant cultural view of sexuality as a source of the highest human fulfillment and its actual capacity to fulfill. According to the dominant cultural view, there is no upper limit to the heights of sexual pleasure and human fulfillment through sex. Accordingly, the culture encourages individuals to be sexual sensation-seekers, searching for ever deeper and more pleasurable sensation. Given the emphasis on sexual pleasure as an end-in-itself and its release from the shackles of reproduction and relational commitment, 'no-strings-attached-sexuality' is not only increasingly acceptable but also encouraged. The difficulty, as Bauman sees it, is that 'liberated' sex – the supposed ticket to the heights of sexual pleasure and the summit of human fulfillment – is limited in its ability to deliver.

Pure sex, Bauman points out, is focused narrowly on orgasm, and, accordingly, the height of the pleasure is limited by the 'inborn monotony and inflexibility of sex (sex, let us remember, being a phenomenon of nature and not of culture)' (2001: 227). Pure sex, if there is such a thing at all, is nothing other than a bodily sensation. Sex, thus, necessarily falls far short of expectations, in much the same way that most objects of consumption in a consumerist society fail to fulfill the illusory images of human power, happiness, well-being, and other desirable states of mind or being that advertising attaches to them. Sex, Bauman argues, is thus not so much liberated as overloaded with expectations beyond its capacity to fulfill (2003: 47).

Yet, in much the same way that unfulfilled consumers keep on shopping, disappointment with sex only seems to fuel the continual chase for more pleasurable sexual sensations. So that contemporary sensation-seekers may be unconstrained in their pursuits, it is essential, Bauman argues, that eroticism not be tied (down) to love or sexual reproduction. In liquid modern fashion, pure sex keeps contemporary men and women 'on the move', maintaining flexibility, freedom to experiment, and openness to ever new and more pleasurable sexual sensations. As sexuality has become so liberated, however, it has simultaneously lost its ability to fulfill the yearning for union with another human being, which Bauman sees as an inherent aspect of the *human* sex drive. In Bauman's view, sex fulfills (beyond the pleasure of bodily sensation) by means of its connection with 'love, security, permanence, immortality-through-continuation of kin' – precisely those things from which pure sex has been liberated.

Not only is sex 'orphaned by Eros' and 'bereaved by the future', as Bauman puts it, in reference to the limitations of pure sex identified above, but even those most committed to 'no-strings attached' sexuality may experience considerable anxiety around sex. One anxiety stems from the ambiguity surrounding any sexual encounter. The 'most fearsome of fears', Bauman says, is the uncertainty of the meaning of a sexual encounter. Pure sex cannot be purely pure, for the simple fact that two human beings, inherently meaning-making creatures, are involved. Given the ambiguity of the cultural emphasis on detached sexuality, however, sexual partners are provided with no clear, shared framework through which to interpret their shared sex (at least not unless or until they establish a patterned relationship). Anxiety in the 'no-strings-attached' sexual encounter, however, stems from not knowing what the other has in mind, from uncertainty as to one's own interpretation or wishes, and from concern about the consequences of a mismatch of expectations. 'The entitlements of sexual partners have become the prime site of anxiety. What sort of commitment, if any, does the union of bodies entail?' (2003: 51). In the marital bedroom or in the brothels of the earlier modern age, the meaning of sex was clear. Today, however, as an increasing amount of sex occurs outside of these clearly defined contexts, the meaning of the sexual encounter may be a source of uncertainty and anxiety. Marriage may banish the uncertainty, Bauman points out, but at a price that may seem to an increasing number of people as too high, given the cultural emphasis on liberated sexual sensation-seeking.

Freedom of sexual experimentation and the indeterminacy of sexual identity, for Bauman, is another source of anxiety for liquid modern men and women. Gender and sexual indeterminacy, in liquid modernity, become a source of anxious soul-searching, both because they are increasingly viewed as open to individual choice but also because of the fear that a wrong choice might cause missing out on heightened pleasure (2001: 232). According to the culture of liquid modernity, sexual identities, like other aspects of postmodern identities, should remain flexible; fixed or stable sexual identities are, according to this cultural view, a sign of maladjustment. Insofar as sexuality is no longer normatively regulated and sexual pleasure is pursued for its own sake, Bauman argues, there is no reason that the pursuit of new and more pleasurable sexual sensation should not lead to experimentation with other-than-heterosexual activities, as there is always the possibility that 'alteration of gender/sexuality might be the solution' to unsatisfactory sexual sensations (2001: 232). The liquid modern sensation-seeker, Bauman suggests, stretches his or her bodily sexual equipment to its maximum potential 'by trying one by one all known kinds of "sexual identity", and perhaps inventing still more on the way' (2004: 85).

But, once again, we return to the basic contradiction of liquid sexualities: how free, detached, flexible, and 'on the move' can contemporary sexual sensation-seekers be and still expect to find in sexuality the summit of human fulfillment? The failure of liquid sexualities to fulfill, as Bauman sees it, stems fundamentally from the application of consumer rationality to human sexuality and intimacy. In the same way that contemporary shoppers fail to find fulfillment in a purchase that is any deeper than the momentary pleasure of wish fulfillment, shopping for new and better sexual sensation tends towards the same shortcomings. 'Today's agonies of homo sexualis are those of homo consumens. They have been born together. If they ever go away, they will march shoulder to shoulder' (2003: 49).

Consumerism, inequality, and the limits of identity politics

As we have seen, the dominance of consumer rationality is crucial for understanding the deregulation of identity and desire, the emergence of the 'pure relationship' and the 'liberation' of sexuality, and the increasing flexibility and fragility of identities and relationships in the contemporary age. Bauman's lack of enthusiasm about increasing deregulation around gender and sexuality can be understood, accordingly, in terms of his more general analysis of the limits of consumer choice. Freedom of consumer choice is no freedom at all when one does not have the money, and has no reasonable prospects of gaining the money, to buy what one wants. Speaking generally of the limits of increased individualization and choice, Bauman states:

> The self-assertive ability of individualized men and women falls short, as a rule, of what genuine self-constitution would require. As Leo Strauss has observed, the other face of unencumbered freedom is insignificance of choice – the two faces conditioning each other: why bother to prohibit what is anyway of little consequence? A cynical observer would say that freedom comes when it no longer matters. There is a nasty fly of impotence in the sweet ointment of the kind of freedom that has been shaped through the pressures of individualization: that impotence is felt as all the more odious and upsetting in view of the empowerment that freedom was expected to deliver and guarantee.
> (Bauman 2001: 48)

Although this point is well understood by social scientists and social critics, this sort of critique of individualization and freedom of choice is much more readily applied when thinking about class and economic inequalities. Could it also be helpful, however, for thinking about the gains of gender and sexual liberation movements? Would it also be accurate to say that the (partial) lifting of restrictive norms around gender and sexuality came when they no longer mattered or mattered less – i.e. at precisely the moment of the global elite's escape from local and national boundaries, as social inequality and injustice intensified on a global scale, and as the economic lives of most men and women became increasingly vulnerable since the early 1970s.

Bauman's cynical stance towards the value of gender and sexual deregulation can be understood not only in terms of his critique of deregulation as a basis of freedom but also in terms of his critique of 'identity politics'. Bauman views the emergence of identity politics as a reflection of the splintering of social discontent, the increasing inability of contemporary individuals to envision a 'good society' and the increased tendency to focus on smaller group or category-related causes. The tendency and limitation of identity politics, in Bauman's view, is to focus on stigma and recognition but to pay relatively little attention to issues of money and class. Bauman finds Richard Rorty's (1998) critique of the cultural left and the identity-based movements, in this regard, on the mark. As Rorty puts it in reference to the cultural left and those who practice identity politics, 'they prefer not to talk about money', focusing more on a cultural mindset rather than a set of economic arrangements. In Rorty's view, as in Bauman's, we need to talk less about stigma and more about money.

Bauman portrays a world in which individuals, at least the more privileged of them, have ample opportunity to experiment with a wide range of identities and styles of gender and sexuality. Identity politics' focus on recognition, or the challenge of hierarchical gender/sexuality dichotomies, as evident in the work of Judith Butler and others, reflects a socio-economically privileged position, in Bauman's view. Recognition, he argues, may be what one or other sector of the successful misses most, as they struggle to 'raise the respect and adulation they enjoy to the level of the economic heights they have already gained' (2004: 37). For a large and growing portion of the planet, Bauman argues, '"recognition" is a nebulous idea and will remain nebulous as long as money is shunned as a topic of conversation' (2004: 37).

For Bauman, the core issue is not the value attributed to various identities, but rather stratification of access to the (economic and political) resources necessary to make identity choice possible and effective.

> Let me note that identification is also a powerful factor in stratification; one of its most divisive and sharply differentiating dimensions. At one pole of the emergent global hierarchy are those who can compose and decompose their identities more or less at will, drawing from the uncommonly large, planet-wide pool of offers. At the other pole are crowded those whose access to identity choice has been barred, people who are given no say in deciding their preferences and who in the end are burdened with identities enforced and imposed *by others*; identities which they themselves resent but are not allowed to shed and cannot manage to get rid of. Stereotyping, humiliating, dehumanizing, stigmatizing identities . . . . Most of us are suspended uneasily between those two poles, never sure how long our freedom to choose what we desire and renounce what we resent will last, or whether we will be able to keep the position we currently enjoy for as long as we would find it comfortable and desirable to hold it.
>
> (Bauman 2004: 38)

Identity may be a source of anxiety at all socioeconomic levels, but the nature of the anxiety (and the amount of joy added to the mix) differs in crucial ways. Those who are most loosely attached to their identities and who experience the most pleasure in the constructing and reconstructing of their individualized identities with successful outcomes, in Bauman's analysis, are typically located at the top of the global power hierarchy. Even for them, however, anxiety cannot be put to rest. The ability to shed old identities and put on new ones at will requires money, in large part because of the central role of consumption in their construction and reconstruction. For most people, access to the steady flow of money necessary to participate fully and continually in the consumer market requires having a well-paid job. But, since no position in liquid modern society is solid, even those who are more favorably positioned must be concerned (and often are anxious) about maintaining their own 'use-value' in a rapidly changing economic marketplace (Bauman 2005: 2). They must be hyper-vigilant in constructing, revising, and revamping identities, in shifting directions and charting new paths, in an effort to maintain their marketability in the rapidly changing global marketplace. The anxiety of these more favorably positioned individuals, however, stems from the perception that their own choices make a difference, but not always in ways they are able to predict or control. So, while they may feel a freedom to choose their identities and to change them as they wish, their anxiety is in their uncertainty about whether they have made the right or best choices.

For the 'global underclass', however, identity choice is not so much a reality. They, like many of the masses in the middle, remain 'stuck' and 'fixed' in their 'no-choice, no-questions-asked, assigned or imposed but in any case "overdetermined" identities' (2005: 26). Lacking the resources, capacities, and access to consumer markets necessary for the continual re-fashioning of identity, such individuals are likely to find painful the assault on their stable identities that the new individualization represents. They may resist individualization and hold tightly to their existing identities, yet, to the extent that they have been exposed to liquid modern culture, cannot help but feel the devaluation of their 'outdated models' of identity. Their anxiety, or fear, concerns the realistic possibility (or, worse, realization) of being consigned to the waste heap of society, deprived and devalued. For those in the middle, the anxieties are a mixture of those experienced by the privileged and the poor (2005).

Bauman and feminism

Relating his ideas to feminist critiques of identity, Bauman argues that there is nothing particularly new or radical about feminists' idea that identity is provisional, cultural rather than natural, and open to change. This, in his view, is the essence of modern thinking. Even if gender and sexuality were, in the earlier modern era, thought to be natural and held off-limits from modernizing tendencies, Bauman sees no reason why gender, sexuality, and even size, shape, and sex of the body should 'remain for long exceptions resistant to this all-embracing modern tendency' (2004: 84) Rather than viewing the idea of the provisional nature of identity as discordant with common ways of thinking, Bauman suggests, most people today assume identity is provisional. 'The freedom to change any aspect and trapping of individual identity is something most people deem today to be attainable right away, or at least they view it as a realistic prospect for the near future' (2004: 84) In contrast to the earlier modern era, identity transformation is much easier and faster, so long as one has the money to buy the gear 'waiting for you in the shops to transform you in no time into the character you want to be, want to be seen being and want to be recognized as being' (2004: 84). This liquid lightness of being requires not only the money to buy identity paraphernalia, but also assumes a position of sufficient privilege that one is unburdened with the 'identities enforced and imposed by others'.

One of the major aims of feminism and sexual liberation movements has been to 'de-naturalize' gender and sexuality, to show that there is nothing at all natural about either but that both are instead a product of culture. Gender is not something that we *have* or *are*, but rather, to use a well-known idea in feminist theory and the sociology of gender, we 'do gender' (West and Zimmerman 1987). Gender is a product of a culturally guided doings, performances, or enactments in a multitude of settings. Accordingly, if we 'do gender', then we can 'undo gender' as well, as the title of one of Judith Butler's (2004) recent books highlights. For Bauman, however, there are problems with this framework.

Bauman argues that the nature/culture opposition is no longer an appropriate way to think about current issues surrounding gender and sexuality. In the current age, Bauman argues, natural traits are seen as increasingly open to human manipulation, whereas culture increasingly 'stands for the inherited part of identity that neither could nor should be tinkered with' (2003: 54). Culture no longer implies 'it is a matter of choice' and nature no longer implies 'humans cannot help it and can do nothing about it'; the nature/culture debate no longer overlaps with the more central question about choice in the current period. Accordingly, in Bauman's view, the feminist emphasis on denaturalizing gender (or sexuality) is beside the point. 'The true point of contention is the extent to which various types of sexual proclivities/preferences/identities are flexible, alterable, and dependent on the subject's choice' (2003: 54).

In the liquid modern era, in Bauman's view, it is clear that gender/sexuality is flexible, alterable, and dependent on the subject's choice, at least in theory. Insofar as denaturalization (removal of the constraint of nature) and deregulation (removal of the constraint of culture) have been viewed as primary aims of gender and sexual liberation, then, these aims have been (or will be) achieved as a natural outcome of liquid modern rationality. The difficulty for individuals now that these constraints have been removed, however, is the lack of any solid basis of identity – neither biology nor culture, in other words, can authorize identity. The nature/culture question may have bearing on whether individuals choose medical intervention or self-training to alter their identities, behavior, or life-experience. In either case, however, individuals know that their identities and their lives can be otherwise and worry that their chosen identities or life paths are missing something essential to their happiness or well-being.

Implicit in feminist theorizing are quite a range of feminist responses to Bauman's ideas and, in particular, the more specific points he makes about gender and sexuality. Here, I will highlight a few basic issues. In the first place, most contemporary feminists share Bauman's view of the importance of resources, money, and economic arrangements. In fact, contemporary feminists and sociologists of gender focus quite centrally on institutional bases of gender inequality and gender inequalities in resources; feminists and sociologists of gender have long emphasized the insufficiency of approaches to understanding or combating gender inequality that focus only on cultural beliefs, values, and mindsets – e.g. gender socialization, gender ideologies, (gendered) psychic structures. Further, while many feminists and sociologists of gender focus attention on micro-social contexts of gender inequality such as family, intimacy, and sexuality, most do not see changes in these realms to be sufficient to eliminate gender inequality on a broader scale.

However, most feminists and sociologists of gender do find cultural beliefs, values, mindsets, and patterns of relationships in families, intimacy, and sexuality to be important dimensions of gender inequality. While many feminists today agree with Bauman about the limits of identity politics with its focus on issues of stigma and recognition (when these exclude consideration of economic inequality and the need for redistribution), many might also find Bauman's remarks to be overly dismissive of the significance of stigma as a basis of injustice and of the importance of recognition as a priority for people whose lives are shaped by their identification with a devalued or stigmatized social category or group. For most feminist theorists today, cultural injustice *and* economic injustice are both significant and often intertwined dimensions of social inequality, and both recognition *and* redistribution are necessary to address social inequality (Fraser 1996). Certainly, recognition may be unrealizable or elusive for the most economically disadvantaged, if money is ignored. Yet, this does not mean that issues of stigma and recognition are concerns only to those with great economic privilege. Worldwide, women who attempt to gain access to more lucrative male-dominated jobs (e.g. mining, construction) suffer gender-based discrimination, hostility, and harassment; most generally pour into lower paid and female-dominated jobs, at least in part because they know the persecution they would face were they to attempt access to higher paying male-dominated jobs. Stigma is clearly at issue here, and recognition (in contexts such as these, and many others) entails not only an increase in respect but also, perhaps more importantly, an opportunity to make a better living and live a better life.

Further, *if* Bauman is talking about the actual conditions of life in advanced societies today and not about the potential impact (on gender and sexuality) of the expansion of liquid modern rationality into more and more areas of life, most feminist theorizing suggests that he overestimates the extent of normative deregulation of sexuality and gender and that he underestimates the potential benefits for women and non-heterosexuals of such deregulation. The idea of gender as *regulated* – and regulated, at all levels of social life, in ways that reinforce gender inequality – is central in much of feminist thinking about gender and gender inequality. Contrary to Bauman's suggestion that the psychic life of liquid modern men and women is increasingly free of the pressure of authoritative ideals or internalized domination, for example, psychoanalytic-feminist theory and a substantial body of sociological research on gender in families, intimate relationships, and sexuality would suggest otherwise. Further, there is a vast body of feminist theory and sociological research that questions the assumption of psychically internalized domination, but instead finds that gendered patterns of behavior and gender inequality are secured, in large part, by normative social control in a wide variety of social contexts. From feminist theory and sociological research on gender and sexuality, we can derive a long list of the ways in which gender and sexuality are regulated. Even if gender and sexuality are more open to choice now than in the earlier modern era, gender and sexuality, most feminists would argue, are far from deregulated.

Apart from the question of the extent of regulation or deregulation of gender and sexuality, feminists would also be likely to find Bauman overly dismissive of the potential value of the deregulation (or liberation) of gender and sexuality. Bauman does not, of course, deny that the lives of some people may be made better, happier, or more fulfilled as a result of increased freedom and lifting of normative regulation in various spheres of life. His point, instead, is that identity politics tends to splinter social critique, leading to a focus on a 'better life for each today' without any concern for a 'better life for all tomorrow'. Bauman is deeply critical of the tendency within contemporary societies to personalize politics, or, in other words, to make the improvement of the quality of the individual's life the sole aim of politics. If Bauman seems dismissive of the aims and gains of feminism, then, it is likely because he sees within contemporary gender and sexual liberation movements a tendency to personalize the political, ignoring economic and political inequality as well as the relationship between gender inequality and other systems of social inequality. This tendency, of course, is characteristic of *some* but certainly not all feminist perspectives. Internally, feminists have been critical of tendencies within feminism to focus on the 'personal' to the deficit of the 'political', subverting and individualizing the meaning of the 1970s feminist slogan, 'the personal is political'. Many contemporary feminists, thus, share Bauman's critique, reversing Habermas, of the colonization of the political by the personal.

The most significant point of contention between Bauman and feminism, however, is his basic argument that normative deregulation of gender (and sexuality) and increasing freedom of choice represent no threat to global power. From a feminist perspective, this viewpoint must seem to minimize the significance of gender as a system of inequality. It is true that the rich (qua rich, setting aside rich men's gender politics) do not care who is doing what; whether the CEO is a man or woman, for example, matters little to the stakeholders so long as the growth of profits accelerates. But feminists would say that it is also true that men qua men have a stake in protecting their preserve – not just to make symbolic statements about recognition and not just to preserve masculine identity but also to maintain a monopoly of money, wealth, and power. Marx (and until the feminist Marxists came along, most Marxists) argued that the interests of capitalists would trump all other interests . . . from nation to race to (if he had thought about it) gender. Bauman, seemingly, shares the basic Marxist assumption that capitalism is the determining structure of power. Gender and sexual regulation, and perhaps gender and sexual *inequality* as well, seem to be treated, in the fashion of mid-century Marxism, as 'epiphenomenal'. From a feminist perspective, this may be Bauman's great oversight; patriarchy does not appear in Bauman's analysis as a structure of power or inequality in its own right.

From Bauman's perspective, not only does gender and sexual regulation represent no threat to the global elite, but it is even useful by releasing a steady flow of unimpeded desire and wish into the consumer market. The basic tendency of liquid modernity, in Bauman's view, is to reduce any barrier to the free flow of the energies that feed the consumer market. If gender and sexual norms reduce the free flow of desire and wish, then, they must, along with any other restrictive barrier, be subjected to liquid modernity's melting powers – just as Marx had argued. The good news, from the perspective of feminists (or anybody who has suffered under the oppressive weight of restrictive gender and sexual standards), is that, if liquid modern rationality continues to spread, gender and sexual restrictions can be expected to become a thing of the past – at least in those parts of the world where the consumer class lives and where consumerist rationality has taken hold or will take hold in the future. Gender and sexual freedom may be resisted by fundamentalists, whose life circumstances (and limited prospects for joining the consumer class) cause them to resist all things liquid modern, but not by the power-wielders of the world. The bad news, however, is that gender and sexual liberation movements lose their critical edge. From a liquid modern standpoint, Bauman suggests, there is nothing at all subversive about denaturalizing and deregulating gender and sexuality; each are fully compatible with the dominant liquid modern culture (even if the denaturalizing and deregulating of gender and sexuality *do* undermine male and heterosexual privilege). Further, if the gains of gender and sexual liberation occur as global inequality intensifies and as the lives of an ever-growing number of men *and* women become more precarious and vulnerable, then, is there not, as Bauman so eloquently puts it, that 'nasty fly of impotence in the sweet ointment of freedom?'

Reading Bauman: empirical reality or cultural logic?

If we read Bauman's analysis of liquid modernity as a description of people's lives in the current period in advanced capitalist societies, there is much that might seem questionable. In the actual lives of contemporary men and women, for example, there is little evidence to suggest that gender and sexuality typically are experienced as unstable or difficult to 'hold onto'. Even if social norms surrounding gender and sexuality have loosened significantly, expanding the range of socially acceptable options, this does not necessarily mean that, for individuals, gender and sexuality necessarily become any more unstable and open to experimentation and choice. Even if experimentation is more common among adolescents and young adults than it used to be, most people, usually before they reach their thirties, establish a sexual orientation and a gender style and stick with it.

Relatedly, Bauman suggests that, as distinctions between healthy and perverse sexuality blur, 'normal' sexuality increasingly becomes a cause of worry. The new ideal, he suggests, is to experience new and different sensations along diverse avenues. Sticking to one sexual orientation, one gender style or gender-style preference increasingly becomes a sign of limitation, as sexual diversity *within* an individual becomes increasingly desirable. Certainly, this viewpoint is out there, at the very least reflecting the perspective of 'queer theorists' (who emphasize the multiplicity of sexualities and challenge what they see as the dominant dichotomous, hierarchical, and normalizing way of thinking about sexuality). There is no evidence, however, to suggest that this has become the dominant way of thinking. Queer theory exists, it could be argued, precisely because 'normal' sexuality continues to be dominant (and hardly cause for worry for most people). Yet, if liquid modern rationality were to penetrate fully into the realm of sexuality, *might* it become the dominant way of thinking? Accordingly, Bauman might suggest, even if the ideas of queer theory would seem radical to most people today, they could be expected to become common sense in the future, given their compatibility with the dominant rationality of liquid modernity. Perhaps, Bauman might suggest, the emergence of queer theory and related postmodern understandings of sexuality are a *product* of the dominant consumer rationality, not so much radical as merely a few steps ahead of the less liquidly modern sexual understandings of most people today.

Bauman, as we have seen, suggests that the liquid modern imperative to stay 'on the move', unconstrained in the pursuit of more satisfying, pleasurable, or promising alternatives creates especially intense ambivalence and anxiety as they face prospects for marriage, relationship commitment, or having children. Even if these are painful decisions for some, however, the reality is that most people do not doubt that they want to marry (or, if not heterosexual, establish an equally committed relationship with a same-sex partner). They may have doubts about one or another potential partner, but most do not doubt that they want a lifetime mate. Among heterosexual married couples of childbearing age, further, most have children as a matter of course without a great deal of anxiety about the choice itself. Most people choose to marry and have children, and, while everyone knows that there is some decreased personal freedom, most agree that it is worth it.

Certainly, consumer rationality has seeped into the realm of family, intimacy, and interpersonal bonds, even if it has not yet come to dominate. And Bauman may be right, further, that the contradiction between the demands of the consumer rationality (pushing for impermanence and loosely tied relations) and the desires that many people have for durable and trustworthy human bonds is a source of increasing ambivalence. There are *some* people, surely, who feel this ambivalence and anxiety every bit as intensely as Bauman portrays, and for who the choice to marry or have children must seem like a terrible compromise. Perhaps this ambivalence and anxiety is greater in those places and among those segments of the population where liquid modern rationality has most deeply penetrated. But, nonetheless, this ambivalence does not seem to characterize the experience of most people today.

It may be more appropriate, then, to read Bauman's analysis of liquid modernity as a logic or tendency, farther along in its realization in some spheres of life, in some stages of life, in some geographical locations, and in certain social classes more than in others. As a description of changing relations between capital and labor, of the shifting aims of politics and social control, and of the increasing dominance of consumer rationality in the lives and minds of contemporary individuals, Bauman's analysis may seem more fitting as an empirical description. It is less clear, however, that the melting powers of liquid modernity, or the dominant consumer rationality, have penetrated so deeply into the spheres of gender, sexuality, family, and intimacy. Even as he sometimes speaks as though they have, Bauman also indicates that the logic of liquid modernity has not fully captured these realms and enters into them with contradiction. While acknowledging current expansion of freedom and choice with respect to gender and sexuality, Bauman speaks of their complete dissolution as constraining categories only as a logical extension of the dominant rationality of liquid modernity.

If the melting powers of liquid modernity are applied more broadly and *if* liquid modern consumer rationality continues to dominate and to spread into the realms of gender, sexuality, family, intimacy, and relational bonds of all sorts, we could expect that the tendencies that Bauman has described in each of these areas to become a reality to a far greater extent than currently may be the case. As noted, however, Bauman suggests that there may be some human species imperatives – i.e. the human drive reflected in sexuality, intimacy, and parent–child relations for 'love, security, permanence, immortality-through-continuation-of-kin' – that will resist the logic of liquid modernity.

On balance, Bauman accords far greater weight to the anxieties, uncertainties, and miseries of liquid modern life than he does to its potential joys and pleasures, providing further evidence of his belief in contradiction between human imperatives and the imperatives of liquid modernity. 'Today's *agonies* of homo sexualis are the *agonies* of homo consumens' – here, Bauman reveals quite clearly his assessment of liquid modernity's damaging and violating human impact. It is by no means clear, however, that Bauman thinks human imperatives will prevail. He seems much more confident, at least for the foreseeable future, in the powers of global capitalism and the melting powers of liquid modernity.

References

Bauman, Z. (1996) Morality in the Age of Contingency. In P. Heelas, S. Lash, and P. Morris (eds) Detraditionalization: Critical Reflections on Authority *and Identity*. Cambridge, MA and Oxford: Blackwell.
Bauman, Z. (2000) *Liquid Modernity*. Cambridge: Polity Press.
Bauman, Z. (2001) *The Individualized Society.*Cambridge: Polity Press.
Bauman, Z. (2003) *Liquid Love*. Cambridge: Polity Press.
Bauman, Z. (2004) Identity: Conversations with Benedetto Vecchi. Cambridge: Polity Press.
Bauman, Z. (2005) *Liquid Life*. Cambridge: Polity Press.
Butler, J. (2004) *Undoing Gender*. New York: Routledge.
Foucault, M. (1976) *The History of Sexuality*, vol. 1. Harmondsworth: Penguin.
Foucault, M. (1977) Discipline and Punish: The Birth of the Prison. London: Allen Lane.
Fraser, N. (1996) Justice Interruptus: Critical Reflections on the *'Post-Socialist' Condition*. New York and London: Routledge.
Giddens, A. (1992) The Transformation of Intimacy: Sexuality, Love, and Eroticism in Modern Societies. Stanford, CA: Stanford University Press.
Rorty, R. (1998) Achieving Our Country: Leftist Thought in Twentieth-century America. Boston, MA: Harvard University Press.
West, C. and Zimmerman, D. H. (1987) Doing Gender. *Gender and Society* 1(2): 125–51.

CHAPTER 5

Relatively liquid interpersonal relationships in flexible work life

Poul Poder

Humans without social bonds? This is the plight of contemporary individuals living in liquid modernity, according to Bauman. He argues that interpersonal relations in friendship, love and sex and work life increasingly become characterized by disengagement, insecurity, irritability and anxiety. I read Bauman's theory of Liquid Modernity as a vision of novel developments which he perceives as possible defining features of the times to come, rather than being already empirically predominant. The aim of his analysis is to capture central trends and reflect on their significance for identity, community and morality rather than to produce well-balanced overall pictures.

Bauman claims that every form of theorizing always selects certain aspects of reality (Bauman 2004). However, the selectivity can be too selective when Bauman emphasizes merely disintegrating forces in his analysis of contemporary flexible work life. In this chapter I therefore consider integrative forces that contribute to the flexible work life, too.

I shall begin by briefly examining Bauman's overall diagnosis of interpersonal relationships in liquid modernity as background for a discussion of liquid or flexible work life. Bauman develops valuable points concerning the changing nature of work, but liquid work life might not be as corrosive as he implies. This is because post-bureaucratic organization, team work and engaged and empowering relationships between manager and employee counter the dissolving forces defining liquid modernity. Assessing Bauman's analysis of interpersonal relationships in liquid work life I apply his theory of freedom as a social relation. This relational freedom must be understood as generated socially in terms of the energetic emotion of confidence (Poder 2006). Consequently, contemporary individuals are empowered qua their interaction with managers and colleagues and not merely subjected to self-management as Bauman envisions. Empowerment should also be seen as a socially and managerially distributed resource of freedom, I suggest, as a major point that can supplement Bauman's analysis.

Insecure and consumerized interpersonal relationships

The background for understanding Bauman's analysis of contemporary interpersonal relationships is his notion of the 'political economy of insecurity' (Bauman 1999).

This notion refers to a massive de-institutionalization of economic and social conditions that undermine security in three different meanings. Individuals in liquid modernity therefore experience *insecurity* of position, entitlements and livelihood, *uncertainty* as to their continuation and future stability, and *unsafety* of their body, self and their extensions: possessions, neighbourhood and community (Bauman 2000: 161).

At the heart of contemporary life-politics lies an unquenchable desire for security. Bauman argues that people's acting on that desire rebounds in more insecurity, as they seek private and privatizing solutions which strengthen the market's deregulation of society. Thereby more insecurity becomes the end result (Bauman 1999: 23).

To live and act on the condition of insecurity is no news. The news is that almost everybody is significantly influenced by insecurity. This includes the great number of middle-class people who fear how they can support themselves as jobs become more unstable, and everybody has to work hard to maintain and develop employability to get jobs that become more and more episodic in character. Only the strongest minority of people can navigate confidently in this chaos. The world of today is full of fear, and people desperately seek to express their fear in ways which each individual hopes can be shared with others. However, insecurity works mostly as an individualizing force, as it is unclear what the next day will bring and therefore it is impossible to mobilize collectively against this insecurity (Bauman 2000: 207).

Insecurity threatens people's agency, as security is a precondition of actively acting rather than merely reacting. The weakening of any of the three ingredients of the German concept *Sicherheit* has the effect of dissipation of self-assurance, loss of trust in one's own capacity and other people's intentions, growing incapacitation, anxiety, cageyness, and a tendency to fault-seeking and fault-finding, scapegoating and aggression (Bauman 1999: 17).

Furthermore, a consumer syndrome is conquering our social relations. People increasingly perceive the world as a collection of consumer goods and see the aim of life as getting instant gratification. The consumption ethic is so strong in the liquid society that the pleasure principle has won over the reality principle. Today, the pleasure principle is the presiding judge over the reality principle (Bauman 1997: 2; Bauman 2002: 187). The consumer syndrome gradually takes hold of every kind of interhuman relationship, and this makes it more difficult, if not impossible, to establish enduring human bonds (Bauman 2005: 63, 84, 87, 108). According to Bauman this consumerization of the social world is a force of individualization, because the seeking and experiencing pleasurable and exciting moments is a very individual undertaking not easily shared with others. It is not the kind of experience that forms collective identity. In the consumer society freedom is very much defined as freedom to consume and people are caught up in seeking ever new and gratifying experiences.

Summing up, in liquid modernity individuals are abandoned by former socially integrative and institutional forces. The strong de-institutionalizing forces make everything solid disintegrate into thin air and nothing seems strong enough to secure individuals a comforting re-embedding, according to Bauman. Insecurity thus appears as the master emotion of the liquid life.

Bauman's diagnosis of interpersonal relationships contains two different messages. One message is radical in suggesting that people lose their social bonds and their capacity to relate to others. The other message is less dramatic, suggesting that liquid individuals have to establish bonds to others by engaged effort because they can no longer rely on given institutionalized bonds. Both messages can be true with respect to different areas of social life. However, when we talk of liquid work life, I contend that interpersonal relationships do not necessarily vanish. While they become more liquid or flexible they do not become completely de-institutionalized, is my argument in the following assessment of Bauman's analysis.

Aesthetic, disengaged and self-managing relationships in work life

The general features of liquid modernity such as de-institutionalization, individualization and insecurity heavily influence the interpersonal relationships in work life. But Bauman also emphasizes other features that are particularly important in understanding his analysis of liquid work life. These features are an increasingly aesthetic orientation towards work, disengaged relationship between capital and labour, and following from this an increased emphasis on employee's own self-management.

The aesthetic of consumption also increasingly defines peoples' orientation towards work. This does not mean that people value leisure time over work, but that they think of work in the same way as they think and feel about consumption. The point is to experience an exciting, stimulating and challenging form of work, and not just to have a job. Work has lost its ethical value as an activity that made humans dignified and full members of society. Rather than having eschatological trappings and metaphysical roots work has now an aesthetical significance. In liquid consumerist society desire develops desire endlessly, and people primarily worry about living an aesthetically challenging, exciting life. The personal, unique experiencing of exciting work is not easily shared with others and therefore does not contribute to the formation of collective identity. As a consequence of the aesthetic orientation to work people are further individualized (Bauman 1998, 2000).

Solid modernity has worked together with a heavy capitalism of a relatively stable engagement between capital and labour. This engagement has fostered a long-term mentality of dependency. In liquid modernity capitalism is no longer heavy in the sense of being tied to local communities like factories used to be. This condition of disengagement between labour and capital engenders a flexible working market saturated with insecurity. According to Bauman we are now living in the post-panoptical era where capital's primary power techniques are escape, slippage and elision rather than the detailed but engaged forms of surveillance characteristic of heavy modernity (Bauman 2000: 11; 2002: 33).

Disengagement also characterizes the interpersonal relationships on a more concrete level of interaction between humans. Because of the 'spectre of insecurity', which is haunting liquid modern times, people generally fear becoming socially redundant. This fear makes people comply and work 'enthusiastically' to a degree that dissolves the need for managers to apply stick-and-carrot forms of power. Managers need no longer exercise power *over* employees: 'Not much is left of the managers' management once it is up to the managed to prove their mettle and convince the managers that they won't regret hiring them. Employees have been "empowered" – the endowment which boils down to bearing responsibility for making themselves relevant and valuable to the company' (Bauman 2002: 34). As organizations work qua 'integration-by-succession-of-short-term-projects' there is no or only minimal need for control from the top. It is up to the employees to continually prove themselves worthy of employment: 'No other form of social control is more efficient than the spectre of insecurity hovering over the heads of the controlled . . . in skating over thin ice, our safety is in our speed' (Bauman 2002: 35).

This liquid form of domination is lighter compared to continuous surveillance defining the heavy modern and Taylorist organization of space. It is no longer the manager's role to direct the employees. Rather it is up to the subordinates to catch the superior's attention to convince him or her about the value of their performances (Bauman 2002: 34). The power relationship between manager and employee is disengaged and people are thrown upon their own self-management.

All in all, Bauman's analysis of work emphasizes disintegrating forces that characterize contemporary work life. His analysis highlights relevant features of flexible work life, but this deals not merely with de-institutionalization and corrosion of interpersonal relationships.

Integrative forces of flexible work life

In the following I'll discuss the significance of the post-bureaucratic organization, team work and the engaged empowerment relationship between manager and employee as integrative features of contemporary liquid work life. However, I'll start with a maybe trivial objection to Bauman's portrayal of liquid individuals as abandoned. The fact is that people *have to* work, and when people are together in organizations they often build emotional attachments characteristic of communities rather than instrumental organizations (Bauman and May 2001: 54). In work life contexts people are therefore not as 'emancipated' and abandoned as they appear as consumers on the marketplace.

Post-bureaucratic organization inviting equality, homogeneity and intimacy

Compared to traditional bureaucratically organized work life it makes sense to see project-based work life as de-institutionalized and liquid. However, most work still relies on bureaucratic features in one sense or another (Huczynski and Buchanan 2001: 496). Consequently, flexible or liquid work is best understood as situated in what has been called the post-bureaucratic organization, which refers to an organization with reduced bureaucratic structures. Rather than seeing novel features such as absence of rigid division of labour, hierarchy and rules, and decentralization, openness and empowerment as something that is realized in an organization beyond bureaucratic organization (Wilson 2004: 278) it is more reasonable to say that post-bureaucratic organization is just a name given to organizations that self-consciously *reduce* bureaucracy (Tucker 1999: 133).[1] Consequently, the post-bureaucratic organization is defined by such structural features as:

- Decentralization: considerable authority is delegated to employees' teams, which are responsible for many decisions affecting daily operation of the firm. This feature gives rise to equality among individuals working in the post-bureaucratic setting.[2]
- De-specializing, which means reducing the bureaucratic division of work which stimulates distinct subcultures across the organization. Such a reduction of specialization can come about when companies promote a homogeneous culture and can be achieved by creating internal mobility which breaks down functional barriers. It leads to growing homogeneity among individuals (Tucker 1999: 30).
- Reducing the strict separation of members' organizational and personal lives, which for example involves formation of strong interpersonal ties and friendships that extend beyond the work place. Intimacy becomes a central feature of post-bureaucratic work life where people delve into each other's personal lives (Tucker 1999: 16).

In the post-bureaucratic organization the social relations between individuals invite equality, homogeneity and intimacy (Tucker 1999: 28–31) as opposed to differentiation and impersonality in traditional bureaucratic organizations. The post-bureaucratic organization engenders a communalism, as observing others, delving into personal lives and communicating feelings become normal behaviour. In this communalism much of the self is public (Tucker 1999: 125).

Moreover, social control changes its form from discipline to what Tucker calls therapy. Discipline shrinks when inequality and social distance shrink, but social control does not. Rather than being punished, subordinates are likely to receive therapy. Several strategies are involved when management initiates therapy: (a) managers attempt to *understand differences* among employees and what is regarded as their distinctive personalities and backgrounds, (b) superiors let people help themselves as much as possible and often encourage them to talk through problems, and (c) therapy from above can also include attempts at *changing the environment* based on the assumption that self-conflicts are influenced by people's larger surroundings (Tucker 1999: 49). Instead of being disciplinarians, making sure people obey rules, managers act more like psychiatrists. In the post-bureaucratic organization, where social space is small, therapy replaces discipline. The self becomes the focus of downward social control. Psychologies are examined and individuals help themselves and discuss their problems (Tucker 1999: 66–7).

Tucker's conceptualization of the post-bureaucratic organization is based on a theory of how structures of minimized social distance engender more intimate rather than disciplinarian forms of social control (Tucker 1999). The point of stressing such a structural perspective is to suggest that certain possibilities of interaction are more likely than others, not to suggest that social structures completely determine the interaction, as other conditions such as the local history of the organization also influence people's interaction with each other.

Furthermore, the post-bureaucratic organization is characterized by an *inclusive principle* of organization. Traditional bureaucracy excludes individual features falling outside its instrumental schemes. This is not the case with post-bureaucracy which opens itself to individual features and includes them in the networks of practice 'in its urge to harness aspects of the "free spheres" of individuals' lives' (Maravelias 2003: 62). As there are no fixed roles and job descriptions, the post-bureaucratic organization requires that individuals define the tasks and how they are to be solved. This organization demands that the individual contributes to the construction of the organizational culture and the roles and identities which it implies. The post-bureaucratic organizational form cultivates freedom of identity and thereby forces the individuals to engage themselves both personally and socially (Maravelias 2003). The individual has to participate in a dedicated sense, she or he cannot merely submit to a certain role (Allvin *et al.* 2006). The personalities of individuals become more involved when they are part of deciding on the division, form and time of the jobs to be carried out. In absence of standard procedures one has to engage oneself more comprehensively to develop processes that are creative enough to provide satisfying solutions. This more ad hoc work condition produces an intensification of emotion as it can lead to both conflict-oriented emotions and more positive emotions when people succeed in working closely together (Christrup 1993: 92).

In sum, given the inclusive nature of the post-bureaucratic organization individuals are placed in a cultural void which poses challenges to them. Consequently, this type of organization is open to individuals as it invites them to participate and prove their worth. Self-exhaustion is one possibility, but self-actualization is equally so in this game (Maravelias 2003: 561). Whether self-actualization or self-exhaustion is realized depends on other additional circumstances than the organizational form itself. This point is important with respect to Bauman's analysis which stresses how the liquid individuals become overburdened with demands on self-management and lack of reassuring institutional forms.

On the basis of the above-outlined conceptualisation of the post-bureaucratic organization I want to stress that this particular inclusive organizational form pulls individuals together as it engenders equality, homogeneity and intimacy. In short, the post-bureaucratic form has institutionalized and integrative effects that counter the forces of dissolution highlighted in Bauman's analysis.[3]

Team work informally ties people together

Team work is a structural component of flexible work life and can be seen as the organizational form par excellence of flexible work life (Limborg 2002). Therefore, Bauman's analysis is limited by the fact that it does not reflect on the significance of team work organization.[4] In the context of liquid work, my argument is that team work can reduce individuals' feeling of insecurity.

According to the American sociologist Donald Gibson, informal ties become more important due to the contemporary movement toward team-based structures. He suggests that '*informal* ties may take on more importance than the formal dictates of an explicit hierarchy; that is, where in a hierarchy there are explicit rules for promotion (whether they are followed completely or not), now one's success in the organization may be based more on acceptance by informal groups' (Gibson 1997:

247). In this type of organization form 'emotional responses, though somewhat different from the overt emphasis on status differences, will nonetheless be strong, surrounding emotions of love and acceptance on the positive side, disgust and repulsion on the negative' (Gibson 1997: 247). What counts is no longer merely how one can perform in a technical sense, but how one is as a person in a broader sense. Is one attractive, 'positive', dynamic, or rather the opposite? In this form of organization competition becomes more covert with the new emphasis on informal interaction rather than on explicit discrimination on the basis of formal rules of promotion. The persons who do not fit the characteristics of the dominant in-group may face difficulties in achieving success in the team-based organization (Gibson 1997: 47). On the basis of Gibson's argument, I stress the point that the group and informal ties become essential for the recognition of the individuals. Not everybody is part of dominant in-groups, but most individuals are part of some groups and thereby tied together.

Although people work in shifting teams in flexible work life, team organization can generate group emotion and thereby make liquid individuals feel less abandoned and lost to their capacities and fate. Generation of group emotion can be explained by Collins's theory of interaction rituals, which develops a sociological understanding of the phenomenon of emotional contagion. Building on Durkheim's theory of ritual, Collins (2004: 48) argues that ritual interaction consists of four main ingredients or initiating conditions:

1 Two or more persons are assembled in the same place, so that they affect each other by their bodily presence.
2 Participants have a sense of who is taking part, as there are boundaries to outsiders.
3 Participants focus their attention upon a common object or activity, and by communicating this focus to each other they become mutually aware of each other's focus of attention.
4 They share a common mood or emotional experience.

These ingredients feed back upon each participant, and in particular on mutual focus of attention (3) and the common mood (4), and reinforce each other. One of the important outcomes of interaction rituals is group solidarity or emotion, a feeling of membership. This emotion arises when the ingredients combine and build up to high levels of mutually focused and emotionally shared attention (Collins 2004: 49).

In conclusion, the team work organization contributes to the generation of informal ties and group emotion. This can be the basis of intimacy and feeling closely related, and in this sense can be a resource of support which liquid individuals draw on, as they cope with the inbuilt insecurity of liquid modernity.

Engaged and empowering manager–employee relationship

In Bauman's vision employees are left to their own self-management and the relationship between manager and employee becomes disengaged.[5] The relationship between manager and employee is emptied of power. However, the transformation of the relationship between managers and employees is more complicated than a shift from a straightforward authoritarian relationship to a relationship without the exercising of power. The trend toward employees being left to self-management works simultaneously with the tendency that the manager–employee relationships become increasingly personally engaging, I argue, by referring to Sørhaug (1996).

Sørhaug's theory of personalization of contemporary project- and team-oriented work life suggests that employees are becoming more dependent on their leaders while they at the same time become more independent in their ways of working. The manager has less direct control over how the job is effectuated when the organization is decentralized. As more emphasis is placed on continuous learning, plurality, communicative capabilities and self-regulation of work performance, it becomes difficult to imagine or grasp the work performance as a clearly defined role. When employee personality seeks to express itself in work and organization, a circulation of total and infinite needs of recognition and confirmation is activated (Sørhaug 1996: 156).

Due to this situation, managers are to a still higher degree expected to confirm the value of the individual employee and his or her performance. When the employee is asked to devote his or her whole personality to the work, and as tasks are becoming more difficult to define in a clear-cut manner, the employee is increasingly more uncertain as to when the task has been satisfactorily fulfilled. Lacking 'objective' measures to assess job performance, the employee becomes more dependent on the manager's feedback. Moreover, the trend towards an organizational logic based on personal alliance increases the personal vulnerability in these team-oriented processes of work. Some of the trust and dependency that was formerly organized collectively and corporately in for instance clubs and factory/enterprise, is now transferred to leaders as *actual* ('personal') individuals (Sørhaug 1996: 156). This trend in working life places new demands on the leader in terms of performing a confirming and caring function. The manager becomes more important to employees in a personalized sense. The manager functions as a coach in contexts of dialogues concerning performance and wages and development plans of the individual employee (Sørhaug 1996: 156–7). In other words, in flexible work life managers are also dedicated to coaching their employees and not merely letting the 'spectre of insecurity' do the job.

Furthermore, empowerment is not necessarily as shallow as Bauman envisions, when suggesting that empowerment equals managers' abandoning employees to their own self-management. Empowerment is also about contributing to employees' feelings of confidence (and trust and loyalty – see Poder 2004). I argue that the relational nature of freedom must be understood as generated socially in terms of the energetic emotion of confidence. Consequently, empowerment is a resource of freedom which employees strive for.

Bauman underlines the relational nature of freedom, as he explains how freedom or agency is to be understood as a differential capacity of social relations. Freedom is not a generic capacity of all human beings. Rather, the condition that freedom and power are two sides of the same relationship implies that the freedom of one actor in most cases limits the freedom of other actors, as their room for acting is limited by the free action of the first-mentioned actor (Bauman 1988). Bauman's relational perspective on agency/freedom is relevant in understanding how structural positions determine when actions are dependent on others' will/freedom. However, I further develop the relational nature of freedom by theorizing social relationships as emotional in a continuous energetic sense. Certain emotions such as confidence (but also trust and loyalty) are underlying in social relationships, and they can explain how agency is defined by emotional energy, and not merely by material or symbolic resources such as money, knowledge and formal authority (Poder 2006).

My starting point for developing this idea of emotional energy as essential in understanding agency is Barbalet's theory of confidence as a basic emotion contributing to agency on a personal level of action.[6] Barbalet's emotionalization of the concept of agency has significant implications for the understanding of freedom/agency and empowerment, as I shall explain.

Confidence is energized in a fundamental sense: 'All action is ultimately founded on the actor's feeling of confidence in their capacities and the effectiveness of those capacities. The actor's confidence is a necessary source of action; without it, action simply would not occur' (Barbalet 1996: 90). This is because confidence is best understood as an emotion of self-projection that encourages one to go one's own way (Barbalet 1996: 77). Confidence can be described as assured expectation and self-projection. These two features are essential to human agency that is only possible insofar, as the individual projects his capacities into the extensive relationship of the future. According to Barbalet, confidence as an emotion relates essentially to the future, as it has the future as its object. Confidence creates a sense of security vis-à-vis the unknowable future by carrying a possible future into the present. Barbalet describes confidence as the opposite of passive emotional states such as anxiety, sorrow or despair. It is also the opposite of emotions such as shame, shyness or modesty that all operate as limiting possibilities of action (Barbalet 1996: 76). Confidence ensures the opposite of conformity, as it encourages one to follow one's own path.[7]

Confidence might not conventionally be thought of as an emotion. However, Barbalet underscores that confidence has three features normally associated with emotions: (1) a subjectively experiential aspect as one knows when one feels confident; (2) a physiological or behavioural aspect, as others can see if a person appears as confident and (3) an impulsive, motoric aspect indicated by the fact that people feeling confident often report bodily reactions or sensations such as control of muscle, deep and relaxed breathing and other pleasurable sensations. Even though confidence, understood as self-assured projection, can be treated as a purely psychological state of the individual, the phenomenon does not arise only in the consciousness of the individual.

From a sociological viewpoint, it is crucial to stress how confidence arises out of social relations where the person concerned is met with appreciation (Barbalet 1998: 86). Moreover, confidence is predicated on the fact that the acknowledging relation also provides the actor with access to relevant resources. These resources are not important because they are immediately used, but because access to them ensures that they are available in future time (Barbalet 1996: 87). In other words, confidence does not feed on acceptance and acknowledgement alone. Without access to relevant resources, the individual cannot sustain a feeling of being able to act on his or her own towards the unknowable future. Access to resources relates to the temporal point of confidence, as it is resources for *future* use that are important to form confidence. To feel confident about realizing for example a projection of oneself as becoming a manager, one needs to sense that one has access to resources of instrumental significance in such a career development. Barbalet's point about the sense of access to means of action does not concern the actual use of these, but the awareness that one is able to gain access to relevant resources. This sense of action possibilities is what helps the individual feel confident.

The generation of confidence is therefore embedded in dynamic social processes of interaction and dependency. With respect to generation of confidence, individuals are dependent on others in two ways. First, the individual person cannot force the other person to give recognition. Asking another person for his or her recognition or praise is less reassuring than unconditionally receiving this recognition. When given as a 'free' gift, recognition has a stronger impact, as it is more easily believed to be genuine (Clark 2001: 11). When delivered on request, doubts about sincerity may rise; maybe the other person said something nice just to be polite. Second, the individual person is dependent on others with respect to gaining access to the relevant future resources. Consequently, it is not the case that some persons have confidence as a stable feature of their personality and others do not. Confidence is not created by a decision of the individual. Rather, the social basis of confidence generation explains how power is involved in engendering confidence, as it is predicated on the decisions and actions of others. One's confidence, then, is in fact established by one's interaction with others.

It is important to understand how social processes like those mentioned above contribute to the formation of agency. Individuals are not agents per se as explained by Bauman's relational and sociological theory of freedom. The challenging issue is to understand what determines how much or how little agency they acquire. Agency is based on power resources such as knowledge, authority and money, but also on confidence[8]. This kind of emotional energy is a necessary, although not sufficient, constituent of agency. Confidence, though, is a decisive precondition for other power resources to be applied. Individuals who possess conventional power resources can be effectively powerless without any confidence. Such a possible combination of considerable material power resources and low confidence suggests that we conceive of the generation of emotional energy as part of power processes.

Confidence as the energetic constituent of agency is a power resource. But it is not a resource as tangible as money or formal authority. In principle individuals might have an unlimited potential of developing confidence. But on a practical level, generation of confidence must be understood from the perspective of somewhat limited resources. One reason is that unavoidably personal sympathy and antipathy make it unfeasible to acknowledge all others to the same degree. Another reason is that managers have a significant influence on who gets which resources, and thereby they perform a gatekeeper function connected to the social generation of confidence. Here, I emphasize that the capacity to energize others is not equally distributed, but influenced by the social position that individuals occupy. In organizational life superiors have a certain advantage in affecting the level of confidence of others. Managers are in charge of the distribution of resources crucial to the engendering of employees' confidence as illustrated by the example of the employee to whom the manager promised his support, if needed, in carrying out her new task. However, colleagues also energize each other, as they can express recognition, too, and open up avenues to relevant recourses of action. I am *not* suggesting that only managers contribute to the engendering of confidence, but I try to explain how different social positions also influence the generation of this form of emotional energy.[9]

As the generation of confidence is based on social relations of dependency – one cannot make up one's confidence by oneself – empowerment can be seen as an asymmetric form of power, which means that some actors have and get more of it than others. A person's mental or emotional energy is not just a matter of the individual's particular personality. Confidence is extraordinarily required in the context of empowerment, as empowerment is a matter of generating agency in the form of confidence and not merely about liberation from restricting structures. Empowerment in this basic sense is about making individuals capable of acting.

Summing up, 'freedom is privilege and power' (Bauman 1988: 27) Bauman explains. Yes, and emotional energy in the form of confidence, I add. The degree of freedom of individuals, that is how much or how little they are actually actors, depends on their social position in social figurations as underlined by Bauman. But it also depends on how confidence is established relationally. Emotional energy such as confidence is a necessary although not sufficient condition of freedom. Mobilizing of emotional energy is a precondition of bringing other power resources into play. This fact is easily ignored as the energy resource often silently accompanies the possession of the more conventionally understood power resources. People in high positions often appear self-confident. But this emotional feature should be seen as a result of these high status people having continuously received recognition and access to relevant resources of action, rather than as given by nature.

Liquid work life integrated qua reflexive authority and communicative leadership

Bauman envisions erosion of every normative pattern as a consequence of thorough de-institutionalization (Bauman 2001: 212). However, there is reason to doubt this idea of absence of any normative pattern, as I claim that the organization of flexible work links itself to normative expectations of dialogue or communicative rationality. Such new normative pattern is crucial in understanding the integrative forces of liquid work life.

According to Hoogenboom and Ossewarde late modern society produces a novel reflexive form of organization with a particular type of authority. This development is driven by the fact that organizations increasingly have to be highly communicative and political in late modernity, since they are forced to cope with latent and unintended consequences of their actions and their ignorance or contingent character of their knowledge. Consequently, such reflexive organizations can no longer bind their members by the authority of fixed rules. The reflexive organization is different from the rule-bound organization characterized by goal-oriented rationality. It is an organization in which rules are not fixed but created in an ongoing process (Hoogenboom and Ossewaarde 2005: 613). But this does not mean that the possibility of social order and authority is ruled out, rather that it takes a reflexive form.

Reflexive organizations are integrated by the members' collective consciousness of entering a temporary alliance, rather than some stable network of relations. The commitment and empowerment of organizational members come from the collective questioning of how things are organized, rather than from a policy of community building. The integration in reflexive organizations rest on the collective understanding of the situation which their organization is in. The more the reflexive organization can adapt itself to the lives of the organizational members the better it can integrate its members: 'If organizational members come to understand the challenges present in their lives – the inescapable necessity to create subjective "truth" and self-identity – then they can be mobilized and empowered' (Hoogenboom and Ossewaarde 2005: 616). The authors argue that reflexive organizations can only become cohesive through the experiment of self-interpretation, self-observation, self-opening, self-discovery and self-invention of their members. In order to integrate members, reflexive organizations must function as arenas where individuals can shape a future for themselves (Hoogenboom and Ossewaarde 2005: 617). This point links to the point made earlier about post-bureaucratic organization being inclusive by asking members to contribute to the definition of the organization instead of requiring a play-acting prescribed by organizational roles.

In the fluid work life the reflexive organization appears, and the characteristics of this particular form of organization are important in order to understand the integrative and relatively stabilizing features of liquid work life. The reflexive organization fosters what Hoogenboom and Ossewaarde call reflexive authority understood as *'the belief in the ability of institutions and actors to negotiate, reconcile and represent arguments, interests, identities and abilities'* (Hoogenboom and Ossewaarde 2005: 614) which is a form of authority that provides stability amidst the modernizing ruptures of present society. The reflexive authority is located in concrete actors and institutions. Like charismatic authority it rests on the 'aura' of the actor in control. But it also differs from charismatic authority because the reflexively, authoritative person or actor follows the rules which are produced in the process and (also) tries to attain the goals of the other actors, rather than just following his own rules. Like all other types of authority reflexive authority is accepted before the decision-making process starts. It is resting on a belief in the qualities of concrete actors or institutions to lead, without knowing beforehand *how* these actors will perform their task and *what* the nature of the result will be.

In sum, the reflexive organization can become 'authoritative by making the accommodation of competing rationality claims one of the central causal elements of their existence' (Hoogenboom and Ossewaarde 2005: 613). Reflexive organizations owe their authority to their capacity to accommodate reflexive action through the provision of data flows, from which the actor is enabled to form an interpretation of his situation. In this way they shape actors capable of major shifts in their frame of reference and embodying the ability to disavow a permanent social character (Hoogenboom and Ossewaarde 2005: 614).

On an organizational level there is a turn towards more emphasis on communication in the form of reflexive organizations. However the commitment to communication and dialogical reasoning is also taking place on the interactional level of leadership in flexible, decentralized and reflexive organizations, as I argue by drawing on Eriksen's (2001) theory of communicative leadership. Referring to Habermas's theory of communicative rationalization of modern society, Eriksen argues that extra-legal and extra-material aspects play a role in achieving authority in an interaction. There are other forms of motivation than the usually theorized and purely material ones, and the basis for coordination of action consists of more than just the use of physical force, power or sanctions.

Eriksen's theory of communicative leadership implies that leaders can be criticized on four grounds:

1 cognitive-instrumental grounds – when the measures decided upon do not contribute to realization of stipulated goals;
2 moral, legal grounds – when what the leader decides and does is considered unfair;
3 ethical grounds – when the leader is not able to account for the 'collective we' of the organization;
4 on grounds of authenticity – when the leader behaves in ways that creates doubts concerning the real motives of his or her behaviour.

In flexible, decentralized organizations there is an organizational basis for communicative leadership, within which managers become increasingly obliged to provide good reasons for their decisions. Eriksen argues that leaders must be able to agree amongst themselves and gain support for their decisions and new measures in their environment in order to take advantage of the opportunities provided by decentralization: 'This necessitates a communicative turn on interaction. In such a form of interaction there are no recipes or predetermined answers on what constitutes rational action, even though the actors may have clear conceptions of such at the outset . . . What is more, it is not until consensus of some sort is achieved that anything at all can be done in a cooperative context of action' (Eriksen 2001: 28). The communicative way of interaction has epistemic value, because it elicits information and solves collective problems by linking competence and responsibility (Eriksen 2001: 32).

Communicative leadership is a form of leadership that fits into organizations which are based on employees' active participation in problem definition and problem solving. And the effect of the communicative attitude is that it strengthens the leader's legitimacy. Furthermore, it allows for storage of authority which relates to the fact that organizational members know that they can question leaders' decisions by employing the legal structure of the organization (Eriksen 2001: 33).

Summing up, Bauman's theorizing does not deal with how contemporary normativity is influenced by communicative developments. Alternatively, I have stressed a perspective that perceives communicative rationalization as a development which is integrally linked to flexible or liquid organizations. A communicative attitude and a willingness to revise one's goals and actions help getting work organizations to function. Individuals in such an organization are not abandoned to a chaos of absence of normative patterns. Reflexive organizations may owe their authority to their capacity to organize social criticism and to accommodate reflexive action through the provision of data flow from which the actor is enabled to form an interpretation of his situation. Individuals are not abandoned by organizations, if they succeed in providing forms of knowledge that can assist individuals in interpreting their life situation, and if they can adjust their action in accordance with critique voiced by the participating individuals.

Making a meaningful difference

In my view Bauman's theory of the consumption society is an original account of how contemporary modern society is integrated. There are many signs of a shift from a work ethic to an aesthetic of consumption, and his theory can explain how individuals are pushed and drawn towards a work-life regime producing both excitement and insecurity. Bauman stresses the idea of a consumerist syndrome making people into eminent seekers of pleasurable moments. This idea is relevant, I think, but Bauman seems to see contemporary individuals as merely or primarily hedonists. It is worth considering that people are more than hunters of pleasurable experiences. While they are preoccupied with getting exciting sensations they are also preoccupied with realizing personal development and ethical values, going further than experiencing isolated moments of pleasure (Bovbjerg 2001). For example, people divorce because they strive to realize an idea of a better and truer love with a new partner (Beck and Beck-Gernsheim 1990).

In relation to work life, contemporary individuals are also concerned with working with issues which they consider meaningful. People like to feel proud of what they are doing and to work in organizations that have a socially acceptable image or ethical profile. Consequently, their work is not merely assessed with respect to how the outside world considers the value of the work organization and not merely in terms of how it provides exciting personal experiences. Individuals in contemporary liquid society are preoccupied with the idea of 'making a difference' which refers to the notion of participating in a work which is not merely gratifying in a personal aesthetic sense, but is meaningful and valuable in a wider social sense. In sum, it is important to consider how individuals in consumer society also seek to realize ethical meanings and not merely pleasurable and episodic experiences.

Conclusion

Bauman effectively analyses disintegrative forces such as insecurity, self-management and the aesthetic orientation towards work. However, empowerment, engaged relationship between manager and employee, post-bureaucratic organization and team organization are also features of liquid work and they can be understood as integrative forces. In this chapter, I have supplemented Bauman's thesis of radical de-institutionalization of contemporary work life by drawing a complex picture of contradictory pressures of both disintegrative and integrative forces in liquid work life. There is individualization *and* increased emphasis on individuals' capacity for working together in teams. Short-term project jobs can be combined with engaged and empowering manager–employee relationships. For core employees in particular, empowerment can be a resource of freedom and upgrading of one's present and future employability. In particular I have stressed the importance of understanding how empowerment involves the generating of emotional energy in liquid employees. Concerning this issue of power in the relationship between manager and employee, I have supplemented Bauman's analysis by highlighting the trend that managers' task increasingly has become that of empowering employees (Ashkanasy and Tse 2000; Dell 1993; Mark 1997; Pepitone 1998; Potterfield 1999; Scott and Jaffe 1991).

Flexibly working individuals are not necessarily as abandoned and 'emancipated' as Bauman claims. In his analysis individuals seem merely confronted with the abstract and overwhelming forces of globalization, individualization, de-regulation, etc. On a more concrete level, the issue is the presence or absence of resources to handle the liquidity rather than liquidity per se. But analysis on more concrete levels show how individuals in varying degrees and ways are enmeshed in networks of resources or emotional ecologies (Frost 2003), which are crucial for how they handle their insecurity. Relevant resources depend on, for example, managerial support and social support among colleagues, and consideration of such local conditions are essential in order to understand if and how individuals are plagued by insecurity in liquid modernity. Whether self-actualization or self-exhaustion is realized in the game of liquid work life depends on such local circumstances rather than the liquid organizational form itself.

Notes

1. It is difficult to judge the extent of post-bureaucratic organization compared to very traditional bureaucratic work organizations. However, today under the names of e.g. empowerment or learning organization efforts are made at decentralizing, reducing specialization and the strict separation between professional and private life in varying branches of work life (Edwards and Wajcman 2005; Jacobsen and Thorsvik 2002).
2. As an example of how decentralization can lead to equality, I here mention how decentralization has meant a reduction of social distance between different status groups in an organization which I have studied (Poder 2004). In one department the manager wanted to reduce the specialization so that both academics and administratively trained employees could handle some of the same tasks. As individuals from both groups began to work together in a team the social distance between the two groups was minimized.
3. Bauman is not alone in engaging in such one-sided kind of diagnosis – see for example Allwin *et al.* (2006) and Sennett (1998).
4. Sennett's analysis of team work suggests that team work equals lack of real communication, superficiality and disappearance of authority (Sennett 1998). However, his analysis is too one-sided, as more productive effects are also associated with the team work organization as I show in this chapter.

5 Sennett also contends that managers lose significance in terms of performing power since, in the flexible team work, groups allegedly perform the power work that formerly the manager performed in traditional authoritarian rule-based organizations (Sennett 1998: 114).
6 Barbalet underlines that: 'All action functions in terms of outcomes, which have not occurred at the time when the action itself is undertaken. As the future is in principle unknowable, it is not possible for actors to operate in terms of calculations based on information about it. In this sense, calculated reason necessarily gives way to emotion as the basis of action' (Barbalet 1996: 88).
7 Concerning Barbalet's conceptualization of confidence, I argue that a sense of confidence is also involved in what is expected, and in carrying out routine tasks. When doing things that are not new, one is still acting towards an insecure future and needs some feeling of reassurance. Consequently, there may also be a certain form of confidence that is not about going 'one's own way'. However, empowerment is very much premised on employees feeling confidence in the sense of being able to act beyond routine. The empowered employee is very much defined in contrast to an employee working within routine.
8 Agency is also based on individuals' psychobiography which refers to the unique subjective configuration of emotional-cognitive capacities that individuals acquire in the course of their development. The notion indicates that the subjective powers of emotional-cognitive capacities vary with shifting phases of the individuals' lives. Social settings influence significantly upon individual powers and capacities, but this does not mean that one should dissolve the distinctive nature of the inner, subjective life of human beings (Layder 2004: 10). The distinction between internal and external is not a radical one, but underlines that there are crucial differences to do with the locus of individual powers. Here, I particularly emphasize dynamic social processes of generating emotions of agency as part of the formation of agency. My point is not that agency is exclusively a sociological issue.
9 By conceiving the degree of civility of others as a form of power, one can analyse how such capability of action is established rather than merely taking the idea of agency as a generic capacity of individuals (Layder 2004) or the idea of 'free willpower' for granted (Campbell 1999).

References

Allvin, M., Aronson, G., Hagström, T., Johansson, G. and Lundberg, U. (2006) *Gränslöst Arbete – Socialpsykologiska perspektiv på det nya arbetslivet* [Limitless Work – Social psychological perspective on the new work life], Malmø: Liber.
Ashkanasy, N. and Tse, B. (2000) 'Transformational Leadership as Management of Emotion – A Conceptual Review', in N. Ashkanasy, C. Härtel and W. Zerbe (eds) *Emotions in the Workplace – Research, Theory, and Practice*, London: Quorum Books.
Barbalet, J. (1996) 'Social Emotions: Confidence, Trust and Loyalty', *International Journal of Sociology and Social Policy* 16 (9–10): 75–96.
Bauman, Z. (1988) *Freedom*. Milton Keynes: Open University Press.
Bauman, Z. (1997) *Postmodernity and its Discontents*, Cambridge: Polity Press.
Bauman, Z. (1998) *Work, Consumerism and the New Poor*, Buckingham: Open University Press.
Bauman, Z. (1999) *In Search of Politics*, Cambridge: Polity Press.
Bauman, Z. (2000) *Liquid Modernity*, Cambridge: Polity Press.

Bauman, Z. (2001) *Individualized Society*, Cambridge: Polity Press.
Bauman, Z. (2002) *Society under Siege*, Oxford: Blackwell.
Bauman, Z. (2004) 'Zygmunt Bauman: Liquid Sociality' in Nicholas Gane (ed.) *The Future of Social Theory*, London: Continuum.
Bauman, Z. (2005) *Liquid Life*, Cambridge: Polity Press.
Bauman, Z. and May, T. (2001) *Thinking Sociologically*, Oxford: Blackwell.
Beck, U. and Beck-Gernsheim, E. (1990) *Das Ganz Normale Chaos der Liebe* [The Normal Chaos of Love], Frankfurt am Main: Suhrkamp.
Bovbjerg, K. (2001) *Følsomhedens Etik – Tilpasning af Personligheden i New Age og Moderne Management* [The Ethic of Soulfulness – The Personality's Adaption in New Age and Modern Management], Højbjerg, DK: Hovedland.
Campbell, C. (1999) 'Action as Willpower', *Sociological Review* 47 (1): 48–61.
Christrup, H. (1993) *Konflikt og Kærlighed i Adhocratiet*, [Conflict and Love in Adhocracy], Copenhagen: Samfundslitteratur.
Clark, C. (2001) 'Emotional Gifts, Micro politics, and Niceness in the Socio-emotional Economy', Keynote address, Feelings and Emotions: The Amsterdam Symposium, University of the Netherlands, Amsterdam, June.
Collins, R. (2004) *Interaction Ritual Chains*, Princeton, NJ: Princeton University Press.
Dell, T. (1993) Motivating at Work: Empowering Employees to Give Their Best, Menlo Park, CA: Crisp Learning.
Edwards, P. and J. Wajcman (2005) *The Politics of Working Life*, Oxford: Oxford University Press.
Eriksen, E. (2001) 'Leadership in Communicative Perspective' *Acta Sociologica*, 44 (1): 21–35.
Frost, P. (2003) *Toxic Emotions at Work: How Compassionate Managers Handle Pain and Conflict*, Boston, MA: Harvard Business School Press.
Gibson, D. (1997) 'The Struggle for Reason: The Sociology of Emotions in Organizations', in R. Erickson and B. Cuthbertson-Johnson (eds) *Social Perspectives on Emotion*, Vol. 4, pp. 211–56, Greenwich, CT: JAI Press.
Hoogenboom, M. and Ossewaarde, R. (2005) 'From Iron Cage to Pigeon House: The Birth of Reflexive Authority', *Organization Studies* 26 (4): 601–19.
Huczynski, A. and Buchanan, D. (2001) *Organizational Behaviour: An Introductory Text*, Essex: Pearson Education.
Jacobsen, D. and J. Thorsvik (2002) *Hvordan Organizationer Fungerer – Indføring i Organization og Ledelse* [How Organizations Work – Introduction to Organization and Management], Copenhagen: Hans Reitzels Forlag.
Layder, D. (2004) *Social and Personal Identity: Understanding Yourself*, London: Sage.
Limborg, J. (2002) *Den Risikable Fleksibilitet – på vej mod 'nyt' arbejdsmiljø*, [The Risky Flexibility – towards a 'new' working environment], Århus: Frydenlund.
Maravelias, C. (2003) 'Post-bureaucracy – Control Through Professional Freedom', *Journal of Organizational Change Management*, 16 (5): 547–66.
Mark, T. (1997) *Mastering People Management: Build a Successful Team: Motivate, Empower and Lead People*, London: Thorogood.
Pepitone, J. (1998) *Motivating Employees*, Blacklick, OH: McGraw-Hill Professional Book Group.
Poder, P. (2004) 'Feelings of Power and the Power of Feelings: Handling Emotions in Organizational Change', Department of Sociology, University of Copenhagen.
Poder, P. (2006) 'Ingen frihed uden magt, ingen magt uden emotionel energi' in Michael Hviid Jacobsen & Poul Poder (eds) *Om Bauman – kritiske essays* [No freedom without power, no power without emotional energy, in About Bauman – Critical Essays], Copenhagen: Hans Reitzels Forlag.

Potterfield, T. (1999) *Business of Employee Empowerment: Democracy and Ideology in the Workplace*. Westport, CT: Greenwood.
Scott, C. and Jaffe, D. (1991) *Empowerment – Building a Committed Workforce,* Menlo Park, CA: Crisp Learning.
Sennett, R. (1998) *The Corrosion of Character,* New York: W. W. Norton.
Sørhaug, T. (1996) *Om Ledelse – makt og tillit i moderne organizering* [On Leadership – Power and Trust in Modern Organizing], Oslo: Universitetsforlaget.
Tucker, J. (1999) *The Therapeutic Corporation*, Oxford: Oxford University Press.
Wilson, F. (2004) *Organizational Behaviour and Work – A Critical Introduction*, (second edition), Oxford: Oxford University Press.

CHAPTER 6

Liquid love

Psychoanalysing mania

Janet Sayers

Zygmunt Bauman ends his book, Liquid Love, with the joke about the man who, asking how to get to Dublin, is told, 'If I wished to go to Dublin, I wouldn't start from here' (Bauman 2003: 155). Similarly, if we wish to analyse or psychoanalyse the ills involved in the manic individualism described by Bauman in *Liquid Love* we might do well to start elsewhere than with here-and-now appearance and ideology. Yet this is one of Bauman's starting points in which he also draws on psychoanalytic accounts of consuming desire. This, however, leads to a cul-de-sac both in psychoanalysis and in the story of manic consumerism Bauman tells in *Liquid Love*. More promising is another starting point, namely Diotima's account of the creative love on which we depend for our coming into being from non-being, as reported by Socrates via Plato in *The Symposium*. I will explain this further later in this chapter by focusing particularly on ways in which Diotima's account of creative love has been developed psychoanalytically by Julia Kristeva on the basis of the work of the psychoanalysts, Donald Winnicott and Wilfred Bion. I will begin though with the consuming desire of manic individualism described both by Bauman and by Freud.

Consuming desire

As just indicated, one of Bauman's starting points is the manic individualism of consuming desire. 'Desire is the wish to consume. To imbibe, devour, ingest and digest – annihilate', he tells us near the beginning of *Liquid Love* (Bauman 2003: 9). He backs this up with quotations from here-and-now advice columns in *The Guardian* telling us how best to feed our desire for love. Catherine Jarvie advises *Guardian* readers, says Bauman, to maximize their love possibilities by not becoming committed to their present object of desire lest this reduce the further objects of consuming desire to be gleaned from 'hunting out pastures new' (in Bauman 2003: 11). Offsetting the ossification of the libido's liquidity, as though it were cash, by fixing it in one relationship when others might be there for the desiring and consuming, another writer, quoted by Bauman from *The Guardian*, scorns commitment as 'meaningless', as a merely temporary device conditional on whether or not another 'viable alternative' is available to desire and consume (in Bauman 2003: 13). Similarly, says Bauman, Jarvie recommends not allowing relationships to 'acquire rights of tenure' lest this stop one knowing 'it's time to move on' (Bauman

2003: 21, 22). Still another *Guardian* writer quoted by Bauman describes 'internet chatting, mobile phoning, 24-hour texting' replacing introspection with 'frantic, frivolous interaction that exposes our deepest secrets alongside our shopping list' (in Bauman 2003: 35).

This shopping-list focus on, and representation of, desire is akin to Freud's focus on desire and its origin. Nor is this any coincidence. As Terry Eagleton observes, 'it is in late modernity, not fortuitously, that a full-blown science of desire, known as psychoanalysis, first appears' (Eagleton 2005: 106). So what was Freud's account of desire? He argued that it is first brought into being in earliest infancy by the mother giving the baby the breast, thus awakening and giving its sexual desire its first shape and form in also impelling it to find a shopping list, as it were, of substitutes, first in its own body – its lips, fingers, thumb – and then in whatever its surroundings offer for it to find. 'Sucking at the mother's breast is the starting-point of the whole of sexual life,' Freud declared, 'the unmatched prototype of every later satisfaction, to which phantasy often enough recurs in times of need' (Freud 1916–17: 314).

Mania involves just such a recurrence. 'The manic patient returns to a stage in which his impulses had not succumbed to repression,' wrote Freud's first leading psychoanalytic colleague, Karl Abraham. Mania, he said, fulfils Faust's wish: 'Bring back my passion's unquenched fires . . . Bring back the youth I was once more' (Abraham 1911: 149, 150). One of Abraham's patients called it 'gobbling mania'. Abraham equated it with erotic excess. 'We are all familiar with the strength of the erotic cravings of the manic patient,' he told his fellow psychoanalysts. 'The patient 'devours' everything that comes his way' (Abraham 1924: 472).

Inspired by psychoanalysis, surrealists indulged just such excess, notably Georges Bataille in his pornographic novella, *The Story of the Eye*. It begins with the narrator's orgasmic pleasure, together with that of his 15-year-old friend, Simone, sitting, her 'pink and dark' flesh astride a cat's saucer of milk (Bataille 1928: 4). Bataille goes on to recount the succession of substitute shopping list objects of their desire – from cat's saucer of milk to eggs, bull's balls and a bullfighter's eyes. This shopping list of objects of desire is linked to another list of liquids, one substituting for another: 'tears, milk in the cat's saucer-eye, the yolk of a soft-boiled egg, sperm or urine' (Barthes 1963: 121). As for the novella's title centring on the eye, it was inspired, Bataille confessed, by seeing his father 'blind, his whitish globes turned up in their sockets as he pissed in front of the child [he once was]' (Barthes 1963: 122). The shopping lists of manic desire are structured according to Freud by dream-work mechanisms of condensation and displacement, and according to Barthes by the substitutions of metaphor and metonymy in language, each item on the shopping lists of desire acquiring its arousal value from its substitutability by, and contiguity with, other items on the list. 'Everything in it is on the surface; there is no hierarchy,' Barthes observes. 'There is no resistance at the level of common sense,' he explains, 'everything works towards a discourse . . . [with] transfer of meaning from one chain to the other – the "eye sucked like a breast", "drinking my left eye between her lips",' and so on (Barthes 1963: 123, 124, 125). The transgressions of Bataille's pornography consist in demolishing the usual links between objects and liquids. He substitutes and offers new objects of consumption and desire by making new and fresh linkages. He interchanges, says Barthes, 'the functions of obscenity and those of substance (the consistency of the soft-boiled egg, the bloodshot, pearly colouring of the raw balls, the glassy quality of the eye)' (Barthes 1963: 126).

There is no doubting the manic quality of this pornographic cornucopia of substitutions. Barthes contrasts this with sublimation. Bataille, he says, uses the substitutions afforded by condensation and displacement, metaphor and metonymy, 'to transgress sex – which is not, of course, the same as sublimating it, rather the contrary' (Barthes 1963: 126). In fact, however, Freud's theory, beginning as it does with consumption – breastfeeding – and a shopping list of substitutions for our original object of desire – the breast – provides no means of distinguishing sex and sublimation. He rooted both in substitution. Sublimation depends on the sexual instinct's capacity, he said, 'to exchange its originally sexual aim for another, which is no longer sexual but which is psychically related to the first aim' – namely sex (Freud 1908: 187). Quoting this from Freud's essay, 'Civilized sexual morality and modern nervous illness', Bauman comments: 'Freud suggests that civilization rests in great measure on the exploitation and deployment of the natural human capacity to 'sublimate' sexual instincts'. Unchecked by repression, Bauman continues, 'modern society has found a way of exploiting the human propensity/amenability to sublimate sexual instincts . . . guided by seduction by the objects of sexual desire on offer' (Bauman 2003: 56, 57).

This fits in with the dictates of global capitalism aimed at seducing and persuading us to desire and buy whatever promises to swell its profits. Its ethic, or 'fetish', says Bauman, 'rests on an assumption that the sum total of human happiness grows as more money changes hands' (Bauman 2003: 67). Hence, presumably, the market's evaluation of Christmas each year in terms of how much money we spent. We might complain against the cynicism of the market in this respect. Bauman's complaint is more all-embracing. He takes issue with the way the ethic of liquidity – not the substituted liquids of Bataille's pornographic novella, but the ethic of cash flow – free of any fetters or commitments, penetrates our most intimate relations as reflected in the *Guardian* writers he quotes. He is appalled by this. He is also appalled by the ramifications of this ethic of liquidity in severing sex from love, in making nonsense of the Christian commandment to love one's neighbour as oneself, in rendering local politics impotent vis-à-vis the machinations of global free-traders and in exacerbating the process of dismantling 'togetherness' with others by either assimilating or excluding, gobbling or ejecting, 'eating' or 'vomiting' them as alien, other and strange (Bauman 2003: 136, 137). In this its ethic is akin to that of the infant described by Freud as judging between good and bad by saying, as it were, 'I should like to eat this' or 'I should like to spit it out' (Freud 1925: 237).

How, though, is gobbling mania and its spewing out antithesis to be resolved if this is where we begin? Freud noted that substitution of one object of consumption and desire can be obstructed by fixation and repression centring, in his view, on dread of castration. He also noted that substitution of one person or object of our consuming desire comes to a halt when we suffer the death of, separation from, or disappointment in those we love but also hate. Fixated to those we have thus lost, no substitute can attract or seduce us away until our libido is freed from them. It only becomes free, liquid and fluid again through what Freud called 'the work of mourning'. It is a piecemeal business. 'Each single one of the memories and expectations in which the libido is bound to the object is brought up and hyper-cathected,' he explained, 'and detachment of the libido is accomplished in respect of it' (Freud 1917: 245). Or the bereaved may defend against this work of mourning by clinging onto and identifying with those they have loved and hated but also lost as though they were identical with them. Freud explained, in terms of illusory oneness with those who are lost, loved and hated, the melancholic's response to loss with both self-loving self-preoccupation and self-hating reviling of themselves as loathsome and hateful.

So bound up is the melancholic with those they thus cling to in love and hate their libido is not free to be seduced into substituting other objects of consumption and desire. Indeed mourning and melancholia often involve the sufferer becoming thin with grief. Why, then, does melancholia sometimes alternate with manic spending sprees and gobbling mania? Abraham, as I have said, explained this in terms of the manic patient returning to the gobbling eroticism of consuming desire with which, according to Freud, our existence as babies begins. Freud himself suggested another possible cause. 'In mania, the ego must have got over the loss of the object (or its mourning over the loss, or perhaps the object itself),' he speculated, 'and thereupon the whole quota of anticathexis which the painful suffering of melancholia had drawn to itself from the ego and "bound" will have become available'. Freed from the work of mourning and from the melancholic ossification of desire in defensive identification with what is gone, 'the manic subject plainly demonstrates his liberation from the object which was the cause of his suffering,' he added, 'by seeking like a ravenously hungry man for new object-cathexes' (Freud 1917: 255).

But Freud was not satisfied with this explanation. For if his account of melancholia was correct then the melancholic is so fixated in identification with what they love, hate and have lost, their libido is not free to be seduced into manic pursuit of others as objects of their consuming desire. Furthermore, as Freud also observed, those rendered free of those they once desired and have lost through death, once they have completed their work of mourning, seldom evince the mania which for some depressives alternates with their melancholia.

Freud sought, but failed, to find a scientific explanation of this alternation. Bauman is less a scientist than a moralist – a utopian socialist, indeed. In so far as he starts *Liquid Love* with the manic individualism of consuming desire, the only solution he offers is both utopian and moralistic, specifically the plea for us to exert a manic effort of will to counter the dismantling of togetherness of our times by striving instead to achieve what he calls 'the politics of shared humanity' (Bauman 2003: 156).

Creative love

A more satisfactory answer to the mania of consuming desire can be found in starting not with the here-and-now manic individualism conveyed by the advice columns of *The Guardian* from which Bauman quotes. Much better is his also starting with the creative love described by Diotima as quoted by Socrates and reported, as follows, by Plato in *The Symposium*:

Diotima	May we then say without qualification that men are in love with what is good?
Socrates	Yes.
Diotima	And not only its possession but its perpetual possession?
Socrates	Certainly.
Diotima	To sum up, then, love is desire for the perpetual possession of the good.
Socrates	Very true.
Diotima	Now that we have established what love invariably is, we must ask in what way and by what type of action men must show their intense desire if it is to deserve the name of love. . . . The object of love, Socrates, is not, as you think, beauty.
Socrates	What is it then?
Diotima	Its object is to procreate and bring forth in beauty. . . . Look at the behaviour of all animals . . . whenever the desire to procreate seizes them . . . [t]heir first object is to achieve union with one another, their second to provide for their young.

(adapted from Plato n.d.: 86–8)

'By intimate association with beauty embodied in his friend, and by keeping him always before his mind,' Plato continues, quoting Socrates' account of what Diotima told him about the creativity of love, 'he succeeds in bringing to birth the children of which he has been long in labour, and once they are born he shares their upbringing with his friend' (Plato n.d.: 91). Furthermore, when the lover, added Diotima, 'encounters a virtuous soul in a body which has little of the bloom of beauty, he will be content to love and cherish and to bring forth such notions as may serve to make young people better' (Plato n.d.: 92).

'To love is to desire "to beget and procreate", and so the lover "seeks and goes about to find the beautiful thing in which he can beget",' says Bauman, quoting Diotima. 'In other words,' he adds, 'it is not in craving after ready-made, complete and finished things that love finds its meaning – but in the urge to participate in the becoming of such things' (Bauman 2003: 6). No need to tell people, as Christ did, 'Thou shalt love thy neighbour as thyself', and no need for Freud's scepticism about this commandment (Freud 1930: 109). Arguing in this vein, Bauman implicitly rejects the individualistic Cartesian proclamation of self-creation: *cogito ergo sum*. Instead he approves of Hegel's account of our creation by others as self-conscious beings through their conferring recognition on our being. It is just such recognition by others that is the origin of self-love. It is not individually self-generated. By contrast, Freud assumed that individuality is where we begin. 'We say that a human being has originally two sexual objects – himself and the woman who nurses him – and in doing so we are postulating a primary narcissism in everyone,' he wrote (Freud 1917: 88). Contrary to Freud's primary narcissism starting point, Bauman rejects the notion that self-love is where we begin. 'Love thy neighbour as thyself', he says, 'implicitly casts self-love as unproblematically given, as always-already-there' (Bauman 2003: 78). To the contrary, he maintains, self-love is not where we begin. It is not always already there. Its coming into being depends on others loving and conferring recognition on us: 'what we love in our self-love is the selves fit to be loved,' he says, 'being objects worthy of love, being recognized as such' (Bauman 2003: 80).

Quite different from the always-already-there self-love of primary narcissism assumed by Freud, self-love, according to Bauman's Diotima- and Hegel-based account of it, originates developmentally in dependence on the creative love of others bringing it into being. In this Bauman's account of self-love is akin to the account of the origin of the individual ego or psyche described in terms of our 'object' relations with others by the psychoanalysts Donald Winnicott and Wilfred Bion and, before that, by Melanie Klein as her work has been reconceptualized by Jacques Lacan and Julia Kristeva. Like Bauman, Kristeva finds authority for her account of self-love as originating in our relations with others in Diotima's account of our coming into being originating in the loving union of one person with another. 'In contrast with the possession-love that Plato works out in *Phaedrus*,' Kristeva writes, 'Diotima, in the *Symposium*, presented it more along the lines of an idealized object relationship that it takes for granted' (Kristeva 1987: 72).

Like Bauman, Kristeva also cites approvingly the work of the social theorist Hannah Arendt. Having told manic individualism's gloomy tale, Bauman includes, in ending *Liquid Love*, Arendt's conclusion to her essay, 'Humanity in dark times', namely Lessing's advice: 'Let each man say what he deems truth,/ and let truth itself be commended unto God' (in Bauman 2003: 152). This means leaving open the question of truth and who is right, by engaging in talk and dialogue with others. It entails, says Bauman, 'speech unsure-of-the-result-of-the-dialogue', speech in which participants respect and recognize each other 'as a partner-in-conversation', confirm each other's credentials and make 'the outcome of the debate a hostage to fate' (Bauman 2003: 153, 154).

Going further than Bauman, we could argue that just such debate, conversation, dialogue or talk is where we begin. This is implicit in Arendt's adoption of Socrates' characterization of thinking as 'two-in-one' silent talk with ourselves premised on our having previously talked with others about things (Arendt 1971: 185). Characterizing Arendt as a feminine genius, Kristeva asserts: 'The work of a genius culminates in the birth of a subject.' Arendt's writing, she goes on, 'focuses on the miraculous "birth of each person" into the "frailty of human affairs".' In this Arendt reveals, Kristeva adds, 'the irreducible singularity of each person, provided that he finds the courage to partake in the common sense of those around him' (Kristeva 1999: x, xvii).

How, though, does this relate to the creative love, as I have called it, that is the developmental precursor, according to Winnicott, of the individual ego, will or psyche? Perhaps it was because he was not only a psychoanalyst but also a paediatrician whose work involved seeing babies with their mothers that he noted, in effect, that we start life not in manic individualistic separateness but in togetherness with others. 'There is no such thing as an infant,' he repeatedly emphasized, meaning, he said, 'that whenever one finds an infant one finds maternal care, and without maternal care there would be no infant' (Winnicott 1960: 39 n.1). Furthermore, he indicated, it is through the mother's loving identification and preoccupation with her baby, and through her thus being able creatively to anticipate what it might be ready to imagine that enables her to give it the breast just at the right moment, thereby bringing its wishing and desiring into being and giving them shape and form in terms of what is actually available. Or, as he put it

> the infant comes to the breast when excited, and ready to hallucinate something fit to be attacked. At that moment the actual nipple appears and he is able to feel it was that nipple that he hallucinated. So his ideas are enriched by actual details of sight, feel, smell, and next time this material is used in the hallucination.
>
> (Winnicott 1945: 152–3)

It is precisely in this togetherness of mother and baby in the pre-verbal dialogue or talk of the baby ready to imagine, and the mother presenting the breast, that the baby's individuality, ego, will, subjectivity begin.

Winnicott emphasized that this togetherness involves overlap of the world of the mother with that of her baby. He said little, however, about the mother's world of experience prior to, and independent of, that of her baby. Bion was more explicit about this. He implied that self-knowledge, self-love and self-hatred originate in the infant through the impressions made on the mother by its 'harvest of self-sensation' (Bion 1962: 116) mating with, and realizing her already existing preconceptions, this being reflected in her response to her infant. This has the effect, he argued, of transforming its self-sensations into the elementary stuff of meaning without which it cannot psychologically register, know or think about its experience of itself. He also described analytic patients who, it seemed, attacked the processes by which they had learnt through the creative love of their mothers for them in earliest infancy to transform their self-sensations into meaningful knowledge, love and hate of themselves. As a result, said Bion, they lacked the necessary 'I think, therefore I am' transformation of self-sensation into the stuff of self-knowledge such that, for the time being, thought had become impossible for them, and along with this no individuated personality or self-consciousness (Bion 1992: 76). This calls in analysis, he argued, for the analyst to register the analysand's self-sensations, as expressed in impressions they make on the analyst in mating with, and realizing the analyst's already existing preconceptions so the analyst can formulate the result into an interpretation, thereby helping the analysand to recover the ability to do this and think for themselves. If the analyst's interpretations are to be helpful in this they must enable the analysand, Bion argued, 'to "know" that part of himself to which attention has been drawn', this involving them 'being' or 'becoming' that person (Bion 1965: 164).

In this Bion enabled other psychoanalysts, Kristeva included, to reconceptualize Klein's development of child analysis, and the psychoanalysis of adults too, as involving the analyst supplementing the impressions made on them by the child analysand with preconceptions these impressions evoke in them as source of their interpretations. We can reconceptualize in these terms Klein's analysis of a 4-year-old, Dick, who, today, might be diagnosed as autistic so little did he express any interests in, or any sense of knowing about, his own experience, or what things around him meant. Klein, it seems, enabled him to acquire or recover a sense of himself through supplementing the impressions made on her by what she learnt from others about him and his few interests, almost entirely limited to an obsession with stations and trains. At their first meeting she accordingly took up two toy engines. She called one 'Daddy', the other 'Dick', and put them side by side. At this, Dick rolled the Dick-train to the window, saying 'Station'. Supplementing this with the Oedipal preconceptions this evoked in her, Klein said, 'The station is mummy; Dick is going into mummy' (Klein 1930: 225). 'She slams the symbolism on him with complete brutality,' Lacan later commented. 'She hits him a brutal verbalisation of the Oedipal myth, almost as revolting for us as for any reader – You are the little train, you want to fuck your mother' (Lacan 1953–4: 68). Kristeva is more generous. She says, apropos the transformation of psychoanalysis and psychotherapy brought about by Klein's pioneering development of child analysis, 'the therapist's named fantasy, which interprets the proto-fantasy enacted by the child, raises the child's emergent thought to a third level: a level that shall be termed symbolic' (Kristeva 2000: 146).

Kristeva prefaces this by suggesting that, contrary to the assumption of Freud, and also of Klein, that individually given instinct is where we begin, individuated subjectivity and imagination comes into being through others, through what she calls 'the newborn's first drive-based interactions' evoking fantasies in those who first mother them (Kristeva 2000: 145). We could put this in terms of the game in which players take turns making a more or less random pencilled or painted doodle or squiggle in which the other player discerns something meaningful, and completes it accordingly. Or, transposing to earliest infancy Kristeva's account of the creative dialogue between analysand and analyst in their talking cure work together, we could say the earliest dialogue between infant and mother bringing the infant's individual subjectivity into being involves 'the interaction between the two imaginaries [the infant's and mother's] as they focus on bodies and their acts' (Kristeva 2000: 148).

Defying death

If the miraculous 'birth of each person' and their 'irreducible singularity' comes into being, as Kristeva puts it, drawing on the work of both Arendt and Klein, through what could be called the initial creative love and dialogue of others with us in first mothering us, what is the origin of the consuming desire of manic individualism described by Bauman in *Liquid Love*? Whereas Freud, who postulated consuming desire as the starting point of our psychology, was unable, as I have said, to explain the mania alternating with melancholic response to loving and hating those who are lost and dead to us, Klein was more able to explain this through basing her account of the infant's first psychological development in terms of what Kristeva calls Diotima's object relations account of love. Klein argued that mania is defiance and denial of death. It is akin to Don Giovanni's defiant feasting faced with the imminent arrival of his death-dealing guest.

Klein arrived at her equation of mania with defiance of death through noting evidence of very young children's fantasies of destroying their mother's sexual coupling with their fathers and dreading her revenge from which, she said, boys flee through taking refuge in defiant and arrogant 'possession of a penis', and girls flee into 'identification with the father' (Klein 1928: 191, 193). Klein (1935, 1940) went on to argue that this flight to maleness and masculinity is succeeded, developmentally, by the infant facing the fact that it both hates and loves its mother. But this evokes depression, anxiety and guilt lest in hating the mother it loves it might have harmed, lost, destroyed or even done her to death. This might impel it to do the work needed to repair the harm done by hatred to what it loves. Or it might defend against this work with manic defiance and triumph over death through denial, hateful contempt for and omnipotent control of those it might otherwise love. 'Control is a way of denying dependence, of not acknowledging it and yet of compelling the object to fulfil a need for dependence,' Klein's follower, Hanna Segal, explains, 'since an object that is wholly controlled is, up to a point, one that can be depended on' (Segal 1973: 83–4).

Mania defies, mystifes, and negates dependence on relations with others. It negates what Bauman, quoting Levinas, calls the opposite of possession, namely 'a relation with alterity', with 'the insurmountable duality of beings'. We might try to overcome this duality, Bauman adds, 'to tame the wayward and domesticate the riotous, to make the unknowable predictable and enchain the free roaming' (Bauman 2003: 7). This is one solution opted for in manic control of others. The Kleinian-minded political theorist Fred Alford characterizes mania in terms of the violence, described by Levinas, involved in making others 'play roles in which they no longer recognize themselves, making them betray not only commitments but their own substance, making them carry out actions that will destroy every possibility for action' (Alford 2002: 45). Mania involves totalizing others, defensively and omnipotently treating them as things, or as either the negation of, or as the same as, us. 'Levinas assumes in his critique of totality,' explains Alford, 'we reduce the other to the same out of rage at its separateness, its existence beyond the realm of my control' (Alford 2002: 53).

In describing mania as the effect of death-instinct motivated hatred of, and control of, others, Klein lost sight of her earlier account of mania as effect of flight from love and hate of the mother to overvaluing men and masculinity. Not so Lacan. Drawing on Klein's (1928) account of flight from fragmenting love and hate of the mother, he described the resulting fantasies of the 'body in bits and pieces' and the resulting allure of mis-identifying and mis-recognizing oneself as the 'I' or 'ego' reflection of oneself offered by language and by the wholeness we see reflected of ourselves in others and in our mirrored image. 'It is the stability of the standing posture, the prestige of stature, the impressiveness of statues, which set the style for the identification in which the ego finds its starting-point', he added. 'This illusion of unity, in which a human being is always looking forward to self-mastery,' he also pointed out, 'entails a constant danger of sliding back again into the chaos from which he started' (Lacan 1953: 12, 15). It is a defence against the fragmentation and frailty of loving and hating those who first mother us in which we begin. Furthermore, whereas Freud argued that desire first comes into being through the infant's first nutritive sucking at the breast, Lacan argued that our first object of desire is modelled on the objects desired by others. The infant, he argued, adopts as its first object of desire whatever is phallic in so far as this is the first or prime object of the mother's desire. 'If the desire of the mother is the phallus,' he maintained, 'the child wishes to be the phallus in order to satisfy that desire' (Lacan 1958: 289).

For Lacan, psychosis, including mania, involves delusional identification with what he called 'the imaginary object of this [the mother's] desire in so far as the mother herself symbolises it in the phallus' (Lacan 1955–6: 198). Mania was once characterized in terms of Napoleonic delusions of grandeur. Lacan was not optimistic about undoing its self-mystifying defensiveness through psychoanalysis. Kristeva is less pessimistic. She adopts as a model for the psychoanalysis of mania Dostoevsky's account of the resolution of the Napoloeonic grandiosity of Raskolnikov in *Crime and Punishment* faced with the fantasies evoked in his friend Sonia by his confessing to her that he is the murderer of her friend Lisaveta. This evokes a fantasy of identification with Lisaveta, which Dostoevsky describes as follows

> [Sonia] looked at him [Raskolnikov] helplessly for some time, and with the same expression of terror on her face [as Lisaveta] and thrusting out her left hand all of a sudden, she touched his chest lightly with her fingers and slowly began to get up from the bed, moving farther and farther away from him and staring more and more fixedly at him. Her feeling of horror suddenly communicated itself to him: exactly the same expression of terror appeared on his face; he, too, stared at her in the same way, and almost with the same child-like smile.

The effect of this is to break through Raskolnikov's manic defence. Soon after, says Dostoevsky:

> [Raskolnikov] looked at Sonia and felt how great her love for him was, and, strange to say, he felt distressed and pained that he should be loved so much. Yes, it was a queer and dreadful sensation . . . and suddenly now, when all her heart was turned to him, he felt and knew that he was infinitely more unhappy than before.
>
> (Dostoevsky 1866: 424, 435)

'According to Dostoevsky, forgiveness . . . raises the unconscious from beneath the actions and has it meet a loving other,' comments Kristeva, 'who does not judge but hears my truth in the availability of love, and for that very reason allows me to be reborn' (Kristeva 1987: 204–5). The analyst is involved in a similar task of enabling the analysand, as Sonia enables Raskolnikov, to discover the frailty and creativity of one human being for another on which we depend, and which is mystified and defiantly defended against, along with death, in mania.

Kristeva also describes manic defiance of death and non-being as abjection. She writes of how, defying and abjecting frailty of the creative love of each other, and specifically the non-being and death equated with oneness with the bodies of our mothers before our birth into individuated subjectivity and meaning, those on the borderline between psychosis and neurosis take refuge in overvaluing male-dominated culture, symbols and words, stripped and abstracted from the body in which words and symbols as talk and creativity begins. Words are sown in us like seeds by those who first mother and create us through their loving identification with, and bringing into meaning the stuff of our object-directed drives and gestures through the bodily response it evokes in them, not least in talking and dialoguing with us. This forms 'mnemic traces onto which perceptions have been grafted, as well as drives emanating from within the body,' says Kristeva. These traces are then subsequently recoverable from unconsciousness via the intermediary of the words sown in, and now present in, our preconscious psyche as adults, thanks to others.

In mania, however, we defensively sever words from 'the solid terrain that leads to truth' (Kristeva 1996: 49). We treat words and symbols as though they were magical, omnipotent things. 'Delirium', Kristeva asserts, 'takes words for things and fails at symbolisation, while at the same time repudiating the other and projecting drives onto it, the death drive, in particular' (Kristeva 1996: 58). Freud's solution was to return, at least in his *Totem and Taboo* account of the manic or magical thinking of religion, to the material reality of the past, to what Kristeva calls, 'the transpsychical; the transubjective' (Kristeva 1996: 59). The same is true of psychoanalysis. Its aim is to bring to consciousness what is otherwise abjected through the transference and counter-transference experience of analysand and analyst of each other as each embodying their otherwise insubstantial, disembodied-seeming, ethereal and unconscious fantasies. Cutting through the mystifications of mania is achieved in psychoanalysis through its free association method of deconstruction. 'Tell me your fantasies, put the sadomasochism of your drives, your parents, your grandparents, transgenerational and primitive histories in narrative form,' says the analyst, 'make the unrepresentable enter representation' (Kristeva 1996: 59). Psychoanalysis, like art, says Kristeva, also gives substance to what is otherwise treated by mania as the stuff of magic and omnipotent control by, she says, 'resexualizing the sublimatory activity, by sexualizing words, colors, and sounds' (Kristeva 1996: 60). In the dialogue of talking cure psychoanalysis it entails, she adds, 'a broadening of the rhetorical or sublimatory capacities of the analyst and analysand' (Kristeva 1996: 61).

Kristeva illustrates this with the case of an artist, Didier, whose mania took the form of obsession with masturbating and with showing off the results of his art-making to his mother for her to admire. In analysis with Kristeva, however, his talk was mechanical, lifeless and dreary. His psyche only became reanimated, it seems, through Kristeva telling him the free associations and fantasies his art-work evoked in her. '[He] worked with various entities – docile objects that were fractured, cracked, and broken up as if slaughtered,' she tells us, 'not a single face espoused the fragments of these mutilated persons, who were primarily female, and who were shown to have a derisive nature and an unsuspected ugliness' (Kristeva 1993: 19). Telling Didier the fantasies this female-centred destructive mayhem evoked helped. Evidence of this for Kristeva includes Didier giving her, at the end of his analysis, a picture made from a photograph of her smoking from which he had cut out the cigarette. 'Nothing between the hands, no penis, no fetish,' he said, 'I did well, didn't I' (Kristeva 1993: 25).

Mania, fetishizing the phallus included, mystifies and defends against dependence on others, not least on the creative love of those who first mothered and brought us into being. Psychoanalysis seeks to demystify through deconstructing via free association such mystifications understood by Freud as effect of dream-work disguise and repression. This includes the psychoanalytic work of demystifying the disguise afforded by mania which, defying the non-being that precedes and succeeds the creative love and interaction with others on which our being depends, severs words from their origin in talk and dialogue with others and treats them as though they had magical power as things-in-themselves. The work of sociology similarly involves not going along with the here-and-now ideology and fabricated dreams and illusions told us by *Guardian* columnists and others. Rather it involves exposing the fabrication and mystification involved. Bauman does this in exposing the defensive character of liquid love's ideology of free-market individualistic consumerism. 'The principal targets of the assault' – of we could call it 'defence' – 'by the market are humans as producers,' he writes, adding 'in a fully conquered and colonized land, only human consumers would be issued residence permits' (Bauman 2003: 74). The market's manic war on, defiance of and defence against the frailty, non-being and death of ourselves, and our consequent dependence on the creative love and productivity of others, involves mystifying production as consumption, sensuous use-value as cash resulting from selling commodities. Anything that 'resists such commodification is denied relevance to the prosperity of the society of consumers,' says Bauman of this mystifying process, adding 'it is stripped of value in a society trained to measure values in currency and to identify them with the price tags carried by sellable and purchasable objects and services' (Bauman 2003: 74–5).

Terry Eagleton makes more explicit the defiance of death and non-being involved in the manic and wilful globalizing imperialism of today's free-market individualism. 'For those who live by the will alone,' he observes, 'mortality', and we could add its corollary, the creative love of others on which we depend for our coming into being, 'is a denial of self-mastery and hence an intolerable insult' (Eagleton 2005: 111). Terrified of non-being, he goes on, global capitalism has launched an endless project of manic dominance and control. 'Power loathes weakness, since it brings to mind its own frailty,' he points out. 'Yet non-being cannot be destroyed, which is why the whole project of trying to dominate it is both interminable and insanely self-defeating' (Eagleton 2005: 121).

Conclusion

The counter-project of analysing sociologically and psychoanalytically so as to expose the mystifications of the manic individualism, the ills of which Bauman describes in *Liquid Love*, entails not resting content with starting, as I have more than once indicated, with individualism's self-representation, as in the writing of *Guardian* columnists with which Bauman begins. Going beyond this, a useful starting place, as depicted by both Bauman and Kristeva, is the starting point of our existence in the creative love depicted by Diotima as reported by Plato. Philosophers, Diotima and Plato included, have only interpreted the world, as one of sociology's leading founding fathers told us. The point, however, as he also pointed out, is to change it. Doing that entails not merely reiterating ideology. It also involves exposing its deceptions of where we begin, not least in its defiance of death through disguising and occluding from itself and others our emergence from non-being into frailty and consequent dependence on creative and productive interchange with others. It is sadly a mark of the dominance of manic individualism that in the interests, it seems, of marketing, Polity consigned the subtitle of Bauman's book, *On the Frailty of Human Bonds*, to an inner page, behind its defiant cover story and title, *Liquid Love*.

References

Abraham, K. (1911) Notes on the psycho-analytical investigation and treatment of manic-depressive insanity and allied conditions. *Selected Papers*. London: Hogarth, 1968: 137–56.
—— (1924) A short study of the development of the libido, viewed in the light of mental disorders. *Selected Papers*. London: Hogarth, 1968: 418–501.
Alford, C. F. (2002) *Levinas, the Frankfurt School and Psychoanalysis*. New York: Continuum.
Arendt, H. (1971) *The Life of the Mind. I. Thinking*. London: Secker and Warburg, 1978.
Barthes, R. (1963) The metaphor of the eye. *The Story of the Eye*. London: Penguin, 1982: 119–27.
Bataille, G. (1928) *Story of the Eye*. San Francisco, CA: City Lights Books, 1987.
Bauman, Z. (2003) Liquid Love: On the Frailty of Human Bonds. Cambridge: Polity Press.
Bion, W. R. (1962) A theory of thinking. *Second Thoughts*. London: Heinemann, 1967: 110–9.
—— (1965) *Transformations*. London: Heinemann.
—— (1992) *Cogitations*. London: Karnac.
Dostoyevsky, F. (1866) *Crime and Punishment*. Harmondsworth: Penguin, 1951.
Eagleton, T. (2005) *Holy Terror*. Oxford: Oxford University Press.
Freud, S. (1908) Civilized sexual morality and modern nervous illness. *SE9*: 181–204.
—— (1916–17) Introductory lectures on psycho-analysis. *SE16*.
—— (1917) Mourning and melancholia. *SE14*: 243–58.
—— (1925) Negation. *SE19*: 235–9.
Klein, M. (1928) Early stages of the Oedipus conflict. *International Journal of Psycho-Analysis* 9: 167–80. Reprinted 1975 in *The Writings of Melanie Klein*, I. London: Hogarth, 1975: 186–98. (1930) The importance of symbol-formation in the development of the ego. *Love, Guilt and Reparation*. London: Hogarth, 1975: 219–32.
—— (1935) A contribution to the psychogenesis of manic-depressive states of mind. *Love, Guilt and Reparation*. London: Hogarth, 1975: 262–89.
—— (1940) Mourning and its relation to manic-depressive states. *Love, Guilt and Reparation*. London: Hogarth, 1975: 344–69.
Kristeva, J. (1987) *Tales of Love*. Trans. Leon S. Roudiez. New York: Columbia University Press.
—— (1993) *Nations without Nationalism*. Trans. Leon S. Roudiez. New York: Columbia University Press.
—— (1996) *The Sense and Non-Sense of Revolt: The Powers and Limits of Psychoanalysis*. New York: Columbia University Press, 2000.
—— (1999) *Hannah Arendt*. New York: Columbia University Press, 2001.
—— (2000) *Melanie Klein*. New York: Columbia University Press, 2001.
Lacan, J. (1953) Some reflections on the ego. *International Journal of Psycho-Analysis* 34(1): 11–17.
—— (1953–4) *The Seminar of Jacques Lacan. Book I*. New York: Norton, 1988.

—— (1955–6) On a question preliminary to any possible treatment of psychosis. *Ecrits*. London: Tavistock, 1977:179–225.
—— (1958) The signification of the phallus. *Ecrits*. London: Tavistock, 1977: 281–91.
Plato (n.d.) *The Symposium*. Harmondsworth: Penguin, 1951.
Segal, H. (1973) *Introduction to the Work of Melanie Klein*. London: Hogarth.
Winnicott, D. W. (1945) Primitive emotional development. *Collected Papers*. London: Tavistock, 1958: 145–56.
—— (1960) The theory of the parent–infant relationship. *The Maturational Processes and the Facilitating Environment*. London: Hogarth, 1965: 37–55.

PART THREE

LIQUID LIFE

Zygmunt Bauman
TO EACH WASTE ITS DUMPING SITE   171

Zygmunt Bauman
THE REALITY PRINCIPLE AND THE PLEASURE PRINCIPLE
STRIKE A DEAL   187

7 Charles Lemert and Makenna Goodman
   LIQUID WASTE, BEING HUMAN, AND BODILY DEATH   198

8 Michael Hviid Jacobsen
   SOLID MODERNITY, LIQUID UTOPIA – LIQUID MODERNITY,
   SOLID UTOPIA: UBIQUITOUS UTOPIANISM AS A TRADEMARK
   OF THE WORK OF ZYGMUNT BAUMAN   217

9 Iain Wilkinson
   ON BAUMAN'S SOCIOLOGY OF SUFFERING: QUESTIONS FOR
   THINKING   241

ZYGMUNT BAUMAN

TO EACH WASTE ITS DUMPING SITE

Source: Zygmunt Bauman (2004) *Wasted Lives*, Cambridge: Polity Press, pp. 70–93.

Once the modern mode of life stopped being a privilege of selected lands, the primary outlets for human-waste disposal, that is the 'empty' or 'no man's' territories (more precisely, the territories that thanks to the global power differential could be seen and treated as void and/or masterless), have vanished. For the 'redundant humans' now turned out in the parts of the planet that have recently jumped into or fallen under the juggernaut of modernity, such outlets were never in existence; in the so-called 'premodern' societies, innocent of the problem of waste, human or non-human alike, the need for them did not arise. As an effect of that blocking or non-provision of external outlets, societies increasingly turn the sharp edge of exclusionary practices against themselves.

If the excess of population (that is, the part that cannot be reassimilated into normal life patterns and reprocessed back into the category of 'useful' members of society) can be routinely removed and transported beyond the boundaries of the enclosure within which an economic balance and social equilibrium are sought, people who escape transportation and remain inside the enclosure, even if currently redundant, are earmarked for recycling. They are 'out', but only temporarily – their 'staying out' is an abnormality that commands and musters a cure; they clearly need to be helped 'back in' as soon as possible. They are the 'reserve army of labour' and must be put in and held in such a shape as would allow them to return to active service at the first opportunity.

All that changes, however, once the channels for draining human surplus are blocked. As the 'redundant' population stays inside and rubs shoulders with the 'useful' and 'legitimate' rest, the line separating a transient incapacitation from the peremptory and final consignment to waste tends to be blurred and no longer legible. Rather than remaining as before a problem of a separate part of the population, assignment to 'waste' becomes everybody's potential prospect – one of the two poles between which everybody's present and future social standing oscillates. To deal with the 'problem of waste' in this new form the habitual tools and stratagems of intervention do not suffice; nor are they particularly adequate. The new policies soon to be invented in response to the new shape of the old problem will most probably start by subsuming the policies once designed to deal with the problem in its old shape. To be on the safe side, emergency measures aimed at the issue of 'waste inside' will be preferred and sooner or later given priority over all other modes of intervention in the issues of redundancy as such, temporary or not.

All these and similar setbacks and reverses of fortune tend to be magnified and made yet more acute in those parts of the globe that have only recently been confronted with the previously unknown phenomenon of 'surplus population' and the problem of its disposal. 'Recently' in this case means belatedly – at a time when the planet is already full, when no 'empty lands' are left to serve as waste-disposal sites and when any asymmetry of boundaries is turned firmly against newcomers to the family of moderns. Surrounding lands will not invite their surplus nor can be, as they themselves were in the past, forced to accept and accommodate it. Such latecomers to modernity are left to seek a *local* solution to a globally caused problem – though with meagre chances of success.

Where family and communal businesses were once able and willing to absorb, employ and support all newly born humans, and at most times secure their survival, the surrender to global pressures and the laying of their own territory open to the unfettered circulation of capital and commodities made them unviable. Only now do the newcomers to the company of moderns experience that separation of business from households which the pioneers of modernity went through hundreds of years ago, with all its attendant social upheavals and human misery but also with the luxury of global solutions to locally produced problems – an abundance of 'empty' and 'no man's lands' that could easily be used to deposit the surplus population no longer absorbed by the economy emancipated from familial and communal constraints: a luxury not available to the latecomers.

Tribal wars and massacres, a proliferation of 'guerrilla armies' (often little more than barely disguised bandit gangs) busy decimating each other's ranks yet absorbing and annihilating the 'population surplus' (mostly the young, unemployable at home and without prospects) in the process – in short, a 'neighbourhood colonialism' or 'poor man's imperialism' – are among such 'local solutions to global problems' the 'latecomers to modernity' are forced to deploy or rather have found themselves deploying. Hundreds of thousands of people are chased away from their homes, murdered or forced to run for life outside the borders of their country.

Perhaps the sole thriving industry in the lands of the latecomers (deviously and deceitfully dubbed 'developing countries') is the mass production of refugees. It is the ever more prolific products of that industry which the British Prime Minister proposes to unload 'near their home countries', in permanently temporary camps (deviously and deceitfully dubbed 'safe havens'), thereby exacerbating the already unmanageable 'surplus population' problems of immediate neighbours who willy-nilly run a similar industry. The aim is to keep 'local problems' local and so nip in the bud all attempts of latecomers to follow the example of the pioneers of modernity by seeking global (and the sole effective) solutions for locally manufactured problems. As I write these words, in another variation of the same theme NATO has been asked to mobilize its armies to help Turkey to seal its border with Iraq in view of the impending assault on the country. Many a statesperson of the pioneer countries objected, raising many imaginative reservations – but none mentioned publicly that the danger against which Turkey was to be protected was the influx of freshly made homeless Iraqi refugees, not an attack by battered and pulverized Iraqi soldiers.[1]

However earnest, the efforts to stem the tide of 'economic migration' are not and probably cannot be made a hundred per cent successful. Protracted misery makes millions desperate, and in an era of a global frontier-land and globalized crime one can hardly expect a shortage of 'businesses' eager to make a buck or a few billion bucks capitalizing on that desperation. Hence the second formidable consequence of the current transformation: millions of migrants wandering the routes once trodden by the 'surplus population' discharged by the greenhouses of modernity – only in a reverse direction, and this time unassisted (at any rate thus far) by the armies of *conquistadores,* tradesmen and missionaries. The full dimensions of that consequence and its repercussions are yet to unravel and to be grasped in all their many ramifications.

In a brief but sharp exchange of views that took place towards the end of 2001 in connection with the war on Afghanistan, Garry Younge mused on the condition of the planet a day *before* 11 September, that is before the day that by common agreement shook the world and ushered in a completely different phase of planetary history. He remembered 'a boatload of Afghan refugees floating off Australia' (to the applause of 90 per cent of Australians) to be in the end marooned on an uninhabited island in the middle of the Pacific Ocean:

> It is interesting now that they should have been Afghans, given that Australia is very involved in the coalition now, and thinks there is nothing better than a liberated Afghanistan and is prepared to send its bombs to liberate Afghanistan ... Interesting also that we have now a Foreign Secretary who compares Afghanistan to the Nazis, but who, when he was Home Secretary and a group of Afghans landed at Stansted, said that there was no fear of persecution and sent them back.[2]

Younge concludes that on 10 September the world was 'a lawless place' in which the rich and the poor alike knew that 'might is right', that the high and mighty can ignore and bypass international law (or whatever is called by that name) whenever they find that law inconvenient, and that wealth and power determine not just economics but morality and the politics of global space and for that matter everything else concerning life conditions on the planet.

As I am writing, a case is being held in front of a High Court judge in London to test the *legality* of the treatment accorded to six asylum seekers, fleeing regimes officially recognized as 'evil' and/or as routinely violating, or negligent of, human rights, such as Iraq, Angola, Rwanda, Ethiopia and Iran.[3] Keir Starmer QC told the judge, Mr Justice Collins, that the new rules introduced in Britain have left hundreds of asylum seekers 'so destitute that they could not pursue their cases'. They were sleeping rough in the streets, were cold, hungry, scared and sick; some were 'reduced to living in telephone boxes and car parks'. They were allowed 'no funds, no accommodation and no food', and were prohibited from seeking paid work while being denied access to social benefits. And they had no control whatsoever over when, where and if their applications for asylum would be processed. A woman who had escaped from Rwanda after being repeatedly raped and beaten ended up spending the night on a chair at Croydon police station – on condition that she did not fall asleep. A man from Angola who found his father shot and his mother and sister left naked after a multiple rape ended up being denied all support and sleeping rough. Two hundred similar cases are currently waiting for the decision of the courts.

In the case presented by Keir Starmer QC, the judge proclaimed the refusal of social assistance unlawful. The Home Secretary reacted to the verdict angrily: 'Frankly I am personally fed up with having to deal with a situation where Parliament debates issues and the judges then overturn them. . . . We don't accept what Mr Justice Collins has said. We will seek to overturn it.'[4]

The plight of the six whose case Keir Starmer QC presented is probably a side-effect of overcrowding and overflowing in the designed or improvised camps to which asylum seekers are routinely transported at the moment of landing. The numbers of homeless and stateless victims of globalization grow too fast for the designation and construction of camps to keep up.

One of the most sinister effects of globalization is the deregulation of wars. Most present-day warlike actions, and the most cruel and gory among them, are conducted by non-state entities, subject to no state laws and no international conventions. They are simultaneously outcomes and auxiliary but powerful causes of the continuous erosion of state sovereignty and the continuing frontier-land conditions in the 'interstate' global space. Intertribal antagonisms break into the open thanks to the weakening hands of the state, or in the case of the 'new states', of hands never given time to grow strong; once let loose, they render the inchoate or entrenched state-legislated laws unenforceable and practically null and void.

The population as a whole finds itself in a lawless space; the part of the population that decides to flee the battlefield and manages to escape finds itself in another type of lawlessness, that of the global frontier-land. Once outside the borders of their native country, escapees are deprived of the backing of a recognized state authority that could take them under its protection, vindicate their rights and intercede on their behalf with foreign powers. Refugees are stateless, but stateless in a new sense: their statelessness is raised to an entirely new level by the non-existence of a state authority to which their statehood could be referred. They are, as Michel Agier put it in his most insightful study of refugees in the era of globalization,[5] *hors du nomos* – *outside* law; not this or that law of this or that country, but *law as such*. They are outcasts and outlaws of a novel kind, the products of globalization and the fullest epitome and incarnation of its frontier-land spirit. To quote Agier again, they have been cast in a condition of 'liminal drift', with no way of knowing whether it is transitory or permanent. Even if they are stationary for a time, they are on a journey that is never completed since its destination (arrival or return) remains forever unclear, while a place they could call 'final' remains forever inaccessible. They are never to be free from the gnawing sense of the transience, indefiniteness and provisional nature of any settlement.

The plight of Palestinian refugees, many of who have never experienced life outside the camps hastily patched together more than fifty years ago, has been well documented. As globalization takes its toll, though, new camps (less notorious and largely unnoticed or forgotten) mushroom around the spots of conflagration, prefiguring the model Tony Blair wishes the UN High Commission for Refugees to render obligatory. For instance, the three camps of Dabaab, populated by as many people as the rest of the Kenyan Garissa province in which they were located in 1991–2, show no signs of imminent closure, yet till this very day they do not appear on the map of the country. The same applies to the camps of Ilfo (opened in

September 1991), Dagahaley (opened in March 1992) and Hagadera (opened in June 1992).[6]

On the way to the camps, their future inmates are stripped of every single element of their identities except one: that of stateless, placeless, functionless refugees. Inside the fences of the camp, they are pulped into a faceless mass, having been denied access to the elementary amenities from which identities are drawn and the usual yarns of which identities are woven. Becoming 'a refugee' means to lose

> the media on which social existence rests, that is a set of ordinary of things and persons that carry meanings – land, house, village, city, parents, possessions, jobs and other daily landmarks. These creatures in drift and waiting have nothing but their 'naked life', whose continuation depends on humanitarian assistance.[7]

As to the latter point, apprehensions abound. Is not the figure of a humanitarian assistant, whether hired or voluntary, itself an important link in the chain of exclusion? There are doubts whether the caring agencies doing their best to move people away from danger do not inadvertently assist the 'ethnic cleansers'. Agier muses whether the humanitarian worker is not an 'agent of exclusion at a lesser cost', and (more importantly still) a device designed to unload and dissipate the anxiety of the rest of the world, to absolve the guilty and placate the scruples, as well as defuse the sense of urgency and the fear of contingency. Putting the refugees in the hands of 'humanitarian workers' (and closing eyes to the armed guards in the background) seems to be the ideal way to reconcile the irreconcilable: the overwhelming wish to dispose of the noxious human waste while gratifying one's own poignant desire for moral righteousness.

> It may be that the guilty conscience caused by the plight of the damned part of humanity can be healed. To achieve that effect, it will suffice to allow the process of biosegregation, of conjuring up and fixing identities stained by wars, violence, exodus, diseases, misery and inequality – a process already in full swing – to take its course. The carriers of stigma would be definitely kept at a distance by reason of their lesser humanity, that is their physical as well as moral dehumanization.[8]

Refugees are human waste, with no useful function to play in the land of their arrival and temporary stay and no intention or realistic prospect of being assimilated and incorporated into the new social body; from their present place, the dumping site, there is no return and no road forward (unless it is a road towards yet more distant places, as in the case of the Afghan refugees escorted by Australian warships to an island far away from all beaten tracks). A distance large enough to prevent the poisonous effluvia of social decomposition from reaching places inhabited by their native inhabitants is the main criterion by which the location of their permanently temporary camps are selected. Out of that place, refugees are an obstacle and a trouble; inside that place, they are forgotten. In keeping them there and barring all leakage, in making the separation final and irreversible, 'compassion by some and hatred by others' cooperate in producing the same effect of taking distance and holding at a distance.⁹

Nothing is left but the walls, the barbed wire, the controlled gates, the armed guards. Between them they define the refugees' identity – or rather put paid to their right to self-definition. All waste, including wasted humans, tends to be piled up indiscriminately on the same refuse tip. The act of assigning to waste puts an end to differences, individualities, idiosyncrasies. Waste has no need of fine distinctions and subtle nuances, unless it is earmarked for recycling; but the refugees' prospects of being recycled into legitimate and acknowledged members of human society are, to say the least, dim and infinitely remote. All measures have been taken to assure the permanence of their exclusion. People without qualities have been deposited in a territory without denomination, whereas all the roads leading back to meaningful places and to the spots where socially legible meanings can be and are forged daily have been blocked for good.

The exact numbers of refugees scattered around the world is a matter of contention and likely to remain such, given that the very idea of 'refugee' – hiding as much as it reveals – is an 'essentially contested concept'. The most reliable figures available are produced bureaucratically, through registration and filing – primarily by the United Nations High Commissioner for Refugees (UNHCR) in the annual *The State of the World's Refugees* reports. The reports give the numbers of people already recognized as answering the UN definition of a 'refugee' and so of legitimate concern to the UNHCR. The latest report estimated the number of such people at 22.1 million (this figure does not include refugees under the care of other agencies, notably the 4 million Palestinian refugees, and of course the persecuted minorities denied statehood who did not register anywhere or have been denied registration). Of the 22.1 million, 40 per cent were located by the end of 2000 in Asia, nearly 27 per cent in Europe, and slightly over 25 per cent in Africa. The most prolific suppliers of refugees were the territories of tribal conflicts and the target places of global military operations: Burundi, Sudan, Bosnia and Herzegovina, Iraq.¹⁰ Most countries, UNHCR complains, 'do not subscribe to the definition' by which it operates. Even more countries insist on assurances that the temporary protection they are pressed to offer 'is indeed temporary' and that refugees will eventually be returned to their home countries or move elsewhere. 'Being under protection' does not mean 'being wanted' – and everything needed, and much more, is being done to prevent the refugees from confusing the two conditions.

Once a refugee, forever a refugee. Roads back to the lost (or rather no longer existing) homely paradise have been all but cut, and all exits from the purgatory of the camp lead to hell . . . The prospectless succession of empty days inside the perimeter of the camp may be tough to endure, but God forbid that the appointed or voluntary plenipotentiaries of humanity, whose job it is to keep the refugees inside the camp but away from perdition, pull the plug. But they do, time and again, whenever the powers-that-be decide that the exiles are no longer refugees since 'it is safe to return' to a homeland that has long ceased to be their homeland and has nothing to offer them that could be wished for. There are, for instance, about 900,000 refugees from the intertribal massacres and the battlefields of uncivil wars waged for decades in Ethiopia and Eritrea, scattered over the northern regions of Sudan, itself an impoverished, war-devastated country. They are mixed with other refugees who recall with horror the killing fields of southern Sudan.[11] By the decision of the UN agency endorsed by the non-governmental charities, they are no longer refugees and so are no longer entitled to humanitarian aid. They refused to go, however; apparently, they do not believe that there is 'a home' to which they could 'return', since the homes they remember have been either gutted or stolen. The new task of their humanitarian wardens is therefore to *make* them go . . . In Kassala camp, cutting of water supplies was followed by the forceful removal of inmates beyond the perimeter of the camp which just like their homes in Ethiopia has been razed to the ground to bar all thought of return. The same lot was visited on the inmates of Um Gulsam Laffa and Newshagarab camps. According to the local villagers' testimony, about 8,000 inmates perished when camp hospitals were closed, water wells dismantled and food delivery abandoned. It is difficult to verify their fate; though what one can be certain of is that hundreds of thousands have disappeared from the refugee registers and statistics even if they did not manage to escape from the nowhere-land of non-humanity.

Refugees, the human waste of the global frontier-land, are 'the outsiders incarnate', the absolute outsiders, outsiders everywhere and out of place everywhere except in places that are themselves out of place – the 'nowhere places' that appear on no maps used by ordinary humans on their travels. Once outside, indefinitely outside, a secure fence with watching towers is the only contraption needed to make the 'indefiniteness' of the out-of-place hold forever.

It is a different story with the redundant humans already 'inside' and bound to stay inside as the new fullness of the planet bars their territorial exclusion. In the absence of empty places to which they could be deported and the locking up of the places to which they would travel of their own free will in search of sustenance, waste-disposal sites must be laid out inside the locality which has made them supernumerary. Such sites emerge in all or most large cities. They are urban ghettoes; or rather, to follow Loïc Wacquant's insight, 'hyperghettoes'.[12]

Ghettoes, named or unnamed, are ancient institutions. They served the purpose of 'composite stratification' (and in one go 'multiple deprivation' as well), overlapping differentiation by caste or class with territorial separation. Ghettoes might be voluntary or involuntary (though only the latter tend to carry the stigma of the name), the main difference between the two being which side of the 'asymmetrical boundary' they faced – the obstacles piled up, respectively, at the entry to or at the exit from the ghetto territory.

Even in the case of 'involuntary ghettoes' there was, however, a modicum of 'pull' factors added to the decisive 'push' forces. They used to be 'mini societies', replicating in miniature all the major institutions that served the daily needs and life pursuits of those living outside the ghetto boundaries. They also provided its residents with a degree of security and at least a whiff of the feeling of *chez soi,* of being at home, unavailable to them outside. To quote Wacquant's description of the pattern dominant in the black American ghettoes of the last century:

> the black bourgeoisie's [doctors, lawyers, teachers, businessmen] economic power rested on supplying goods and services to its lower-class brethren; and

all 'brown' residents of the city were united in their common rejection of caste subordination and abiding concern to 'advance the race' . . . As a result, the postwar ghetto was *integrated both socially and structurally* – even the 'shadies' who earned their living from such illicit trades as the 'numbers game', liquor sale, prostitution and other *risqué* recreations, were entwined with the different classes.[13]

The orthodox ghettoes might have been enclosures surrounded by insurmountable, even if non-material, barriers [physical and social] and with the few remaining exits exceedingly difficult to negotiate. They might have been instruments of class-and-caste segregation and might have branded their residents with the stigma of inferiority and social rejection. Unlike the 'hyperghettoes' that have grown out of them and took their place towards the end of the last century, they were not however dumping sites for the surplus, redundant, unemployable and functionless population. Unlike its classical predecessor, the new ghetto, in Wacquant's words, 'serves not as a reservoir of disposable industrial labour but a mere dumping ground [for those for who] the surrounding society has no economic or political use'. Abandoned by their own middle classes, who ceased to rely on black clientele alone and chose to buy their way into the higher grade security of the voluntary ghettoes of 'gated communities', the ghetto dwellers cannot create on their own substitute economic or political uses to replace the uses denied to them by the greater society. As a result, 'whereas the ghetto in its classical form acted partly as a protective shield against brutal racial exclusion, the hyper-ghetto has lost its positive role of collective buffer, making it a deadly machinery for naked social relegation.'

In other words: the American black ghetto has turned purely and simply into a, virtually single-purpose, waste-disposal tip. 'It has devolved into a one-dimensional machinery for naked relegation, a human warehouse wherein are discarded those segments of urban society deemed disreputable, derelict, and dangerous.'

Wacquant notices and lists a number of parallel and mutually coordinated processes that bring the American black ghettoes ever closer to the model of prisonlike Goffmanesque 'total institutions': a 'prisonization' of public housing ever more reminiscent of houses of detention, with new 'projects' 'fenced up, their perimeter placed under beefed-up security patrols and authoritarian controls' – and as Jerome G. Miller noted, 'random searches, segregation, curfews, and resident counts – all familiar procedures of efficient prison management';[14] and the transformation of state-maintained schools into 'institutions of confinement' whose primary mission is not to educate but to ensure 'custody and control' – 'Indeed, it appears that the main purpose of these schools is simply to "neutralize" youth considered unworthy and unruly by holding them under lock for the day so that, at minimum, they do not engage in street crime.'

There is a movement in the opposite direction, transforming the nature of American prisons, their manifest and latent functions, their declared and tacit purposes and their physical structures and routines, so that urban ghettoes and prisons meet halfway, their meeting place being the explicit role of a dumping ground for human waste. To quote Wacquant again, 'The "Big House" that embodied the correctional ideal of melioristic treatment and community reintegration of inmates gave way to a race-divided and violence-ridden "warehouse" geared solely to neutralizing social rejects by sequestering them physically from society.'[15]

As far as other urban ghettoes are concerned, and particularly the ghettoes emerging in the great number of European cities with a significant immigrant population, a similar transformation may be fairly advanced but remains incomplete. Racially or ethnically pure urban ghettoes remain a rarity in Europe. Besides, unlike the American blacks, the recent and relatively recent immigrants who populate them are not locally produced human waste; they are 'imported waste' from other countries with a lingering hope of recycling. The question of whether such 'recycling' is or is not on the cards and so whether the verdict of assignment to waste is final and globally binding remains open. These urban ghettoes remain, we may say, 'halfway inns' or 'two-way streets'. It is because of that provisional, undecided, underdefined character that they are the sources and the target of acute tension erupting daily into reconnaissance skirmishes and boundary clashes.

This ambiguity that sets the immigrant and thus far mixed-population ghettoes of European towns apart from the American 'hyperghettoes' may not however last. As Philippe Robert found, French urban ghettoes that originally had the character of 'transit' or 'passage' stations for new immigrants who were expected soon to be assimilated and ingested by established urban structures turned into 'spaces of relegation' once employment was deregulated, becoming precarious and volatile, and unemployment became durable. It was then that the resentment and animosity of the established population grew into a virtually impenetrable wall locking out the newcomers-turned-outsiders. The *quartiers,* already socially degraded and cut off from communication with other parts of the cities, were now 'the only places where [the immigrants] could feel *chez soi,* sheltered from the malevolent looks of the rest of the population'.[16]

Hughes Lagrange and Thierry Pech note in addition that once the state, having abandoned most of its economic and social functions, selected a 'policy of security' (and more concretely of personal safety) as the hub of its strategy aimed at recouping its fallen authority and the restoration of its protective importance in the eyes of the citizenry, the influx of newcomers was overtly or obliquely blamed for the rising uneasiness and diffuse fears emanating from the ever more precarious labour market.[17] The immigrants' *quartiers* were depicted as hothouses of petty criminality, begging and prostitution, which were accused in their turn of playing a major role in the rising anxiety of 'ordinary citizens'. To the acclaim of its citizens desperately seeking the roots of their incapacitating anxiety, the state flexed its muscle, however flabby and indolent in all other domains, in full public view – criminalizing those margins of the population who were the most feeble and living the most precariously, designing ever more stringent and severe 'firm hand' policies and waging spectacular anti-crime campaigns focused on the human waste of foreign origin dumped in the suburbs of French cities.

Loïc Wacquant notes a paradox:

The same people who yesterday fought with visible success for 'less state' to set free capital and the way it used the labour force, arduously demand today 'more state' to contain and hide the deleterious social consequences of the deregulation of employment conditions and the deterioration of social protection for the inferior regions of social space.[18]

Of course, what Wacquant noted is anything but a paradox. The apparent change of heart strictly follows the logic of the passage from the recycling to the disposal of human waste. The passage was radical enough to need the keen and energetic assistance of state power, and the state obliged.

It did it first by dismantling collective forms of insurance to cover individuals who fell off the productive treadmill (temporarily, it was assumed). It was the kind of insurance that made obvious sense to both left and right wings of the political spectrum as long as the fall (and thus the assignment to productive waste) was deemed to be a temporary mishap, ushering in a brief stage of recycling ('rehabilitating', then returning to active service in the industrial force). But it quickly lost its 'beyond left and right' support once the prospects of recycling started to look remote and uncertain and the facilities of regular recycling looked increasingly incapable of accommodating all who had fallen or who had never risen in the first place.

Second, the state obliged by designing and building new secure waste-disposal sites – an endeavour certain to command ever growing popular support as the hopes of successful recycling faded, as the traditional method of human-waste disposal (through the exportation of surplus labour) ceased to be available, and as the suspicion of human universal disposability deepened and spread wider, together with the horror that the sight of 'wasted humans' evoked.

The social state is gradually, yet relentlessly and consistently, turned into a 'garrison state', as Henry A. Giroux calls it, describing it as a state that increasingly protects the interests of global, transnational corporations 'while stepping up the level of repression and militarization on the domestic front'. Social problems are increasingly criminalized. In Giroux's summary,

> Repression increases and replaces compassion. Real issues such as a tight housing market and massive unemployment in the cities – as causes of homelessness, youth loitering and drug epidemics – are overlooked in favour of policies associated with discipline, containment and control.[19]

The immediate proximity of large and growing agglomerations of 'wasted humans', likely to become durable or permanent, calls for stricter segregationist policies and extraordinary security measures, lest the 'health of society', the 'normal functioning' of the social system, be endangered. The notorious tasks of 'tension management' and 'pattern maintenance' that, according to Talcott Parsons, each system needs to perform in order to survive presently boil down almost entirely to the tight separation of 'human waste' from the rest of society, its exemption from the legal framework in which the life pursuits of the rest of society are conducted, and its 'neutralization'. 'Human waste' can no longer be removed to distant waste-disposal sites and placed firmly out of bounds to 'normal life'. It needs therefore to be sealed off in tightly closed containers.

The penal system supplies such containers. In David Garland's succinct and precise summary of the current transformation, prisons which in the era of recycling 'functioned as the deep end of the correctional sector' are today 'conceived much more explicitly as a mechanism of exclusion and control'. It is the walls, and not what happens inside the walls, that 'are now seen as the institution's most important and valuable element'.[20] At best, the intention to 'rehabilitate', to 'reform', to 're-educate' and to return the stray sheep to the flock is only paid an occasional lip service – and when it is, it is countered with an angry chorus baying for blood, with the leading tabloids in the role of conductors and leading politicians singing all the solo parts. Explicitly, the main and perhaps the sole purpose of prisons is not just any human-waste disposal but a final, definitive disposal. Once rejected, forever rejected. For a former prisoner on parole or on probation, a return to society is almost impossible and a return to prison almost certain. Instead of guiding and easing the road 'back to the community' for prisoners who have served their term of punishment, the function of probation officers is keeping the community safe from the perpetual danger temporarily let loose. The interests of convicted offenders, insofar as they are considered at all, are viewed as fundamentally opposed to those of the public.'[21] Indeed, offenders tend to be viewed as 'intrinsically evil and wicked', they 'are not like us'. All similarities are purely accidental . . .

> There can be no mutual intelligibility, no bridge of understanding, no real communication between 'us' and 'them' . . .
> Whether the offender's character is the result of bad genes or of being reared in an anti-social culture, the outcome is the same – a person who is beyond the pale, beyond reform, outside the civil community . . .
> Those who do not or cannot fit in must be excommunicated and forcibly expelled.[22]

In a nutshell, prisons, like so many other social institutions, have moved from the task of recycling to that of waste-disposal. They have been reallocated to the front line of the battle to resolve the crisis in which the waste-disposal industry has fallen as a result of the global triumph of modernity and the new fullness of the planet. All waste is potentially poisonous – or at least, being defined as waste, it is deemed to be contaminating and disturbing to the proper order of things. If recycling is no longer profitable and its chances (at any rate in the present-day setting) are no longer realistic, the right way to deal with waste is to speed up its 'biodegradation' and decomposition while isolating it as securely as possible from the ordinary human habitat.

> Work, social welfare, and family support used to be the means whereby ex-prisoners were reintegrated into mainstream society. With the decline of these resources, imprisonment has become a longer-term assignment from which individuals have little prospect of returning to an unsupervised freedom . . .
> The prison is used today as a kind of reservation, a quarantine zone in which purportedly dangerous individuals are segregated in the name of public safety.[23]

Building more prisons, making more offences punishable by imprisonment, the policy of 'zero tolerance' and harsher and longer sentences are best understood as so many efforts to rebuild the failing and faltering waste-disposal industry – on a new foundation more in keeping with the novel conditions of the globalized world.

There is also another kind of waste directly linked to the globalization process in its present form: a kind of waste whose origins can be traced back to globalization's 'frontier-land' conditions and one that globalization in such a form cannot but turn out daily in Manuel Castells's 'space of flows'.

As has been already suggested, under classical 'frontier-land' conditions cattle barons and outlaws were in tacit agreement: neither of them wished the lawlessness and the rule of the quickest and the shrewdest and the least scrupulous to grind to a halt and be replaced with the government of law. They both thrived on the absence of routine, on fluidity of alliances and front lines and on the overall frailty of commitments, rights and obligations. Such a convergence of interests did not augur well for the personal safety of everyone inside the frontier-land, whatever precautions residents or travellers took to insure themselves against the danger. It made the frontier-land a site of perpetual uncertainty and at the same time made insecurity immune to all effective intervention. Insecurity could not be confronted at its source; like the coalitions and the battlefields, the resulting anxiety was free-floating, unsure of its targets and selecting them at random. Frontier-land conditions are best conveyed by Jurij Lotman's metaphor of the minefield, of which one can say with a high degree of certainty that explosions will occur there, but can only guess at their timing and location.

In the present-day rendition of frontier-land conditions the place of cattle barons has been taken by global manufacturing, trade and capital companies, while the free-roaming bandits, single or in gangs, have been replaced by terrorist networks and an indefinable number of scattered individuals who spy in terrorist acts an archetype for their own private battles with individually suffered traumas or simply a hint as to how even a snubbed and spurned wretch can go down with a bang.

The acts of both major adversaries/partners in the frontier-land game add profusely to the production of human waste. The first are most active in the 'economic progress' branch of the industry, the second in the 'creative destruction of order' branch – a thoroughly deregulated version of the coercive undertakings in which modern states used to be engrossed from the start even while claiming monopoly on designing and building social order.

No authority can claim today an exclusive grip over its ostensibly sovereign territory. Even the most closely guarded borders are porous and prove easy to penetrate; courtesy of shock-greedy media, the massive forces summoned to protect borderlines against leaks and break-ins (like the widely publicized sight of tanks at Heathrow) daily remind the public of the ultimate vanity of the effort. Strikingly different and often incompatible ideas of the right and proper order of things meet and clash inside each ostensibly sovereign territory, their champions and foot soldiers vying with each other to lift the world to the height of their idea – though invariably at the expense of the residents, transformed in the process into thoroughly disposable props of the battle scene, the 'collateral damage' of the actions of war.

In the era of globalization, the 'collateral damage' and 'collateral casualties' left behind by the continuously sizzling and occasionally erupting enmities between the liquid modern versions of cattle barons and mounted bandits turn gradually into the staple and most voluminous products of the waste industry. While (in theory at least, if not in practice) one can fight tooth and nail against an adverse verdict delivered by the authority in judgement, fight to reverse the verdict, argue to prove one's case, appeal to a higher court in case your argument is rejected, try to arouse public indignation and protest, and if all that fails seek rescue in an escape from the realm of the court's sovereignty – none of such expedients are available to the victims of 'collateral damage'. There is no authority they may resist, sue, lay charges against, or demand compensation from. They are the waste of the ongoing creative destruction of global legal, political and ethical order.

Under such circumstances no line drawn to separate 'the waste' from a 'useful product' is likely to remain uncontested and no sentence condemning to a life-on-a-refuse-heap is likely to hold for long without an opposition trying hard to overthrow and reverse it. And so no one feels truly secure amidst the uncounted number of competing design-and-build projects. No one can rely on a recent or currently enforced verdict, however powerful the authority that delivered it might be. No one can assume that the spectre of a disposal tip has been once and for all exorcized and the danger of being rejected and consigned to waste definitely averted. The overall impression is one of randomness, unalloyed contingency, blind fate – and against haphazard sequences, unaccountable accidents and *non sequiturs,* just as against ad hoc alliances of powers held together or dismantled by bribery or blackmail, there is no conceivable defence. One can possibly avoid being a victim, but nothing can be done to escape the fate of being a 'collateral casualty'. That adds a wholly new sinister dimension to the spectre of uncertainty that hovers above the world remade into a global frontier-land.

The 'social state', that crowning of the long history of European democracy and until recently its dominant form, is today in retreat. The social state based its legitimacy and rested its demands for the loyalty and obedience of its citizens on the promise to defend them and insure against redundancy, exclusion and rejection as well as against random blows of fate – against being consigned to 'human waste' because of individual inadequacies or misfortunes; in short, on the promise to insert certainty and security into lives in which chaos and contingency would otherwise rule. If hapless individuals stumbled and fell, there would be someone around ready to hold their hands and help them to their feet again.

Erratic conditions of employment buffeted by market competition were then, as they continue to be, the major source of the uncertainty about the future and the insecurity of social standing and self-esteem that haunted the citizens. It was primarily against that uncertainty that the *social* state undertook to protect its subjects – by making jobs more secure and the future more assured. For the reasons already discussed this is however no longer the case. The contemporary state cannot deliver on the social state's promise and its politicians no longer repeat the promise. Instead, their policies portend a yet more precarious, risk-ridden life calling for a lot of brinkmanship while making life projects all but impossible; they call on the electors to be 'more flexible' (that is, to brace themselves for yet more insecurity to come) and to seek individually their own individual solutions to the socially produced troubles.

A most urgent imperative faced by every government presiding over the dismantling and demise of the social state is therefore the task of finding or construing a new 'legitimation formula' on which the self-assertion of state authority and the demand of discipline may rest instead. Being felled as a 'collateral casualty' of economic progress, now in the hands of free-floating global economic forces, is not a plight which state governments can credibly promise to stave off. But beefing up fears about the threat to personal safety from similarly free-floating terrorist conspirators, and then promising more security guards, a denser net of X-ray machines and a wider scope for closed-circuit television, more frequent checks and more pre-empting strikes and precautionary arrests to protect that safety, looks like an expedient alternative.

By contrast with the all-too-tangible and daily experienced insecurity manufactured by the markets, which need no help from political powers except to be left alone, the mentality of a 'besieged fortress' and of individual bodies and private possession under threat must be actively cultivated. Threats must be painted in the most sinister of colours, so that the *non-materialization of threats* rather than the advent of the foreboded apocalypse can be presented to the frightened public as an *extraordinary* event, and above all as the result of the exceptional skills, vigilance, care and goodwill of state organs. And this is done, and to spectacular effect. Almost daily, and at least once a week, the CIA and the FBI warn Americans of imminent attempts on their safety, casting them into a state of constant security alert and holding them there, putting individual safety firmly into the focus of the most varied and diffuse tensions – while the American President keeps reminding his electors that 'it would take one vial, one canister, one crate slipped into this country to bring a day of horror like none we have ever known'. That strategy is eagerly, even if so far with somewhat less ardour (less because of lack of funds rather than will), copied by other governments overseeing the burial of the social state. A new popular demand for a strong state power capable of resuscitating the fading hopes of protection against a confinement to waste is built on the foundation of *personal* vulnerability and *personal* safety, instead of *social* precariousness and *social* protection.

As in so many other cases, so also in the development of that new legitimation formula America plays a pioneering, pattern-setting role. There is little wonder that many a government facing the same task looks towards America with sympathetic anticipation, finding in its policies a useful example to follow. Underneath the ostensible and openly aired differences of opinion on the ways to proceed there seems to be a genuine 'union of minds' between the governments, not at all reducible to the momentary coincidence of transient interests; an unwritten, tacit agreement of state power holders on a common legitimation policy. That this may be the case is shown in the zeal with which the British Prime Minister, watched with rising interest by other European prime ministers, embraces and imports all American novelties related to the production of a 'state of emergency' – such as locking up the 'aliens' (euphemistically called 'asylum seekers') in camps, giving 'security considerations' unquestioned priority over human rights, writing off or suspending many a human right that has stayed in force since the time of the Magna Carta and habeas corpus, a 'zero tolerance' policy towards alleged 'budding criminals', and regularly repeated warnings that *somewhere, sometime, some* terrorists will most surely strike. We are all potential candidates for the role of 'collateral casualties' in a war we did not declare and to which we did not give our consent. When measured against that threat, hammered home as much more immediate and dramatic, it is hoped that the orthodox fears of social redundancy will be dwarfed and possibly even put to sleep.

'Collateral damage' was a term that might have been specifically invented to denote the human waste specific to the new planetary frontier-land conditions created by the impetuous and unrestrained globalization drive that thus far effectively resists all attempts at taming and regulating it. Fears related to that variety of modern waste production seem to overshadow the more traditional waste-related apprehensions and anxieties. Little wonder that they are most eagerly employed in the construction (and so also in the attempts at deconstruction) of new planet-wide power hierarchies.

These new kinds of fear also dissolve trust, the binding agent of all human togetherness. Epicurus, the ancient sage, already noted (in the letter to Menoeceus) that 'it is not so much our friends' help that helps us as the confident knowledge that they will help us'. Without trust, the web of human commitments falls apart, making the world a yet more dangerous and fearsome place. The fears aroused by the frontier-land variety of waste tend to be self-reproducing, self-corroborating and self-magnifying.

Trust is replaced by universal suspicion. All bonds are assumed to be untrustworthy, unreliable, trap-and-ambush like until proven otherwise; but in the absence of trust the very idea of a 'proof, let alone a clinching and final proof' is anything but clear and convincing. What would a credible, really trustworthy proof be like? You wouldn't recognize it if you saw it; even staring it in the face, you wouldn't believe that it was indeed what it was pretending to be. The acceptance of proof, therefore, needs to be postponed indefinitely. The efforts at tying up and fastening bonds line up in an infinite sequence of experiments. Being experimental, accepted 'on a trial basis' and perpetually on trial, always of a provisional 'let's wait and see how they work' kind, human alliances, commitments and bonds are unlikely to solidify enough to be proclaimed fully and truly reliable. Born of suspicion, they beget suspicion.

Commitments (employment contracts, wedding agreements, living together arrangements) are entered into with a 'cancellation option' in mind; and by the firmness of the 'opt out' clauses is their quality judged and desirability measured. In other words, it is clear from the very start that a waste-disposal site will indeed be, as it should and as it is bound to be, their ultimate destination. From the moment of their birth, commitments are seen and treated as prospective waste. Frailty (of the biodegradable sort) is therefore seen as their advantage. It is easy to forget that the bond-tying commitments were sought in the first place, and continue to be sought, for the sake of putting paid to that mind-boggling and blood-curdling fragility of human existence . . .

Bereaved of trust, saturated with suspicion, life is shot through with antinomies and ambiguities it cannot resolve. Hoping to get on under the sign of waste, it stumbles from a disappointment to a frustration, each time landing at the very point it wished to escape when starting its journey of exploration. A life so lived leaves behind a string of faulty and abandoned relationships – the waste of the global frontier-land conditions notorious for recasting trust as a sign of naivety and as a trap for the unresourceful and gullible.

Notes

1 At the time of the Gulf War, 'when Saddam turned his helicopter gunships on the Iraqi Kurds, they tried to flee north over the mountains into Turkey – but the Turks refused to let them in. They physically whipped them back at the border crossings. I heard one Turkish officer say. 'We hate these people. They're fucking pigs.' So for weeks the Kurds were stuck in the mountains at 10 below zero, often with only the clothes they were wearing when they fled. The children suffered the most: dysentery, typhoid, malnutrition . . .', see Maggie O'Kane, 'The most pitiful sights I have ever seen', *Guardian*, 14 Feb. 2003, pp. 6–11.
2 Garry Younge, 'A world full of strangers', *Soundings* (winter 2001–2), pp. 18–22.
3 See Alan Travis, 'Treatment of asylum seekers "is inhumane"', *Guardian*, 11 Feb. 2003, p. 7.
4 See Alan Travis, 'Blunkett to fight asylum ruling', *Guardian*, 20 Feb. 2003, p. 2.
5 See Michel Agier, *Aux bords du monde, les réfugiés* (Flammarion, 2002), pp. 55–6.
6 Ibid., p. 86.
7 Ibid., p. 94.
8 Ibid., p. 117.
9 Ibid., p. 120.
10 See Sharon Stenton Russell, 'Refugees: risks and challenges world-wide', *Migration Information Source*, 26 Nov. 2002.
11 See Fabienine Rose Émilie le Houerou, 'Camps de la soif au Soudan', *Le Monde Diplomatique*, May 2003, p. 28.
12 See Loïc Wacquant, 'Urban outcasts: stigma and division in the black American ghetto and the French urban periphery', *International Journal of Urban and Regional Research* 3 (1993), pp. 365–83; 'A black city within the white: revising America's black ghetto', *Black Renaissance* (fall/winter 1998), pp. 142–51.
13 See Loïc Wacquant, 'Deadly symbiosis: when ghetto and prison meet and mesh', *Punishment and Society* 1 (2002), pp. 95–134.
14 Jerome G. Miller, Search and Destroy: African-American Males in the Criminal Justice System (Cambridge University Press, 1996), p. 101.
15 Wacquant, 'Deadly symbiosis'.
16 See 'Une généalogie de l'insécurité contemporaine', entretien avec Philippe Robert, *Esprit* (Dec. 2002), pp. 35–58.
17 See Hughes Lagrange and Thierry Pech, 'Délinquance: les rendezvous de l'état social', *Esprit* (Dec. 2002), pp. 71–85.
18 Wacquant 'commet la "tolerance zero" vint à l'Europe', p. 40. In *Manière de Voir* (Mar./Apr. 2001), pp. 38–46.
19 See Henry A. Giroux, 'Global capitalism and the return of the garrison state', *Arena Journal* 19 (2002), pp. 141–60.
20 David Garland, The Culture of Control: Crime and Social Order in Contemporary Society (Oxford University Press, 2001), pp. 177–8.
21 Ibid., p. 180.
22 Ibid., pp. 184–5.
23 Ibid., p. 178.

ZYGMUNT BAUMAN

THE REALITY PRINCIPLE AND THE PLEASURE PRINCIPLE STRIKE A DEAL

Source: Zygmunt Bauman (2002) *Society Under Siege*, Cambridge: Polity Press, pp. 187–200.

The 'reality principle', as Sigmund Freud famously declared, was the limit set to the 'pleasure principle' – the boundary over which the seekers of pleasure could trespass only at their own peril. The two principles were at cross-purposes; it did not occur to either the managers of capitalist factories nor the preachers of modern reason that the two enemies could strike a deal and become allies, that pleasure could be miraculously transmogrified into the mainstay of reality and that the search for pleasure could become the major (and sufficient) instrument of pattern maintenance. That, in other words, fluidity could be the ultimate solidity – the most stable of conceivable conditions. And yet this is precisely what the consumer society is about: enlisting the 'pleasure principle' in the service of the 'reality principle'; harnessing the volatile, fastidious and squeamish desires to the chariot of social order, using the friable stuff of spontaneity as the building material for the lasting and solid, tremor-proof foundations of routine. Consumer society has achieved a previously unimaginable feat: it has reconciled the reality and pleasure principles by putting, so to speak, the thief in charge of the treasure chest. Instead of fighting vexing and recalcitrant but presumably invincible irrational human wishes, it has made them into faithful and reliable (hired) guards of rational order.

How did this wondrous transformation come about?

First came the reclassification of human desires; once the irritating though unavoidable costs of production, they have been transferred in the accountancy books to the side of profits. Capitalism discovered that the morbid urge for distraction, that major scourge of profit-making from the exploitation of productive labour, may become the largest and perhaps an inexhaustible source of profit once it is the turn of the consumers, rather than the producers, to be exploited. As George Ritzer points out,

> the focus in contemporary capitalism, at least in the United States, seems to have shifted from the valorization and control processes, indeed from production as a whole, to consumption. The essence of modern capitalism, at least as it is practiced by the core nations, may not be so much maximizing the exploitation of workers as the maximization of consumption.[1]

Far from needing taming and incarcerating, desires should be set free and made to feel free; better still, encouraged to run wild, to ignore all limits and go on the rampage. 'Acting on impulse', that epitome of irrationality in the world of producers, savings books and long-term investments, is destined to become the major factor of rational calculation in the universe of consumers, credit cards and instant gratification.

Then, the fragility and precariousness endemic to the pleasure-and-distraction-seeking life have been reclassified from being the major threats to the stability of social order into being its chief support. Modernity has discovered that the condition of volatility which results in the perpetual insecurity of actors may be made into the most reliable of pattern-maintaining factors. The politics of normative regulation has been replaced by the 'policy of precarization': the flexibility of human conditions pregnant with the insecurity of the present and uncertainty of the future has been found to be the best raw material for the construction of a tough and resilient order; life sliced into episodes with no strings to the past and no bind on the future eliminates the challenge to order more radically than the most elaborate (and exorbitantly costly) institutions of panoptical surveillance and day-in, day-out management. As Pierre Bourdieu points out, 'those who deplore the cynicism which in their opinion marks the men and women of our time should not omit to mention the economic and social conditions which favour or demand, as well as reward it.'[2]

Bourdieu coined the term 'Flexploitation' for the strategy deployed (whether deliberately or matter-of-factly) by that novel policy of social integration and conflict prevention. Flexploitation no longer promotes rationality of behaviour, nor is it meant to: after all, while the ability to make future projections is the condition *sine qua non* of all rational behaviour, making future projections all but impossible (except in the shortest of terms) is the principal objective, and most conspicuous effect, of the 'policy of precarization'. Whatever the rationality of consumer society may mean, it does not aim to rest – in stark opposition to the society of producers of the 'solid' stage of modernity – on the universalization of rational thought and action, but on a free reign of irrational passions (just as its routine rests on catering for the desire of diversion, its uniformity on the recognition of diversity, and its conformity on its agents' liberation). The rationality of consumer society is built out of the irrationality of its individualized actors.

Holism made fallacy

Speaking of 'policy', we tacitly assume the presence of 'policymakers': there must be someone (or something) for who the happy reunion of the reality and pleasure principles was an objective to be systematically pursued or a strategem consistently deployed, being calculated to suit their interests best. Many studies of consumer facilities and habits bear an uncanny resemblance to detective novels: in the stories told of the birth and ascendancy of consumer society, the plots tend to grind relentlessly to the unmasking of the scheming culprit(s). There is hardly a piece without some singly or severally acting villains – be it a conspiracy of merchandisers, the sly intrigues of their advertising henchmen, or brainwashing orchestrated by media moguls. Explicitly or implicitly, the shoppers/consumers emerge from the story as victims of collective brain damage: gullible and duped victims of crowd hypnosis.

The stories in question are misleading without necessarily being false. They carry a lot of truth (none of the appointed villains is without guilt: if not as an accomplice, then at least as an accessory-after-the-fact) – and yet vital chunks of the truth remain untold and unaccounted for. What is missing in the argument and left out of consideration is a possibility that, far from being deceived and falling into a skilfully laid trap, the members of consumer society try hard, just as all human beings do, to respond sensibly to the conditions of life which may be, but may not be, rational and suitable for rational conduct and render rational strategies effective: that, in other words, under certain conditions irrational behaviour may carry many a trapping of rational strategy and even offer the most immediately obvious rational option among those available.

As we know from Karl Marx, one thing which is not for choosing is the conditions under which the choices are made and which sort out the few realistic and effective choices from the many that are nebulous and abortive. People do make history – but seldom if ever is the history they make 'made to order' and seldom does it resemble the end-state they divined and pursued in their labours. Sociologists have chosen to call that disparity between rationally conceived ends and the kinds of realities that emerge in the course of pursuing them the 'unanticipated consequences' of human action, pointing out that whatever is there in the world people inhabit is a consequence of their deeds yet not the kind of consequence they expected or desired. The conditions which made the consumer society feasible, and the actions of its major protagonists effective, are the unanticipated consequences of the history of modern capitalism over more than two centuries. The sellers of goods and of their images may be earnestly and vigorously cultivating the conditions under which their own and their addressees' actions make sense and bring results, but no one planned these conditions in advance 'in order to' create the setting in which present-day practices would become viable. If anything, the conditions in question belied the projections and dashed the hopes of the most insightful thinkers and people of action of the 'solid modernity' era.

In her eye-opening study of the way in which social scientists compose and share their stories, Barbara Czarniawska considers the reasons why writing a novel of the classic 'realist' type, until recently identified with the novel as such, has nowadays become all but impossible. The realist novel, she says,

> celebrated holism as the only proper perspective on both society and the individual . . . This kind of narrative presupposed, as a scene on which public action by moral agents could unfold, a stable social order, a clear-cut political economy, and a collective psychology in which personal character and public conduct were assumed to be inseparable. When such assumptions became untenable, some proclaimed 'the end of the novel'.[3]

The holistic assumptions of the intimate link between personal conduct and society at large have however become untenable, and writing a 'realist' novel, which drew a line between the solid world out there and fickle and error-prone humans desperately trying to find their way through the labyrinth by choosing all the right turns and omitting all the wrong ones, has become a daunting, perhaps an impossible task. The holistic assumptions were not the private property of the 'realist' novelists; they shared them with the enlightened opinion of their time (as well as with the common human experience of the 'solid modernity' era), notably with the most reputable psychologists, who in order to learn more about human behaviour used to send hungry rats through the corridors of a maze and recorded the time the rodents needed to learn the quickest way leading through fixed and inflexible passages to the pellet of food permanently placed in one, and always the same, of the many cells of the labyrinthine edifice. The conduct of the laboratory rats, much like that of the characters of *Bildungsromane,* was all about learning, and learning fast, and being rewarded by learning well and punished for neglect or sloth in learning. But to conceive of conduct in such a fashion, the walls of the twisted corridors of the maze had to retain their shape, if not forever then at least long enough for the learning to reach completion; and the norms and institutions of society (those equivalents of the maze passages) which the heroes of the realist novels had to learn to follow and obey had to be resistant to change and steady enough to be projected into the undefinable future.

Indeed, for Émile Durkheim, it was 'an undoubted fact' that

> we need to believe that our actions have consequences which go beyond the immediate moment: that they are not completely limited to the point in time and space at which they are produced, but that their results are, to some degree, of lasting duration and broad in scope. Otherwise they would be too insignificant: scarcely more than a thread would separate them from the void, and they would not have any interest for us. Only actions which have a lasting quality are worthy of our volition, only pleasures which endure are worthy of our desires.[4]

All people, Durkheim insisted, 'aspire to detach themselves from the present'. That applies to a child and the savage and to the 'civilized man' (whether 'of average culture' or 'more developed') alike; they differ only in how far ahead they look and think – in the length of that 'future' which stretches beyond the fleeting present that makes the present worthy of their attention and effort. 'The perspective of nothingness', Durkheim seems to repeat after Pascal, 'is an intolerable burden to us.' But unlike Pascal, Durkheim believed in tune with the hopes and intentions of 'solid modernity' that rather than trying to divert and distract ourselves and drown our fears in fleeting pleasures, we would tend to escape the dread by 'living in the future'. Diversion is not a solution: 'what value are our individual pleasures, which are so empty and short?'; but fortunately, individual pleasures are not the only option; it is our good luck that 'societies are infinitely more long-lived than individuals' and thus 'they permit us to taste satisfactions which are not merely ephemeral'.

We may all be 'mortal and miserable', but societies are 'infinitely more long-lived' than any of the mortals: to our transient individual life they represent eternity. To the mortals, they are bridges into immortality. We may trust societies as a secure shelter for our life accomplishments. Investing in the perpetuation of society, we may participate in things eternal; through society, we can recast our transcience into duration, and so stop our mortality making us miserable. Those who can say in good conscience, 'in thee, my Society, have I put my trust', may also hope that the verdict 'unto dust shalt thou return' can be averted or quashed.

Contemplation of society's immortality may be a highly gratifying pastime for philosophers. When embraced from the philosophical perspective, itself defiant to the eroding powers of time, it looks today (and will tomorrow and the day after tomorrow) as 'infinitely more long-lived' (immortal when measured by brief individual existence), as it did in Durkheim's time. But at the dawn of the twentieth century, philosophers could pride themselves on striking a chord in 'human, all too human' experience. They spoke in the name of a society busily composing solid frames in which transient human deeds could be inscribed to last forever and promising to make such frames rock-hard. Durkheim's words were recorded at a time when (in Alain Peyrefitte's words)[5] self-reliance, confidence in the others around, and trust in the longevity of social institutions combined and gelled into the courage to act and the long-term resolve to see the action through. To the ears of his contemporaries, Durkheim's words sounded therefore anything but abstract or far-fetched: they restated the beliefs daily corroborated by everyone's experience.

The triune trust documented by Peyrefitte has by now been broken, and it has become clear to anyone (except perhaps those living in philosophy, the art of conjuring continuity out of discontinuity – that 'epistemological premise' of 'continuous time') that none of the three trusts can survive, let alone thrive, on its own. Self-confidence, the audacity to set one's life as a project, and the determination to see that project to completion through thick and thin, is unlikely to appear unless prompted and bolstered by trust in the long-term stability of the world around, of its demands and of the rules that tell, and tell authoritatively, how to go about meeting them. 'The conditions of time in the new capitalism', Richard Sennett observes, 'have created a conflict between character and experience, the experience of disjointed time threatening the ability of people to form their characters into sustained narratives.'[6] Such conflict is only to be expected, given that uncertainty, though always a ubiquitous accompaniment of human existence, has nowadays acquired novel, previously unexperienced features: it is now 'woven into the everyday practices of a vigorous capitalism. Instability is meant to be normal . . .'

Were there a long-term logic behind the torn and mangled experience of a world changing with little or no warning, humans would hardly glean it from their daily experience; unlike birds and philosophers, they seldom rise above the ground they tread high enough to spy it out. 'Society', firm and whole as it may appear in the social-scientific studies, makes itself present to most of us mediated by occasions which do not necessarily connect into continuous and coherent experience. For most of us, most of the time (except when we fall into philosophical mood), 'society' is a summary name for the people we meet in the place where we earn our living, the partners we live with under one roof, the neighbours with which we share the street, and the ways and means of dealing with all of them which we think will meet with approval and bring proper effects. And the snag is that of none of those constituents of the idea of 'society' can we say now, judging from our experience, that they are 'infinitely more long-lived' than ourselves and that therefore they offer us 'satisfactions that are not merely ephemeral'. *Pace* Durkheim, it is now each of us, individually, that is the 'longest living' of all the bonds and institutions we have met; and the only entity whose life expectation is steadily rising rather than shrinking.

Indeed, there are few if any reference points left which could reasonably be hoped to lend a deeper and longer-lasting significance to the moments we live. If trust is the hinge attaching the mobile (and transient) to the steady (and durable), it would seek a frame in vain. It is myself, my living body or that living body which is me, which seems to be the sole constant ingredient of the admittedly unstable, always until-further-notice composition of the world around. My life may be too short for comfort, but the lifespan of anything else seems disconcertingly brief by comparison. Few if any partnerships are entered into with a belief that they will last 'until death us do part'. Fewer and fewer families can be vouched to outlive its members. Few if any painstakingly acquired skills may be hoped to last for the lifetime of their proud owner. No places of work can be anticipated to sustain the job currently performed, or for that matter to offer any kind of job, until the retirement of its current holder. Few if any neighbourhoods are likely to withstand for long the irrepressible vigour of developers, and if they do they would hardly resist the virus of slow yet relentless dilapidation and demise. Few if any among hard-won possessions are likely to retain their allure for long, surpassed as they tend to be by new, more seductive attractions. Few if any hard-learned styles and habits will go on bringing satisfaction and esteem for long. In this world, putting all one's eggs in one basket is no longer the ultimate imprudence. Baskets as such, however many, should be looked at with suspicion: few people of sane mind would entrust any eggs to any of them.

Whoever chains themselves to an unseaworthy vessel risks going down with it at the next tide. By comparison, surfing seems a safer option. 'Eternity' acquires a sinister flavour, unless it means an uninterrupted string of episodes: the perpetual ability to 'finish quickly and begin from the beginning'. If the assets of long-term security are not available, long-term commitments are liabilities. The future – the realistic future and the desirable future – can be grasped only as a succession of 'news'. And the only stable, hopefully unbreakable continuity on which the beads of episodes could conceivably be strung together so that they won't scatter and disperse is that of one's own body in its successive avatars.

Niklas Luhmann wrote of modern society that it is 'modern' in as far as it 'marks its newness by relegating the old':

> Whether we like it or not, we are no longer what we were, and we will not be what we are now . . . [T]he characteristics of today's modernity are not those of yesterday and not those of tomorrow, and in this lies modernity. The problems of contemporary society are not problems in maintaining a heritage, whether in education or elsewhere. Much more important is the constant creation of otherness.[7]

In the *Lebenswelt* around as much as in its only epicentre, the self, continuous discontinuity is the only form continuity may take – the only one to be found and the only one to be sensibly – realistically – coveted. In the game of life, 'society' has moved from the role of a caring albeit exacting warden/keeper into the position of one of the players (not even *primus inter pares*). Once the mainstay of stability and the warrant of assurance, it has now become the prime source of surprise and of a diffuse, frightening because unknowable, danger. It is erratic, as all players are: it keeps its cards close to its chest and likes its moves to take people unawares, time and again catching its partners napping. In the game of life, its constantly changing rules are themselves the major stake. There is next to nothing that the individual players can do to escape surprising moves and their consequences; the only thing individuals can do is to practice one-upmanship, struggle to outsmart the prankster, try their best to stay alert and be ready to change tack when the wind shifts; try never to be left behind or caught napping.

To stay seaworthy seems the only realistic purpose: the one task which the individual may – just may – take responsibility for and responsibly carry on. History, says Ulrich Beck,

> shrinks *to the (eternal) present;* and everything evolves around the axis of one's personal ego and personal life . . . The proportion of life opportunities which are fundamentally closed to decision-making is decreasing and the proportion of biography which is open and must be constructed biographically is increasing.[8]

The overall result of all this is the 'subjectivization and individualization of risks and contradictions produced by institutions and society'. In short, individuals are doomed to seek 'biographical solutions to systemic contradictions'. An impossible task to be sure, one that defies logic and one that cannot be undertaken in anything remotely reminiscent of a coherent and systematic way. Since there is not personal strategy which can arrest (let alone prevent) the vagaries of 'life opportunities', or short of arresting them can defuse or outweigh their impact, fragmentation of the big task which one cannot tackle into a plethora of small tasks which one can handle is the only reasonable way to proceed. Let's take one thing at a time, and let's worry about crossing that other bridge, out there in the foggy future, when it emerges from the fog and we know for sure that there is indeed a bridge to cross.

It is here, in this predicament of individuals doomed to compensate for the irrationality of their *Lebenswelt* by resorting to their own wits and acumen (to quote Beck once more, 'experts dump their contradictions and conflicts at the feet of the individual and leave him or her with the well-intentioned invitation to judge all of this critically on the basis of his or her own notions'), that 'consumer society' comes into its own; that life turns into a shopping spree and is neither more nor less consuming than the excitement, adventure, and manage in practice, to be.

Choosing reassurance, reassuring choice

There is a 'mutual fact', an 'elective affinity' between the inanities of the consumer market and the incongruities of the task which the individuals are presumed to perform on their own: their duty to compose individually the continuity which society can no longer assure or no longer intends to promise. Indeed, one is tempted to say that the marriage between the two protagonists has been made in heaven and that no man or woman, certainly not when acting singly or severally as they do, can tear it apart. There is a nearly 'perfect fit' between the characteristics of the commodities the consumer market offers, the fashion in which it offers them, and the kinds of anxieties and expectations which prompt individuals to live their lives as a string of shopping expeditions. Two irrationalities meet, cooperate and jointly self-reproduce through the rationality of sellers' calculations and the rationality of buyers' life strategies.

The consumer market has achieved the uncanny feat of reconciling and blending two mutually contradictory values which are both avidly sought by the members of individualized society: it offers, in one package deal, a badly missed reassurance and the guarantee that is keenly desired yet unavailable elsewhere of goods replacement, even a money-back guarantee, in the event that the presently sought reassurance wears off and a new reassurance needs to be put in its place. The consumer market promises, and delivers, a comforting certainty of the present without the frightening prospect of mortgaging the future. It supplies durability through the transcience of its offerings – a durability which no longer needs to be painstakingly built piece by piece, through perpetual effort and occasional self-sacrifice. It proffers eternity in instalments, each bit coming ready for immediate use and meant to be disposed off without regret or remorse once it is used up.

The consumer market sets the finishing lines close enough to prevent desire from exhausting itself before the goal is reached, but frequently enough for the runners never to worry about the durability of the spoils' value and for desire never to ponder frustration but always be eager to start afresh and never lose its vigour; and as Pascal observed a long time ago, it is the hunting not the hare that people call happiness. Admittedly, temporary identities can only be conjured up from a differentiation from the past: 'today' derives its meaning from cutting itself off from a 'yesterday'. The never-ending process of identification can go on, undisturbed by the vexing thought that identity is the one thing it is conspicuously unable to purvey. And so, on the one hand, the spectre of durability, and indeed of direction, is rising out of the rapidity and swiftness with which diverse transient states succeed each other. On the other hand, there is no worry that the objects of desire might outstay their welcome and that their refusal to vacate the stage for the yet-unscripted plays of the future might spoil the joy of the future chase.

The consumer market offers choice complete with the reassurance that the choice is right: the authority of experts and of the recondite knowledge they are trusted to possess, or the authority of great numbers of satisfied buyers, or the authority of huge demand that exceeds the offer, tend to be as a rule attached to the products on the department stores' shelves. At the same time, the sellers make no secret of the fact that the goods currently on offer will be, inevitably, superseded by some as yet unknown 'new and improved' ones, and for their customers the awareness that this must sooner rather than later happen is not at all off-putting. On the contrary, that knowledge is a vital part of the reassurance they seek: it is comforting to know that no decision is final, that none has irreversible consequences, that each one can be safely taken since like all other decisions it will bind the decision-maker only 'until further notice'. Let us note that since such awareness is shared by the sellers and the buyers, no disappointment is ultimate and conclusive enough to invalidate the rationality of the game and the wisdom of playing it. The game of 'finishing quickly and beginning from the beginning' is self-propelling and self-propagating, securely defended against adversary tests and the *experimentum crucis* of ultimate futility.

Feeding uncertainty, feeding on uncertainty

The game is self-perpetuating for one more reason. It is addictive: protracted participation in the consumerist game results in an instilled incapacity to seek 'biographical solutions to systemic contradictions' in any other way. To become a consumer means to be dependent for one's survival, even for the keeping of simple daily routines, on the consumer market. It means to forget or fail to learn the skills of coping with life challenges, apart from the skills of seeking (and, hopefully, finding) the right object, service or counsel among the marketed commodities (in a New Year version of *Cinderella* staged by Channel Four in 2000, the Prince matter-of-factly assumes that the magic mountain where Cinderella acquired her ball-dress must be a shopping mall). The chronic deficit of certainty may be recompensed by consumers in one way only: by pursuing the avenues laid out and made passable by marketing and shopping. We all live in a society of spare (and disposable) parts, and in such a society the art of repairing malfunctioning objects, characters or human bonds is all but uncalled for and obsolete.

George Ritzer grasps perfectly the dual attraction of market-mediated consumerism when he discusses the 'action holidays' pre-scripted and pre-packed by travel agencies – when he observes that 'most inhabitants of a postmodern world might be willing to eat at the campfire, as long as it is a simulated one on the lawn of the hotel.'[9] Tourists of the consumer society want their holidays to be escapes from daily routine – but also to be escapes from the hazards, confusions and uncertainties endemic to their daily life; the holidays they would gladly pay for should be predictable, calculable, efficient and controlled. The holiday companies, just like McDonald's restaurants, are expected to provide, first of all, shelters of security and predictability. Adventures should be carefully planned to include a happy end, excitements should be sanitized and pollution-free, the 'far away from everywhere' must be located no more than a car drive's distance from shops and restaurants, the wilderness ought to have exits that are well mapped and signed, wild beasts should be either tamed or locked in secure enclosures, and snakes, if encountered, should have their poisonous teeth removed.

What makes the dreamed-of holidays alluring to the seekers of adventures and strong emotions is the certainty (included in the package and protected by travel insurance) that someone, somewhere, knows exactly what is going on and how it is going to end, so no shock will be 'for real', being 'an experience' of rather than the thing itself. Nothing really disastrous, let alone irrevocable, will occur, and if (God forbid) it does occur due to someone's mistake or neglect, opting out is not just conceivable, but on the whole easy, while the dissatisfied customer can always sue for compensation even if the 'money-back guarantee' was missing from the contract. Cinema goers made *The Blair Witch Project* an astounding box-office success as they flocked to see their innermost fears vividly, and horrifyingly, portrayed: being cut off from the nearest socket for portable computers and from access to the internet, finding that mobile telephones are unusable or absent, suspecting that the game is 'for real', that the ending of the spectacle has not been fixed in advance and that there is no switch-off button – these are the most awesome of the nightmares that haunt the 'incapacitated-by-training' consumers. *The Blair Witch Project* made the ineffable anxiety tangible, gave visible shape to misty apparitions – but, let us note, not just any shape, but one that sets consumer society firmly in the role of the exorcist-in-chief and the last shelter for the perplexed and the ignorant.

As fears go, the consumer market may legitimately contest and refute its responsibility for parenthood. As has been argued before, the anxieties of uncertainty offer a potentially fertile soil for the marketeers to cultivate. But the crops – the *names* of the fears on which the dispersed anxiety would eventually focus – are products of farming and depend on the techniques the farmers deploy and the materials they use. The choice of techniques and materials is, in its turn, dictated by the farmers' understanding of 'best gain'. In addition, no farmer worth his salt would rely on the natural fertility of the soil and even less would he allow the fertility found to be exhausted by drawing from the soil all its nutritional substances in one go. Good farmers (and marketeers are better than most) would take care to ensure that fertility could continually recuperate and grow by the skilful use of fertilizers, whether natural or artificial.

Uncertainty-generated anxiety is the very substance that makes the individualized society fertile for consumerist purposes; it needs therefore to be carefully and lovingly cared for, and must on no account be allowed to dry up or evaporate. More often than not, the production of consumers means the production of 'new and improved' fears. The affair of the millennial (hum)bug offers a pattern daily and ubiquitously repeated: no one could say for sure that the bug was a figment of the imagination, and even less could one call the bluff of those who insisted on being in the know even if the surmise that they were bluffing was correct. Most reasonable people would therefore follow Pascal's advice of the 'safe bet'. A multibillion pound industry of computer-system testing and reprogramming would be created in a truly Divine manner, *ab nihilo,* and the act of its creation would be almost universally greeted with a sigh of relief. When the day of reckoning finally comes, the failure of the prophesized catastrophe to materialize will be, again universally or almost, the proof that it was averted thanks to the purveyors of the anti-bug services, and as another clinching test of the omnipotence of marketable expertise. The whole episode would anyway be soon forgotten as other fears came to usurp the headlines, but the memory of that omnipotence would stay, making the ground yet more fertile for the next panic-production.

Let us note that – wisely – consumer markets seldom offer cures or preventive medicines against natural dangers, like earthquakes, hurricanes, floods or avalanches; promises of protection and salvation focus as a rule on dangers artificially created. The latter have a clear advantage over the former, since they allow the fears to be cut to the measure of the available cures, rather than vice versa.

The trained incapacity of the consumers is by far the best of the weapons of consumer goods suppliers. American giants of genetic engineering finance research which 'proves beyond reasonable doubt' that without genetically modified crops the feeding of the world's population will shortly become impossible. What the research reports tend to be silent about is that their pronouncements bear all the marks of self-fulfilling prophecies; or, rather, that what they do is to provide a gloss on their sponsors' practices, while making such practices more palatable through reversing the order of causes and effects. The introduction of 'genetically improved' seeds casts great numbers of farmers out of business and makes the rest incapable of producing their own seeds for next year since the 'improved' grains are as a rule infertile. Once that happens, the assertion that without a constant and rising supply of GM stuff the feeding of humankind won't be possible acquires the authority of an 'empirically proven truth' and can no longer be questioned. The practices of the genetic engineering industry may well serve as a pattern of the paramount function in a consumer society – that is the production of (willing or unwilling, yet cooperative) consumers. George Ritzer's 'McDonaldization' would not work unless it was complemented by 'Monsantization'.

To conclude: the powers and the weaknesses, the glory and the blight of the consumer society – a society in which life is consuming through a continuous succession of discontinuous consumer concerns (and itself consumed in its course) – are rooted in the same condition: the anxieties born of and perpetuated by institutional erosion coupled with enforced individualization. And they are shaped and reproduced by the response led by the consumer market to that condition: the strategy of the rationalization of irrationality, the standardization of difference, and the achievement of stability through an induced precariousness of the human condition.

Notes

1 George Ritzer, *The McDonaldization Thesis* (Sage, 1998), p. 68.
2 See Pierre Bourdieu, *Contre-feux* (Raisons d'Aguir, 1998), pp. 97–9.
3 Barbara Czarniawska, *Writing Management: Organization Theory as a Literary Genre* (Oxford University Press, 1999), p. 53.
4 Émile Durkheim, 'La science positive de la morale en Allemagne', *Revue Philosophique* (1987); here quoted from *Émile Durkheim: Selected Writings*, ed. and trans. Anthony Giddens (Cambridge University Press, 1972), pp. 93–4.
5 Alain Peyrefitte, *La société de confiance* (Odile Jacob, 1998), pp. 514–16.
6 Richard Sennett, *The Corrosion of Character* (W.W. Norton, 1998), p. 31.
7 Niklas Luhmann, *Observations on Modernity*, trans. William Whobrey (Standford University Press, 1998), p. 3.
8 Ulrich Beck, *Risk Society*, trans. Mark Ritter (Sage, 1992), pp. 135–7.
9 Rtizer, *The McDonaldization Thesis*, pp. 146, 138.

CHAPTER 7

Liquid waste, being human, and bodily death

Charles Lemert and Makenna Goodman

Among social theorists and others of their kind, Zygmunt Bauman is something of an eighth wonder of the world. What sets him apart from the rest is neither the improbable mass of his writings since, say, 1987, when *Legislators and Interpreters: On Modernity, Post-modernity and Intellectuals* initiated a break of sorts. Before then, Bauman wrote more as the sociologist, though hardly one obedient to the norms; after, his writings became something more, eventually transcending the terms of his academic discipline. Among sociologists who took note of him in those days, he was seen still as a sociologist of the postmodern[1]. What many missed was that, far from being a certain kind of progressive theorist, Bauman was already inventing a way of thinking about what lay behind the theories and beyond what meets the eye. As the list of his writings grew, it soon became clear to those willing to notice that, while the sociology remained, the beyond had taken over. Just the same, prescience and originality are not Bauman's chief claim on our attentions.[2]

In the end, to begin to explain Bauman's special place in the history of social thought one might consider the distinctive literary quality of his later writings; in particular, the ease with which they float on their author's prodigious learning. Typically, the learned never tire of reminding the reader that they know better, and more. By contrast, Bauman, while not a moralist himself, seems to have taken on the responsibilities of one who is humbled but not diminished by the demands his subject, the tumultuous liquid worlds, makes on his learning. There could hardly be a quality of character more necessary for writing the kind of social theory Bauman writes in a time like the one in which he writes. The troubled nature of the world after the transformations of 1989–91, made acute a decade later by the terrors of 9/11, requires just the sort of aboriginal courage that won Bauman the Polish Cross of Valor. This he won for his daring as a young man in the struggle to rid Poland of its military and ideological occupiers – a formation that cannot help but stiffen the spine against the terrors of these latter years.

Bauman is nothing if not a realist before the limits of what one can do, while also being tough-mindedly determined to do what needs doing – or, in the case of his writing, to say what needs saying and to say it against the grain of common expectations.

It is a moral world in which the responsibility for another goes as far as the readiness to die. It is a cruel, inhuman and immoral world in which that readiness is called, and required, to be acted upon. Such is the world at war. Such was, more than any other world, the world of the Holocaust, of the Gulag, of the genocide. The moral actors of those worlds were not heroes at all. Or, rather, they acted heroically because they were moral – it was not the act of heroism that grounded their morality. They were, purely and simply, the 'morally awakened', caring people. People who just could not make themselves live at the expense of their responsibility for Others, and hence were ready to make their lives – even their lives – the price of that responsibility. They did not see themselves as heroes. And they would not be heroes, if the circumstances had not put an equals sign between being human and acting heroically.[3]

Here, as on nearly every page, is literary grace, the elegance of which lies in the simplicity with which the author contradicts without abandoning modern culture's all-too-naive faith in the hero as the one who wards off the tragedy of evil. Whether in writing these lines Bauman was thinking of his own experience of holocausts and gulags is hard to say[4]; but it is evident that he understands the experience of the hero as the one called, against resistance and fear, to be human by acting bravely before the realities as they are.

Such, also, is the grace of thinking outside his chosen vineyard, sociology, with its closely guarded recipes for analytic methodologies that reduce away the fine bitters that give zest to human history. Bauman defines his approach to these things as a *sociological hermeneutic*. He is quick to distinguish his sociological hermeneutic from hermeneutic sociology; or, for that matter, from all other of the regularizing methods of academic sociology[5]. It is possible that one can only write and think as Bauman does by shedding the responsibilities of academic instruction and administration. It is certain, however, that such an approach is not possible unless the thinker is freed of the desire to obey the norm, yet freed not by virtue of the wish to be different as by the necessity of being serious.

Strictly speaking Bauman's hermeneutic is not sociology at all in the usual sense, but an interpretative cast on the social waters that he insistently goes beyond – beyond the social realities as they are customarily thought; beyond the worlds as they present themselves to the naked eye; beyond the theorists all-too-human aptitude for making what is said about the external realities a tribute to the luminous brilliance of the one having his say. The rigors of interpreting the secrets of the social orders soften before their hard demand that we make sense of them, when we can, by the ways we live and act – both of which are bound inextricably to how and when we are willing to die.

Thus, Bauman's method of thinking and writing, far from being directed at the local as many interpretative methods are, is in fact a hermeneutic of global things. Bauman thinks globally as opposed to thinking *about* globalization. To appreciate his manner of global thinking one must embrace the dual meanings of the root term – he thinks in terms of wholes; he thinks concretely of the geographic and historic whole of the worlds as they are becoming. This is a striking departure from a good deal of social theory which, on the one hand, views thinking in wholes as a kind of structuralism (for which Marx, Lévi-Strauss, Parsons, Luhmann, Wallerstein are among the examples usually given) and, on the other, thinking globally as an occasion for theories of the global situation (for which: Giddens, Castells, Fukuyama, Beck, Wallerstein after 1991, among others). Bauman somehow manages to collapse the two. How he does this is, honestly, a bit of a mystery. In fact, it is hard to come by an analogue, though at least one homologue comes to mind. Good poetry somehow manages by a parsimonious condensing of words to bring interior personal experience into line with the shadow of universal humanity. But here the historical aspect is lost. Bauman could hardly be accused of being either a poet (though his words are often poetic) or parsimonious (though when necessary, he can be).[6] In the end one must grant his language its due for what it is in its effect. The reader soon enough recognizes that she is being lifted to a kind of global perspective that somehow avoids the notorious 'view from nowhere'.[7] It is not quite that Bauman presents himself in his writing as grounded or embedded in the world as it is. More, as the passage on true morality suggests, he offers his ideas as a prudent elder of the tribe who is familiar with, if not quite implicated in, the dirty business of modernity as it is betrayed by globalization. Again, there is the touch of moral duty that comes short of moralism – the sense of being faced with realities not at all pleasing yet also being willing and able to take them into lively account. This, we think, gives the writings their mysteriously powerful empirical aspect – mysterious because he does not deal in data so much as the refiguring of history and of what others have said of that history.

One effect of this global-thinking-that-does-not-essentialize-global-things is that it is consistent with his theory of the modern individual. Borrowing from Elias's *The Society of Individuals*, Bauman has said (with a nod to Marx): 'Casting members as individuals is the trademark of modern society.'[8] He means, we think, somewhat less the act of fishing in moving water than 'casting' in the theatrical sense (though without the Goffmanian twist that, relatively speaking, tends to formalize the dramatic role).[9] In the same place, he borrows more heavily from Marx to say that the modern individual is fated, not chosen; bound, not free.

> Let there be no mistake: now, as before, individualization is a fate, not a choice: in the land of individual freedom of choice the option to escape individualization and to refuse to participate in the individualization game is emphatically *not* on the agenda.[10]

To social theorists accustomed to the tired and untrue formula of the individual as an ontic thing separable from social things, the emphasis on individualization as an aspect of modernity's civilizing process will seem strange, even repulsive.

Bauman of course was not the first to make moves of this kind. But he did see the game board as a whole better than others, thus to advance his position with moves more daring than those of others. Granting, for instance, Bauman's appreciation of the theorists of reflexivity – Anthony Giddens and, especially, Ulrich Beck[11] – he opens a strategically more interesting attack in sociology's losing attempt to protect the modernity's conceptual queen, the autonomous individual. Whereas both Beck (to a lesser extent Giddens as well) and Bauman see individualism as a 'social form' they part ways on the role of the individual in response to the uncertainties and risks of second or liquid modernity. For example, Beck:

Let us call the autonomous, undesired and unseen transition from industrial to risk society *reflexivity* (to distinguish it from and contrast it with *reflection*). Then 'reflexive modernization' means self-confrontation with the effects of risk society that cannot be dealt with and assimilated in the system of industrial society – as measured by the latter's institutionalized standards. The fact that this very constellation may later, in a second stage, in turn become the object of (public, political and scientific) reflection must not obscure the unreflected, quasi-autonomous mechanism of the transition: it is precisely abstraction which produces and gives reality to risk society.[12]

Like Giddens (ever more the optimist), Beck holds out hope that, though the terms of life-politics are drastically changed, the individual is able to 're-embed' himself somewhere, somehow in the risk society. Hence, the conclusion that modernity in its second stage is capable of becoming self-critical, thus casting off the blinders of first modernity.[13] On this point Bauman complains that Beck is too much the optimist, a charge he denies.[14] But Beck's denial falters on the difference between a risk society and a liquid one.

Metaphors are not everything to be sure, but they can be telling. To be at risk is to hold out for the heroic possibility of overcoming the tragic outcome. To be swept away in a sea of liquids is, in a word, to be swept to no place certain. Beck, thus,

Modernity becomes *reflexive*, which means concerned with its unintended consequences, risks and their implications for its foundations. Where most postmodern theorists are critical of grand narratives, general theory and humanity, I remain committed to all of these, but in a new sense.[15]

The new idea, for Beck, seems to be that the old foundations must be defended and can be. No tsunami here. Bauman, who for the most part respects and draws upon Beck, demurs on the crucial point of the prospect for an emancipatory critical theory in the wash of liquid society that casts (now in the angling sense of the word) the individual in a sea full of fish with neither rod nor hook. Bauman:

The modernizing impulse, in any of its renditions, means the compulsive critique of reality. Privatization of the impulse means compulsive *self*-critique born of perpetual self-disaffection: being an individual *de jure* means having no one to blame for one's own misery, seeking the causes of one's own defeats nowhere except in one's own indolence and sloth, and looking for no remedies other than trying harder and harder still.[16]

In short, Bauman sees the self-critical aspect of the individual in a liquid society as anything but a reflexive response to threat. For Bauman self-criticism is a pathology of modernization's deep *and* foundational commitment to individualization as a social form of modernity's early attempts to present itself as solid when in fact it was always liquid – a melting away of human freedoms in the coke furnaces and sweatshops of modern enterprise. Where Beck (and surely Giddens as well) holds dear to a liberal faith in the recovery of freedom, Bauman, while not entirely a pessimist, takes on the more tragic realities as if they were what in fact history has shown them to be. For Beck critique is a norm; for Bauman it is a pathology that must be cured if there is to be any possibility of de facto as distinct from *de jure* individualization.[17]

> To diagnose a disease does not mean the same as curing it – this general rule applies to sociological diagnoses as much as it does to medical verdicts. But let us note that the illness of society differs from bodily illnesses in one tremendously important respect: in the case of an ailing social order, the absence of an adequate diagnosis . . . is a crucial, perhaps decisive part of the disease.[18]

The social body is different from the body proper. Lesions and infections of the flesh may be hard to diagnose, but not so hard as in the social body. It is the nature of modern culture to mask the signs of its terminal disorder. Modern culture injures but it does not hurt, until it is too late. The human body is the site of disease or injury. Culture, in the modern social body, is the disease of requiring individuation of human beings who cannot, within that culture, be individuals. In this respect, Bauman has moved beyond even the more determined attempts to rethink the individual's relation to the social and structural. Bauman's scheme is post-analytic and one that can only be arrived at from outside the scientific desire to settle the categories by which social things are cut and parsed, mercilessly.

Bauman, thus, moves perceptibly away from Beck and Giddens, who on the surface seem to be playing much the same type of game. Giddens, of course, is the shifter on these matters. In the debate over second modernity, he may well have been the signifier that brought Beck and Bauman together. Just so, though less directly, Giddens inconspicuously put Bourdieu into relief against the American-dominated sociology he was, in his youth, intent upon reworking to the same degree that Bourdieu meant to put himself at an ever more salient distance from it. With a minimum of contact, Bourdieu and Giddens, in the 1980s, established a distinctively European sociology – one that did not lapse into exegesis as Habermas by then had.[19]

Nearly three decades ago, now, Bourdieu and Giddens, in their different ways, first set out to get around the, by then, age-old conceptual opposition of the force of social and cultural structures to the autonomous and moral authoritative subject. Bourdieu in *Outline of a Theory of Practice* (1972; 1977, English) put forth *habitus* and practice as the modalities of social interpretation that could get social thought out of the subjectivism/objectivism straightjacket which at the time was preoccupying French social theory as the post-structuralisms were vaporizing the moral subject in ways ever more severe than the earlier structuralisms, in prior turn, had attacked the existential historical individual.[20] Similarly, Giddens, in *Constitution of Society* (1984), took a more classically sociological approach to the recursivity of structures and the discursive practices of agents as the energizing poles of his theory of structuration. In retrospect both were more sensible at the time than their putative straw men – the French structuralisms in Bourdieu's case, American sociology in Giddens's. Of the two, Bourdieu adjusted less well to the changes in the fate of the modern individual that became clear after 1991. Giddens of course became a key player in the movement in Europe that owes visibly to Beck (who in turn owes much to Giddens). Giddens largely accepted Beck's attempts to redefine Giddens's own reflexive modernity as what he, Beck, came to call second modernity. The crucial pact between the two, adumbrated more explicitly by Beck, was that, against the claim of a postmodernity, the history of modernity can and should be parsed into its own interior stages in which the socially charged individual comes to understand that his is the history of risks generated by the wheel of reflexive uncertainty.[21]

Bauman, who, evidently, reads everyone with no important exception, came out closer to the Beck–Giddens nexus than to Bourdieu's position.[22] Yet, with a difference that begins to suggest his edge on the fields of social theory, Bauman states:

> Our society – a society of 'free individuals' – has made the critique of reality, the disaffection with 'what is' and the voicing of disaffection, both an unavoidable and an obligatory part of every member's life business. As Anthony Giddens keeps reminding us, we are all engaged nowadays in 'life-politics'; we are 'reflexive beings' who look closely at every move we take, who are seldom satisfied with its results and always eager to correct them. Somehow, however, that reflexion does not reach far enough to embrace the complex mechanisms in full swing. We are perhaps more 'critically predisposed', much bolder and intransigent in our criticism than our ancestors managed to be in their daily lives, but our critique, so to speak, is 'toothless', unable to affect the agenda set for our 'life-political' choices. The unprecedented freedom which our society offers its members has arrived, as Leo Strauss warned a long while ago, together with unprecedented impotence.[23]

The free individual is an artifact of modern civilization – and just as inert as any relic of a civilization past its prime.

In the tiresome controversy as to whether somewhere in the last quarter of the twentieth century modernity came to an end or transformed itself into something similar but different from its old self, Bauman stands very much by himself in driving to the heart of the matter. Whatever one thinks about the theoretical debates, few possessed of a scrap of common sense (by which I exclude most of the political Right in my country who seem to have lost their minds altogether[24]) would deny that *something* has changed. This is the symbolic significance of 9/11 and its *sequelae* that have been anything but merely symbolic. The fall of the towers brought home the realities that had long been there under the visible surface of modern cultures. In a word, Bauman distinguishes himself from theorists of second modernity or reflexive modernity by taking to heart one of their theoretical dispositions – that, whatever the changes, modernity still has the upper hand – while moving on to an independent judgment as to disjunctures that vitiate modernity as such.

Fine points of controversy aside, where Bauman comes fully into the power of his position is in the books of the 2000s that followed upon *Liquid Modernity* (2000) and the subsequent books in the liquidities series. Of these, *Wasted Lives: Modernity and its Outcasts* (2004) is particularly judicious; for example:

> If the premodern life was a daily rehearsal of the infinite duration of everything except mortal life, the liquid modern life is a daily rehearsal of universal transience. Nothing is truly necessary, nothing is irreplaceable. Everything is born with a branding of imminent death; everything leaves the production line with a 'use-by-date' label attached; constructions do not start unless permissions to demolish (if required) have been issued, and contracts are not signed unless their duration is fixed or their termination allowed depending on the hazards of the future. No step and no choice is once and for all, none is irrevocable. No commitment lasts long enough to reach the point of no return. All things, born or made, human or not, are until-further-notice and dispensable. A spectre hovers over the denizens of the liquid modern world and all their labours and creations: the spectre of redundancy.[25]

'Nothing is truly necessary.' The poetic power of Bauman's language could not be more in evidence. If, as Marx first said, with Engels, in 1848 in the *Manifesto*, 'all that is solid melts into air' then indeed, as Marx continued, 'all fixed, fast-frozen relations are swept away'. If, in Bauman's logic, everything is waste, then nothing is necessary and all things are dispensable. Liquid modernity, the figure Bauman takes directly from Marx, opens social thought to the realities modernity would wish away. Progress is at the price of life itself. Death is the mortgage paid on a house of cards that stood firm for so long, only to collapse when it could no longer hide the fatal flaw at its foundation.

Death, furthermore, is the consideration that prevents Bauman's affirmation of the liquidity of modern life from constituting a kind of break of its own.[26] In fact, in 1992, nearly a decade before the liquidity series, in *Mortality, Immortality, and Other Life Strategies*, there appears an early use of this key metaphor:

> Now, as Lyotard says, it is the modern way of living-with-the-project, in-the-shadow-of-a-project, toward-a-project – that today has been not so much abandoned or forgotten or forcefully suppressed, as *liquidized*. It lost, so to speak, its former solidity, 'Liquidization is', in Lyotard's words, a 'way of destroying the modern project while creating an impression of its fulfillment.' To create the impression could not be easier: it was enough to accept that *future is now*. Or, rather that the bliss future once promised – liberty, democracy, equality, wealth, security and what not – has . . . arrived. No more history.[27]

Though tucked away in a corner of this most philosophical of Bauman's books, the early reference to liquid modernity already portends the full-blown ideas to come – the ruse of solidity, the false hope of individual freedoms, the lie of history as promise. Just as important is where the passage occurs in his meditation on death in modern culture. On the page following, Bauman explicitly associates liquidity with death in a remarkable passage that not only extends the earlier intimation of the solid/liquid modernity figure, but elaborates the 'no more history' dictum into a full-blown prophecy of the end of the modern as being already contained in modernity's deceptions, of which the denial of death is first and foremost:

> If modernity deconstructed death into a bagful of unpleasant but tameable illnesses, so that in the hubbub of disease fighting which followed mortality could be forgotten and not worried about – in the society that emerged at the far end of the modern it is the majestic yet distant immortal bliss that is being deconstructed into a sackful of bigger or smaller, but always within-reach, satisfactions, so that in the ecstasy of enjoyment the likeness of the ultimate perfection may dissolve and vanish from view. Time still runs, but the pointer has been lost in the flow.[28]

'No more history' / 'Time still runs, but the pointer has been lost in the flow.' Though death reappears in later books,[29] nowhere is human mortality so forceful a social fact as in Bauman's analysis of the duplicity of modernity. The very culture that invented history as progress and time, as running forward on the legs of the free individual, is here said to be based in the displacement of death to the remote nether regions of consciousness. Modernity's preoccupation with the sciences and technologies of life – like its vapid promises of progress and the entire kit and caboodle of its illusions – is a deceit of the worst sort. The obsession with life-maintaining measures is but a nasty distraction from the first fact of human being – that of endings, which of course are poisonous to the principle of unending historical progress.

Indeed, one of the ways to account for modernity is to see that its every move sooner or later comes back to the need, as Bauman puts it, to deconstruct mortality – to slowly and unrelentingly demonstrate the indemonstrable final limits on human possibility. The demonstration is of course beyond the reach of mere denial. Modernity resorts instead to 'holding it off the agenda'.[30] Against which, the postmodern deconstructs *immortality* by the ironic work of attenuating modernity's willful ignorance; this by, in effect, putting everything, including mortality, *on* the agenda. When all things in these worlds are taken for what they are without blinders then human being is left to make history in the absence of history. When every little social thing is on the agenda then reification reduces the all and every to as similarly puny prominence. History as it was portrayed under modernity depended wholly on the ability of its true believers to produce and be reproduced by the distractions that kept death at spiritual bay. Since death cannot be denied, it cannot then be forever kept in limbo. This, thus, is the fatal flaw in the modern synthesis. The postmodern deconstructs immortality – the false life that by making history we will be remembered and live on – which of course puts death back on the agenda; not as the looming social fact so much as the final fact among the others, among which there can be no sure demarcation.

> The deconstructing of mortality made the presence of death more ubiquitous than ever: it made survival into the meaning of life, and anti-death magic into life's pattern. The deconstructing of immortality, on the other hand, seems to subvert the meaning and deny the need of a pattern. The paradoxical outcome of modernity's project is that the work of modernity is being undone. Death is back – un-deconstructed, unreconstructed. Even immortality has now come under its spell and rule. The price of exorcising the spectre of mortality proved to be a collective incapacity to construct life as reality, to take life seriously.[31]

Hence, the religious paradox that human beings can only take life seriously by overcoming the urge to make one's survival the prime object of its affections. The ordinal sin is selfishness, beginning with the self-preoccupied need to hold fast to the hope of eternal life. Hold a false hope too tightly and the heat of the anxious hand melts it away. Only those without could chant keep hope alive; those with are the ones to be pitied.

Here, behind the liberties we take with his formulation, it is all the more evident that Bauman is wellnigh to being a theologian. *Mortality, Immortality* begins with a concept that could have been taken directly from Augustine, if not Reinhold Niebuhr.

> Humans are the only creatures who not only know, but also know that they know – and cannot 'unknow' their knowledge. In particular, they cannot 'unknow' the knowledge of their mortality.[32]

Bauman's theology, if it can be called that, is surely drawn from Levinas.[33] Still, Christian thinkers like Augustine and the Jewish crypto-theologian understood self-knowledge in relation to the knowledge of death, of God, and, not inconsequentially, of human awareness of and frustrations in life with Others. Living with death is living with others; hence, the uncertainties of liquid love. In a passage that leads into the lines on the modern hero, quoted earlier, Bauman offers a forceful denunciation of modernity's utilitarian calculus, framed in the shadow of human mortality:

> The most altruistic of loves is also the most selfish.. . . But, one can also be *ready to die* for the Other not 'in order to', not at all as a means to an end, not as a trade-off of a lesser good for a more precious one; as a matter of fact, not in the result of any calculation at all and not out of desire for any achievement. Without thinking. Without justifying. Without rationalizing. Without arguing – with others, or with oneself. Without gratifying belief in the 'effectiveness' of one's death. And without *wishing* to die. One can be ready to die for another just because one is ready to see one's responsibility for the Other through to its end, whatever the end may be – and if that responsibility has a price tag of death attached to it, so be it. The devastating irony is (but one that makes such a death truly, self-deprecatingly disinterested) is that the death, if and when it comes, may not save the Other for who the sacrifice has been made.[34]

Here, as in the idea of the modern hero, is revealed Bauman's social ethic, which, we would venture, is at the heart of his developing sociological hermeneutic of modern things. The modern, secular ideal of the individual in history making progress *must* hold off human mortality, because progress cannot embrace definitive endings. Here again the sharp differences from the theorists of the reflexive individual in second modernity. Their idea, while by no means naively accepting of liberal culture, still holds out for the possibility of an individual, even if a social form, who is able, both generically and concretely, to come to terms with modernity. Those terms, for Beck especially, are the terms of a critical theory, which Bauman sees as highly problematic.[35] Whether it is fair to describe Bauman's alternative as crypto-religious is hard to say. But, at the least, he could not have come to his ethical ideal of the one who dies for another – out of responsibility, without prospect of gain, without wanting to die, without an assurance of immortality – were it not for his own version of a Levinasian perspective on time, death, and the Other.

In death, there are no individuals. Whatever may be in the after, this after is neither modern nor liberal. Death does not cast individuals into a mold, which is what believers on this side of the grave do, they hold on to overdetermined convictions as to the resurrection or the eternal soul or the impermanent consciousness as such. Death, as Bauman makes shockingly clear, when taken with utter seriousness, destroys the modern individual fated to pursue a freedom she can never attain. Hence also, this is the source of the ontic individual so indispensable to modern philosophies including sociologies with their worries about preserving the individual as the agent of her own salvation. Death destroys the instrumentally rational ethic that makes everything, including altruism and self-sacrifice, a maximizable benefit of some measurable kind. Death destroys tragedy, supplanting it with the irony of life itself – human being is to die. How we die may make a difference, but not one from which we can benefit. If there is a We in the varieties of human difference, it is the We of our deaths, not of the ideal community of good men and women serving the common good according to vague rules of civil conduct which are supposed to permit the free thought that envelopes human freedom in the veil of a beatitude without pain or suffering. Against which is the startling image of the postmodern community as, in effect, preoccupied with the pain of death. 'The life of postmodern community is itself a daily rehearsal of mortality; or, of the irrelevance of immortality for the business of life – which amounts, as it were, to the same.'[36]

Bauman is nothing if not the master of paradox. But the paradoxical tales he spins are not Zen riddles of the eternal verities anymore than they are clever ironies of inscrutable humanity. Bauman remains very much the sociologist. His instincts, thereby, are directed at the historical contradictions of actual, existing modernities. As a result, the postmodern is anything but a triumphant passing into a new and better dispensation. On the contrary, the postmodern is the decomposition of the modern under the pressure exerted by its inherent dead weight. There is no revolution from below. No particular historical actor. No poignant conjuncture. Nothing but the raw details of worlds made of straw stanchions laced with too fine a thread.

This, therefore, is what establishes Bauman's credentials in the historical study of modernity – and what, thereby, sets him apart from those, like Beck and Giddens and ever more so Habermas, whose nostalgia for the emancipatory might of liberal culture chains them to figments of the modern imaginary in which critique renewed, third ways, and transcending universals were fountains of leftish hope. Liquid modernity is a both/and that is also a neither/nor. It is decidedly not a scheme for parsing the history of modernity. Nor is the case for liquid modernity a psalm to the promises or possibilities of a new and better version of the modern ideal. Liquids are melted solids. The solid modernity of heavy industry through, say, the 1960s, is not the *before* of the liquid flows of light technologies in the *after* in which, in principle, we live today. There is no ordinal position in this history – no first and second modernity; no first and second globalization, and the like. The solid modern was in effect the condensation of organic structures forged in the hope for progress in the time of reason. The liquid state was always there in the organic bonds of the solid, waiting for a time to come from nowhere to smash this history at just the right point, thus to dissolve the thing into the unrecognizably fluid state it always was and ever will be. Thus also, with Bauman, the postmodern is part and parcel of the modern paradox and, thereby, nothing worthy of celebration. It is, in effect, the social facts as they are, no longer organized by the legends and myths of liberal history. They offer, thus, not so much a gloomy prospect as the hard-to-swallow promise of seeing things for what they are in all their various finitudes and fragments.

Postmodern liquidity is, furthermore, the explosive excrement of modern constipation. These liquids do not quench the thirst for meaning. They are, at least as much, vile-smelling shit – a kind of metaphoric diarrhea that empties the body of its poisons at the risk of dehydration. Thus what remains of the modern in the postmodern is liquid waste. Though Bauman does not use the phrase 'liquid waste' in *Wasted Lives: Modernity and its Outcasts* (2004), it is in its way a key to liquid modernity argument.[37] Wasted lives is a way of describing the expulsion for all to see of modernity's bulimic appetites:

> As the triumphant progress of modernization has reached the furthest lands of the planet and practically the totality of human production and consumption has become money and market mediated, and the processes of the commodification, commercialization and monetarization of human livelihoods have penetrated every nook and cranny of the globe, global solutions to locally produced problems, or global outlets for local excesses are no longer available.[38]

Bauman never leaves his ideas unmarked by paradox. Modernity's eating disorder is classic. It stuffs the gut to feed the feeling of emptiness stimulated by the unquenchable wish to be lean in order to run the forward race. In due course, the body is full to the point of explosion. Vomit then empties the body so that, thinned down again, it can run after its desires, which can never be satisfied, to the point of stuffing again, and again.

> Our planet is full . . . as technological progress offers . . . new means of survival in habitats that were previously deemed unfit for human settlement, it also erodes the ability of many habitats to sustain the populations they previously used to accommodate and feed. Meanwhile *economic* progress renders once effective modes of making a living unviable and impracticable, thereby adding to the size of wastelands laying fallow and abandoned.[39]

Hence the paradox of the full and the empty: the bulimic pathology of the modern empties it of all real value. 'Empty spaces are first and foremost empty of *meaning*.'[40] Here again the theme of modernity's averted gaze. It is not that there is no meaning to rapacious progress, but that, in its time, it is '*seen* as without meaning' which he adds is the same as not being seen at all, from which the literalness of the word waste derives:

> The story we grow in and with has no interest in waste. According to the story it is the product that matters, not the waste. Two kinds of trucks leave factory

yards daily – one kind of truck proceeds to the warehouses and department stores, the other to the rubbish tips. The story we have grown with has trained us to note (count, value, care for) solely the first kind of truck. Of the second, we think only on the (fortunately not-yet-daily) occasions when the avalanche of leftovers descends from the refuse mountains and breaks through the fences meant to protect our own backyards. We do not visit those mountains, neither in body nor in thought, as we do not stroll through rough districts, mean streets, urban ghettoes, asylum-seekers' camps and other no-go areas. We carefully avoid them (or are directed away from them) in our compulsive tourist escapades. We dispose of leftovers in the most radical and effective way: we make them invisible by not looking and unthinkable by not thinking.[41]

One interesting, if gratuitous, observation is that in the telling of the story of our times, Bauman composes the tale as if writing a children's book – the repetitive care to distinguish the two trucks, the plain almost toneless language, the factory/store/mountain chain of images. But then, soon upon naming the dumping sites, he returns to his usual more lively 'adult' style of extended instances and nuance phrasings such as visible/invisible and thinkable/unthinkable. It is likely that he meant to tell the folk tale *with which we have grown up* as if speaking to children too innocent to follow the hard line of the story. Either way, the point is made that waste is just as basic to modernity as is production. It is the excrement of the body wasted by indulgence.

Just as death is put out of sight (off the agenda), so too is waste rendered invisible and unthinkable; and just as death intrudes in its time, so too do the mountains spill over onto the streets of the living. The waste is identified as the walking dead of modernity – those designed out of order building, the superfluous ones of little or spent utility to progress, those consigned by globalization to their separate dumping sites.[42] And here the full/empty opposition is in play. The dumping sites he mentions (a short list of the many alluded to) – rough districts, mean streets, urban ghettoes, asylum-seeks camps and other no-go areas (of which crucially, prisons) – are the formerly empty spaces of the modern world where the wasted lives are left to rot. Bauman always brings his metaphors down to the dirty truth of the worlds.

> Refugees, the displaced, asylum seekers, migrants, the *sans papiers*, they are the waste of globalization. But they are not the only waste turned out in ever rising volumes in our times. There is also the 'traditional' industrial waste which accompanied modern production from the start. Its disposal presents problems no less formidable than the disposal of human waste, and ever more horrifying – and for much the same reasons: the economic progress that is spreading to the most remote nooks and crannies of the 'filled up' planet, trampling on its way all remaining forms of life alternative to the consumer society.[43]

Human waste, in all senses of the term, is the waste of modern humanity. Human being is, at its most vile, shit. Modernity excretes not just the denatured by-products of its consumptive appetite, but even of human being itself. We wish to say 'human being' – the generic term – without ignoring the actual beings forced to flee to camps and empty cities, or confined by force in prisons and ghettoes.

The terms by which human being was defined under the modern regime are changed. Humanity was born in the Enlightenment, baptized by the hand of a humanism meant to protect the soul of human worth from death. But it was born, if not still, already soiled. The gentle prospect of human rights, liberal humanisms, universal man, and all the other euphemisms by which human being itself has been denatured, like industrial wastes, turns out to be little more than a veil by which generic man was blinded to the reality of her actual, uninverted social condition. It is only when the refugees, the homeless, the beggars, the prisoners and the growing number of others spill out from their camps and dark corners that those not-yet wasted come to their senses. The empty spaces themselves are filled to overflowing. They give a few coins to the beggars as down payment against the day when all will be wasted, excreted, vomited. To see fecal being, as today it is impossible not to, is to realize that we too will die on the mountain of shit toward which liberal progress leans. Oddly, we did not see the invisible in the time of heavy modernity, even though the deadly factory system loomed larger still than today's light informational mode of production. The perverse benefit of globalization is that the lightness of its being crushes humanity by the touch of the reaper who comes to take us away to that place, once empty, where all must go – the place that is no place because it is filled with the specific gravity of the situation we are in with no relief in sight.

There are reservations to hold against Bauman, but they are themselves thin against the shear weight of his logic. For one, and perhaps most importantly, he shrinks from a full exposition of the human body. Bodies too often (and atypically for him) are treated abstractly. Bodies shit in order to live. Their waste stinks, as do rotting corpses. Graveyards, it is true,[44] are museums to the dead and wasted, but beyond the monuments in most cities are the pauper fields, the mass graves, the decomposing flesh of the nameless and forgotten who are, in fact, the forerunners in the race for progress.

For another, it is fair to wonder why with all of Bauman's historical sensibility, he does not engage the question of just when, exactly, heavy modernity revealed itself in the lightness of being. Naturally he must have wished to maintain the difference from Beck and Giddens and the others who seek to hold tight to modernity by periodizing it into stages that permit the modern to salvage itself from its deeply structured illusion. Still, there would be a benefit to examining the point of departure as more specific than the shift from heavy industry to light. Plus which, heavy industry has not so much been overcome as redistributed into the economic peripheries where, as in China's Pearl River Delta, industrial production, however light, pollutes the rural countryside and imprisons the millions locked out of Hong Kong or Shanghai. More to the point, it is possible to locate the historical moment when this shift took place in the period between 1949, when modernity's global colonies began to rebel, and 1968, when the revolutions entered the core states of the European Diaspora. The primal empty places of the modern era, after it had settled the new world, were the colonized regions of the South and East in which the modern prison system was perfected in its current form. As valuable as

Foucault's notion of the carceral society that evolved from Bentham's panopticon may be, the fact remains that the global system of modern capitalism had long before organized the empty global spaces, beginning with the notorious dark continent, as prison regimented, factory-like, for the production of natural wealth and the wasting of superfluous humanity.

For a third reservation, Bauman might sharpen his liquidity figure were he to develop the idea of haunting which, not incidentally, appears in close textual proximity to Marx's refiguring of the modern as a melting away of the solids. The ghosts haunting Europe in 1848 were not necessarily political ones, as Marx and Engels thought; the revolutionary movements of that time were put down. What was not was the inexorable movement of heavy modernity toward the point where its denials and deflections could no longer be hidden. Liquidity is a powerful literary figure, but it still does not quite do what the ghost figure might. If it is true, and Bauman is at his best on this point, that the melting of solid modernity was in the chemical structures of the thing itself, then what remains is the need for a somewhat more nuanced interpretation of just how this works in the whole.

What haunting permits, apart from its connotative possibilities in respect to Bauman's almost religious ethic, is a way of tying death to the body. Ghosts frighten because, though dead, they come in bodily form. Hauntings, thus, would permit a somewhat more systematic tying together of the dumping grounds of liquid modernity. For one example, is not the supermarket the ghost of the farm which in turn was a key element in the global prison-house wrought by capitalism beginning with the long sixteenth century? And does not the body still now remains, as on the harvest of agricultural production, available for consumption in places that, even in the ghettoes, are made up and organized to appear as, if not a farm, at least a grazing field for the satiation of human appetites. And is it not at the doors of the supermarkets, coffee shops, diners, and other wonders of belly stuffing temptations, that the walking dead gather to beg a few coins, to dive the dumpsters, to find some warmth and shelter, to bum a ride to visit their loved ones in prison? If the supermarket is the ghost of the farm, the commercial center is the ghost of the lost community, and the prison and other such asylums are the ghosts of the global past from whence came modernity's myths of the free, natural, human being who worked his body to produce his human worth, without the constraints and confines that modernity introduced.

If the modern social body is haunted by the apparitions of modernity's dead, then it must be that the modern cannot be buried, if it be dead in fact, until it reckons with the ghosts of Bauman's wasted humans. But what does it mean to reckon? We must look in between the crevices of social things; as Avery Gordon, the foremost theorist of ghostly matters, says:

> Haunting is an encounter in which you touch the ghost or the ghostly matter of things: the ambiguities, the complexities of power and personhood, the violence and the hope, the looming and receding actualities, the shadows of our selves and our society . . . to be sure, haunting terrorizes but it gives you *something you have to try for yourself*.[45]

These are the challenges those living in a haunted modernity face. It is the untangling of an information web and the localization of each and every Other in relation to it. Where do I fit in? How am I implicated? What can be done?

> When you see . . . the ghostly matter . . . when you have a profane illumination of these matters, when you know in a way you did not know before, then you have been notified of your involvement. You are *already* involved, implicated, in one way or another, and this is why, if you don't banish it, or kill it, or reduce it to something you can already manage, when it appears to you, the ghost will inaugurate the necessity of doing something about it.[46]

When Marx himself wrote with Engels of the specter then haunting Europe, he wrote as one already involved, for those who themselves were already involved, because that ghost of communism was in fact the spirits of the dead and dying who were already then suffering the heavy weight of modern capitalist manufacture. The ghost brings the dead into relation with the walking dead, thus bestowing on all, even those of inverted consciousness, an engagement with the real consequences of modernity's waste production. The deeds of its dead past come back to haunt, even if farcically.

One of the limitations of the liquidity figure is that liquids never fully escape the possibility that they may be returned to the solid state. As a result the lightness of modernity's being, if, as Bauman says, it was always there from the beginning, so too must the heavy solidity of its industrial dispensation. Factually, at least for the time being, the displacements of heavy industry may be less visible, like death itself, but they remain; they may be unthinkable, as waste itself, but factory-system and its entailments, even if information-based, still crush the life out of the workers who assemble the micro-parts and parcels by which the system as a whole produces its chips and widgets.

Is Bauman's liquid waste, then, capable of addressing the historical structure built on the parasitically infected body, captive in effect to the instruments of their destruction – fated thereby not for freedom but for excretion caused, internally, by the germ that produces modernity's diarrheic quality. The infected social body feeds off itself, one body engorging itself on the bodies of others. Liquid waste, thus, may not have been avoided out of scrupulous inattention. It may be that when it comes to death and waste, liquidity does not quite work. It does not allow a sharp definition of the way that the dead past haunts the present; or, even, how the liquid present, if already then in the heavy past, maintains itself apart from that to which, in chemical principle, it might return. Again, Gordon illustrates the way around this dilemma:

> Disappearance is an exemplary instance in which the boundaries of rational and irrational, fact and fiction, subjectivity and objectivity, person and system, force and effect, conscious and unconscious, knowing and not knowing are constitutively unstable. Nothing characterizes a terroristic society where the state, in the name of a patriarchal, nationalistic, Christian capitalism, is disappearing people more than haunting does. Haunting, however, is precisely what prevents rational detachment, prevents your willful control, prevents the

LIQUID WASTE, BEING HUMAN, AND DEATH

disaggregation of class struggle and your feelings, motivations, blind spots, craziness, and desires. A haunted society is full of ghosts, and the ghost always carries the message – albeit not in the form of academic treatise, or the clinical case study, or the polemical broadside, or the mind-numbing factual report – that the gap between personal and social, public and private, objective and subjective is misleading in the first place . . . it is making you see things you did not see before . . . your relation to things that seemed separate or invisible is changing.[47]

The ghost makes the invisible visible, but spooking those who would not think or see to throw off their blinders. The dead disappeared buried in unknown mass graves are us, one day, in effect if not in fact. Their corpses deliquesce in the dirty rains that wash their remains into the never, any longer, pure waters by which the still living are one day infected with the parasites that will kill them soon enough.

Yet these reservations are little more than hints of how we and others, who would not have thought what we think without him, might press the case beyond. What Bauman does so well is show the specific gravity of the *logic* of the progress-waste system that it produces wealth at the necessary risk of human wastage. Even, then, prisoners and other captive people are 'productive'. They are the fast-food refuse that stuff the market dumpsters. Bauman shows us that it is the deconstruction of the system logic that demonstrates, as not even Marx was able, the way endemic exclusion and waste are *productive* necessities.

Yet, we think, it is this logic itself that creates ghosts by forcing we who are already involved to face the unthinkable realities that, the natural laws of bodily death aside, our deaths are foreordained by the system itself. What is required is that we reckon with the spooks that terrify us so. What world will this generation inherit? How have the adults of the previous generations failed the current one? How are the people to feel about this black-hole inheritance?

Notes

1 One of the earliest and most astute readings of Bauman by an American sociologist was Steven Seidman, *Contested Knowledge* (Oxford: Blackwell, 1994), 294–303. Sadly, here, as all too often, when one speaks of academic sociology it is American sociology that comes to mind – notwithstanding its peculiar resistance to the sort of thinking one associates with Bauman; hence, the credit due Seidman for beginning, then, to see the possibilities beyond the norm.
2 Nor, even, can our awe of him arise singularly from the biographical oddity that the more familiar (to us who do not read Polish) of Bauman's works were written *after* retirement from the universities of Warsaw and Leeds in 1990. These works are, indeed, many in number (and still growing), but they are not yet so great in number as to dwarf the bulk of some twenty five books written *before* retirement.
3 Bauman, *Morality and Immorality and other Life Strategies* (Cambridge: Polity, 1992), 208.
4 In a 1990 interview, Bauman makes the astonishing statement that 'for most of my life and the greatest part of it, Jewishness played a very small role, if at all. The first time it was brought to my awareness, was in 1968 – this eruption of anti-semitism', 'Sociology,

postmodernity, and exile: an interview with Zygmunt Bauman' (by Richard Kilminster and Ian Varcoe), in Bauman, *Intimations of Postmodernity* (London: Routledge, 1992), 226.

5 This was his response to a question I [CL] asked him in Oxford (June 2005). Notably, believing that I was American, he was quick to add, in effect, that he did not mean 'hermeneutic sociology' or any other methodology. As a measure of Bauman's emergence in a position beyond sociology compare his 1978 book, Bauman, *Hermeneutics and Social Science* (London: Routledge, 1978), which is mostly a disquisition of the contributions of hermeneutics to a method of understanding in sociology. Yet, even here, at the very end of a relatively traditional book (p. 246), he signals what would come years later: 'The practical success of sociology so understood [as a method of interpretation] can only be measured by the degree to which the opposition between consensus and truth is gradually reduced, and the problem of understanding as an activity distinct from communal life gradually disappears.'

6 One such instance is an address given in the Netherlands in 2004 to an audience of practitioners of the art of 'supervising and coaching' in which he condenses the whole of his theory of liquid modernity to a very few, plain spoken words; 'Liquid Modernity' ANSE (Leiden, the Netherlands, 7 May, 2004), downloaded from: http://www.supervision-eu.org/anse/bauman%20englisch.pdf

7 The phrase comes from Thomas Nagel, *The View from Nowhere* (Oxford University Press, 1986), but it took on its bite from feminist theorists who use the phrase to characterize masculinist determined social science. For the classic instance of a feminist use, see Susan Bordo, 'Feminism, Postmodernism, and Gender-Skepticism', in Linda Nicholson (ed.) *Feminism/Postmodernism* (New York: Routledge 1990).

8 Bauman, *The Individualized Society* (Cambridge: Polity, 2001), 45. Notably, on the page following, Bauman remarks on Ulrich Beck's theory of individualization in a risk society: 'It can be said that, just as Elias "historicized" Sigmund Freud's theory of the "civilized individual" by exploring the civilization as an event in (modern) history, so Beck historicized Elias's account of the birth of the individual by re-presenting that birth as an aspect of continuous and continuing, compulsive and obsessive *modernization*.' As a clue as to how prescient Elias was on this point, consider the 1939 title essay of *The Society of Individuals* (Oxford: Blackwell, 1991) in which rather snidely he refers (p. 54) to the debate in modern societies of the west over the primacy of the individual versus that of the social as a 'curious party game'.

9 Erving Goffman is usually interpreted as an early sociologist of the human freedom to make the self in the conditions of a setting. Yet, from the early essays on face work and interaction rituals to the later ones on framing he casts himself in the role he chose – that of a Durkheimian of contexts. As we will show later, Bauman's liquidity metaphor allows him a greater fluidity in the interpretation of a much wider range of social wholes.

10 *Individualized Society*, 46–7.

11 Among their many writings, too numerous to catalogue, see the contributions of Beck and Giddens to U. Beck, A. Giddens, and S. Lash, *Reflexive Modernization: Politics, Tradition and Aesthetics in the Modern Social Order* (Cambridge: Polity, 1994).

12 Beck, 'The Reinvention of Politics', in *Reflexive Modernization*, 6.

13 *Ibid*. 5–23; after which follows an almost upbeat section 'Paths to New Modernity' in which he talks of such prospects as 'rationality reform', 33ff. Likewise, in response to his critics, Beck speaks of the 'opportunities of the risk society': Beck, *World Risk Society* (Oxford: Blackwell, 1999), 152.

14 *Ibid*. 10 (which cites Bauman's criticism in 'The solution as problem', *Times Higher Education Supplement* (13 November 1992), 25).

15 Beck, *World Risk Society*, 152.

16 Bauman, *Liquid Modernity* (Cambridge: Polity, 2000), 38. In this respect, I [CL] must confess to having too much lumped Bauman in with Beck and Giddens in the sections I wrote for my book with Anthony Elliott; Elliot and Lemert, *The New Individualism: The Emotional Costs of Globalization* (London: Routledge 2006). In my defense, I would say that one of Bauman's qualities of character is that he may have set the standard for generosity in praising and using the thoughts of others even when he deplores some of what they say.
17 On de facto individualism, see *Liquid Modernity*, 38–41.
18 *Ibid.* 214–15.
19 In regard to Habermas, whose earlier writings were, if not exactly empirical, at least amenable to the concerns of an empirical sociology, in the 1980s he put forth a magnum opus that is little more than commentary: *The Theory of Communicative Action* (two volumes, 1981; 1984 and 1987, English editions). There are those who might say much the same of Giddens's *Constitution* (1984), but the fact is that this book does engage, if at a distance, empirical issues at play in the social sciences (its enormous influence of cultural geography and the sociology of cities, for one instance). At the same time, Bourdieu's most important empirical work, *Distinction* (1979), had already established his original approach to research in the field of culture.
20 Bourdieu, *Outline of a Theory of Practice* (Cambridge University Press, 1977).
21 Beck and Johannes Willms, *Conversations with Ulrich Beck* (Cambridge: Polity, 2004), 11–61. Giddens, *Consequences of Modernity* (Stanford University Press, 1990).
22 Yet, where Bourdieu and Beck are closer is their respective methods which are both rooted in an aesthetic sensibility that allows them to visualize the spaces of social relations in non-linear, even three-dimensional, ways. The difference is that Bourdieu's is more intently a reworking of sociology as critique of aesthetic judgment, while Beck's approach is more a literary critique of modernity and its entailments.
23 Bauman, *Liquid Modernity*, 23.
24 The locution owes to Charles Barkley, one time professional basketball star and long-time member of the Republican Party.
25 Bauman, *Wasted Lives: Modernity and its Outcasts* (Cambridge: Polity, 2004), 96–7.
26 These references to breaks and non-breaks are decidedly not in the Althusserian sense of epistemological breaks. Even in the shift, if that is the word, around 1988–90, Bauman clearly builds on his earlier more sociological work. But, here, in the evolution of the liquidity figure Bauman suggests more an epiphany of what had been hidden from the foundations than a departure within modernity.
27 Bauman, *Mortality, Immortality*, 164–5. The Lyotard reference is *Le postmoderne expliqué aux enfants* (Paris : Galilée, 1988), 36.
28 *Mortality, Immortality*, 164.
29 Notably in *Liquid Fear* (2006, chapter 1) as well as *Wasted Lives* (2004, especially chapter 3).
30 *Mortality, Immortality*, 137; compare the whole of chapter 4.
31 *Ibid.* 199; compare the whole of chapter 5.
32 *Ibid.* 3.
33 See Augustine, *On the Trinity* (400–416 CE). The most succinct explanation and application of Augustine's theory of the self is Reinhold Niebuhr, 'Augustine's Political Realism', in Niebuhr, *Christian Realism and Political Problems* (New York: Scribner's, 1953). Whether Bauman has read Augustine, we cannot say, but he has read a good bit of Niebuhr who he occasionally cites. The source however is certainly Emmanuel Levinas whose *Otherwise than Being* (The Hague: Martinus Nijhoff, 1981) figures prominently in *Mortality, Immortality*.

34 *Mortality, Immortality*, 207.
35 *Liquid Modernity*, 38–52.
36 *Mortality, Immortality*, 199; hence, in the same place, the replacement of the modern ideal of a universal human community with localized and distinguished communities as havens for survival against the odds.
37 Naturally, *Liquid Modernity* is in its way more systematic in the way it addresses the differential implications of the idea. Still, *Wasted Lives*, even without firm association with the liquidity theme is the clearest and most bracing interpretation of the meaning and history of Marx's idea of the modern as melting solids. One can only speculate as to why *Wasted Lives* was not explicitly identified with the liquidity series. Perhaps it was, as we say later, because the metaphoric connotation was too coarse.
38 *Wasted Lives*, 6.
39 *Ibid*. 5.
40 Li*quid Modernity*, 103; phrase below, same place.
41 *Wasted Lives*, 27.
42 The three elements in the series are the topics of the key chapters in the book: waste as order-building, the waste of economic progress, the waste of globalization.
43 *Ibid*. 58–9.
44 *Ibid*. 120.
45 Avery Gordon, *Ghostly Matters, Haunting and the Sociological Imagination (*University of Minnesota Press, 1997), 124.
46 *Ibid*. 205.
47 *Ibid*. 98.

CHAPTER 8

Solid modernity, liquid utopia – liquid modernity, solid utopia

Ubiquitous utopianism as a trademark of the work of Zygmunt Bauman

Michael Hviid Jacobsen

'As utopian oases dry up, a desert of banality and bewilderment spreads.'
Jürgen Habermas (1989: 68)

'To be human really means to have utopias.'
Ernst Bloch (quoted in J. R. Bloch 1988: 33)

The death and dearth of utopia? – An assessment of contemporary utopianism

In his politically provocative as well as thought-provoking 1999 book *The End of Utopia*, American social critic Russell Jacoby, as the title of his book suggests, dramatically declared the intellectual meltdown or at least the eclipse of utopianism in contemporary social, political and academic life. Hereby he suggested that a previously strong utopian impulse among intellectuals, planners and politicians had faded and resulted or culminated in an 'age of apathy'. According to Jacoby's pessimistic thesis, social critics and writers, previously the most vociferous of utopians, had now moved from utopia to myopia. He went on to suggest, after presenting a depressing diagnosis of the state of contemporary utopianism:

> World events and the *Zeitgeist* militate against a utopian spirit – and have for decades. If not murderous, utopianism seems unfashionable, impractical and pointless. Its sources in imagination and hope have withered. The demise of radicalism affects even the unpolitical and the unconcerned, who viscerally register a confirmation of what they always intuited: This society is the only possible one.
>
> (Jacoby 1999: 179–80)

Especially the intellectuals and social thinkers as critics of contemporary Western society have apparently banished the utility of the notion of utopia which has now turned into a liability because of being associated with matters of social control, state intervention and totalitarianism. Moreover, to make matters even worse, the advance of neo-liberalism in recent years and its alleged hostility to social alternatives as well as the lessons learned from totalitarianism or fundamentalist terrorism have now, perhaps inredeemably, put utopia into disrepute.

This relatively recent tendency indeed inaugurates an intellectual landslide and paradoxical change in the status and situation of utopianism. For centuries, intellectuals and social critics were among the most valiant and vociferous exponents of utopian ideals and imaginings. Not surprisingly, there has been some controversy over the veracity of the aforementioned declaration of the 'end of utopia' (as concerning all the other current fads of prognosticating the end of something – be it history, ideology, politics, etc. – at the threshold of the new millennium). Some have in fact claimed that utopian thought today encounters a heretofore new and much more fertile soil. For example, George Slusser remarked that 'there are more utopias being conceived and written than ever before, a frenzy of them' (Slusser 1999: xiii). On the other hand, however, Bruce Mazlish recently observed that 'the social context in which we live is not favourable to utopias' (Mazlish 2003: 43) and Krishan Kumar some years ago noted that 'utopia as a form of the social imagination has clearly weakened – whether fatally we cannot say' (Kumar 1987: 423). Naturally, both claims can hardly be true at one and the same time – or can they? It appears as if there is some uncertainty as to the status of utopian thinking in these, what Zygmunt Bauman (2000) described as, 'liquid modern' times. This uncertainty apparently pertains, as we will seek to illustrate below, to the inherent ambivalence of the notion of utopia as simultaneously possibility *and* reality, counterfactuality *and* negation, constantly receding horizon *and* final destination, latency *and* actuality, immanence *and* transcendence, alternative *and* embodied end-state, telos *and* nomos, etc. Thus, any declaration of the state of utopianism must take into account what is actually meant by 'utopia'.

As a consequence of this conceptual welter, utopia has perhaps been one of the most widely used and misused concepts within social theory and social philosophy throughout the last couple of centuries and something suggests that the original content of the notion has been somewhat diluted or at least swelled in contemporary usage. Utopia has attracted as many enemies as supporters throughout the years. The catalogue of critiques aimed against utopianism includes its potential realisation of totalitarianism, the irrationality of thinking about – not to mention planning – the future, the idleness of dreaming and the impracticality of its political propositions (Kateb 1963; Goodwin and Taylor 1982: 92–115). Supporters of utopia, on the other hand, have emphasised the normative necessity of reaching beyond the actually existing reality and the empirically factual, the power of pointing to the 'ought' rather than the 'is', and the desirability of visionary daydreaming and creative imagination. Such conflicting positions, inner ambiguity or conceptual multivalency of the concept of utopia and its warranty, are also reflected in the treatment of utopia in the writings of Zygmunt Bauman who throughout his lifelong career continually has visited and revisited the strange land of utopia. Especially since the turn of the millennium, and thus since the publication of *Liquid Modernity*, one can witness a revival or resurgence of utopian concerns in Bauman's writings. This resurfacing of utopianism seems to coincide with the terminological shift from 'postmodernity' to 'liquid modernity' at the threshold of the new millennium. After extended absence, approximately ranging from the mid-1970s to the late 1990s, the term utopia as well as an underpinning of utopianism in his sociology has resurfaced most persistently in his work. Despite being cursorily treated in many recent introductory or biographical texts (Blackshaw 2005; Beilharz 2000; Jacobsen 2004a; Smith 1999; Tester 2004), the seminal importance of utopia, however, still remains a relatively overlooked yet integral part of any appreciation of Bauman's writing (see Jacobsen 2004b, 2006a, 2006b).

The purpose of this chapter is therefore threefold. Initially we will explore and document the development and transformation of the utopian perspective within the writings of Zygmunt Bauman throughout the years. His diagnosis of the possibility and necessity of utopian thinking in contemporary (dystopian) liquid modernity will also be outlined. Finally, we will attempt to summarise and draw perspectives from the perpetual yet usually unspoken presence of utopianism within the sociology of Zygmunt Bauman and present certain points of criticism that may be raised against his perspective.

The early years: socialism and culture as utopia

Socialist pioneer Karl Kautsky once remarked that 'with the utopia modern socialism begins'. Paradoxically, however, utopianism has ever since the conception of socialism been a thorn deeply buried in its flesh, a blemish in its pedigree; part and parcel of many especially early and exotic variants of Marxism (Geoghegan 1987; Ulam 1973), yet relentlessly condemned by Karl Marx and Friedrich Engels in their *The Communist Manifesto* as well as by Engels (1976) in his critique of the utopian socialists and their futilitarian and utterly unscientific predilection for the anticipated future instead of preoccupation with the urgency of the present situation. Marx, for example, in personal correspondence blatantly labelled utopianism 'silly, stale, and basically reactionary' (Marx in Padover 1979: 320). Therefore, the classic as well as contemporary band of Marxist-inspired utopian writers – such as Charles Fourier, Robert Owen, Mikhail Bakunin, Pierre Joseph Proudhon, Oskar Negt, André Gorz, Ernst Bloch, Herbert Marcuse, Wilhelm Reich and Rudolf Bahro, just to mention a few – often found themselves at the margins of conventional Marxism and their writings were deemed either idiosyncratic or heretic by the prevailing economic determinist strand or more realist variants of Marxist social theory. As Ernst Bloch famously and poetically noted on this development of socialism: 'There appeared now and then an excessive progress of Socialism from utopia to science, so that not only the cloud but also the flame of utopia, which paves the way, was extinguished' (Bloch in Bayertz 1984: 100). Bauman's work presents no exception to the fate of this company of socialist utopians, as he was expelled from the University of Warsaw in March 1968 on charges of dissidence and corrupting Polish youth, leading to his lifelong exile in Britain. Therefore, his early writings upon arrival in Leeds in 1971 illustrate how he sought to dissociate his more humanistic and indeed utopian variant of socialism from the structural, 'scientific' and economic determinist

Marxism, hostile to utopianism, practised in his abandoned Polish homeland as well as to a certain degree among many of his new British colleagues within sociology. Thus, Bauman's oeuvre, from the early years, can be read as a repristination or reappraisal of utopia.

Apart from Marxism, or perhaps rather because of Marxism, sociology in general has always stayed hostile to and suspicious of utopianism because it challenged the conventional notions of value-neutrality, empirical documentation, verification and the norms of scientificity. Utopianism was concerned with the 'ought' rather than the 'is', the speculative rather than the empirically observable or logically deducible. As a consequence, utopianism can be, and historically has been, roundly criticized for its normativity and dubious objectivity, its lack of concrete scientific procedures and methodology, its blurred understanding of ontology and thus of reality, its absolutist epistemology, its prognostications lingering beyond proof, its prescriptive utilising of social theory, its narrow view of human nature, its insistence on intervention in the world and so forth (Goodwin 1978: 174–201). One would therefore be on solid ground if proposing the incompatibility of social scientific practice and utopianism. However, Robert Nisbet debunked this, in his opinion, artificial opposition between social science and utopianism by commenting that 'utopianism and social science may seem to be incompatible. But they are not. Utopianism is compatible with everything but determinism, and it can as easily be the over-all context of social science as can any other creative vision' (Nisbet 1962: xvii). Upon his arrival in Britain, Bauman especially and strongly objected to the determinism of much conventional Marxist theory. From early on he embraced a utopian understanding of the role of socialism as opposed to utopianism as an iron-clad Marxian ideological programme, and he recently indicated how he believed his deep-seated hostility to and suspicion of the latter tendency to stem from a narrow-minded conceptualisation and appreciation of utopianism within Marxism as well as within sociology:

> I suspect that in our social-scientific usage all too often we unduly narrow down the concept of 'utopia' to the early modern blueprints of the good society, understood as a kind of totality which pre-empts its members' choices and determines in advance their goodness, however understood . . . I am now inclined to accept that utopia is an undetachable part of the human condition . . . I now believe that utopia is one of humanity's constituents, a 'constant' in the human way of being-in-the-world.
>
> (Bauman in Bauman and Tester 2001: 48–50)

As such an 'undetachable part of the human condition', a 'constituent of humanity' and a 'constant in the human way of being-in-the-world', utopia quickly became an integral part of Bauman's showdown with those positions within conventional sociology or Marxism hostile to human activity, creativity and choice. His alternative vision of 'the active utopia' countered the prevalent understandings of utopia as order, blueprints, conformity and coercion into happiness. In short, Bauman reinterpreted utopia as something that critically challenged common sense, habit, the present state of affairs, heteronomy and obsessive order thereby seeking to salvage and resurrect its critical edge.

Bauman's early acquaintance with utopia was ushered in by the publication of *Socialism: The Active Utopia*. This book marks his third volume released in English (anticipated by *Between Class and Elite* (1972) and *Culture as Praxis* (1973)). In the book, Bauman defines utopia as an 'activating presence' (Bauman 1976) which has many similarities to what fellow Polish thinker and exile Leszek Kołakowski (1981) described as an 'imaginative incentive' guiding human creative and critical activity, something defying reason, logic and prediction. The four cornerstones of this 'active socialist utopia' as an activating presence were defined by Bauman in the following way:

1 'Utopias relativise the present . . . By exposing the partiality of current reality, by scanning the field of the possible in which the real occupies merely a tiny plot, utopias pave the way for a critical attitude and a critical activity which alone can transform the present predicament of man';
2 'utopias are those aspects of culture . . . in which the possible extrapolations of the present are explored . . . The driving force behind the search for utopia is neither the theoretical nor the practical reason, neither the cognitive nor the moral interest, but the principle of hope';
3 'utopias split the shared reality into a series of competing project-assessments. The reality in which utopia is rooted is not neutral toward conflicting perspectives generated by social conflicts . . . Utopias scan the options open to society at the current stage of its history; but by exposing their link to the predicament of various groups, utopias reveal also their class-committed nature. In other words, utopias relativise the future into a bundle of class-committed solutions, and dispel the conservative illusion that one and only one thread leads from the present . . . Utopias weaken the defensive wall of habit'; and finally,
4 'utopias do exert enormous influence on the actual course of historical events . . . They just linger in the public mind as guides for social action, as criteria marking off the good from the evil, and as obstinate reminders of the never-plugged gap between the promise and the reality . . . Utopias enter reality not as the aberrations of deranged intellects, but as powerful factors acting from within what is the only substance of reality, motivated human action.'

(Bauman 1976a: 12–17)

Thus, the active utopia envisaged by Bauman in this specific period was clearly a particularly socialist utopia by his pointing to the class-related and thus conflict-oriented nature of utopianism, but it also contained more universal humanistic aspirations as a constant reminder of the more general possibility of retrieving forgotten hopes, neglected alternatives and missed chances. In short, Bauman's notion of the 'active utopia' represents an iconoclastic, critical, counter cultural, transformative alternative and action-oriented antipole to the common-sense vision of utopia as a conservative and consensual 'graveyard' where nothing new ever happens (Dahrendorf 1958: 117).

Socialism as an active utopia wanted to honour all the conflicting hopes and contradictory intentions and ideals contained within modernity – liberty, equality and brotherhood – without distorting them as did capitalism through its inhuman exploitation and alienation. In vain, it aspired to square the unsquarable circle, to dissolve all the antinomies (freedom versus equality, state versus community, historical laws versus free agency) of modern existence (Bauman 1976: 49–64). The socialist utopia itself ran out of steam and ended in death throes exactly when it was seeking to enforce and legislate a utopian reality by sacrificing liberty at the altar of equality, when autonomy was subjugated to the demands for social conformity and absolute obedience, when community was crushed by the state and when autonomous human agents were eliminated from the logics of history. Socialism was, as a start, the modern utopia par excellence. However, it was a utopia, when turned or forced into flesh and blood, which destroyed itself as utopia:

> Socialism shares with all other utopias the unpleasant quality of retaining its fertility only in so far as it resides in the realm of the possible. The moment it is proclaimed as accomplished, as empirical reality, it loses its creative power; far from inflaming human imagination, it puts on the agenda in turn an acute demand for a new horizon, distant enough to transcend and relativise its own limitations.
>
> (Bauman 1976: 36)

The Stalinist or Communist aspirations to legislate the socialist utopia as state power in the Soviet Union and its satellite states meant the absorption of the counter-cultural potency of socialism under the banner of thorough and inhuman industrialism as well as political pacification of most parts of the population. It was now a new incarnation of the capitalist utopia, 'a capitalist utopia with no room for capitalists . . . a "populist" version of the old bourgeois utopia' (Bauman 1976: 91). Leszek Kołakowski stated on this central opposition between utopianism as 'regulative' and as 'constitutive' ideas that 'they serve us better if they are signposts which show the direction towards an unattainable goal, instead of asserting that the goal has been, or is about to be, reached' (Kołakowski 1983: 236).

Against this historical tragedy of the socialist utopia, Bauman muses: 'One can say that the history of socialism has come full circle. It started, in the [utopian] work of Mably, Morelly, Saint-Simon or Fourier, as an idea in search of a constituency; it has become recently a constituency in search of an idea' (Bauman 1976: 109). Socialism ceased to be utopian once its 'constituency' lost the guiding vision of the good and just society and instead, at all costs, attempted to enforce or legislate social and political order. Bauman, however, never abandoned socialism and still regards his sympathies as thoroughly socialist. Socialism as an active utopia has not come to the end of the road despite the severe distortions of numerous failed social experiments embarrassingly exposed to the tests of empirical scrutiny and moral assessment:

> The role of socialism as a constantly critical leaven within the texture of present society has never changed. The desire for a just society, coupled with the

renunciation of the present one as unjust, is the most constant feature of socialism, as well as the key to the understanding of its historical role in modern society ...]The utopian function of the socialist project can be retained, in the circumstances, only on condition that its critical edge is directed against *all* reality.

(Bauman 1976a: 51, 130)

Socialism, not just as a specific counter-culture of modernity or capitalism aimed at creating the just society, but as culture in itself, as an ongoing creative human activity, is utopian because it seeks to breach the boundaries of nature, necessity, inevitability and order. Culture, in Bauman's perspective, means living forwards, striving and confronting that which is in order to realize that which could or should be. In this way, culture is utopian and utopia is cultural: 'Social life cannot in fact be understood unless due attention is paid to the immense role played by utopia. Utopia shares with the totality of culture the quality – to paraphrase Santayana – of a knife with the edge pressed against the future' (Bauman 1976: 12).

Especially throughout these early years, Bauman persistently turned against notions of inevitability, necessity and predictability and thus his book on socialist utopianism, as well as his book on culture, annoyed more deterministic Marxists who in the laws of historical materialism discovered a universal logic of historical development and teleological evidence of a predetermined future just patiently waiting to be realized, legislated or brought about by working-class revolution. Bauman did not entertain the certainty or predictability of such a position but through the idea of the active utopia explored the still unfulfilled potentials of socialism and the alternatives open to human creativity and ingenuity.

The later years: the Other and morality as utopia

The utopian impulse did not vanish altogether when Bauman passed from the early years of conversation with and reconstruction of socialism and Marxism to a more postmodern perspective throughout the latter parts of the 1980s. As Keith Tester remarks: 'In the 1970s, Bauman identified utopia with culture and socialism' (Tester 2004: 147). Later in his writings, in his so-called 'moral' or 'postmodern' phase ranging from the early to the late 1990s (Jacobsen 2004a), other notions and ideas supplemented and eventually substituted the previous priority of culture and socialism as the prime carriers of utopian aspirations. However, the idea of caring for and defending the weak, implied also in the socialist utopia, did not disappear but took on new meanings. Towards the end of *Socialism: The Active Utopia*, Bauman prophetically professed that 'attempts to emancipate utopian imagination from the shallow sands of daily realism tend inevitably to stray into the hanging gardens of moral and artistic criticism' (Bauman 1976: 113). Thus, not surprisingly, art, especially postmodern art, morality and the generic notion of the Other and the more specific concept of the stranger increasingly became the new focus of utopian attention in his work. Everything defying the obsessive modern quest for order, transparency, purity, predictability and systemness were suddenly seen as carrying utopian connotations or containing utopian potentials.

The publication of the postmodern moral manifesto *Postmodern Ethics* revealed Bauman's intimate engagement with the metaphysical phenomenology of French-Lithuanian thinker Emmanuel Levinas in whose work 'the Other' constituted the centre of analytical and moral attention (Bauman 1993). In the original version of this moral phenomenology, Levinas ascribed morality and thus also the Other to the realm of 'infinity' marked by infinite possibilities, infinite responsibility and infinite being-for-the-Other, standing in sharp opposition to the realm of 'totality' in which order, system and coercion ruled supreme (Levinas 1961). To Levinas, as well as to Bauman, the subjectivity of the Other (and especially the 'face' of the Other) represents that which cannot and ought not be objectified or reduced to the means to an end. The Other is a perpetual aporia, and it is exactly the weakness of the Other which urges the self to take unconditional responsibility for the well-being of the Other. Levinas's moral ontology is constituted by the transindividual universe of two and his ethics are constructed around the biblical story of the Good Samaritan helping the needing stranger. Bauman utilises Levinas's terminology to create a more sociological understanding of the nature of human morality. Contrary to modern universal and foundational ethics, externally enforced by the coercive powers stemming from the church pulpit or state bureaucracies, Bauman believes postmodernity potentially promises a moral incentive, a new moral awakening, a possibility of being-*for*-the-Other rather than merely being-*besides*-the Other or being-*with*-the-Other because solid foundations are no longer available or plausible and because contingency and ambivalence prevail. Clearly, there is a utopian element in Bauman's and Levinas's priority of the Other over the self in moral relationships and in the unspoken ethical demand imposed by the weakness and vulnerability of the Other. Stefan Morawski, Bauman's lifelong friend and fellow exile, pondered on the notion of 'being-for-the-Other' in Bauman's work: 'Can there be a more utopian blueprint of humankind that "being-for" taking priority over "being-beside" or "being-with"?' (Morawski 1998: 35). The answer must be a resounding 'no'. In a universe, as that of Levinas and Bauman, in which 'ethics come before ontology', in which moral responsibility pre-empts lawful obligations, utopia reigns supreme. Therefore, Levinas in an interview also confessed the utopianism immanent in his metaphysical philosophy when stating: 'There is a utopian moment in what I say; it is the recognition of something which cannot be realized but which, ultimately, guides all moral action . . . There is no moral life without utopianism – utopianism in this exact sense that saintliness is goodness' (Levinas 1988: 178).

The aforementioned Levinasian opposition between 'infinity' and 'totality' is equally evident in Bauman's own moral reinterpretation of the Bible stemming from the two primordial stories, or so-called 'etiological myths', of Adam and Eve expelled from the Garden of Eden and Moses and the law-giving act on Mount Sinai resulting in the Ten Commandments being handed down from God to humankind. The latter story became the mould from which most modern ethical and moral understandings were subsequently conceived within Western philosophical and political thought. Bauman, however, prefers the so-called 'morality of choice' to a 'morality of conformity' by privileging the former story to the latter as the harbinger or expression of postmodernity and postmodern morality. Whereas the latter etiological myth of conformity spells out a life lived in the shadow of abiding by the letter of the Law, a life of coercion into conformity, of authority, obedience and of strict subjugation and submission (but also of security, certainty and safety), the former myth of choice rather depicts the existential and moral condition as a cruel ambivalent predicament, eternal uncertainty and perpetual agony (but also of autonomous human responsibility, freedom of choice and the knowledge of the existence and necessity of making such a choice). The trouble with the morality of choice, which is pre-societal, arises with the arrival of the third, or with the constitution of Society. Then the intimate primal relationship of proximity between the self and the Other (which need not be physical) becomes diluted, delicate, complex and potentially excluding. Protracted negotiations and contractual obligations elbow out unmediated moral responsibility, formal rules erode spontaneous identification, written principles of justice supplant unspoken and unconditional moral responsibility and politics and ethics become the locus of legislative ambitions undermining the original moral impulse. Bauman therefore requests that justice, the 'pupil of the school of morality', remains true to its deep-seated moral roots, however utopian. Although 'justice is first and foremost the matter of *politics*, not morality' (Bauman 1998: 21), justice itself also contains strong utopian connotations and implications: 'Justice, one may say, must exist perpetually in a condition of *noch nicht geworden*, setting itself standards higher than those already practiced' (Bauman 1999b: 155). Justice, in a paradoxical way, is only alive and kicking through its negation injustice, through its own unfulfilled potential of not being just enough. In a similar sense as utopia which when enforced turned dystopian, justice worthy of its name is always inches short of reaching the ultimate goal line:

> For all that we know today, history does not seem to run towards 'just society', and all attempts to force it to run in this direction tend to add new injustices to the one's they were bent on repairing. It seems more and more likely that justice is a movement, rather than a goal or any describable 'end state'; that it manifests itself in the acts of spotting and fighting injustices ... Justice means always wanting more of itself.
>
> (Bauman 1997: 242)

Justice can never 'be done'. One may also surmise that justice as well as morality, as guiding principles, must always remain short of and shy away from their full-blown promises and potentials in order to perform the continuous task of critical knife edges pressed against the throat of the present as well as the future.

In *Life in Fragments*, another book from the 1990s on postmodern moralities, Bauman expanded and elaborated his position from *Postmodern Ethics* by testifying how 'art and the Other of moral relationship – the Other of being-for, the Other as *the face* – share the same status: when they are, they are in the future; when they are not in the future, they are no more. They are what they are only as a challenge to what already is and has been' (Bauman 1995: 67). The future constituted the 'absolute Other' in Levinas's writings and the future also concerns Bauman because it is open, indeterminable, unpredictable and aporetic. *Futura*, not *facta*, constitutes the core of Levinas's and Bauman's utopianism because *futura*, and thus the majority of human history, is characterized by the possible whereas *facta* is entirely determined by the probable and thus rooted in past experiences. As Bauman states, 'each moment of human history is, to a greater or lesser degree, an open-ended situation; a situation which is not entirely determined by the structure of its own past, and from which more than one string of events may follow' (Bauman 1976: 10). Apart from art, the future and the Other, especially the persona of the stranger, and within this category particularly the Jew, mark the embodiment of otherness, of puzzling idiosyncrasy, of the mind-blowing diversity, surprise and unpredictability of modern and postmodern existence. The stranger's ambivalence was an 'activating presence' in modernity, but also an annoying presence. Two active ways of dealing with the presence of the stranger were typical of modernity; one strategy, still prevalent in various guises today, is assimilation, by Bauman sometimes referred to as the 'anthropophagic' strategy, which seeks to reduce or eliminate the element of unpredictability and uncertainty in strangers by making 'them' identical to 'us', by devouring their strangeness; the second strategy, sometimes called the 'anthropoemic' strategy, also still present in certain places, consists of excluding the strangers – expelling, incarcerating or ultimately exterminating them. According to Bauman, 'all utopias, these crystallized precipitations of diffuse longings and scattered hopes of the modern mind, followed the first of the two "rational" strategies: they were utopias of an orderly, transparent and predictable, "user-friendly" world. And they were all architectural and "urban-planning" utopias' (Bauman 1995: 128). However, the first strategy was sometimes supplemented by the second, as in Hitler's concentration camps or in Stalin's gulags. Therefore, the modern ambition of mental eradication of the unwelcome presence and existence of strangers often led to spatial segregation, sometimes even physical extermination, of individuals or groups of people not fitting in with the utopian image of the world, annoyingly signalling that things *can* be different.

From gamekeeping utopia via gardening utopia to hunting utopia

Zygmunt Bauman has not only dealt with utopia as a cognitive undercurrent, a fanciful figment of the mind, or as an ignition tube for the human imagination. He recently also presented a compressed historiography of the practical bearings of utopian ideas within and upon Western societies from premodernity via modernity to postmodernity or liquid modernity. He utilises some of the same notions originally developed in *Legislators and Interpreters* (1987) and *Modernity and Ambivalence* (1991) such as the 'gamekeeping state' and the 'gardening state' in order to describe the transformation of the utopian spirit and practice throughout the epoch of modernity, the dialectics between ideas and reality. As Bauman claims, 'modernity is also a social and psychological phenomenon . . . One can only surmise that however the advent of modernity affects the dimensions and the content of yearnings and utopias, the impact is mediated by these latter phenomena more than anything else' (Bauman 1976: 38). Thus, a good place to start any comprehension of the transformation of modernity would be to look at modernity's many and shifting utopias, to regard utopia as an optics through which not only the dreams and illusions of that era can be glimpsed but also through which modernity's concrete realisations and embodiments of its concomitant utopian aspirations can be seen.

Modernity was, as mentioned above, the epoch when new types of utopia initially and emphatically saw the light of day because the advancing modern society provided the two necessary preconditions for the advancement of utopianism: first, an overwhelming feeling that the world was not functioning properly or optimally; and, second, that humans possess the ability and potency to perform this task of recalibrating the social world (Bauman 2005b). This did not mean, however, that all modern utopias were identical; socialism and capitalism were two distinct types of modern utopia. It does suggest, though, that throughout the modern era, numerous utopias were feverishly conceived, construed, written and constructed based on the belief in the omnipotence of Man in shaping the present and in forestalling the future. Utopia was thus a particularly and thoroughly modern invention, a figment of modern imagination, a creation of modern mind. However, it was never merely a figment of the imagination or utterly idle or 'simple dreaming', as Krishan Kumar (1991) pointed out. Rather, modern mentality was bent on embodying and embedding utopia in concrete and actual reality.

In a recent manuscript, 'Living in Utopia', Bauman testifies how the modern mentality – in its early infancy, its full-blown realisation as well as after its loss of illusions – comprised and embraced different notions of utopia which can be divided into three somewhat historically overlapping yet analytically distinct phases. The first utopia is by Bauman labelled the 'gamekeeping utopia'. The premodern or early modern gamekeeping state, passively regarding the surrounding world as a natural wilderness and infused with performing merely the function of a gamekeeping utopia, concentrated primarily on supervising the porous borders between wilderness and civilisation and upholding the superhumanly designed universe (Bauman 1987: 51–68). Therefore, gamekeepers, based on their predominantly metaphysical or religious perspective on the world, only rarely tinkered with the natural and divine order of things and mainly maintained the status quo: 'Gamekeeper's services rest on the belief that things are at their best when not interfered with; that the world is a divine chain of being in which every creature has its rightful and useful place, even if human abilities are too limited to comprehend the wisdom, harmony and orderliness of God's design' (Bauman 2005b). Thus, the premodern utopia of the gamekeepers was in essence a non-utopia, in which the future was merely seen as and expected to be a smooth and gradual extension of the present or as something not to worry about. No, or only a few, visionary dreams on behalf of mankind were dreamt, pipe dreams were regarded with suspicion, and nothing seemed to guide human imagination which could not be obtained immediately in the daily grind. As a consequence, most things were left entirely in divine hands.

The advent of modernity, later labelled 'solid modernity' by Bauman, signalled a much more potent, active and confident attitude embodied in the notion of the 'gardening utopia'. This was the nursery of the great political and economic ideologies of capitalism, liberalism and socialism alike. As the metaphor suggests, gardeners are concerned with cultivating, ordering, planning and structuring activities – they seek a beautiful, symmetrical, harmonious and homogenous human garden in which the weeds and unwanted waste have been removed by root. The modern Promethean mentality, inspired by the humanistic impulse of the Enlightenment and aided and abetted by *les philosophes*, was self-confident and determined. The thoroughly modern, deliberate and secular utopia, contrary to the religious gamekeeping utopia of premodernity, was guided by dreams of purity, progress, perfection and predictability that one wishes to translate from the realm of dreams to the realm of reality. As Bauman noted in *Society Under Siege* on the ambition and aspiration of the specifically modern utopian urge that distinguished it from its premodern stepping stone:

> Utopia was to be the fortress of certainty and stability; a kingdom of tranquillity. Instead of confusion – clarity and self-assurance. Instead of the caprices of fate – a steady and consistent, surprise-free sequence of causes and effects. Instead of the labyrinthine muddle of twisted passages and sharp corners – straight, beaten and well-marked tracks. Instead of opacity – transparency. Instead of randomness – a well-entrenched and utterly predictable routine ... Utopias were blueprints for the routine hoped to be resurrected.
>
> (Bauman 2002a: 229)

The practical vehicles used by the gardening utopia to obtain these chromium-plated ideals and blueprints were primarily the progress of modern natural science and the political or social engineering emanating from the State as the natural and legitimate nucleus of society. It took the shape of political reform, social organization, economic activity, architectural planning and scientific development. The modern gardening utopia was an obsessively activist, restless and manic modern phenomenon trying to make tomorrow today: 'Impatience is an integral part of the utopian attitude', as Bauman (1976: 25) observed. Such impatience several times proved dangerous or even deadly to those who could, would or should not become part of the promised utopia for example, as when the gardeners started using their herbicide on humans. The dividing line between utopia and dystopia then became increasingly strained until the point of breaking. Bereaved of God and left to their own human and supposedly rational devices, the moderns desperately sought a thoroughly secular and earthly order, a new artificial totality named 'society' in which all the debris and disorder abandoned by the gamekeepers' utopia, the *l'ancien régime*, would, in an act of creative destruction, be wiped away: 'The new, modern order took off as a desperate search for structure in a world suddenly denuded of structure. Utopias that served as beacons for the long march to the rule of reason visualized a world without margins, leftovers, the unaccounted for – without dissidents and rebels' (Bauman in Beilharz 2001: 195).

Modern utopias, contrary to their passive premodern predecessors, were actively and practically involved on all levels of systemic reproduction, social integration and the constitution of individual and cultural life-worlds. Nothing escaped attention and nothing was left entirely to coincidence. The Great Society required that the population was continuously held at bay either by the external and coercive presence of the State or by the conscientious 'policeman in the back of the mind'. The architectural structure of the Panopticon of Jeremy Bentham and Michel Foucault embodied this vision of constant surveillance and supervision, and thus a catflap was inadvertently left open not merely to serve the noble cause of 'ordinary' social control, law and order, but also to excessive totalitarianism and its desire to eradicate unpredictability, opaqueness and freedom of choice:

> A remarkable feature of modern utopias was the attention devoted to the meticulous planning of the environment of daily life . . . Utopian inventions were strikingly similar to each other bearing vivid testimony to the shared obsession that gave birth to all of them: that of transparency and unequivocality of setting, capable of healing or warding off the agony of risky choice.
> (Bauman 2001a: 64)

When modern utopias turned into 'blueprints' or 'projects' for a world to be brought about by force, the totalitarian, destructive and repressive side of the double-edged sword of utopianism, the 'totalitarian temptation' as Hannah Arendt once called it, overshadowed its opposite more progressive, democratic and humanistic potential.

Like its premodern gamekeeping predecessor, the modern ambitious gardening utopia ultimately also ran out of steam and was overtaken by a radically different utopian, or some would say anti-utopian or dystopian, outlook. The coming of liquid modernity heralded the abandonment of the grand-designing illusions and ambitions of solid modernity: 'If one hears today phrases like "the demise of utopia" or "the end of utopia" or "the fading of utopian imagination", repeated often enough to take root and settle in common sense and so be taken for self-evident, it is because the gamekeeper's and gardener's postures are giving nowadays way to that of the *hunter*' (Bauman 2005b). The 'hunting utopia' differs radically from the utopias of premodernity or modernity because it is utterly devoid of any ambitions of controlling the present or of shaping the future. Bauman continues: 'Unlike the preceding types, hunters could not care less of the overall "balancing of things", whether "natural" or designed and contrived. The sole task they pursue is another "kill", big enough to fill their game-bags to capacity' (Bauman 2005b). Contrary to the collective and long-term focus of the utopias of modernity, hunting utopias are hyper-individualised and thoroughly short term; grand designs or lofty ideals appear as anachronisms in the deregulated atmosphere of liquid modernity. Individuals are socialised and interpellated as hunters and act like hunters – constantly looking for prey and for that extra amount of sensation to stimulate, however unsuccessfully or short term, their insatiable appetite for ever more.

Unlike the controlling ambitions embodied in the Panopticon of the modern age, in which the few guardians (or gardeners) successfully supervised and cultivated the many, in contemporary so-called Synopticon – a term proposed by Norwegian criminologist Thomas Mathiesen (1997) – the many watch the few and uncritically emulate, imitate and celebrate their way of life. As Bauman observed in *Identity*: 'Millions and hundreds of millions watch and admire the same film stars or pop celebrities, move simultaneously from "heavy metal" to rap, from flared trousers to the last word in trainers, fulminate against the same (global) public enemy, fear the same (global) villain or applaud the same (global) saviour' (Bauman 2004a: 97). Consequently, people today are primarily socialised and interpellated as consumers through the mass media and through their daily mediated confrontation with celebrities and lifestyle experts on display. There is no longer any need for panoptical guardians – only in connection to those unfortunate 'flawed consumers' incapable of participating in the hunters' utopia. Liquid modern society valorises the never-ending search for stimulation. As a consequence, disengagement rather than lifelong loyalty, forgetting rather than remembering, escaping rather than committing, dismantling rather than constructing is the name of the game for hunters. The reification of human relationships, however, is the heavy price to be paid. In recent years, Bauman often quotes Ralph Waldo Emerson's words that 'in skating on thin ice, our safety is our speed' as the philosophy permeating contemporary social life. The hunting utopia is also similar to George Steiner's (1971: 73) notion of 'utopias of the immediate': they are utterly concentrated on the *hic et nunc*, and they are post-cultural in the sense that they have abandoned every comprehensive cultivating ambition of gardening utopias and appear satisfied with managing merely the surfaces of social life such as lifestyle choices and the accessibility of consumer goods.

Consequently, after having closely examined the many hits on the internet when searching for the contemporary use of the term 'utopia', Bauman claims that the concept today has been appropriated by fashion houses, cosmetics corporations, holiday providers or interior design companies (Bauman 2005b). In *Liquid Life* he declared how 'utopias have become the game and the prey for lone rangers, hunters and trappers; one of the many spoils of the conquest and annexation of the public by the private. The grand social vision has been split into a multitude of private, strikingly similar but decidedly not complementary portmanteaus' (Bauman 2005a: 152). As described above, the arrival of the hunting utopia signals the dissolution and disillusion of the conventional collective or public utopia of solid modernity. Does this signal the end of utopia, a eulogy of utopianism? Only in the conventional sense of the term:

> Strange, unorthodox utopia it is – but utopia all the same, as it promises the same unattainable prize all utopias brandished, namely the ultimate and radical solution to human problems past, present and future, and the ultimate and radical cure for the sorrows and pains of human condition. It is unorthodox mainly for having moved the land of solutions and cures from the 'far away' into the 'here and now'. Instead of living *towards* the utopia, hunters are offered a living *inside* the utopia.
>
> (Bauman 2005b)

Indeed is it a new type of utopia, an ultra-utopia, a realized utopia or, perhaps, rather a dystopia? In *Liquid Modernity*, Bauman defined the contemporary state of affairs in the following dramatic way: 'This seems to be a dystopia made to the measure of liquid modernity – one fit to replace the fears recorded in Orwellian and Huxleyan-style nightmares' (Bauman 2000: 15). So this is where we currently reside – but is there a way out of the trap of dystopia?

SOLID/LIQUID MODERNITY/UTOPIA

The path from liquid modern unorthodox utopia to ubiquitous pantopia

Bauman's description of contemporary liquid or hunting utopia as a sort of dystopia is certainly not an appraisal of this new type of utopia but rather substantiates the many claims of the current disenchantment of conventional utopia described above. Despite being pessimistic about the presence and prospects of the hunting utopia currently 'enjoying the luxury of an unchallenged status', Bauman, however, is not defeatist. The present-day prevalence of the hunting utopia may eventually help bring about those unfulfilled promises and hopeful alternatives of its dormant socialist counterpart. The values of the socialist utopia are as important today, at the threshold of the twenty-first century, perhaps even more so, as when they were first conceived in the nineteenth century. There are several reasons for this.

First, despite valorising unlimited freedom of choice, hunting-style utopia is an utterly stratified experience exemplified by the bottomless abyss between the protagonists of the consumerist utopia, the so-called 'tourists' and their avant-garde exterritorial elite of celebrities or 'light capitalists', on the one hand, and the flawed consumers and 'vagabonds', the human waste of liquid modernity, on the other. Whereas the former are entirely free to make their moves and choices and escape their commitments, the latter, as Bauman vividly illustrated in books such as *Globalization: The Human Consequences* (1998), *Work, Consumerism and the New Poor* (1998), *Community* (2001) as well as in *Liquid Love* (2003), are increasingly marginalised and incarcerated in involuntary ghettos or refugee camps. The utopia of the few turns dystopian for the many. Already in *Socialism: The Active Utopia* did Bauman anticipate such stratified experience that later became a central tenet in his work when stating that today a lot of the socialist utopian potential has been extinguished, expropriated or absorbed by a self-contained intellectual elite with no real regard for the suffering and which

> is practically confined to the ultra-developed fringes of the modern world; and within this affluent suburb of the globe it is still further expropriated by the thin stratum of the educated elite. The links of this stratum with the actual victims of whatever injustice and exploitation the modern society may be guilty of . . . is, to say the least, tenuous. The virtual absence of such links permits the producers of utopia to spread their wings and fly high as never before.
> (Bauman 1976: 128)

The higher the producers and inventors of new glittering hunting utopias fly, be they self-contained intellectuals or product promoters for the affluent, the further away from the daily suffering, humiliation and misery of millions of people around the world they seem to move and an iron-curtain or gulf of incomprehension rises between them.

Second, the hunting utopia is exclusive in a dual and self-perpetuating sense of the term, first, it is an offer directed solely to those who already possess the means or the powers to pursue their prey and continue the hunt; and, second, it simultaneously and mercilessly marginalises those who have been deemed useless, flawed or undeserving. Therefore, only the pristine socialist utopia with its insistence on actual equality of opportunity, positive freedom and unlimited and inclusive solidarity, the humanistic tripod of Enlightenment philosophy, can counter the anti-social and socially unjust consequences of the liquid modern hunting utopia. As Bauman noted in *Community*, 'if the idea of the "good society" is to retain its meaning in the liquid modernity setting, it must mean a society concerned with "giving everybody a chance", and so with the removal of the many impediments to such a chance being taken' (Bauman 2001b: 79). Therefore, the socialist utopia described in the early years is still very much part and parcel of Bauman's perspective on the social world – the desire and demand for a just, fair and democratic world.

According to Bauman in his recent *Liquid Life*, the advancement of liquid modernity marks a bad omen for conventional utopias (and especially the socialist variant) because 'the advent of liquid modern society spelled the demise of utopias centred on society and more generally of the idea of the "good society"' (Bauman 2005a: 11). Liquid modern hunting utopia rests on a thorough individualisation and privatisation of means and ends, of life chances, life choices and life projects, so 'no wonder that it was the *public* or *social* utopia that fell as the first casualty of the dramatic change undergone by the public sphere these days' (Bauman 2005a: 152). This view of privatisation and individualisation of the 'good life' is also supported by German social thinker Oskar Negt who described how 'social utopias have crawled into the individual; the quite overwhelmed individual must now understand all chasms to society as creative possibilities for a recreation of objective conditions' (Negt 2001: 62). In the stratified hunting utopia, however, the 'chasms to society' more often than not become a dead end and a burden for many and seem impossible for most rather than appearing as 'creative possibilities for a recreation of objective conditions'. It is therefore increasingly left to the lone hunters to 'seek biographical solutions to systemic contradictions', as Bauman as an echo of Ulrich Beck often suggests.

Today we experience not only the individualisation and privatisation of the utopia of the living but also of the utopia of the dead – immortality, which once upon a time meant eternity, has in contemporary liquid modernity meticulously been cut into digestible pieces of consumer satisfaction designed, in the memorable phrase of George Steiner, for 'maximal impact and immediate obsolescence'. The ideology of *siempre viva* (the forever) has been replaced by the ideology of *carpe diem* (the here and now) as the guiding principle for people's quest for immortality (see Jacobsen 1997). As Bauman emphatically stated in *Mortality, Immortality and Other Life Strategies*:

> If modernity deconstructed death into a bagful of unpleasant, but tameable illnesses . . . in the society that emerged at the far end of the modern era it is the majestic yet distant immortal bliss that is being deconstructed into a sackful of bigger or smaller, but always-within reach, satisfactions, so that in the ecstasy of enjoyment the likeness of the ultimate perfection may dissolve and vanish from view . . . Each moment, or no moment, is immortal. Immortality is here – but not here to stay. Immortality is as transient and evanescent as the rest of things.
>
> (Bauman 1992b: 164)

'The majestic moment', 'the eternal now', replaces the forevermore of premodernity and modernity, holistic health is substituted for bodily fitness and survivalism ousts immortality. When immortality was the privilege of the few – artists, kings, scribes and certain nobilities – it was a cherished and valuable possession. When immortality, in the shape of the notorious 'fifteen minutes of fame' announced by Andy Warhol, became public property, when the bridges leading from earthly to immortal life were overcrowded, when national heroism obtained in war service was replaced by the popular idolatry of celebrities on the silver screen, when notoriety outcompetes fame, the promise of lasting individual immortality was irreparably dissolved. In the carnivalesque TV culture of today in which a multitude of ordinary people continuously pop up in quizzes, shows and competitions only to disappear as swiftly again from the screens, immortality as collective remembrance and (inter)national admiration or indebtedness is doomed. Liquid modernity liquefies the durability, continuity and stability which previously constituted the precondition of immortality. As Peter Beilharz observed: 'If the older, modern utopias valued stasis, the new, postmodern image demands speed, restlessness, dizziness not as an end-state so much as a way of life' (Beilharz 2000: 133). Utopia as such a liquefied way of life, a life lived towards yet ignorant of death, ushers in the end of immortality as we know it. But in the same way as utopia has not vanished but has been transformed, immortality has not disappeared either – it has merely changed. Utopia itself has now become immortal:

> Utopia brought from the misty 'far away' into the tangible 'here and now', utopia *lived* rather than being *lived towards*, is immune to tests; for all practical intents and purposes, and it is immortal. But its immortality has been achieved at the price of frailty and vulnerability of all and each one of those enchanted and seduced to live it.
>
> (Bauman in Jacobsen *et al.* forthcoming)

How do we possibly counter this concomitant frailty and vulnerability of living inside immortal utopia, a utopia of no alternatives? Instead of trying to conjure up a new 'nowhere' (the original semantic meaning of *utopia*) either in the shape of a solidified social system or a specific island-state or by building phantasmagorical castles in Spain, Bauman seems to be searching for and envisaging what Uruguayan writer Fernando Ainsa (1997) poignantly termed 'pantopia', the place of 'everywhere'. The closest one comes to an approximation of the content of such a pantopia envisioned by Bauman is presented throughout the book *In Search of Politics*. In it he describes the political pantopia that may propose a counter-cultural alternative to the present state of apathic and anti-social affairs. The book depicts the classical Greek, and Republican, phenomenon of the *agora* – in which private (*oikos*) and public (*ecclesia*) concerns are peacefully resolved, in which autonomous individuals as citizens engage with each other in an autonomous democratic society, in which universal rights and obligations are united, in which the actual quality of welfare is measured by the standards of the weakest members of society, and in which the gnawing fear of insufficiency, strangers and the future is eradicated – as such, a pantopia (Bauman 1999a). The *agora* as pantopia in many ways represents and resembles a politics of proximity in much the same way as Bauman's preferred ethics, as we saw above, was a morality of proximity. We must, however, not confuse physical proximity or personal propinquity with moral or political proximity. Bauman's political and moral pantopia does not require the intimate or constant co-presence of people; it is by nature necessarily global – 'there are no local solutions to global problems', as he persistently proclaims. Pan-utopianism means the ubiquity of utopia, simultaneously the everywhere and the nowhere of utopia. Such a ubiquitous pantopia, as idea and possibility, must continuously counter the merciless forces of globalisation and individualisation and revive the spirit of hope instead of surrendering it to defeatist despair, smug self-confidence, self-sufficiency and political apathy. As Bauman warns: 'We tend to be proud of what we perhaps should be ashamed of, of living in the "post-ideological" or "post-utopian" age, of not concerning ourselves with any coherent vision of the good society and of having traded off the worry about the public good for the freedom to pursue private satisfactions' (Bauman 1999a: 8). Pan-utopianism means the revival of the social and public utopia, the collective and democratic idea of the 'good society', while ridding it of its 'totalitarian tendency' (Bauman 1999a: 87).

In the bygone solid phase of modernity, utopia seemed liquefied, unnecessary, superfluous and even ridiculed in a society confident that it 'by its boot-straps', as it were, could embody and realize the ideals of 'the good society'. In the contemporary liquid modern phase of human history, the need for a solid utopian alternative becomes increasingly urgent because nobody, no agency and no institutional arrangement, appears interested, determined or powerful enough to seek to steer our world clear of dystopian disasters waiting ahead. According to Bauman, we currently live in the age of the TINA syndrome ('There Is No Alternative'); a paradoxically solid age which, although liquid, is utterly resistant to critique, change and dialogue: 'Utopia, on the other hand, is manifestly and self-consciously stripped of the right to demand obedience; and particularly a blank-cheque, unquestioning obedience. Utopia aims at setting imagination in motion, inspiring thought and prompting speech. Unlike TINA . . . utopia cannot but be an invitation to dialogue' (Bauman 2002b: 183–4). It is this dialogue, Bauman aspires to initiate, and this imagination, he insists on setting in motion.

The dawn of utopia? – An assessment of Bauman's utopianism

Having traced and delineated the ubiquitous utopian presence in the writings of Zygmunt Bauman – sometimes explicitly stated, at other times hidden between the lines – from the early books published upon arrival in Britain in the 1970s and their somewhat obscure status to the latest much more popular publications, it is now time to attempt briefly to summarise what we, social thinkers and sociologists, can possibly learn and deduce from his utopianism and what it can tell us about the state of utopianism in contemporary society and social science. As the title of this chapter suggests, in solid modernity, despite constituting the cradle of many grand utopian designs, utopian thought was roundly ridiculed and appeared liquefied within most sections of sociology because society, as such, through its social engineering and political planning efforts, desperately sought to embody utopian ideas, to turn idealism into materialism, to make fantasy flesh and blood. In contemporary liquid modernity, however, with utopian ambitions and dreams fast drying out, a more solid utopia must be advanced but apparently seems nowhere in the offing. Over a couple of decades ago, Ruth Levitas observed how 'it has not become impossible to imagine utopias; but it has become difficult to imagine utopia as possible – which paradoxically makes it possible to be more utopian. The problem is not lack of utopias, but the lack of hope; and the cause of this lies not in imagination but in the real conditions of the present' (Levitas 1979: 31). These lines are today as true as when they were first written. The stubborn opposition of the 'real conditions of the present' to utopianism does not mean, however, that all hope has vanished and evaporated from contemporary social thought. Neither does it suggest that we should give up on utopia; on the contrary. Bauman, now together with a growing band of equally concerned critical social thinkers (see Jacobsen 2005), has throughout the years remained a valiant champion of hope, sometimes perhaps of 'hopeful despair' in the words of Paul Gilroy, but always representing a critical voice in an age increasingly characterized by a deadly limitation of intellectual mind and social critique.

So how is Bauman a utopian thinker? If we unduly narrow down the concept of utopia to the modernist notions of an enforced state of affairs, he most certainly is not. In fact, in such case, he might be labelled anti-utopian. However, as Ruth Levitas observed, 'any general definition needs to accommodate to the fact that utopian scholarship does encompass a wide variety of approaches and questions, and this multi-dimensional approach is itself fruitful' (Levitas 1990: 179). In this more general, and indeed fruitful, sense of the term, Bauman *is* utopian, although he never proposes any applied utopistics, as so many hardcore utopians. Bauman is a critical utopian thinker because he is concerned with improving our present and future plight and because he refrains from insisting that such improvement emanates from following any systematic methodology, iron-clad political ideology or predetermined path of events. Amitava Ray once insisted that the utopian thinker 'is free to imagine and create a world without being tied up to any particular type of methodology' (Ray 1979: 76). This is Bauman's position in a nutshell – the free imagination rummaging every nook and cranny for possibilities, the 'gaseous and corpuscular utopia' hiding in the shadowy folds, in Italo Calvino's (1986: 255) wonderful words – which promises no answers or solutions but incessantly raises ever new questions. As mentioned above, Bauman seldom substantiates his utopian vision, hardly ever proposes concrete propositions, and almost never offers definitive illustrations of his ideal society. Is this a strength or a weakness? As Henry David Thoreau famously remarked in *Walden*: 'If you built castles in the air, your work need not have been lost; that is where they should be. Now put the foundations under them' (Thoreau 1854/1960: 215). Bauman's utopian work may still be found lacking in this respect, as the foundations are only conspicuous by their absence, but it has not been conceived in vain.

Many criticisms can be and have been voiced against utopianism in general; criticisms that may also be directed against Bauman's variant of utopian thinking. Social science, perhaps inevitably, lingers uneasily between normativity and objectivity, nostalgia and progressivism, utopianism and dystopianism (see Mendelsohn and Nowotny 1984), and Bauman's position in many respects is no exception to this rule. The claims of nostalgia, dystopianism and normativity have regularly been heard in discussions of Bauman's oeuvre, especially in recent years, as a way of delegitimising his type of theorising, thinking or diagnosing. But is Bauman, apart from being a utopian, also a nostalgic, a dystopian, a normative thinker?

If we look at the nostalgic dimension first, nostalgia would conventionally mean a desire for reviving or retrieving something from the past in the present, or as a way of handling contemporary fears and anxieties by resorting to habitual practices of yesteryear (Davis 1979). Bauman, however, is not a nostalgic suffering from what Christopher Yorke (2004) captured by the phrase 'malchronesis' – a longing or yearning for times and places we never lived in and that perhaps never existed. Malchronesis, according to Yorke, is not an expression of utopianism but of the opposite, the failure of utopianism. But a certain kinship between utopia and nostalgia, or at least an elective affinity, is unavoidable within any kind of theorising critically looking back or ahead such as Bauman's. Thus he, when asked in conversation about the claims of nostalgia, responded: 'Due to the "pendulum like" trajectory to historical sequences, a close proximity of "forward and backward" or "utopia" and "nostalgia" pregnant with confusion is virtually inevitable' (Bauman in Jacobsen, *et al.* forthcoming). However, Bauman's continuous and consistent critique of communitarianism and its attempt to pre-empt members' choices and by building the perfect future on the shoulders of the apparently perfect past is merely one example of his merciless showdown with malchronetic nostalgia. His equally scathing critique of modernity's propensity for totalitarianism is but another.

The same goes for claims of dystopianism, frequently uttered after the publication of Bauman's critique of liquid modernity. Here there is an equally thin and blurred line between the hopeful vision, the utopian imagination, and the tragic vision, the dystopian or anti-utopian imagination. Bauman may be criticised for not presenting a tangible utopia, and for representing contemporary liquid modernity as dystopia without posing a counter-image of a desirable society. However, as Krishan Kumar suggested, utopianism and anti-utopianism are inextricably linked and necessarily in mutual fashion influence and stimulate each other: 'As nightmare to its dream, like a malevolent and grimacing *doppelgänger*, anti-utopia has stalked utopia from the very beginning. They have been locked together in a contrapuntal embrace, a circling dance, that has checked the escape for either for a very long time' (Kumar 1987: 99). This is also the case in Bauman's writings – by embracing utopianism, he also, perhaps inadvertently, ventures into the realm of anti-utopianism and its negative description, and its distorted image of contemporary society is more often than not presented as a caricature rather than a reflection, a deliberate overstatement more than an 'objective analysis', an exaggeration more than a mirror image.

Apart from containing certain nostalgic and dystopian undercurrents, Bauman's utopian sociology is also highly normative – perhaps normative because utopian, utopian because normative – which has been the reason behind quite a lot of the criticism waged against it from the quarters of mainstream sociology throughout the years. In recent years, Bauman has sought to solidify his somewhat gaseous or liquid yet normative utopianism by proposing certain, admittedly vague, institutional and political arrangements (such as a basic income presented towards the end of *In Search of Politics* (1999)) in order for society to be able to stem the disastrous tidal waves of globalisation and individualisation. This solidification can equally be witnessed in the gradual shift from a morality of proximity to the concern with global justice (Bauman 1997, 1999b), in the attempt to carve out a place for utopian universalistic and republican politics (Bauman 1999a), as well as in his recent description of Europe as a utopian adventure, as something, in Polish poet Alexander Wat's apt description, that always 'tends to run ahead of the "really existing Europe"' (Bauman 2004b: 5), and, in Denis de Rougemont's words, as something that 'exists through its search for the infinite' (Bauman 2004b: 1). Contemporary utopia-hostile liquid modernity must be countered by some solidity – solid politics, solid solidarity and solid humanity – without, however, reifying social reality. In this sense, Bauman's work is and remains highly normative; for better and for worse, depending on personal predilections.

So Bauman's utopianism is to some extent nostalgic, dystopian and normative. But it is, perhaps first and foremost, necessary. Contrary to the one-dimensional, myopic and specialised visions of many contemporary liquid modern utopias, what Yaron Ezrahi (1984) poignantly labelled depoliticised 'micro-utopias' (see also Jacobsen 2005), Bauman instead proposes an inclusive, comprehensive, multifaceted and indeed critically and politically potent utopia with universalistic underpinnings, although the political dimension still appears somewhat underdeveloped. Therefore, despite his recent attempts to forge concrete politics out of corpuscular utopian visions, Bauman's utopia still remains more liquid than solid, more ethereal than tangible. Obviously, this may serve as a launching pad for the aforementioned criticisms. There are, however, good reasons why Bauman refrains from engaging in the utopian construction of ideal societies or envisaging the happy end-state of history. Twice in his personal life has he experienced what the fatal consequences may be when totalitarian systems or regimes strive to force utopia through; the first time when the Nazis in their quest for world domination sought to annihilate all human diversity and on that account murdered six million European Jews; the second time, later in his life, when the Communists, fuelled by anti-Semitism and the fear of disobedience, in their quest for total order sought to eradicate political dissidence and critique by expelling and eventually eliminating any unwanted opposition. Both ethnic cleansings and political purges were examples of modern totalitarianism going berserk in its ambition to force utopia from its ethereal and imaginary existence down to earth, to turn latency into manifest reality, and to embody utopia in specific social structures or institutions. Utopia can potentially lead to the good life, but it can equally destroy every chance of ever coming close to the good society; it may obsessively strive towards order, but it may also liberate and even disrupt order; it may imprison the mind, but may equally set the imagination free. Utopia is ambivalent and full of inner tensions, and, like sociology – which Bauman once described as inherently schizophrenic and organically dual (Bauman 1992a: 209) – is, according to Paul Ricoeur (1986: 1), also schizophrenic because it equally proposes an ideal society as well as a dystopian image of the worst possible place, it is ambiguously constructive and destructive, constitutive and pathological. Dystopia, as mentioned, is the perpetual *doppelgänger* of utopia, its evil twin. Utopias turning dystopian, promises being corrupted, dreams going sour, illusions charred, hopes fading – these constitute the horrendous historical evidence of most modern utopias and, as Bauman once remarked, 'with too many successive dreamworlds remembered mostly for the painful scars they left, the very activity of dreaming has been cast into disrepute' (Bauman 1992c: 101). He, however, has retained the activity of dreaming.

Obviously, this conclusion must necessarily turn out as inconclusive as Bauman's own ubiquitous utopianism described above. On this background, it seems appropriate to end the chapter, penultimately, with the magnificent words of Karl Mannheim, who, towards the end of his classic *Ideology and Utopia*, as Bauman, remained thoroughly ambivalent – equally optimistic and sceptic – about utopia, however still wanting to preserve the imaginative incentive inherent in utopianism:

> The complete disappearance of the utopian element from human thought and action would mean that human nature and human development would take on a totally new character. The disappearance of utopia brings about a static state of affairs in which man himself becomes nothing more than a thing.
> (Mannheim 1936/1976: 236)

And, as true utopians of hope, let us recall the first wonderful utopian words of Ernst Bloch's *The Spirit of Utopia*:

> I am. We are. That is enough. Now we have to begin. Life has been put into our hands. For itself it became empty already long ago. It pitches senselessly back and forth, but we stand firm, and so we want to be its initiative and we want to be its ends.
> (Bloch 2000: 1)

References

Ainsa, Fernando (1997) *La Reconstruction de l'utopie*. Paris: Unesco.
Bauman, Zygmunt (1976) *Socialism: The Active Utopia*. London: Allen and Unwin.
Bauman, Zygmunt (1987) *Legislators and Interpreters: On Modernity, Post-Modernity and Intellectuals*. Cambridge: Polity Press.
Bauman, Zygmunt (1991) *Modernity and Ambivalence*. Cambridge: Polity Press.
Bauman, Zygmunt (1992a) *Intimations of Postmodernity*. London: Routledge.
Bauman, Zygmunt (1992b) *Mortality, Immortality and Other Life Strategies*. Cambridge: Polity Press.
Bauman, Zygmunt (1992c) 'Love in Adversity: On the State and the Intellectuals, and the State of the Intellectuals'. *Thesis Eleven*, 31: 81–104.
Bauman, Zygmunt (1993) *Postmodern Ethics*. Oxford: Blackwell.
Bauman, Zygmunt (1995) *Life in Fragments: Essays in Postmodern Morality*. Oxford: Blackwell.
Bauman, Zygmunt (1997) 'Morality Begins at Home – Or: Can There Be a Levinasian Macro-Ethics?', in Harald Jodalen and Arne Johan Vetlesen (eds) : *Closeness – An Ethics*. Oslo: Scandinavian University Press.
Bauman, Zygmunt (1998) 'What Prospects of Morality in Times of Uncertainty?'. *Theory, Culture and Society*, 15 (1): 11–22.
Bauman, Zygmunt (1999a) *In Search of Politics*. Cambridge: Polity Press.
Bauman, Zygmunt (1999b) 'The World Inhospitable to Levinas'. *Philosophy Today*, 43 (2): 151–67.
Bauman, Zygmunt (2000) *Liquid Modernity*. Cambridge: Polity Press.

Bauman, Zygmunt (2001a) *The Individualized Society*. Cambridge: Polity Press.
Bauman, Zygmunt (2001b) *Community: Seeking Safety in an Insecure World*. Cambridge: Polity Press.
Bauman, Zygmunt (2002a) *Society Under Siege*. Cambridge: Polity Press.
Bauman, Zygmunt (2002b) 'Pierre Bourdieu – or the Dialectics of Vita Contemplativa and Vita Activa'. *Revue Internationale de Philosophie*, 220: 179–93.
Bauman, Zygmunt (2004a) *Identity: Conversations with Benedetto Vecchi*. Cambridge: Polity Press.
Bauman, Zygmunt (2004b) *Europe: An Unfinished Adventure*. Cambridge: Polity Press.
Bauman, Zygmunt (2005a) *Liquid Life*. Cambridge: Polity Press.
Bauman, Zygmunt (2005b) 'Living in Utopia'. Published by the Czech Internet journal *Respekt* at: www.respekt.inway.cz
Bauman, Zygmunt and Keith Tester (2001) *Conversations with Zygmunt Bauman*. Cambridge: Polity Press.
Bayertz, Kurt (1984) 'From Utopia to Science? The Development of Socialist Theory Between Science and Utopia', in Everett Mendelsohn and Helga Nowotny (eds) *Nineteen Eighty-Four: Science Between Utopia and Dystopia*. Dordrecht: Reidel.
Beilharz, Peter (2000) *Zygmunt Bauman: Dialectic of Modernity*. London: Sage.
Beilharz, Peter (ed.) (2001) *The Bauman Reader*. Oxford: Blackwell.
Blackshaw, Tony (2005) *Zygmunt Bauman*. London: Routledge.
Bloch, Ernst (2000) *The Spirit of Utopia*. Stanford, CA: Stanford University Press.
Bloch, Jan Robert (1988) 'How Can We Understand the Bends in the Upright Gait?'. *New German Critique*, 45: 9–39.
Calvino, Italo (1986) *The Uses of Literature*. New York: Harcourt Brace Jovanovich.
Dahrendorf, Ralf (1958) 'Out of Utopia: Toward a Reorientation of Sociological Analysis'. *American Journal of Sociology*, 64 (2): 115–127.
Davis, Fred (1979) *Yearning for Yesterday: A Sociology of Nostalgia*. New York: Free Press.
Engels, Friedrich (1976) *Anti-Dühring*. Peking: Foreign Language Press.
Ezrahi, Yaron (1984) 'Science and Utopia in the Late 20th Century Pluralist Democracy', in Everett Mendelsohn and Helga Nowotny (eds) *Nineteen Eighty-Four: Science Between Utopia and Dystopia*. Dordrecht: Reidel.
Geoghegan, Vincent (1987) *Utopianism and Marxism*. London: Methuen.
Goodwin, Barbara (1978) *Social Science and Utopia: Nineteenth-Century Models of Social Harmony*. Atlantic Highlands, NJ: Humanities Press.
Goodwin, Barbara and Keith Taylor (1982) *The Politics of Utopia: A Study in Theory and Practice*. London: Hutchinson.
Habermas, Jürgen (1989) 'The New Obscurity: The Crisis of the Welfare State and the Exhaustion of Utopian Energies', in *The New Conservatism: Cultural Criticism and the Historians' Debate*. Cambridge, MA.: MIT Press.
Jacobsen, Michael Hviid (1997) 'The Myth of Homo Immortalis – A Thanatology of Radicalized Modernity'. Unpublished thesis in sociology, Aalborg University.
Jacobsen, Michael Hviid (2004a) *Zygmunt Bauman – den postmoderne dialektik*. Copenhagen: Hans Reitzels Forlag.
Jacobsen, Michael Hviid (2004b) 'From Solid Modern Utopia to Liquid Modern Anti-Utopia? Tracing the Utopian Strand in the Sociology of Zygmunt Bauman'. *Utopian Studies*, 15 (1): 63–87.
Jacobsen, Michael Hviid (2005) 'Into Utopia. Towards a Reorientation of Sociological Analysis'. *Sosiologisk Årbok/Yearbook of Sociology*, 10 (1): 31–56.
Jacobsen, Michael Hviid (2006a) 'Den underfundige utopi som rød tråd i Zygmunt Baumans sociologi', in Michael Hviid Jacobsen and Poul Poder (eds) *Om Bauman – kritiske essays*. Copenhagen: Hans Reitzels Forlag.

Jacobsen, Michael Hviid (2006b) '"The Activating Presence" – What Prospects of Utopia in Times of Uncertainty?'. *Polish Sociological Review*, 3 (155): 337–356.

Jacobsen, Michael Hviid, Sophia Marshman and Keith Tester (forthcoming) *Bauman Beyond Postmodernity: Critical Appraisals, Conversations and Annotated Bibliography 1989–2005*. Aalborg: Aalborg University Press.

Jacoby, Russell (1999) *The End of Utopia: Politics and Culture in an Age of Apathy*. New York: Basic Books.

Kateb, George (1963) *Utopia and Its Enemies*. London: Free Press.

Kołakowski, Leszek (1981) 'A Conversation with Leszek Kołakowski by George Urban: The Devil in History'. *Encounter*, 56 (1):9–26.

Kołakowski, Leszek (1983) 'The Death of Utopia Reconsidered', in Sterling M. McMurrin (ed.) *The Tanner Lectures on Human Values IV*. Cambridge: Cambridge University Press.

Kumar, Krishan (1987) *Utopia and Anti-Utopia in Modern Times*. Oxford: Blackwell.

Kumar, Krishan (1991) *Utopianism*. Milton Keynes: Open University Press.

Levinas, Emmanuel (1961) *Totality and Infinity*. Pittsburgh, PA: Duquesne University Press.

Levinas, Emmanuel (1988) 'The Paradox of Morality: An Interview with Emmanuel Levinas', in Robert Bernasconi and David Wood (eds) *The Provocation of Levinas: Rethinking the Other*. London: Routledge.

Levitas, Ruth (1979) 'Sociology and Utopia'. *Sociology*, 13 (1): 19–33.

Levitas, Ruth (1990) *The Concept of Utopia*. Syracuse, NY: Syracuse University Press.

Mannheim, Karl (1936/1976) *Ideology and Utopia: An Introduction to the Sociology of Knowledge*. London: Routledge and Kegan Paul.

Mathiesen, Thomas (1997) 'The Viewer Society: Michel Foucault's "Panopticon" Revisited'. *Theoretical Criminology*, 1 (2): 215–34.

Mazlish, Bruce (2003) 'A Tale of Two Enclosures: Self and Society as Settings for Utopia'. *Theory, Culture and Society*, 20 (1): 43–60.

Mendelsohn, Everett and Helga Nowotny (eds) (1984) *Nineteen Eighty-Four: Science Between Utopia and Dystopia*. Dordrecht: Reidel.

Morawski, Stefan (1998) 'Bauman's Way of Seeing the World'. *Theory, Culture and Society*, 15 (1): 29–38.

Negt, Oskar (2001) *Arbeit und menschliche Würde*. Göttingen: Steidl.

Nisbet, Robert (1962) *Community and Power*. New York: Oxford University Press.

Padover, Saul (1979) *The Letters of Karl Marx*. Englewood Cliffs, CA: Prentice-Hall.

Ray, Amitava (1979) *Political Utopianism: Some Philosophical Problems*. Calcutta: Minerva.

Ricoeur, Paul (1986) *Lectures on Ideology and Utopia*. New York: Columbia University Press.

Slusser, George (1999) 'Proteus and the Phoenix: Transformations of Utopian Experience', in George Slusser, Paul Alkon, Roger Gaillard and Danièle Chatelain (eds) *Transformations of Utopia: Changing Views of the Perfect Society*. New York: AMS Press.

Smith, Dennis (1999) *Zygmunt Bauman: Prophet of Postmodernity*. Cambridge: Polity Press.

Steiner, George (1971) *In Bluebeard's Castle: Some Notes Towards the Re-definition of Culture*. London: Faber.

Tester, Keith (2004) *The Social Thought of Zygmunt Bauman*. London: Palgrave/Macmillan.

Tester, Keith and Michael Hviid Jacobsen (2005) *Bauman Before Postmodernity: Invitation, Conversations and Annotated Bibliography 1953–1989*. Aalborg: Aalborg University Press.

Thoreau, Henry David (1854/1960) *Walden*. New York: New American Library.

Ulam, Adam (1973) 'Socialism and Utopia', in Frank E. Manuel (ed.) *Utopias and Utopian Thought*. London: Souvenir Press.

Yorke, Christopher (2004) 'The Normative Role of Utopianism in Political Philosophy'. *New Thinking*, 2 (1): 2–11.

CHAPTER 9

On Bauman's sociology of suffering

Questions for thinking

Iain Wilkinson

Introduction

The social theory of Zygmunt Bauman resonates with morality. Whilst working to present sociology as a moral discourse on 'the way the world appears to us now' and 'how we are made to live in it', he maintains an emphasis upon our moral capacity before the possible futures that await us. When explaining the moral purpose of his writing he openly declares that, above all else, he is committed to exposing the social production of human suffering and disclosing the better ways in which we might live together so as to limit the harms we inflict on one another (Bauman 2000: 202–16). It is with reference to populations rendered superfluous in events of industrial genocide and the 'vagabond' majorities of the world existing under conditions of material scarcity that he underlines the importance of his work. Certainly, it is by emphasising the ways in which Bauman's sociology bears witness to the problem of suffering in our times that a number of commentators commend its manner of exposition and moral design (Abrahamson 2004; Bauman and Gane 2004; Gane 2001; Tester and Jacobsen 2005).

A number of attempts have been made to debate the value of Bauman's work for ethical thinking but, as yet, his approach to writing about human suffering has not been addressed as a cause for concern (Junge 2001; Lyon 2001). In the hope of encouraging further enquiries along these lines, I offer a series of critical reflections on the forms of vocabulary and categories of representation by which Bauman works to highlight the reality of human affliction. I analyse the extent to which the possibilities afforded by Bauman's work for recognising the ties of moral responsibility that bind our actions to the fates of others are shaped by the ways in which the suffering of others is framed for our attention. I contend that the character and direction of the moral debates that are to be found in Bauman's work are incisively influenced by his style of writing about human suffering.

As a means to draw out some of the wider ethical and political implications of this venture, I compare Bauman's approach to writing with that of Hannah Arendt and I take the further step of contextualising the works of both of these authors in relation to contemporary research and writing on the phenomenon of 'social suffering'. A key point that I would raise for further 'thinking' (in the Arendtian sense of the word), concerns the extent to which an explicit debate over the moral hazards and political risks inherent in writing about the suffering of others has the potential to bring readers to the point of recognising common ties of humanity, and engage them in the struggle to build more humane forms of society. I contend that whereas this insight is shared by writers such as Hannah Arendt and Pierre Bourdieu and is an explicit component of their struggles to write about the experience of human affliction, it does not feature in the work of Zygmunt Bauman. For this reason, whilst I recognise that Bauman's social theory refers us to some of the ways in which the culture of modernity is implicated within extreme events of human suffering, I argue that his style of writing affords little space for *thinking with suffering*.

There are long-established traditions of writing on the problem of suffering so as to provoke critical thinking about accepted beliefs, values and practices. Arguably, these traditions may be traced all the way back to the Book of Job (Nemo 1998). In such writing we are encouraged to reflect upon the brute facts of intense experiences of adversity that seem to exceed the bounds of moral justification. The indignation of those seeking an explanation for experiences of human suffering is aroused not by a lack of reasons, but rather by the understanding that there is *too much* suffering to explain. It is with an appeal to the ways in which excessive experiences of cruelty, violence, terror and loss appear to render reason radically questionable, and even absurd, that writing on the problem of suffering seeks to have us debate the primal meaning and value of our cultural reality.

I identify the work of Hannah Arendt and more recent collections of writing on 'social suffering' as modern developments within these traditions. Whilst considerable disagreements remain as to the most effective ways by which it is possible to fashion a style of writing that provokes readers to think with suffering, nevertheless, these researchers share in the understanding that this task amounts to a mode of critical praxis that has the potential to impress upon us the vital need for intellectual, moral and political reform. In my own work I place an emphasis upon the extent to which this involves confessing to a sense of failing to make proper sense of the pains of others and giving vent to the frustration of failing to find a sufficient moral meaning for what suffering does to people (Wilkinson 2005). It is by dwelling upon the intellectual and moral *shortcomings* of symbolic forms of meaning that steps are taken towards a broader acknowledgement of the negative force of suffering in human life and the moral significance this holds for our social relationships with others. Hannah Arendt addresses this matter in terms of an attempt to infect her readers with the 'difficulties of understanding' that animate her writing (Arendt 1994a). By presenting us with a manner of writing about human affliction that at the same time 'solves no problems and assuages no suffering', she aims to provoke us into a process of critical thinking about the social and political conditions that allow people to be treated as superfluous waste material. For Arendt, the difficulty of assigning a sufficient moral meaning to human suffering is seized as an opportunity for learning and political thinking. Her hope is that where readers are made to encounter the 'terminal aporia' of human suffering there is the possibility that they shall be moved to take action against worlds made inhuman (Arendt 1968: 27–9; Ricoeur 1995; Wilkinson 2005).

As my analysis develops I raise the possibility that Bauman's style of writing is ill-suited to uphold this ambition. Paradoxically, while he represents the quest for order within the intellectual and political culture of modernity as a form of social pathology, he does not venture to reflect upon the extent to which this is (paradoxically) a necessary part of his own diagnostic language. In marked contrast to writers such as Arendt and Bourdieu, he does not openly attend to the intellectual hazards and moral dangers that are courted through his chosen methods of writing. He does not appear to be reflexively oriented towards the capacity for the language of social theory to abolish our moral proximity to others. He does not dwell upon the potential for his own style of communication to deny us the possibility of recognising 'alterity' in human existence. In face of the brute fact of human suffering, this might be taken as a serious failing; for it could serve to withhold a proper acknowledgement of how the problem of suffering takes place in human experience. The pain of suffering appears to thrive upon the struggle to constitute our lives with positive meaning; it seems to gather its power to torment us by forcing us to bear the analytical frustration of continually failing to find a sufficient moral and social meaning for experiences that are wholly against us. Thinking with suffering is initiated at the point where we venture to pay heed to this fact; and further, allow this to temper our approach to ethics and politics. On my reading, this does not feature within Bauman's approach to writing and thinking.

What is Bauman's sociological purpose?

Bauman's writings have inspired an industry of secondary scholarship. Numerous special editions of journals, scholarly studies and textbook commentaries have been devoted to debating and evaluating his main propositions and concerns (Best 1998; Beilharz 2000; Blackshaw 2005; Kilminster and Varcoe 1998; Smith 1999; Tester 2004; Tester and Jacobsen 2005). Accordingly, when it comes to an assessment of his theories one is not only presented with the task of studying the narrative style, form and content of his many publications, but also, with a call to comment on the Bauman commentary; and these problems of assessment are further exacerbated by the fact that in recent years Bauman himself has directed many comments back towards his commentators (Bauman and Tester 2001; Bauman and Gane 2004). Indeed, his various responses to the critical readings of his work now amount to a significant portion of his output, and appear to be implicated within some of the recent developments in his theoretical language. Under these circumstances, it is all too easy to be overwhelmed by the amount of conceptual and analytical 'ground clearing' that must take place before one arrives in a position to offer any comprehensive and informed points of view on what makes his writing most valuable, provocative or troublesome.

Bauman does not provide us with a conventional form of sociology. He does not align himself to a particular school of sociological theory or systematically work to develop answers to a categorical list of questions. He is more an essayist than a clinical analyst. Bauman comments upon a considerable diversity of topics and in his writing makes passing reference to a wide range of sources from a great variety of literary, academic and cultural contexts. In so doing, he appears to hold no respect for accepted analytical practices or disciplinary divisions. Those that promote his work tend to regard this as a deliberate move on his part to have his writing hold a mirror up to an experience of social life which is resolutely indeterminate, heterogeneous and contingent. For example, Pieter Nijhoff argues that Bauman 'is demonstrating in a stylistic way that our reality is multitudinous' and he is attempting to show us 'what living at peace with ambivalence may look like' (Nijhoff 1998: 97; Bauman 1991: 15). Similarly, Tony Blackshaw maintains that Bauman seeks to demonstrate an approach to sociological thinking that is 'alert to life as it is lived: relentless, unpredictable, ambivalent' (Blackshaw 2005: 15).

Nevertheless, while Bauman's preferred style of sociological writing may draw upon the understanding that the common cultural experience of modernity is 'eclectic', 'pluriform' and 'fluid', at the same time, he is also concerned to present his readers with a definitive stance towards, or overarching perspective on, the times in which we are made to live. In the process of drawing our attention to diverse ways of living, he works to highlight the common elements within our existential situation. In each new departure in language and theme, he is inclined to return over and again to a two-fold message about life in modern times; namely, that the greatest danger facing humanity is that we fail to recognise our social and individual potential for self-determination and change, and that in this we also fail to heed our moral responsibility to care for the suffering of others. Whilst on the one hand he is openly concerned to advance a form of sociological enlightenment that promotes 'the cause of the autonomous individual', on the other hand, he consistently works to emphasise that in this we should be morally opposed to the social conditions that give rise to human suffering. Indeed, when explaining the moral purpose of his approach to sociological writing, Bauman states:

> Whoever willingly or by default partakes of the cover-up, worse still, denial of the human-made, non-inevitable, contingent and alterable course of the nature of social order, notably of the kind of order responsible for unhappiness, is guilty of immorality – of refusing to help a person in danger. Doing sociology and writing sociology are aimed at disclosing the possibility of living together differently, with less misery or no misery: the possibility daily withheld, overlooked or unbelieved.
>
> (Bauman 2000: 215)

This message is proclaimed along with a repeated warning about the dehumanising consequences of the ordering practices and mentalities inherent within processes of modernisation. From the mid-1950s to the present day, Bauman has endeavoured to draw critical attention towards the multiple ways in which conditions of modernity are legitimated and maintained via oppressive forms of culture that stand opposed to individual freedoms (Marotta 2002; Tester and Jacobsen 2005). For Bauman, modernity is essentially concerned with 'the production of order'; and further, he would leave us in no doubt that this is an exclusionary and pernicious form of ordering that is inclined toward the suppression of human possibility. Whilst this warning is most forcefully expressed in works such as *Modernity and the Holocaust* (1989), *Modernity and Ambivalence* (1991) and *Wasted Lives: Modernity and its Outcasts* (2004), it is the constant refrain throughout his writings. Bauman maintains that 'an obsession with ordering' is the 'common denominator' within all facets of modernity, and this always involves the imposition of restrictive rules and regulations upon individual lifestyles, identifications and behaviours. On this account, 'the purpose of ordering is the elimination of situational ambiguity and behavioural ambivalence' (Bauman and Tester 2001: 79). Whilst the cultural logic of modernity was pushed to its most horrific extremes in the Holocaust, he contends that it remains within the dull compulsion and administration of everyday life where individuals find themselves trapped and humiliated by (seemingly) immovable social boundaries, institutional obligations and consumerist expectations. He would have us understand that the cultural codes at work within 'the final solution' persist whenever any moves are made to conform human behaviour to ideals of 'the good society', 'the model citizen' and 'the exemplary consumer'; a 'totalitarian temptation' is an ever-present force within the culture of modernity (Bauman 2001a: 123; Arendt 1951).

In this regard, Bauman revisits some of the political and existential concerns that were central to Hannah Arendt's thinking. There are a number of instances where he openly acknowledges her influence upon his thought (Bauman 1988: 96–7; 1989: 177–9; 1999: 86–100; 2001a: 123; 2005: 129–53). First, his various discussions of the repressive ordering tendencies of processes of modernisation echo many of Arendt's insights into the cultural proclivities and structural conditions that give rise to the phenomenon of totalitarianism (Arendt 1951). Second, Bauman's (utopian) emphasis upon, and celebration of, human possibility, may be interpreted as strongly aligned with Arendt's appreciation for human plurality and individual spontaneity (Arendt 1958). Third, they are both committed to reinvigorating the political realm on the understanding that our free participation in public debate is necessary for the goal of self-realisation (Marotta 2002). Finally, through their respective studies of the totalitarian tendencies of modern societies, they both draw the conclusion that we need to radically revise western traditions of ethics so as to rediscover how to a lead a moral life under conditions where human beings are continually being rendered 'superfluous'.

Yet while Bauman and Arendt may be united in their efforts to bring these issues to our attention, their respective approaches to writing are markedly different. Most notably, Arendt is far more concerned than Bauman to reflect upon the potential strengths and limitations of different genres of writing about human experience. In many of her works she confesses to her ongoing reservations towards the forms of expression and narrative style by which she seeks to engage us with the task of thinking; and never more so than when it comes to addressing the acute forms of suffering experienced by people subjected to forces of totalitarian domination (Wilkinson 2005: 79–107). Arendt is prepared to confess to the extent to which language contributes to her difficulties of understanding; and even relies on this as a means to provoke further thinking amongst her readers (Fine 2001; Arendt 1994a). Her struggles with (and against) language are a constant theme throughout her writings, and in this regard she works to make known to her readers the extent to which she considers herself to be teetering on the point of failure when taking up the task of shining any light of 'truth' through our 'dark times'. By contrast, it is only on rare occasions that Bauman seems troubled by the potential for his trains of thought to be derailed by the deficiencies of language. Certainly, when announcing his 'liquid turn', he pauses to reflect upon the possibility that the increasing conflict of interpretations surrounding the concept of 'postmodernity' may confuse the message of his work, but, for the most part, we never find him expressing any reservations about the tone and character of the authorial voice by which he seeks to provoke his readers into a moral engagement with questions of humanity and politics (Bauman and Tester 2001: 96–8; Bauman and Gane 2004: 17–18). Arguably, whilst Arendt is always suspicious of the potential for words to obscure more than they explain about the lived reality of our human condition, by contrast, Bauman places much more confidence in the potential for his writing to communicate the existential force of the questions that animate his thinking.

In the space that remains, I aim to explore this matter in more detail; for I contend that from here it is possible to raise more far-reaching questions of morality, politics and human meaning. In so doing, I am not seeking to pronounce judgement upon the virtues of Bauman's work or offer a political evaluation of the life it has acquired within the realms of social theory and public discourse. I would rather approach this as an opportunity to outline some parameters of debate concerning the symbolic forms of communication by which we venture to make known the brute facts of human suffering and as a point from which to encourage more reflexive thinking over the ways in which narratives are designed to make us dwell upon our ties of moral responsibility towards 'the other'. Moreover, I maintain that the significance of these issues extends beyond the immediate concerns of this book so as to place the wider purposes and value of sociological writing in question.

Writing on the problem of suffering

The writings of Hannah Arendt display a pronounced struggle to make known harsh realities in human experience that have either been left 'undescribed', or have been presented to us in fixed categories that prevent us from grasping the full force of their political and moral meaning (Canovan 1974: 7). When reflecting back upon the many events of extreme human suffering that marked the first half of the twentieth century, she warns us that all too often an 'efficient talk and double-talk' have been used to explain away the existential meaning of political oppression, economic hardship and mass violence. She exhorts us to take heed of the moral calamity of 'speech that does not disclose what is but sweeps it under the carpet, by exhortations, moral and otherwise, that, under the pretext of upholding truths, degrade all truth to meaningless triviality' (Arendt 1968: 8).

Under this imperative, she never arrived at a satisfactory form of words for describing the 'evils' done to people under the brutalising force of totalitarian regimes. However, at the very least, she appears to have arrived at the conclusion that any 'poetic' or 'metaphysical' form of language is wholly unsuited to provide a morally appropriate account of the Nazi crimes. In a letter dated 19 October 1946, Karl Jaspers first works to persuade Arendt that we should aim to 'see these things in their total banality, in their prosaic triviality, because that is what truly characterises them' (Arendt and Jaspers 1992: 62). With this emphasis on the 'banality of evil', he is concerned to alert Arendt to the danger of bestowing a 'streak of satanic greatness' upon those responsible for perpetrating mass murder, lest any support be given to the notion that the explanation for such atrocity lies beyond the realm of human understanding. Accordingly, Jaspers seeks to persuade her that we should resist any temptation to represent these events in a manner that obscures the potential for gathering sociological and psychological insight into the conditions under which large numbers of 'ordinary' people will thoughtlessly lend their support to political regimes that design social systems for the purposes of genocide.

Although this exchange left Arendt with many lasting doubts as to how to devise an ethically sufficient form of language for writing about events such as the Holocaust, at the very least she was moved to declare that: 'One thing is certain: we have to combat all impulses to mythologize the horrible and to the extent that I can't avoid such formulations, I haven't understood what actually went on' (Arendt and Jaspers 1992: 69). With this conviction, and to the moral outrage of her critics, she worked at eliminating all elements of pathos or fury from her account of the Eichmann trial (Arendt 1963). Whilst convinced that in the figure of Eichmann she was confronted with unprecedented phenomena that defied categorisation in terms of conventional notions of a 'corrupted will', sinful motive or metaphysical evil, at the very least she appears to have been convinced that it was by applying a 'rational vocabulary' of social science to the work of thinking that some progress could be made towards understanding the proper nature of his criminality. Moreover, towards the end of her life, she even celebrated the offence caused by her emphasis on the 'banality of evil' for she came to recognise that through such heated responses to her tone of writing it was possible to infect others with the perplexities of her thinking (Arendt 1978: 3–16).

In her essay 'On humanity in dark times; thoughts about Lessing', Arendt was more willing to acknowledge a role for emotionally laden and poetic forms of language within the record of human history, but still warned that, for the sake of 'mastering' the past, we are all too ready to 'suppress the memory of a seemingly unendurable reality' and allow pathos to smother the terrible truths disclosed by events of mass destruction (Arendt 1968). She concedes that a process of lamentation is a necessary part of the means by which people struggle to find the cultural resources to live with and beyond traumatic events in their lives, but still maintains that we should be most concerned by the potential for people's struggle for emotional healing to lead them to hide themselves and others from the reality of the harms we do to one another. Accordingly, whilst prepared to account for her own work in terms of an effort to prepare the way for 'poetry' as a 'human potentiality', at the same time, she reaffirms her commitment to the development of a method of writing that 'solves no problems and assuages no suffering', so as to keep alive to memory events that require us to rethink the proper grounds for ethics and human meaning (Arendt 1968: 29).

In recent years, some of the debates raised by Arendt over the forms of writing by which we might venture to represent problems of human suffering have been revisited by researchers committed to bringing public attention to the phenomena of 'social suffering' (Bourdieu et al. 1999; Graubard 1996; Kleinman and Kleinman 1997; Wilkinson 2001, 2004, 2006). From a number of directions in cultural anthropology and sociology writers have been drawn to conclude that we lack forms of language that are sufficient to convey the moral significance of what extreme suffering *does* to people's lives. In fields of social science, the work of Pierre Bourdieu and colleagues in *The Weight of the World* (1999), along with numerous publications by the anthropologist and medical practitioner Arthur Kleinman, have attracted most attention (Bourdieu *et al.* 1999; Kleinman 1999, 2006; Kleinman *et al.* 1997). Here we are presented with ethnographic scripts that are designed to make known some part of the *experience* of suffering individuals living in various states of acute distress and/or under conditions of extreme hardship. In the words of Veena Das, such literatures attempt to produce 'a body of work that lets the pain of the other happen to it' (Das 1997: 572). Accordingly, the team of sociologists working with Pierre Bourdieu make a special effort not only to record the precise words, but also to detail the specific points of emphasis, intonation and gesture that people use to communicate their suffering, on the understanding that it is only in so far as we acquire some appreciation for the 'expressive intensity' with which people talk about their experience that we can venture to 'see' the world from their particular points of view. In a similar vein, Arthur Kleinman aims to produce a form of 'empathic witnessing' that, whilst alerting us to the social constraints under which individuals struggle to live through painfully traumatic experiences, also provides a space in which we might attend to the cultural grammar of the everyday forms of language with which they speak of their suffering.

As in the case of Hannah Arendt, under the effort to convey some part of the violation of human dignity that takes place in events of extreme suffering, such works aim to engage readers in a process of critical thinking about the forms of morality and politics that serve to build humane forms of society. They share in her conviction that by working to make explicit the ethical frustrations and intellectual tensions borne under the struggle to make human suffering intelligible to reason, it is possible to provoke readers into taking action against the social conditions that wreak havoc on human life. Accordingly, as a mode of critical praxis, writing on 'social suffering' works to make clear a sense of failing to make proper sense of the pains of others and does not shy away from giving vent to the frustration of failing to find a sufficient moral meaning for what suffering does to people. Whilst this manner of writing 'solves no problems and assuages no suffering', it is carried out on the understanding that where readers are made to encounter the 'terminal aporia' of human suffering there is the possibility that they shall be moved to take action against worlds made inhuman (Arendt 1968: 27–9; Ricoeur 1995; Wilkinson 2005).

However, there are some matters raised in the new writing on social suffering that mark this out as attuned to a set of interests that do not directly enter into Arendt's work. In works of 'social suffering' we are also encouraged to dwell upon the capacity of literature to contribute some part to processes of healing and recovery in the lives of individual sufferers. Accordingly, at the same time as writers seek to advance a 'politics of recognition' they also aim to explore the ways in which cultural narratives provide individuals with the psychic and moral resources to live through and beyond their suffering. In practice, this leads researchers to take an interest in the ways in which ethnography might be incorporated within our writing so as, not only to make known the suffering voice of others, but also, to allow those 'in' suffering to know that their voice is being heard. Whilst documenting the suffering of others, writers such as Arthur Kleinman also aim to provide a space in which individuals can both reflexively engage with the moral meaning of their experience and draw a measure of comfort from the knowledge that, in some part, this is being communicated to a wider audience (Kleinman 1988, 2006). As a result, one tends to find researchers being particularly attentive to the ways in which symbolic forms of communication acquire moral and intellectual authority in public life; and, in particular, much critical attention has come to be focused on the ways in which both practitioners of social science and wider publics might be educated to act morally on sentiments of compassion (Kleinman and Kleinman 1997; Nussbaum 1996, 2001; Spelman 1997; Wilkinson 2005: 108–35). In contrast to the themes of Arendt's work, those with an interest in aspects of social suffering are more willing to concede that there are occasions where emotive frames of reference have a positive role to play within the social representation of human affliction and that political movements for social reform are fuelled as much by moral feeling as by intellectual conviction.

Such concerns open on to debates that are beyond the scope of this chapter; indeed, many hold that by developing new ways of *thinking with suffering*, we might arrive in a position to radically reform the practices and values of social science (Graubard 1996; Wilkinson 2005; Das 1997; Kleinman 1999). Writing on 'social suffering' has been approached as the grounds from which to address the moral responsibility of western social science towards the plight of the poor in developing societies (Farmer 1997, 2005). It has been taken as a point of departure into debates over the cultural politics of compassion and the strength of the popular appeal of global humanitarianism (Bauman and Tester 2001; Cohen 2001; Cohen and Seu 2002; Ignatieff 1998; Kleinman 1995; Spelman 1997). Moreover, for those working in the field it is readily understood to give rise to debates over the potential for the concepts and methods of social science to be implicated in acts of 'symbolic violence' upon the experience of those we study (Bourdieu *et al.* 1999; Skultans 1998).

On the character of Bauman's witness to suffering

Where might we locate the work of Zygmunt Bauman within this context? If we accept that his concern for moral outlook and behaviour is underlined with reference to the brute facts of human suffering and the need for us to work against this, then what should we make of the form of writing by which he seeks to engage us with this project? How does he bear witness to human suffering and what does this possibly imply for his sociological ambitions?

Bauman's writings represent one of the most forthright attempts at articulating the existential situation of individuals in our current period of modernity. Read as a whole, the last twenty years of his writing might be approached in terms of a concerted effort to forge new concepts for describing and narrating key transitions in the socio-cultural history of industrial nations. A great deal of Bauman's writing is devoted to advancing sociological/literary representations of dominant modes of cultural experience, moral outlook and social disposition in contemporary western society. To this end, he works with the assumption that a bipolar narrative is central to the art of writing social theory and, indeed, is an integral part of the act of sociological disclosure. At one level of analysis, his works might be approached as an extended debate over the heuristic merits of a series of narratives constructed around binary cultural divisions. Perhaps with the example of Georg Simmel in mind, he invites us to attend to the meaning of human existence with the aid of sociological dualisms (Bauman and Tester 2001: 10–11). Accordingly, Bauman writes about the politics of knowledge in a cultural milieu where 'gamekeepers' are converted into 'gardeners' and 'legislators' are opposed to 'interpreters' (Bauman 1987, 1992). On his account, the social world is divided into 'tourists' and 'vagabonds', 'the seduced' and 'the repressed'; a privileged 'society of consumers' intent on holding a 'surplus population' of 'wasted outcasts' at bay (Bauman 1998a, 1998b, 2004). Arguably he has devoted more space and time than any other social theorist to legitimise the juxtaposition between 'modernity' and 'postmodernity' as a common currency of cultural analysis and ethical debate; and in an effort to clarify the distinctive message of this work, he now encourages us to dwell upon this in terms of a comparison between a 'solid' and 'liquid' state and/or experience of modernity (Bauman 2000, 2005; Bauman and Tester 2001: 70–5; Bauman and Gane 2004).

This form of writing accounts for common experiences and cultural outlooks through opposing categories of generalisation. The common experience of humanity is diametrically framed in terms of the values that unite and divide; the essential traits that distinguish our belonging or non-belonging to distinct social groupings and the core values that give rise to opposing cultural interests. His peculiar brand of 'sociological hermeneutics' appears to be grounded in the presumption that it is by counterpoising abstract idealisations of prevailing lifestyles and world views that some clarity of vision is brought to bear upon the flux of everyday life. Bauman's manner of writing seems to be developed on the understanding that where human beings may be inspired to work at changing their world, then the role of sociologist is to provide them with a moral script that makes clear core principles of social identification and ethical injunction.

In this manner of sociological writing, Bauman tends to address the brute facts of human suffering as follows: first, as a means to introduce modes of metaphorical thinking about major social divisions in society, he refers us to global metrics of suffering gathered by international non-governmental organizations and UN agencies. Accordingly, the headline statistics from reports on average income per head in developing countries as compared to the richest nations of the earth and accounts of the appalling differences in levels of consumption, comparative rates of HIV infection, malnutrition and life expectancy between sub-Saharan Africa and Western Europe are cited when introducing us to the central characters in his stories (Bauman 1998a: 70–4; 2001b: 114–15; 2004: 41–6). Thereafter, he tends not to concern himself with detailing the *quality of life* experienced by individuals living under conditions of extreme material scarcity and social deprivation but, rather, concentrates the greater part of his efforts on developing sociological caricatures of the 'winners' and 'losers' in a modern 'morality play'. He appears to be not so much interested in having us attend to the voice of individuals 'in' suffering as he is to bring moral resonance to abstract characterisations of modernity presented through ideal-typical models of 'productive' and 'wasted' lives. Bauman is not so much concerned with conveying the individual standpoints of those categorised as the 'vagabonds' and 'outcasts' of modernity, as he is with establishing such stylised identifications as part of a grand narrative on the moral meaning and fate of our times.

In his defence, one might argue that Bauman's approach to writing has the potential to perform an important role within the translation of people's personal troubles into public issues. If it is the case that the majority of those living in the more institutionally privileged and affluent sectors of society are too easily able to ignore or deny human suffering, then one might argue that Bauman's style of sociology is well designed for the purpose of alerting us to the common ties of humanity that induce care for 'the other' and the moral choice to act on this impulse. Indeed, a number of Bauman commentators are readily prepared to celebrate his works in these terms. For example, Peter Abrahamson declares that whilst Bauman reminds us that 'the road liquid modernity is going down currently leads to unbearable human suffering' he also makes it abundantly clear that 'we are at the crossroads' and have the choice to work against this (Abrahamson 2004). Similarly, Nicholas Gane takes Bauman's references to global metrics of suffering as a cue to debate the moral meaning of new class hierarchies and the possibility of democratising the public sphere (Gane 2001: 273; Bauman and Gane 2004: 26–7). Finally, when summarising the overriding purposes of Bauman's writing Keith Tester and Michael Jacobsen readily declare that:

> Bauman's sociological and moral mission is always, categorically and unconditionally, to side with the weakest members of society and to show us, the better off part of the planet, that our moral obligations must be equally unconditional and unwavering if human suffering is to be avoided or overcome.
> (Tester and Jacobsen 2005: 24)

However, it is also possible to find writers expressing critical reservations towards the strategies adopted by Bauman as a means to highlight the suffering of others. For example, with reference to objective measures of human suffering such as the World Bank's Disability Adjusted Life Years index, Arthur and Joan Kleinman argue that, whilst this allows for standardised comparisons to be made across societies, it also 'thins out' the lived experience of suffering so that a 'language of efficiency and cost' tends to be privileged above the everyday languages with which individuals seek to make known the violation of their human dignity (Kleinman and Kleinman 1997). Similarly, Paul Farmer argues that whilst statistics and graphs 'note' the existence of suffering, they fall woefully short of conveying the negative force of suffering in human life (Farmer 1997). Accordingly, both the Kleinmans and Farmer contend that if we are to properly attend to what suffering does to people, then we should be particularly concerned with the potential for ethnography to provide a social space for individuals to make known their experience, and for ethnographic writing to be fashioned as a mode of critical praxis (Kleinman 1999). Indeed, in his essay on 'Understanding' which is included as an analytical postscript to *The Weight of the World* (1999), Pierre Bourdieu pursues this argument by confessing to the extent to which he has become alarmed by the capacity for sociology to 'gloss over' human experience through its privileging of 'scientific' forms of language and criteria of 'objectification'. Here Bourdieu maintains that sociological writing risks becoming a form of 'symbolic violence' that, despite the good faith of individual researchers, colludes with oppressive structures of power and privilege so as to keep us from properly listening to the voice of suffering in everyday life and from taking moral responsibility for the harms we inflict on one another.

The key issue at stake here concerns both the potential for our manner of writing to make known the brute fact of human suffering in everyday life and for this knowledge to contribute to wider processes of political thinking and moral decision. The fears expressed by writers such as Bourdieu are directed towards the understanding that, in order to have our work resonate with a language of 'expert authority', we might unwittingly collude with the 'silencing' of people living under the yoke of extreme hardship; that is, by adopting the cultural grammar of academic styles of writing, we arrive at the point of eclipsing the face of 'the other'. What is encouraged here is more reflexive thinking about the ways in which our styles of writing cue readers to adopt particular forms of moral response towards the suffering of others; and, in this regard, we are also challenged to work on enhancing the potential for symbolic forms of communication to be fashioned as a means to challenge collective 'states of denial' (Cohen 2001).

Bauman makes clear his faith in a form of sociological writing that draws attention to the suffering of others so as to highlight the extent to which the structural violence of everyday life (which at the same time contributes to events of extreme suffering) is a product of moral decision (Bauman 2000: 202–16). However, at no point does he venture to explain his understanding of the relative virtues of his style of approach to this task; neither does he explain the moral and political risks he understands himself to be taking through the literary tactics he deploys to provoke our thinking. It seems that the forms of methodological reflexivity that we find in Bourdieu's writing on 'social suffering' and in Arendt's accounts of her thinking on the evils of totalitarianism are not permitted to intrude upon his work. Here I would raise the contention that such open expressions of professional self-doubt and critical introspection might not only serve to engage us in a deeper appreciation for Bauman's sociological ambition, but also serve to fire our moral imagination in face of the problem of human suffering in social life.

Conclusion: for thinking

One of the underlying assumptions in Arendt's method of writing is that it is through our experience of 'border situations', that is via encounters with critical events in human life, that we are driven to dwell on the meaning of human existence and our ties of moral responsibility towards others (Arendt 1994b). For Arendt, proper 'thinking' is both difficult and dangerous; for not only does it speak of a personal encounter with the borderlands of life but, at the same time, it involves a form of critical introspection whereby all hitherto accepted values and opinions can be brought into question (Arendt 1971). We risk being undone by thinking; and yet in face of the 'evils' of totalitarianism she expects us to take this risk and works to encourage this through her writing. Her purpose is to infect us with the perplexities of her thinking and at every turn she is concerned to work against the potential for language to serve not so much as a means to further this critical process, but rather as a 'flight from reality' (Arendt 1994c).

In this chapter, I have argued that by giving open expression to the 'difficulties of understanding' that animate her writing, Arendt provides us with a pioneering example of how literary struggles to convey the moral meaning in human suffering can be developed into a mode of critical praxis. Moreover, I have outlined some of the ways in which I understand the more recent 'turn' to research and writing on the phenomenon of 'social suffering' as a further elaboration upon this tradition. My overriding objective has been to provide readers with some questions for 'thinking' about the possible ways in which Bauman's style of sociological engagement with human suffering either compliments or departs from this.

I value the sociological ambition of Bauman's work; however, I have taken the opportunity to highlight a paradox in this style of writing, namely that, whilst declaring a commitment to human possibility and celebrating the presence of multiple social and cultural arrangements, under the effort to get his message across, he does not appear to be too worried by the extent to which his narrative style risks reducing the complexity and plurality of lived experience to abstract categories and broad generalisations. At no point does Bauman express any moral concern with regard to the potential for his own favoured accounts of the world to create obstacles to thinking about the multiple possible configurations of human experience. Moreover, one might argue that at the same time as he is inclined to represent the quest for order within the intellectual and political culture of modernity as a form of social pathology, he has not ventured to reflect upon the extent to which this is a necessary part of his own diagnostic language. In this respect, he does not openly attend to the intellectual hazards and moral dangers that are courted through his chosen method of writing.

On my reading, Bauman does not appear to be particularly worried about the capacity for the language of social science to abolish our moral proximity to others; neither does he appear too concerned with the potential for his own style of communication to deny us the possibility of recognising 'alterity' in human existence. Whilst working to frame human suffering for sociological attention, he does not seek to analyse the ways in which the moral economy of our collective response to the suffering of others is shaped and modified through the shifting lens of culture. He does not provide us with any political or moral defence of the particular forms of cultural representation through which he seeks to draw our attention to the bounds of human affliction. On this account I suggest that, whilst Bauman provides us with an idiosyncratic style of writing about the social injustice of the world, the problem of finding a sufficient moral/rational explanation for the negative force of suffering in human life does not appear to impact upon his approach to thinking. Whilst writing about human suffering, he does not appear to be *thinking with suffering*.

References

Abrahamson, P. (2004) Liquid Modernity: Bauman on Contemporary Welfare Society, *Acta Sociologica*, 47(2): 121–9.
Arendt, H. (1951) *The Origins of Totalitarianism*, New York: Meridian Books.
Arendt, H. (1958) *The Human Condition*, Chicago, IL: Chicago University Press.
Arendt, H. (1963) *Eichmann in Jerusalem: A Report on the Banality of Evil*, Harmondsworth: Penguin.
Arendt, H. (1968) *Men in Dark Times*, Harmondsworth: Penguin.
Arendt, H. (1971) Thinking and Moral Considerations: A Lecture, *Social Research* 38(3): 417–46.
Arendt, H. (1978) *The Life of the Mind: Thinking*, London: Secker and Warburg.
Arendt, H. (1994a) Understanding and Politics (The Difficulties of Understanding), in *Essays in Understanding 1930–1954*, New York: Harcourt Brace, pp. 307–27.
Arendt, H. (1994b) What is Existential Philosophy?, in *Essays in Understanding 1930–1954*, New York: Harcourt Brace, pp. 163–87.
Arendt, H. (1994c) Nightmare and Flight, in *Essays in Understanding 1930–1954*, New York: Harcourt Brace, pp. 133–5.
Arendt, H. and Jaspers, K. (1992) *Correspondence 1926–1969*, New York: Harcourt Brace.
Bauman, Z. (1987) *Legislators and Interpreters*, Cambridge: Polity Press.
Bauman, Z. (1988) *Freedom*, Milton Keynes: Open University Press.
Bauman, Z. (1989) *Modernity and the Holocaust*, Cambridge: Polity Press.
Bauman, Z. (1991) *Modernity and Ambivalence*, Cambridge: Polity Press.
Bauman, Z. (1992) *Intimations of Postmodernity*, London: Routledge.
Bauman, Z. (1998a) *Globalization: The Human Consequences*, Cambridge: Polity Press.
Bauman, Z. (1998b) *Work, Consumerism and the New Poor*, Buckingham: Open University Press.
Bauman, Z. (1999) *In Search of Politics*, Cambridge: Polity Press.
Bauman, Z. (2000) *Liquid Modernity*, Cambridge: Polity Press.
Bauman, Z. (2001a) Identity in the Globalising World, *Social Anthropology*, 9(2): 121–9.
Bauman, Z. (2001b) *The Individualized Society*, Cambridge: Polity Press.
Bauman, Z. (2004) *Wasted Lives: Modernity and its Outcasts*, Cambridge: Polity Press.
Bauman, Z. (2005) *Liquid Life*, Cambridge: Polity Press.
Bauman, Z. and Tester, K. (2001) *Conversations with Zygmunt Bauman*, Cambridge: Polity Press.
Bauman, Z. and Gane, N. (2004) Zygmunt Bauman: Liquid Sociality, in N. Gane (ed.) *The Future of Social Theory*, London: Continuum.
Beilharz, P. (2000) *Zygmunt Bauman: Dialectic of Modernity*, London: Sage.
Best, S. (1998) Zygmunt Bauman: Personal Reflections within the Mainstream of Modernity, *British Journal of Sociology* 49(2): 311–20.
Blackshaw, T. (2005) *Zygmunt Bauman*, London: Routledge.
Bourdieu, P. *et al.* (1999) *The Weight of the World*, Cambridge: Polity Press.
Canovan, M. (1974) *The Political Thought of Hannah Arendt*, London: J. M. Dent and Sons.
Cohen, S. (2001) *States of Denial: Knowing about Atrocities and Suffering*, Cambridge: Polity Press.
Cohen, S. and Seu, B. (2002) Knowing Enough Not to Feel Too Much: Emotional Thinking and Human Rights Appeals, in M. P. Bradley and P. Petro (eds) *Truth Claims: Representation and Human Rights,* New Brunswick, NJ: Rutgers University Press, pp. 187–201.

Das, V. (1997) Suffering, Theodicies, Disciplinary Practices, Appropriations, *International Journal of Social Science* 49, 563–72.

Farmer, P. (1997) On Suffering and Structural Violence: A View From Below, *Social Suffering*, Berkeley: University of California Press.

Farmer, P. (2005) *Pathologies of Power: Health, Human Rights and the New War on the Poor*, Berkeley: University of California Press.

Fine, R. (2000) Hannah Arendt: Politics and Understanding After the Holocaust, in R. Fine and C. Turner (eds) *Social Theory after the Holocaust*, Liverpool: Liverpool University Press.

Fukuyama, F. (1992) *The End of History and the Last Man*, London: Penguin.

Gane, N. (2001) Zygmunt Bauman: Liquid Modernity and Beyond, *Acta Sociologica* 44(3): 267–75.

Graubard, S. R. (1996) Preface to the issue 'Social Suffering', *Daedalus*, 125(1): v–x.

Ignatieff, M. (1998) *The Warriors Honors: Ethnic War and the Modern Conscience*, New York: Henry Holt.

Junge, M. (2001) Zygmunt Bauman's Poisoned Gift of Morality, *British Journal of Sociology* 52(1): 105–19.

Kilminster, R. and Varcoe, I. (1998) Three Appreciations of Zygmunt Bauman, *Theory, Culture and Society* 15(1): 23–38.

Kleinman, A. (1988) *Illness Narratives: Suffering, Healing and the Human Condition*, New York: Basic Books.

Kleinman, A. (1995) Pitch, Picture, Power: The Globalization of Local Suffering and the Transformation of Social Experience, *Ethnos* 20(3–4): 181–91.

Kleinman, A. (1999) Experience and its Moral Modes: Culture, Human Conditions and Disorder, in G. B. Peterson (ed.), *The Tanner Lectures on Human Values*, Salt Lake City: University of Utah Press, pp. 355–420.

Kleinman, A. (2006) *What Really Matters: Living a Moral Life Amidst Uncertainty and Danger*, Oxford: Oxford University Press.

Kleinman A. and Kleinman, J. (1997) The Appeal of Experience; the Dismay of Images: Cultural Appropriations of Suffering in our Times, in A. Kleinman, V. Das and M. Lock (eds) *Social Suffering*, Berkeley: University of California Press, pp.1–23.

Lyon, D. (2001) Everyday Life in Informational Societies: Uncertainties, Morals and Zygmunt Bauman's Sociology, *International Review of Sociology* 11(3): 383–93.

Marotta, V. (2002) Zygmunt Bauman: Order, Strangerhood and Freedom, *Thesis Eleven* 70(August): 36–54.

Nemo, P. (1998) *Job and the Excess of Evil*, Pittsburgh, PA: Duquesne University Press.

Nijhoff, P. (1998) The Right to Inconsistency, *Theory, Culture and Society* 15(1): 87–112.

Nussbaum, M. (1996) Compassion: The Basic Social Emotion, *Social Philosophy and Policy* 13(1): 27–58.

Nussbaum, M. (2001) *Upheavals of Thought: The Intelligence of Emotions*, Cambridge: Cambridge University Press.

Ricoeur, P. (1995) Evil, a Challenge to Philosophy and Theology, in *Figuring the Sacred: Religion, Narrative, and Imagination*, Minneapolis, MN: Augsburg Fortress, pp. 249–61.

Skultans, V. (1998) *The Testimonny of Lives: Narrative and Meaning in Post-society Latvia*, London: Routledge.

Smith, D. (1999) *Zygmunt Bauman: Prophet of Postmodernity*, Cambridge: Polity Press.

Spelman, E. V. (1997) *Fruits of Sorrow: Framing our Attention to Suffering*, Boston, MA: Beacon Press.

Tester, K. (2004) *The Social Thought of Zygmunt Bauman*, Basingstoke: Palgrave Macmillan.

Tester, K. and Jacobsen, M. H. (2005) *Bauman Before Postmodernity*, Aalborg: Aalborg University Press.
Wilkinson, I. (2001) Thinking With Suffering, *Cultural Values* 5(4): 421–44.
Wilkinson, I. (2004) The Problem of 'Social Suffering': The Challenge to Social Science, *Health Sociology Review* 13(2): 113–21.
Wilkinson, I. (2005) *Suffering: A Sociological Introduction*, Cambridge: Polity Press.
Wilkinson, I. (2006) Health Risk and Social Suffering, *Health Risk and Society* 8(1): 1–8.

AFTERWORD

Zygmunt Bauman
ON WRITING; ON WRITING SOCIOLOGY   257

ZYGMUNT BAUMAN

ON WRITING; ON WRITING SOCIOLOGY

Source: Zygmunt Bauman (2001) *Liquid Modernity*, Cambridge: Polity Press, pp. 202–16.

The need in thinking is what makes us think.
Theodor W. Adorno

Quoting the Czech poet Jan Skácel's opinion on the plight of the poet (who, in Skácel's words, only discovers the verses which 'were always, deep down, there'), Milan Kundera comments (in *L'Art du roman,* 1986): 'To write, means for the poet to crush the wall behind which something that "was always there" hides.' In this respect, the task of the poet is not different from the work of history, which also *discovers* rather than *invents:* history, like poets, uncovers, in ever new situations, human possibilities previously hidden.

What history does matter-of-factly is a challenge, a task and a mission for the poet. To rise to this mission, the poet must refuse to serve up truths known beforehand and well worn, truths already 'obvious' because they have been brought to the surface and left floating there. It does not matter whether such truths 'assumed in advance' are classified as revolutionary or dissident, Christian or atheist – or how right and proper, noble and just they are or have been proclaimed to be. Whatever their denomination, those 'truths' are not this 'something hidden' which the poet is called to uncover; they are, rather, parts of the wall which the poet's mission is to crush. Spokesmen for the obvious, self-evident and 'what we all believe, don't we?' are *false poets,* says Kundera.

But what, if anything, does the poet's vocation have to do with the sociologist's calling? We sociologists rarely write poems. (Some of us who do take for the time of writing a leave of absence from our professional pursuits.) And yet, if we do not wish to share the fate of 'false poets' and resent being 'false sociologists', we ought to come as close as the true poets do to the yet hidden human possibilities; and for that reason we need to pierce the walls of the obvious and self-evident, of that prevailing ideological fashion of the day whose commonality is taken for the proof of its sense. Demolishing such walls is as much the sociologist's as the poet's calling, and for the same reason: the walling-up of possibilities belies human potential while obstructing the disclosure of its bluff.

Perhaps the verses which the poet seeks 'were always there'. One cannot be so sure, though, about the human potential discovered by history. Do humans – the makers and the made, the heroes and the victims of history – indeed carry forever the same volume of possibilities waiting for the right time to be disclosed? Or is it rather that, as human history goes, the opposition between discovery and creation is null and void and makes no sense? Since history is the endless process of human creation, is not history for the same reason (and by the same token) the unending process of human self-discovery? Is not the propensity to disclose/create ever new possibilities, to expand the inventory of possibilities already discovered and made real, the sole human potential which always has been, and always is, 'already there'? The question whether the new possibility has been created or 'merely' uncovered by history is no doubt welcome nourishment to many a scholastic mind; as for history itself, it does not wait for an answer and can do quite well without one.

Niklas Luhmann's most seminal and precious legacy to fellow sociologists has been the notion of *autopoiesis* – self-creation (from Greek ποιείη, do, create, give form, be effective, the opposite of πασχειη – of suffering, being an object, not the source, of the act) – meant to grasp and encapsulate the gist of the human condition. The choice of the term was itself a creation or discovery of the link (inherited kinship rather than chosen affinity) between history and poetry. Poetry and history are two parallel currents ('parallel' in the sense of the non-Euclidean universe ruled by Bolyai and Lobachevski's geometry) of that autopoiesis of human potentialities, in which creation is the sole form discovery can take, while self-discovery is the principal act of creation.

Sociology, one is tempted to say, is a third current, running in parallel with those two. Or at least this is what it should be if it is to stay inside that human condition which it tries to grasp and make intelligible; and this is what it has tried to become since its inception, though it has been repeatedly diverted from trying by mistaking the seemingly impenetrable and not-yet-decomposed walls for the ultimate limits of human potential and going out of its way to reassure the garrison commanders and the troops they command that the lines they have drawn to set aside the off-limits areas will never be transgressed.

Alfred de Musset suggested almost two centuries ago that 'great artists have no country'. Two centuries ago these were militant words, a war-cry of sorts. They were written down amidst deafening fanfares of youthful and credulous, and for that reason arrogant and pugnacious, patriotism. Numerous politicians were discovering their vocation in building nation-states of one law, one language, one world-view, one history and one future. Many poets and painters were discovering their mission in nourishing the tender sprouts of national spirit, resurrecting long-dead national traditions or conceiving of brand-new ones that never lived before and offering the nation as not-yet-fully-enough-aware-of-being-a-nation the stories, the tunes, the likenesses and the names of heroic ancestors – something to share, love and cherish in common, and so to lift the mere living together to the rank of belonging together, opening the eyes of the living to the beauty and sweetness of belonging by prompting them to remember and venerate their dead and to rejoice in guarding their legacy. Against that background, de Mussel's blunt verdict bore all the marks of a rebellion and a call to arms: it summoned his fellow writers to refuse co-operation with the enterprise of the politicians, the prophets and the preachers of closely guarded borders and gun-bristling trenches. I do not know whether de Musset intuited the fratricidal capacities of the kind of fraternities which nationalist politicians and ideologists-laureate were determined to build, or whether his words were but an expression of the intellectual's disgust at and resentment of narrow horizons, backwaters and parochial mentality. Whatever the case then, when read now, with the benefit of hindsight, through a magnifying glass stained with the dark blots of ethnic cleansings, genocides and mass graves, de Musset's words seem to have lost nothing of their topicality, challenge and urgency, nor have they lost any of their original controversiality. Now as then, they aim at the heart of the writers' mission and challenge their consciences with the question decisive for any writer's *raison d'être*.

A century and a half later Juan Goytisolo, probably the greatest among living Spanish writers, takes up the issue once more. In a recent interview ('Les batailles de Juan Goytisolo' in *Le Monde* of 12 February 1999), he points out that once Spain had accepted, in the name of Catholic piety and under the influence of the Inquisition, a highly restrictive notion of national identity, the country became, towards the end of the sixteenth century, a 'cultural desert'. Let us note that Goytisolo writes in Spanish, but for many years lived in Paris and in the USA, before finally settling in Morocco. And let us note that no other Spanish writer has had so many of his works translated into Arabic. Why? Goytisolo has no doubt about the reason. He explains: 'Intimacy and distance create a privileged situation. Both are necessary.' Though each for a different reason, both these qualities make their presence felt in his relations to his native Spanish and acquired Arabic, French and English – the languages of the countries which in succession became his chosen substitute homes.

Since Goytisolo spent a large part of his life away from Spain, the Spanish language ceased for him to be the all-too-familiar tool of daily, mundane and ordinary communication, always at hand and calling for no reflection. His intimacy with his childhood language was not – could not be – affected, but now it has been supplemented with distance. The Spanish language became the 'authentic homeland in his exile', a territory known and felt and lived through from the inside and yet – since it also became remote – full of surprises and exciting discoveries. That intimate/distant territory lends itself to the cool and detached scrutiny *sine ira et studio,* laying bare the pitfalls and the yet untested possibilities invisible in vernacular uses, showing previously unsuspected plasticity, admitting and inviting creative intervention. It is the combination of intimacy and distance which allowed Goytisolo to realize that the unreflexive immersion in a language – just the kind of immersion which exile makes all but impossible – is fraught with dangers: 'If one lives only in the present, one risks disappearing together with the present.' It was the 'outside', detached look at his native language which allowed Goytisolo to step beyond the constantly vanishing present and so enrich his Spanish in a way otherwise unlikely, perhaps altogether inconceivable. He brought back into his prose and poetry ancient terms, long fallen into disuse, and by doing so blew away the store-room dust which had covered them, wiped out the patina of time and offered the words new and previously unsuspected (or long-forgotten) vitality.

In *Contre-allée,* a book published recently in co-operation with Catherine Malabou, Jacques Derrida invites his readers to think *in travel* – or, more exactly, to 'think travel'. That means to think that unique activity of departing, going away from *chez soi,* going far, towards the unknown, risking all the risks, pleasures and dangers that the 'unknown' has in store (even the risk of not returning).

Derrida is obsessed with 'being away'. There is some reason to surmise that the obsession was born when the 12-year-old Jacques was in 1942 sent down from the school which by the decree of the Vichy administration of North Africa was ordered to purify itself of Jewish pupils. This is how Derrida's 'perpetual exile' started. Since then, Derrida has divided his life between France and the United States. In the USA he was a Frenchman; in France, however hard he tried, time and time again the Algerian accent of his childhood kept breaking through his exquisite French *parole*, betraying a *pied noir* hidden under the thin skin of the Sorbonne professor. (This is, some people think, why Derrida came to extol the superiority of writing and composed the aetiological myth of priority to support the axiological assertion.) Culturally, Derrida was to remain 'stateless'. This did not mean, though, having no cultural homeland. Quite the contrary: being 'culturally stateless' meant having more than one homeland, building a home of one's own on the crossroads between cultures. Derrida became and remained a *métèque,* a cultural hybrid. His 'home on the crossroads' was built of language.

Building a home on cultural crossroads proved to be the best conceivable occasion to put language to tests it seldom passes elsewhere, to see through its otherwise unnoticed qualities, to find out what language is capable of and what promises it makes it can never deliver. From that home on the crossroads came the exciting and eye-opening news about the inherent plurality and undecidability of sense (in *L'Écriture et la différence*), about the endemic impurity of origins (in *De la grammatologie),* and about the perpetual unfulfilment of communication (in *La Carte postale*) – as Christian Delacampagne noted in *Le Monde* of 12 March 1999.

Goytisolo's and Derrida's messages are different from that of de Musset: it is not true, the novelist and the philosopher suggest in unison, that great art has no homeland – on the contrary, art, like the artists, may have many homelands, and most certainly has more than one. Rather than homelessness, the trick is to be at home in many homes, but to be in each inside and outside at the same time, to combine intimacy with the critical look of an outsider, involvement with detachment – a trick which sedentary people are unlikely to learn. Learning the trick is the chance of the exile: *technically* an exile – one that is *in,* but not of the place. The unconfinedness that results from this condition (that *is* this condition) reveals the homely truths to be man-made and un-made, and the mother tongue to be an endless stream of communication between generations and a treasury of messages always richer than any of their readings and forever waiting to be unpacked anew.

George Steiner has named Samuel Beckett, Jorge Luis Borges and Vladimir Nabokov as the greatest among contemporary writers. What unites them, he said, and what made them all great, is that each of the three moved with equal ease – was equally 'at home' – in several linguistic universes, not one. (A reminder is in order. 'Linguistic universe' is a pleonastic phrase: the universe in which each one of us lives is and cannot but be 'linguistic' – made of words. Words lit the islands of visible forms in the dark sea of the invisible and mark the scattered spots of relevance in the formless mass of the insignificant. It is words that slice the world into the classes of nameable objects and bring out their kinship or enmity, closeness or distance, affinity or mutual estrangement – and as long as they stay alone in the field they raise all such artefacts to the rank of reality, the only reality there is.) One needs to live, to visit, to know intimately more than one such universe to spy out human invention behind any universe's imposing and apparently indomitable structure and to discover just how much human cultural effort is needed to divine the idea of nature with its laws and necessities; all that is required in order to muster, in the end, the audacity and the determination to join in that cultural effort *knowingly,* aware of its risks and pitfalls, but also of the boundlessness of its horizons.

To create (and so also to discover) always means breaking a rule; following a rule is mere routine, more of the same – not an act of creation. For the exile, breaking rules is not a matter of free choice, but an eventuality that cannot be avoided. Exiles do not know enough of the rules reigning in their country of arrival, nor do they treat them unctuously enough for their efforts to observe them and conform to be perceived as genuine and approved. As to their country of origin, going into exile has been recorded there as their original sin, in the light of which all that the sinners later may do may be taken down and used against them as evidence of their rule-breaking. By commission or by omission, rule-breaking becomes a trademark of the exiles. This is unlikely to endear them to the natives of any of the countries between which their life itineraries are plotted. But, paradoxically, it also allows them to bring to all the countries involved gifts they need badly even without knowing it, such gifts as they could hardly expect to receive from any other source.

Let me clarify. The 'exile' under discussion here is not necessarily a case of physical, bodily mobility. It may involve leaving one country for another, but it need not. As Christine Brook-Rose put it (in her essay 'Exsul'), the distinguishing mark of all exile, and particularly the writer's exile (that is the exile articulated in words and thus made a communicable *experience*) is the refusal to be integrated – the determination to stand out from the physical space, to conjure up a place of one's own, different from the place in which those around are settled, a place unlike the places left behind and unlike the place of arrival. The exile is defined not in relation to any particular physical space or to the oppositions between a number of physical spaces, but through the autonomous stand taken towards space as such. 'Ultimately', asks Brooke-Rose,

> is not every poet or 'poetic' (exploring, rigorous) novelist an exile of sorts, looking in from outside into a bright, desirable image in the mind's eye, of the little world created, for the space of the writing effort and the shorter space of the reading? This kind of writing, often at odds with publisher and public, is the last solitary, non-socialized creative art.

The resolute determination to stay 'nonsocialized'; the consent to integrate solely with the condition of non-integration; the resistance – often painful and agonizing, yet ultimately victorious – to the overwhelming pressure of the place, old or new; the rugged defence of the right to pass judgement and choose; the embracing of ambivalence or calling ambivalence into being these are, we may say, the constitutive features of 'exile'. All of them – please note – refer to attitude and life strategy, to spiritual rather than physical mobility.

Michel Maffesoli (in *Du nomadisme: Vagabondages initiatiques,* 1997) writes of the world we *all* inhabit nowadays as a 'floating territory' in which 'fragile individuals' meet 'porous reality'. In this territory only such things or persons may fit as are fluid, ambiguous, in a state of perpetual becoming, in a constant state of self-transgression.

'Rootedness', if any, can there be only dynamic: it needs to be restated and reconstituted daily – precisely through the repeated act of 'self-distantiation', that foundational, initiating act of 'being in travel', on the road. Having compared all of us – the inhabitants of the present-day world – to nomads, Jacques Attali (in *Chemins de sagesse,* 1996) suggests that, apart from travelling light and being kind, friendly and hospitable to strangers who they meet on their way, nomads must be constantly on the watch, remembering that their camps are vulnerable, have no walls or trenches to stop intruders. Above all, nomads, struggling to survive in the world of nomads, need to grow used to the state of continuous disorientation, to the travelling along roads of unknown direction and duration, seldom looking beyond the next turn or crossing; they need to concentrate all their attention on that small stretch of road which they need to negotiate before dusk.

'Fragile individuals', doomed to conduct their lives in a 'porous reality', feel like skating on thin ice; and 'in skating over thin ice', Ralph Waldo Emerson remarked in his essay 'Prudence', 'our safety is in our speed'. Individuals, fragile or not, need safety, crave safety, seek safety, and so then try, to the best of their ability, to maintain a high speed whatever they do. When running among fast runners, to slow down means to be left behind; when running on thin ice, slowing down also means the real threat of being drowned. Speed, therefore, climbs to the top of the list of survival values.

Speed, however, is not conducive to thinking, not to thinking far ahead, to long-term thinking at any rate. Thought calls for pause and rest, for 'taking one's time', recapitulating the steps already taken, looking closely at the place reached and the wisdom (or imprudence, as the case may be) of reaching it. Thinking takes one's mind away from the task at hand, which is always the running and keeping speed whatever else it may be. And in the absence of thought, the skating on thin ice which is the *fate* of fragile individuals in the porous world may well be mistaken for their *destiny*.

Taking one's fate for destiny, as Max Scheler insisted in his *Or do amoris,* is a grave mistake: 'destiny of man is not his fate . . . [T]he assumption that fate and destiny are the same deserves to be called fatalism.' Fatalism is an error of judgement, since in fact fate has 'a natural and basically comprehensible origin'. Moreover, though fate is not a matter of free choice, and particularly of the individual free choice, it *'grows up* out of the life of a man or a people'. To see all that, to note the difference and the gap between fate and destiny, and to escape the trap of fatalism, one needs resources not easily attainable when running on thin ice: a 'time off to think, and a distance allowing a long view'. 'The image of our destiny', Scheler warns, 'is thrown into relief only in the recurrent traces left when we turn away from it.' Fatalism, though, is a self-corroborating attitude: it makes the 'turning away', that *conditio sine qua non* of thinking, look useless and unworthy of trying.

Taking distance, taking time – in order to separate destiny and fate, to emancipate destiny from fate, to make destiny free to confront fate and challenge it: this is the calling of sociology. And this is what sociologists may do, if they consciously, deliberately and earnestly strive to reforge the calling they have joined – their fate – into their destiny.

'Sociology is the answer. But what was the question?' states, and asks, Ulrich Beck in *Politik in der Risikogesellschaft.* A few pages previously Beck had seemed to articulate the question he seeks: the chance of a democracy that goes beyond 'expertocracy', a kind of democracy which 'begins where debate and decision making are opened about whether we *want* a life under the conditions that are being presented to us . . . '.

This chance is under a question mark not because someone has deliberately and malevolently shut the door to such a debate and prohibited an informed decision-taking; hardly ever in the past was the freedom to speak out and to come together to discuss matters of common interest as complete and unconditional as it is now. The point is, though, that more than a formal freedom to talk and pass resolutions is needed for the kind of democracy which Beck thinks is our imperative, to start in earnest. We also need to know what it is we need to talk about and what the resolutions we pass ought to be concerned with. And all this needs to be done in our type of society, in which the authority to speak and resolve issues is the reserve of experts who own the exclusive right to pronounce on the difference between reality and fantasy and to set apart the possible from the impossible. (Experts, we may say, are almost by definition people who 'get the facts straight', who take them as they come and think of the least risky way of living in their company.)

Why this is not easy and unlikely to become easier unless something is done Beck explains in his *Risikogesellschaft: aufdem Weg in eine andere Moderne*. He writes: 'What food is for hunger, eliminating risks, *or interpreting them away*, is for the consciousness of risks.' In a society haunted primarily by material want, such an option between 'eliminating' misery and 'interpreting it away' did not exist. In our society, haunted by risk rather than want it does exist – and is daily taken. Hunger cannot be assuaged by denial; in hunger, subjective suffering and its objective cause are indissolubly linked, and the link is self-evident and cannot be belied. But risks, unlike material want, are not subjectively experienced; at least, they are not 'lived' directly unless mediated by knowledge. They may never reach the realm of subjective experience – they may be trivialized or downright denied before they arrive there, and the chance that they will indeed be barred from arriving *grows* together with the extent of the risks.

What follows is that *sociology is needed today more than ever before*. The job in which sociologists are the experts, the job of restoring to view the lost link between objective affliction and subjective experience, has become more vital and indispensable than ever, while less likely than ever to be performed without their professional help, since its performance by the spokesmen and practitioners of other fields of expertise has become utterly improbable. If all experts deal with practical problems and all expert knowledge is focused on their resolution, sociology is one branch of expert knowledge for which the practical problem it struggles to resolve is *enlightenment aimed at human Understanding*. Sociology is perhaps the sole field of expertise in which (as Pierre Bourdieu pointed out in *La Misère du monde*) Dilthey's famed distinction between *explanation* and *understanding* has been overcome and cancelled.

To understand one's fate means to be aware of its difference from one's destiny. And to understand one's fate is to know the complex network of causes that brought about that fate and its difference from that destiny. To *work* in the world (as distinct from being 'worked out and about' by it) one needs to know how the world works.

The kind of enlightenment which sociology is capable of delivering is addressed to freely choosing individuals and aimed at enhancing and reinforcing their freedom of choice. Its immediate objective is to reopen the allegedly shut case of explanation and so to promote understanding. It is the self-formation and self-assertion of individual men and women, the preliminary condition of their ability to decide whether they want the kind of life that has been presented to them as their fate, that as a result of sociological enlightenment may gain in vigour, effectiveness and rationality. The cause of the autonomous society may profit together with the cause of the autonomous individual; they can only win or lose together.

To quote from *Le Délabrement de l'Occident* of Cornelius Castoriadis,

> An autonomous society, a truly democratic society, is a society which questions everything that is pre-given and by the same token *liberates the creation of new meanings*. In such a society, all individuals are free to create for their lives the meanings they will (and can).

Society is truly autonomous once it 'knows, must know, that there are no 'assured' meanings, that it lives on the surface of chaos, that it itself is a chaos seeking a form, but a form that is never fixed once for all'. The absence of guaranteed meanings – of absolute truths, of preordained norms of conduct, of pre-drawn borderlines between right and wrong, no longer needing attention, of guaranteed rules of successful action – is the *conditio sine qua non* of, simultaneously, a truly autonomous society and truly free individuals; autonomous society and the freedom of its members condition each other. Whatever safety democracy and individuality may muster depends not on fighting the endemic contingency and uncertainty of human condition, but on recognizing it and facing its consequences point-blank.

If orthodox sociology, born and developed under the aegis of solid modernity, was preoccupied with the conditions of human obedience and conformity, the prime concern of sociology made to the measure of liquid modernity needs to be the promotion of autonomy and freedom; such sociology must therefore put individual self-awareness, understanding and *responsibility* at its focus. For the denizens of modern society in its solid and managed phase, the major opposition was one between conformity and deviance; the major opposition in modern society in its present-day liquefied and decentred phase, the opposition which needs to be faced up to in order to pave the way to a truly autonomous society, is one between taking up responsibility and seeking a shelter where responsibility for one's own action need not be taken by the actors.

That other side of the opposition, seeking shelter, is a seductive option and realistic prospect. Alexis de Tocqueville (in the second volume of his *De la démocratie en Amérique*) noted that if selfishness, that bane haunting humankind in all periods of its history, 'desiccated the seeds of all virtues', then individualism, a novel and typically modern affliction, dries up only 'the source of public virtues'; the individuals affected are busy 'cutting out small companies for their own use' while leaving the 'great society' to its own fate. The temptation to do so has grown considerably since de Tocqueville jotted down his observation.

Living among a multitude of competing values, norms and lifestyles, without a firm and reliable guarantee of being in the right, is hazardous and commands a high psychological price. No wonder that the attraction of the second response, of hiding from the requisites of responsible choice, gathers in strength. As Julia Kristeva puts it (in *Nations without Nationalism*), 'It is a rare person who does not invoke a primal shelter to compensate for personal disarray.' And we all, to a greater or lesser extent, sometimes more and sometimes less, find ourselves in that state of 'personal disarray'. Time and again we dream of a 'great simplification'; unprompted, we engage in regressive fantasies of which the images of the prenatal womb and the walled-up home are prime inspirations. The search for a primal shelter is 'the other' of responsibility, just like deviance and rebellion were 'the other' of conformity. The yearning for a primal shelter has come these days to replace rebellion, which has now ceased to be a sensible option; as Pierre Rosanvallon points out (in a new preface to his classic *Le Capitalisme utopique*), there is no longer a 'commanding authority to depose and replace. There seems to be no room left for a revolt, as social fatalism *vis-à-vis* the phenomenon of unemployment testifies.'

Signs of malaise are abundant and salient, yet, as Pierre Bourdieu repeatedly observes, they seek in vain a legitimate expression in the world of politics. Short of articulate expression, they need to be read out, obliquely, from the outbursts of xenophobic and racist frenzy – the most common manifestations of the 'primal shelter' nostalgia. The available and no less popular alternative to neotribal moods of scapegoating and militant intolerance – the exit from politics and withdrawal behind the fortified walls of the private – is no longer prepossessing and, above all, no longer an adequate response to the genuine source of the ailment. And so it is at this point that sociology, with its potential for explanation that promotes understanding, comes into its own more than at any other time in its history.

According to the ancient but never bettered Hippocratic tradition, as Pierre Bourdieu reminds the readers of *La Misère du monde,* genuine medicine begins with the recognition of the invisible disease – 'facts of which the sick does not speak or forgets to report'. What is needed in the case of sociology is the 'revelation of the structural causes which the apparent signs and talks disclose only through distorting them *[ne dévoilent qu'en les voilant]*'. One needs to see through – explain and understand – the sufferings characteristic of the social order which 'no doubt pushed back the great misery (though as much as it is often said), while . . . at the same time multiplying the social spaces . . . offering favourable conditions to the unprecedented growth of all sorts of little miseries'.

To diagnose a disease does not mean the same as curing it – this general rule applies to sociological diagnoses as much as it does to medical verdicts. But let us note that the illness of society differs from bodily illnesses in one tremendously important respect: in the the case of an ailing social order, the absence of an adequate diagnosis (elbowed out or silenced by the tendency to 'interpret away' the risks spotted by Ulrich Beck) is a crucial, perhaps decisive, part of the disease. As Cornelius Castoriadis famously put it, society is ill if it stops questioning itself; and it cannot be otherwise, considering that – whether it knows it or not – society is autonomous (its institutions are nothing but human-made and so, potentially, human-unmade), and that suspension of self-questioning bars the awareness of autonomy while promoting the illusion of heteronomy with its unavoidably fatalistic consequences. To restart questioning means to take a long step towards the cure. If in the history of human condition discovery equals creation, if in thinking about the human condition explanation and understanding are one – so in the efforts to improve human condition diagnosis and therapy merge.

Pierre Bourdieu expressed this perfectly in the conclusion of *La Misère du monde*: 'To become aware of the mechanisms which make life painful, even unliveable, does not mean to neutralize them; to bring to light the contradictions does not mean to resolve them.' And yet, sceptical as one can be about the social effectiveness of the sociological message, the effects of allowing those who suffer to discover the possibility of relating their sufferings to social causes cannot be denied; nor can we dismiss the effects of becoming aware of the social origin of unhappiness 'in all its forms, including the most intimate and most secret of them'.

Nothing is less innocent, Bourdieu reminds us, than *laissez-faire*. Watching human misery with equanimity while placating the pangs of conscience with the ritual incantation of the TINA ('there is no alternative') creed, means complicity. Whoever willingly or by default partakes of the cover-up or, worse still, the denial of the human-made, non-inevitable, contingent and alterable nature of social order, notably of the kind of order responsible for unhappiness, is guilty of immorality – of refusing help to a person in danger.

Doing sociology and writing sociology is aimed at disclosing the possibility of living together differently, with less misery or no misery: the possibility daily withheld, overlooked or unbelieved. Not-seeing, not-seeking and thereby suppressing this possibility is itself part of human misery and a major factor in its perpetuation. Its disclosure does not by itself predetermine its use; also, when known, possibilities may not be trusted enough to be put to the test of reality. Disclosure is the beginning, not the end, of the war against human misery. But that war cannot be waged in earnest, let alone with a chance of at least partial success, unless the scale of human freedom is revealed and recognized, so that freedom can be fully deployed in the fight against the social sources of all, including the most individual and private, unhappiness.

There is no choice between 'engaged' and 'neutral' ways of doing sociology. A non-committal sociology is an impossibility. Seeking a morally neutral stance among the many brands of sociology practised today, brands stretching all the way from the outspokenly libertarian to the staunchly communitarian, would be a vain effort. Sociologists may deny or forget the 'world-view' effects of their work, and the impact of that view on human singular or joint actions, only at the expense of forfeiting that responsibility of choice which every other human being faces daily. The job of sociology is to see to it that the choices are genuinely free, and that they remain so, increasingly so, for the duration of humanity.

Notes

1 This essay was first published in *Theory, Culture and Society* 1 (2000).

Index

Abraham, K. 155, 157
Abrahamson, P. 251
activistic image 91
Adorno, T.; and Horkheimer, M. 20, 21
agency/freedom; Bauman 144
Agier, M. 174
Agrippa, M. 36
Ainsa, F. 233
Alford, F. 162
ambivalence 10
anti-utopian 235
Arendt, H. 83, 159, 229, 241, 242, 247, 249, 252; and Bourdieu, P. 243; and Klein, M. 161
association; free 164, 165
Attli, J. 109
authenticity; grounds 148

Barbalet, J. 145
Barthes, R. 15, 155, 156
Bataille, G. 155
Baudrillard, J. 6
Bauman, Z. 3, 10, 11, 12, 14, 15, 46, 72–3, 74, 76, 122, 154–66; agency/freedom 144; before and after postmodernity 4–12; liquid modern world 107–16; liquid turn 4, 12–18; sociological scope (critique) 51–60; utopianism 234–8; and Welzer, H. 64–75; will/freedom 144
Baxter, R. 103
Beck, U. 50, 73, 193, 200, 201, 202, 203, 206, 232, 264; and Giddens, A. 16, 207, 210; liquid individuality 69; and Rutherford, J. 32; and Urry, J. 63
Beck–U. 23
Beilharz, P. 84, 233
Bell, D. 36, 48
Benjamin, W. 34
Best, S. 53
Bion, W.R. 16, 160
Bloch, E. 238

blueprint; utopian 224
bond: identity 20; institutionalized 138; social 20, 138
Bourdieu, P. 202, 251, 252, 267, 268; and Arendt, H. 243
Branaman, A. 117–35
Broch, H. 82; and Kundera, M. 83
Brodsky, J. 111
Brook-Rose, C. 263
Butler, J. 128, 130

Calvinos, I. 38, 102, 235
capital 39, 40; labour 48, 138; punishment 110; social 69
capitalism 18, 50, 59, 138, 187, 222, 227, 231; consumer 51; global 49, 156, 165; globalized 57; heavy 42; light 42; modern 189, 211; modernity 223; multinational global 7; new 191; software 36
career paths 36
Carlyle, T. 30
caste; class 177
Castells, M. 182
Castoriadis, C. 19, 52, 57, 267
casualty; collateral 184
change: global institutional 53; social 54, 59
children; fantasy 161
choice: free 264, 266; freedom 31, 127, 225, 231; identity 128; lifestyle 230; reassuring 193–5
chronophonism 67, 76
citizen; model 5
civilization; modern 203
class 74; caste 177; power 9; system 72
cognitive *a priori* 90, 91, 93, 94
cognitive mapping 7
Cohen, D. 36
collateral damage 182, 183
colonialism 172
colonialization: private 24; public 24
colonization 31, 35

INDEX

commitment 102
commodity 39
communalism 140
Communism 66, 75
communitarianism 236
community 136
condensation 155, 156
conditions; frontier-lands 182
confidence 144, 145
connections 58, 103
consumer: capitalism 51; objects of consumption 113
consumerism 74; manic 154
contact; social 74
contemporary liquid; work life 139
control 88; hierarchy 55; manic 162; politics and social 134; power 35; social 119, 120, 139, 140
control processes 187
creative destruction 108
crisis; meaning 68
critical theory 20, 21, 22, 24, 25
critique: consumer-style 20; producer-style 20
Crozier, M. 38, 40
cruelty; liberal 87
culture: desire 15; global 71; repression 15
Czarniawska, B. 189

de-civilizing process 75
de-industrialization 138, 146
de-institutionalization 139, 150
de-specializing 140
death of the social 6
Debord, G. 44
decentralization 140
deregulation: privatization 9, 49; sexual 118
Derrida, J. 37, 261, 262
desire: consuming 154, 154–7; culture 15; object of 156; objects 194; sexual 155
Didier 164
Discipline and Punish (Foucault) 119
discourse: apodoctic and dogmatic 94; modernity 29; public 246
displacement 155, 156
division; social 38, 39
domestication 35
domination; political 9
Dostoevesky, F. 163
dream-work 165
drives; object-directed 164
Drucker, P. 23
Durkheim, E. 64, 72, 87, 142, 190, 191, 192

Eagleton, T. 155, 165
economic balance 171

economy; global 15
ego 157; individuality 160; personal 193; psyche 159
Elias, N. 75, 200
Elliott, A. 13, 46–63
Emerson, R.W. 230, 264
empowerment 143, 150
equality 6, 139–41
equilibrium 91; social 171
Erbring, L.; and Nie, N. H. 69
Erikson, E. 148
Eros 126
eroticism 124–5
ethical grounds 148
exile 263
expectation; assured 144
experiences; social 65
extra-legal 148
extra-material 148

fantasy: children 161; unconscious 164
Farmer, P. 251
fatal strategy 6
fatalism 264
feminism 124, 129–33
fetishism; value 36
Flew, A. 41
flexibilization 31
flexible liquid organisation 149
flexible working; market 138
fluid; modernity 33, 38
force; individualizing 137
Foucault, M. 120
foundations; ironic 90–3
fragmentation; tolerance 109
free will 110
freedom 6, 38, 39, 71, 88, 91, 110, 126, 129, 132, 136, 137, 145, 146, 180, 202, 232; choice 31, 123, 225, 231; human 83, 268; identity 141; imagination 235; individual 204, 244; relationship 123; self-determination 117; speak 265
Freud, S. 15, 121, 155, 158, 159, 161,165, 187
Friedson, E. 72
frontier-land; global 177

game keeping; state 226
gamekeepers 250
gamekeeping; premodern 229
gardening: state 226; utopia 227, 228
Garland, D. 180
Gates, B. 41, 109; style 42
gender: inequality 117, 131; sexual indeterminancy 126; sexuality 133

genocide 247; industrial 241
ghetto: prison 210; urban 177, 179
Gibson, D. 141, 142
Giddens, A. 2, 123, 200, 201, 203; and Beck, U. 16, 207, 210
Gilroy, P. 235
Giroux, H.A. 115
global colony; modernity 210
globalism 11, 13
globalization 3, 14, 17, 46, 51, 59, 72, 74, 77, 84, 150, 174, 199, 200, 209, 210, 237; individualisation 234; process 182; second 207; unrestrained drive 185; Western 8
Globalization (Bauman) 70
Goffman, E. 200
Goodman, M.; and Lemert, C. 16
Gordon, A. 211, 212
Goytosolo, J. 261, 262
Gross, N. 55

Habermas, J. 76, 148, 202; and Parsons, T. 65
Hamlet rule; Shakespeare, W. 113
Hampton, K.; and Wellman, B. 69
hardware: modernity 34, 55; quality 35
Harrington, C. 64
heavy-liquid; metaphor 67
Hegelians 64
hermeneutics; sociological 250
hierarchy: control 55; global power 129; power 124
Hilton, J. 34
Hochfield, J. 91
holism 188
Holocaust 4
homogeneity 139–41
Hoogenboom, M.; and Ossewarde, R. 146, 147
Horkheimer, M.; and Adorno, T. 20, 21
human: freedom 83; rights 23; waste 209, 231
humanitarianism; global 249
hunting-style; utopia 231
hyperghetto 177

identification; delusional 163
identity 5, 50, 52, 59, 74, 112, 117, 130, 136, 229; bond 20; collective 138; freedom 141; liquid 58; national 72, 260; politics 58, 128; privatized 50, 58; selfhood 15; sexual 122, 126; subjectivity 58–60
imagination: free 235; sociological 13; tradition 85–90
immigrant 179
imperialism 172
incentive; imaginative 221

individual; fragile 263
individualisation: globalisation 234; privatisation 232
individualism 266; free-market 165; manic 58, 154, 157, 166
individuality 158; ego 160
individualization 23, 24, 25, 50, 51, 101, 129, 137, 138, 193, 200
inequality: gender 117, 131, 132; political 132; social 131
instant living 41–4
instinct; sex 156
intimacy 139–41
Invisible Cities (Calvino) 102, 109
ironism; liberal 89, 90
ironization 88
irony; uses 2–5

Jacobsen, M.H. 17, 251
Jacobson, F.; and Tester, K. 52
Jacoby, R. 217
Jameson, F. 7, 11
Jamous, H.; and Pelloille, B. 72
Jarvie, C. 154; on Walton, G. 104
Jaspers, K. 246, 247
just society 23
justice 225

Katz, J.; *et al* 69
Kautsky, K. 219
Kilminster, R.; and Varcoe, I. 84
Klein, M. 160, 161; and Arendt, H. 161
knowledge 206
Kolakowski, L. 222
Kraut, R.; *et al* 69
Kristeva, J. 16, 160, 161, 163, 165, 267
Kumar, K. 218, 227, 236
Kundera, M. 13, 86, 94, 259; and Broch, H. 83

labour; capital 48, 138
Lacan, J. 162, 163
Lagrange, H.; and Pech, T. 179
leadership: communicative 146–9; reflexive authority 146–9
Lemert, C. 76; and Goodman, M. 16, 17
Lessing, G. 22
Levinas, E. 206, 207, 224
Levitas, R. 235
Lewin, L. 43, 44
liberty 6
libido 157
life: personal 193; politics 19, 33, 137
lifestyle; choice 230
light; capitalist 231

INDEX

liquefaction 30, 47
liquid: identity 58; Life 16, 58; love 154–66; mode 9; modern 102, 218; modernity 4, 17–18, 137, 200; moderns 50–1; one 201; sexuality 127; state 207; waste 212; work 149; work life 138; worlds 198
liquid individuality; Beck 69
Liquid Love 15
liquid modern; society 113, 114
liquid modern life 108
liquid modern world; Bauman 107–16
Liquid Modernity 218
liquid modernity: gender and sexuality 117–35; liquid life 107; postmodernity 63–77
liquid organisation; flexible 149
liquid turn 245; Bauman, Z. 4, 12–18
liquid waste 198–213
liquidity 211; postmodern 208
liquidization 3, 13, 49, 50, 204; global 5; postmodernity 56–8; societal 47, 48
liquidizing; power 33
Lisaveta 163
Lotmans, J. 182
love: Bauman, Z. 101–6; confluent 122; creative 157–61
Luckmann, T. 68
Luhmann, N. 192, 260
lumpenproletariat; spiritual 111

Maffesoli, M. 263
Malabou, C. 261
malchronesis 236
manager-employee; relationship 143
mania 162; psychoanalysing 154; recurrence 155
Mannheim, K. 238
manpower 40
manufacture; capitalist 212
market; flexible working 138
Marx, K. 94, 132, 189, 200, 204, 211, 212, 213
Marxism 220
masculinity; maleness 162
Mathiesen, T. 229
meaning; crisis 68
melting power; modernity 32, 118
melting of solids 30, 31
Melucci, A.; and Giddens, A. 50
metaphor; heavy-liquid 67
micro-utopias 237
Miller, J.G. 178; and Bollard, ?. 101
model; citizen 5
modern; liquid 101, 102
modern life; liquid 103

modernisation 244; process 245
modernity 13, 22, 29, 31, 46, 57, 76, 84, 119, 192, 205, 209, 250; capitalism 223; discourse 29; fluid 33, 38; global colony 210; hardware 34, 55; heavy 34–44, 50, 72, 118; light 34–44, 118; liquid 4, 17–18, 46–63, 136, 137, 200; melting power 118; melting powers 32; melting of solid 211; second 206; solid 38, 42, 138, 190, 227, 229, 266; solid phase 234; solid/liquid 204; solid 230; theory 47–50; tradition and the vicissitudes 75–6
Modernity and the Holocaust (Bauman) 4
modernization 208
morality 136; utopia 223–6
Morawski, S. 224
movement; sexual liberation 127

narcissim; primary 158
Negt, O. 232
network 103; social 69; style 20
new relational model 123
Nie, N. H.; and Erbring, L. 69
Nijhoff, P. 244
Nisbet, R. 220
nonsocialized 263

object-cathexes 157
objects of consumption; consumer 113
Occam's Razor 93
Offe, C. 31
oppression; social 9
order: political 222; social 199, 222, 244, 268
organization 142; post-bureaucratic 140; reflexive 147; rule-bound 147; team based 142
Orwell, G. 21
Ossewarde, R.; and Hoogenboom, M. 146, 147
Ossowski, S. 91, 95

Paolini, A. 53–4
Parsons, T. 180; and Habermas, J. 65
Pech, T.; and Lagrange, H. 179
Pelloille, B.; and Jamous, H. 72
perpetuum mobile 114
Peyrefitte, A. 191
phallus 164
Plato 165
pleasure 155; individual 190; principle 137
pluralism; self-reflexive 5
Poder, P. 16
polarization; rich and poor 8
policy 188

politics: identity 128; life 24, 33, 137; power 25; recognition 248; solid 237
Polyani, K. 39
population; surplus 172, 173
post-bureaucracy 141; organization 140
postcolonialism 53
postmodern 223; theory 10
postmodernism 3
postmodernity 12, 13, 46, 57, 219, 226, 246, 250; liquid modernity 63–77; liquidization 56–8
postmodernization 52
poverty 88
power 50, 72, 77, 119, 145, 146, 165, 191, 218; class 9; control 35; economic 177; global 108, 108–9, 171; hierarchy 124; liquidizing 33; melting 134, 135; political 184; politics 25; privilege 252; state 180, 184; wealth 34, 173
precarization; policy 188
preconceptions; Oedipal 161
premodernity 226
principle; pleasure 137
prison; ghettoes 210
privatization 201; deregulation 9, 49; individualisation 232
privatized identity 14
privilege 146; power 252
process; social 72
Protestant Ethic and the Spirit of Capitalism (Weber) 65
psychoanalytic eye 16
public choice theory 43
punishment; capital 110
pyramid; social 111

quality; hardware 35

rational choice 44
rational order 187
Ray, L. 13, 53, 63–77
reality: principle 137; respect 86
reality principle 187–97
recognition; politics 248
recurrence; mania 155
reflexive authority; leadership 146–9
reflexive beings 19
refugees 175, 209
rejection; social 178
relation; time/space 37
relational model 123
relations: global social 70; social 69, 76
relationship 103, 104, 124; contemporary 124; episodic sexual 15; freedom 123; liquid interpersonal 136–50; manager-employee 143; object 159; power 139; pure 122; social 12, 144; spirit 105; Top-pocket 104; virtual 103
relationships insecure and interpersonal 136–8
Rengger, N. 65
repression: culture 15; sexual 120
respect; reality 86
revolution; East European 3
Ricoeur, P. 237
Riley, A. 107–8
ritual; interaction 142
Ritzer, G. 187, 195, 197
Robert, P. 179
Rockefeller 41
Rorty, R. 57, 87, 89, 90, 92, 95, 115, 128
Rosanvallon, P. 267
Rougemont, de D. 237
Rousseau, J-J. 44
Rutherford, J.; and Beck, U. 32

Sayers, J. 16, 154–66
SDC model 106
segregation; caste-and-class 178
self-actualization 141
self-assertion 23
self-conciousness 160
self-confidence 191
self-conscious stage 10
self-consciousness 10, 160
self-control 55, 86
self-creation 158
self-criticism 86
self-determination; freedom 117
self-disaffection 201
self-distantiation 264
self-esteem 74
self-exhaustion 141
self-expression 14
self-hating 157
self-hatred 160
self-identification 23
self-identity 14, 67, 118, 147
self-images 115
self-knowledge 160, 206
self-love 157, 159, 160
self-management 23, 143
self-perpetuating 195
self-preoccupation 157
self-reform 114
self-sensations 160
self-sufficiency 23
selfhood; identity 15
Sennett, R. 109, 191
sex: instinct 156; liberated 124; pure 124, 126

INDEX

sexual indeterminancy; gender 126
sexual liberation; movement 127, 130, 132
sexuality 121, 122; gender 133; liquid 127; normal 122; plastic 122
Shakespeare, W.; Hamlet rule 113
Shipman, B.; and Smart, C. 55
Simmel, G. 36
Skácel, J. 259
Sklair, L. 74
Slusser, G. 218
Smart, C.; and Shipman, B. 55
social bonds 136
social conditions; transformation 46
social hierarchy 9
social order 182, 188
social process 50, 52
social state 183
social system 56
social theory 12; Marxist 219
socialism 227
society: capitalist 66; individualized 194, 196; liquid modern 113, 114, 121; modern 192; post-panoptical 119–22; postmodern 171; risk 201; self 3
sociological hermeneutic 199
sociology: kings 93–5; mechanistic 94; Warsaw 87; writing 259–68
software; capitalism 36
solid modernity 38, 227, 229
solid phase 48; modernity 234
space: global 173; social 267; time 50–1
space of flows 182
spirit; relationship 105
Stasjuk, A. 111
state: game keeping 226; gardening 226; liquid 207; social 180, 183
status; system 72
Stauss, L. 19
Steiner, G. 230, 232
strategy: anthropophagic 226; merger/downsizing 40, 41
Strauss, L. 127, 203
structure: social 50; team based 141
subjectivity; identity 58–60
subjectivization 193
suffering 242, 249–52; creative 248; human 251; social 17, 242, 253
system: class 72; social 46, 66; status 72; value 82
systematic style 20
Szahaj, A. 110

team based; organization 142
team work 141–2

Tester, K. 13, 14, 81–96, 251; and Jacobson, F. 52
thinking: disobedient 95; reflexive 252
Thompson, M. 42
Thoreau, H.D. 235
time/space 50–1; relation 37
Tocqueville, de A. 30, 266
Todorov, T. 75
tolerance; fragmentation 109
topical relevances 37
tradition; imagination 85–90
transformation: global 4, 8; global capitalist 6, 7; social 65; social conditions 46
transnational families 55
transphysical 164
transubjective 164
truth 6
Tucker, J. 140
Tullocy, G. 43
Twain, M. 22

unconsciousness 14
underclass; global 129
universe; linguistic 262
Urry, J.; and Beck, U. 63
utopia: capitalist 222; gardening 227, 228; hunting-style 231; morality 223–6; public/social 232
utopianism 85; Bauman, Z. 234–8; class-related 221; conflict-orientated 221; contemporary 217–19

value system 82
Varcoe, I.; and Kilminster, R. 84
violence; hidden 124
volume 50

Waquant, L. 177, 178, 179, 180
Warsaw; sociology 87
waste; liquid 212
Wat, A. 237
waters; social 199
wealth 35; power 34, 173
Weber, M. 20, 22, 30, 37, 75
Weberian-Marxism 9
Wellman, B.; and Hampton, K. 69
Welzer, H.; and Bauman, Z. 64–75
Wilkinson, I. 17
will/freedom; Bauman 144
Winnicot, D.W. 16, 160
work life: contemporary 139; contemporary liquid 139; flexible 141; integrative forces 139–49; liquid 138; project-and-team orientated 143

worlds; liquid 198
Wright Mills, C. 13, 81, 83, 86, 87, 91, 93, 94, 95

Yorke, C. 236

Zeitgeist 65
zero tolerance 181–2, 184
zombie categories 32, 63
zombie institutions 32

eBooks – at www.eBookstore.tandf.co.uk

A library at your fingertips!

eBooks are electronic versions of printed books. You can store them on your PC/laptop or browse them online.

They have advantages for anyone needing rapid access to a wide variety of published, copyright information.

eBooks can help your research by enabling you to bookmark chapters, annotate text and use instant searches to find specific words or phrases. Several eBook files would fit on even a small laptop or PDA.

NEW: Save money by eSubscribing: cheap, online access to any eBook for as long as you need it.

Annual subscription packages

We now offer special low-cost bulk subscriptions to packages of eBooks in certain subject areas. These are available to libraries or to individuals.

For more information please contact webmaster.ebooks@tandf.co.uk

We're continually developing the eBook concept, so keep up to date by visiting the website.

www.eBookstore.tandf.co.uk